International Investment Law and the Right to Regulate: A Human Rights Perspective

The book considers the ways in which the international investment law regime intersects with the human rights regime, and the potential for clashes between the two legal orders. Within the human rights regime states have an obligation to regulate, a duty to adopt regulation aiming at improving social standards and conditions of living for their population. Yet, states are increasingly confronted with the consequences of such regulation in investment disputes, where investors seek to challenge regulatory interferences for example in expropriation claims. Regulatory measures may for instance interfere with the investment by imposing conditions on investors or negatively affecting the value of the investment. As a consequence, investors increasingly seek to challenge regulatory measures in international investment arbitration on the basis of an investment treaty, such as a bilateral investment treaty.

This book sets out the nature and the scope of the right to regulate in international investment law. The book examines bilateral investment treaties (BITs) and ICSID arbitrations, looking at the indicative parameters that are granted weight in practice in expropriation claims delimiting compensable from non-compensable regulation. The book places the potential clash between the right to regulate and international investment law within a theoretical framework that describes the stability–flexibility dilemma currently inherent within international law. Lone Wandahl Mouyal goes on to set out methods that could be employed by both BIT negotiators and adjudicators of investment disputes, allowing states to exercise their right to regulate while at the same time providing investors with legal certainty.

The book serves as a valuable tool, an added perspective, for academics as well as for practitioners dealing with aspects of international investment law.

Lone Wandahl Mouyal is Assistant Professor in international economic law at the Law Faculty at the University of Copenhagen, Denmark.

Routledge Research in International Economic Law

Available:

Recognition and Regulation of Safeguard Measures Under GATT/WTO
Sheela Rai

The Interaction between WTO Law and External International Law
The Constrained Openness of WTO Law
Ronnie R.F. Yearwood

Human Rights, Natural Resource and Investment Law in a Globalised World
Shades of Grey in the Shadow of the Law
Lorenzo Cotula

The Domestic Politics of Negotiating International Trade
Intellectual Property Rights in US–Colombia and US–Peru Free Trade Agreements
Johanna von Braun

Foreign Investment and Dispute Resolution Law and Practice in Asia
Vivienne Bath and Luke Nottage (eds.)

Improving International Investment Agreements
Armand De Mestral and Céline Lévesque (eds.)

Public Health in International Investment Law and Arbitration
Valentina Vadi

The WTO and the Environment
Development of Competence beyond Trade
James Watson

International Investment Law and
the Right to Regulate
A Human Rights Perspective

Lone Wandahl Mouyal

Routledge
Taylor & Francis Group

LONDON AND NEW YORK

First published 2016 by Routledge

2 Park Square, Milton Park, Abingdon, Oxfordshire OX14 4RN

711 Third Avenue, New York, NY 10017

Routledge is an imprint of the Taylor & Francis Group, an informa business

First issued in paperback 2018

British Library Cataloguing in Publication Data
A catalogue record for this book is available from the British Library

Library of Congress Cataloging-in-Publication Data
Names: Mouyal, Lone Wandahl, author.
Title: International investment law and the right to regulate : a human
   rights perspective / Lone Wandahl Mouyal.
Description: New York : Routledge, 2016. | Series: Routledge
   research in international economic law | Includes bibliographical
   references and index.
Identifiers: LCCN 2015040265 | ISBN 9781138924970 (hbk) |
   ISBN 9781315684055 (ebk)
Subjects: LCSH: Investments, Foreign (International law) |
   Investments, Foreign—Law and legislation. | Human rights. |
   International commercial arbitration.
Classification: LCC K3830 .M68 2016 | DDC 346/.092—dc23
LC record available at http://lccn.loc.gov/2015040265

ISBN: 978-1-138-92497-0 (hbk)
ISBN: 978-1-138-61422-2 (pbk)

Typeset in ITC Galliard
by Apex CoVantage, LLC

To Isabella and Caroline from whom I learn so much every day.
And to David without whom I could not have done it.

Contents

Preface

As an LL.M. student at Geneva Academy in the year 2008–2009 I had the privilege to meet the late Professor Antonio Cassese, who taught several courses at that time. His considerations on the formation of international law, how it developed and in which directions it moved really made a deep impression on me. One thing that struck me was how he encouraged us to make positive contributions to the development of international law. *"You should not be hesitant to disagree on legal reasoning,"* he said and added, *". . . as long as it is well reasoned."* Creativity to the law can be allowed if it is well reasoned and it benefits common universal values. That was his view. As Professor Cassese made clear *"Law is developed in the dissenting opinions, whereas the majority opinions just state what the law is."* Inspired by his holistic approach to the law and his view that international law should be beneficial to higher common or universal values, I later approached the work of John Ruggie, the Special Representative of the UN Secretary-General on business and human rights. The work of John Ruggie made me aware of the need for research into intersections of human rights and international economic law. Thanks to the Law Faculty at University of Copenhagen, this was made possible as I started off in 2010.

First and foremost, I thank my supervisor Professor Jens Schovsbo for confidence and interest in my academic explorations, for fruitful discussions that made me sharpen my arguments and for a hearty laugh when it was most needed. My gratitude goes to all my wonderful colleagues at the Law Faculty in Copenhagen for their support and confidence in me. Special thanks to Jeanette Høj Jensen and Alexander Stig Vishart Gryholm for their assistance with footnotes and bits of BITs. My thankfulness also goes to friends and colleagues abroad that I met at the Geneva Academy and at the Graduate Institute of Development Studies in Geneva, the UNCTAD and at King's College London, for rewarding discussions and encouragement along the way. I also thank Director of the Danish Institute for Human Rights, Jonas Christoffersen, LL.D. and Chief Advisor at the Trade Council, Danish Ministry of Foreign Affairs, Sven Gad, LL.M., for thorough and insightful criticism at my evaluation seminar and for their comments on drafts of my writing. Finally, my warmest thanks goes to my family for their priceless support and for their unconditional love for which I am deeply grateful.

This book is a revised version of my doctoral dissertation that I defended at University of Copenhagen, January 2014. A special thanks to my assessment committee, Professor Linda Nielsen, Professor Sten Schaumburg-Müller and Dr Federico Ortino for their comments and suggestions. Any mistakes remain my own.

Copenhagen, 2015.
Lone Wandahl Mouyal

1 Foreign investments and public policies

1. Introduction

Picture the following scenario . . .

State X and State Y have concluded a bilateral investment treaty (BIT) with the aim of promoting and protecting foreign investments. According to the BIT, the states commit to compensate investors for expropriations or interferences tantamount to expropriation. The BIT reciprocally allows investors of the other state to submit a dispute over the investment to international arbitration.

A corporate investor from State X with worldwide profitable investments in the natural resource industry sets up an iron mine in State Y through a local subsidiary with an initial pre-production capital investment of more than $2 billion. The investment mainly covers the building of the mine, infrastructure and the building of a cargo airport nearby. The mine is expected to be operational for at least 30 years. According to the taxation scheme laid down in the exclusive exploitation licence granted to the local subsidiary, the government take is 37% in company taxes. After three years of exploitation the government of State Y decides to change the tax scheme by imposing 2% production royalties to the benefit of the local community. Is the investment expropriated? No, the government does not interfere with the ownership of the company. Is there a loss of expected profits? Yes. Should the investor then be compensated? Yes, that is highly likely.

Would the legal response to this question be different if the same company is not subject to tax regulation but to labour regulation, since it employs workers at an hourly salary 50% lower than what a new law imposed on State Y concerning sustainable business practices requires? Or what if new environmental regulation imposes CO_2 quotas or obliges the company to change its production process due to a ban on the use of a chemical that recent tests show is likely to cause cancer? What if the same mining company had been granted a licence to exploit uranium and technical analyses later revealed that it was harmful to the local environment and public health? Or what if a newly elected government wants to impose a zero-tolerance policy towards uranium mining? Does it make a difference if the company has voluntarily committed to report annually on their social responsibility?

What weight should be given to the *purpose* of the regulatory measure, if any? Does the *type* of regulation imposed have an impact on whether investors should be compensated or not? Or to what extent?

This research seeks to assist in developing a methodology that on the one hand protects large-scale investments from the will of governmental haphazardness, while at the same time ensuring that states can exercise their legislative function to enhance development and social welfare or at least ensure that foreign investment is not detrimental to these aims.

International investment law is a branch of international law governing the rules protecting foreign investments in a global context. This introductory part seeks to explain the rationale behind this research concerning international investment law and states' right to regulate.

2. Background and methodological considerations

This research transpires from a basic thought of collision of two legal regimes of international law, the international investment law regime and the human rights regime encompassing a collision of norms, policies and values. The overall objective of this research is to examine the right to regulate in international investment law, focusing on the determination of the *nature* and *scope* of the right to regulate. Whereas the nature of the right to regulate focuses on what states can do under this right, the scope of the right to regulate is largely concerned with the practical applicability of the right. The human rights perspective basically underlines that this is a study of the human rights implications on the international investment law regime.

This study of the right to regulate in international investment law is based on a perception of international law as a system, where the principle of coherence serves as the overall guideline. Coherence is attached to the idea that a system should *"make sense as a whole"*.[1] Making sense as a whole is a precondition of intelligibility, which in turn is considered an essential characteristic of law. When considering international law as a system, coherence plays an important role providing normative order. This is because that what is coherent forms a well-organized structure. In the contrary, international law would appear with disorder and inconsistent normative statements. Though the idea of a coherent international legal order is a theoretical ideal, which in practice faces many obstacles, this research – nevertheless – approaches international law from the perspective of creating international legal order.

International law is not only subject to deliberate change (e.g. through legislation and administrative orders). Also, the law changes pursuant to developments in morals and values in society.[2] Norms are not domestically fixed but may

---

1 Stefano Bertea, "The Arguments from Coherence: Analysis and Evaluation," *Oxford Journal of Legal Studies* 25, no. 3 (2005): 385.
2 See generally Antonio Cassese, *Realizing Utopia: The Future of International Law*, 1st ed. (Oxford: Oxford University Press, 2012).

transcend the national sphere becoming international norms or concepts. Said norms, due to their established role in society and morals, are becoming absorbed by the law. Perceiving international law as an open process ensures the ability to maintain a perspective of law as an authoritative process displaying and reinforcing policies and fundamental societal values. This approach is in contrast to a more traditional perspective on legal analysis as a construction of norms determined by reference to formal sources of international law. This is not to say, however, that the following represents a revolutionary theory about international law. The perception of international law as a dynamic body of law is neither new nor controversial. In essence, law reflects the ideologies of its place and time. At the same time, integrity of law is linked with a political obligation on law-appliers to make their decisions cohere with the expectations of the community whose law they administer.[3]

All in all, the task of legal reasoning is to establish the systemic relationships between law and policy. The role of the legal researcher is therefore twofold. On the one hand, the researcher must determine what the law is by rationally reconstructing the norms in the most coherent and convincing way possible. On the other hand, the researcher must seek to develop the law so as to serve as a means for social justice. The method employed thus consists of two steps by both analysing the law as it is, as well as the law as it should be when taken into account its particular policy context.

From an overall perspective, law is perceived as being closely linked with justice. Some of the earliest thinking about justice is found in Aristotle, who distinguished between 'corrective justice' and 'distributive justice'. This research employs a method that comprises aspects of both law and policy to enhance distributive justice, i.e. the appropriate distribution of goods.[4] The purpose of law is here considered to be both practical ('solving problems') and ideal ('realising our potential as a society'). At the practical level, we could treat justice as the outcome of decisions by courts and arbitral tribunals. At the ideal level, law can be the means to social justice. Justice must be done and be seen to be done through the use of legal means. Law has therefore to seek and demonstrate justice at all times.[5] It may be said that states, which seek to promote public policies in an attempt to serve broader community interests, are pursuing justice. Serving a higher goal of justice thereby becomes the link between public policies and the formation of the law.

---

3 In his legal theory, Dworkin draws attention to 'integrity' as a political ideal, which requires governments to speak with one voice and to act in a principled and coherent manner towards all their citizens; see Ronald Dworkin, *Law's Empire*, 1st ed. (Cambridge, Massachusetts: Harvard University Press, 1986), 165. See also the Report of the Study Group of the International Law Commission finalized by Martti Koskenniemi "Fragmentation of International Law: Difficulties Arising from the Diversification and Expansion of International Law," *The United Nations*, 13 April 2006, A/CN.4/L.682 at 24, para. 35, <http://legal.un.org/ilc/documentation/english/a_cn4_l682.pdf>.

4 See further on theories of justice in Michael Freeman, *Lloyd's Introduction to Jurisprudence*, 8th ed. (London: Sweet & Maxwell, 2008), 583–632.

5 Stephen Riley, *Legal Philosophy*, 1st ed. (Harlow: Pearson, 2012), 8–9.

The interaction between law and policy is under scrutiny in this research. As to methodology, the research relies largely on a classical dogmatic legal analysis of the law as it is (*de lege lata*), since it describes, systematizes and interprets existing rules relating to the protection of foreign investments and the right for states to regulate. In addition hereto, this research includes suggestions for improvements to enhance the unification of international investment law (*de lege ferenda*). For this purpose, the research draws on methods from political science, such as policy analysis and the use of statistical data in order to determine which rules should be employed to achieve an outcome in the application of the law, which corresponds to the policy goals endeavoured. In the main this research embarks on a *prospective approach* to the law through the analysis of trends and developments in contrast to adopting a *retrospective approach*, which historically explains how the law has developed until now. The reason for this is the ambition to make a qualified contribution to the development of international investment law. As it appears, merely depicting the dysfunction of the international investment law regime from the human rights perspective is a demanding task.

The ambition of this research is to provide a theoretical foundation, which can be useful for both policy makers, negotiators of International Investment Agreements (IIAs) as well as practitioners advising foreign investors and arbitrators tasked with the settlement of investment disputes.

The data of this research comes from a variety of sources, whereas the collection of BITs and model BITs, the review of practice from arbitral tribunals and courts as well as the literature review account for the main sources. These sources are greatly supported by supplementary sources in the form of statements and reports by key policy makers, informal interviews with scholars, negotiators, arbitrators as well as researchers at the United Nations Conference on Trade and Development (UNCTAD).

While examining states' right to regulate, the object of examination is limited in three ways:

1) to an examination of BITs, which makes up the major group of IIAs;
2) to an examination of arbitral practice in investor–state disputes, mainly focusing on disputes initiated at the International Centre for Settlement of Investment Disputes (ICSID);
3) to an examination of expropriation claims.

The BITs examined are selected so as to cover a geographical representative extract, which allows for consideration to various cultural and regional interests, economy as well as level of development. BITs examined thus cover North–South BITs (between countries traditionally perceived as developed and developing countries), South–South BITs (between countries traditionally perceived as developing countries) and BITs between the BRIC countries and European states as well as BITs between BRIC countries and developing countries. The scope is further limited to BITs drafted in English, German, French or Spanish. In total, a sample of 293 BITs and 13 model BITs have been examined. BITs examined can be found at the webpage of the UNCTAD.[6] Model BITs can be found either at the webpage of Investment Treaty Arbitration[7] or in the book C. Brown (ed.) *Commentaries on Selected Model Investment Treaties* (Oxford: Oxford University Press, 2013).

The analysis of practice in investment disputes focuses on ICSID claims since ICSID arbitration is the most frequently used institutional course of action for solving investment disputes. Furthermore, many decisions and awards are published on the official webpage with the consent of both disputing parties.[8] Arbitral practice is primarily used on the basis of identification of key cases. Since many investment disputes are based on complicated facts and agreements, the approach in this research project is to reproduce the facts in a simplified manner where they are deemed relevant or as to set the scene for the legal analysis.

The case study focuses on expropriation claims. There are substantial reasons for this focus. Some scholars suggest for example that unlawful interference with the interest of foreign investors first and foremost trigger the contemplation of a potential expropriation claim,[9] or that expropriation – apart from violence toward the person of the investor – is *"the most serious infringement of an investor's rights"*.[10] In some BITs, the investor–state arbitration provision applies only to alleged expropriations.[11] Moreover, linking public policy concerns with cases of expropriation allows for comparison with the standard of protection under customary international law as well as protection of property under human rights law. As to the human rights perspective, the European Court of Human Rights (ECtHR) is a relevant institution due to an extensive and well-established practice dealing with expropriation claims. The relevance of ECtHR jurisprudence links back to the focus on ICSID arbitrations since arbitrators have chosen to refer to practice from the ECtHR, even in cases not involving member states to the ECHR.[12]

On this basis, the research disseminated in this book is intended to contribute to the basic – but highly needed – scientific research on the right to regulate in international investment law. Other perspectives on the right to regulate in

---

6 See http://investmentpolicyhub.unctad.org/IIA. Many times, BITs are also published on the webpage of the countries' Ministry of Foreign Affairs.

7 See http://www.italaw.com/resources/investment-treaties.

8 See <http://icsid.worldbank.org>.

9 See Martins Paparinskis, "Regulatory Expropriation and Sustainable Development," in *Sustainable Development in World Investment Law*, ed. Marie-Claire Cordonier, Markus W. Gehring, and Andrew Newcombe, Global Trade Law Series (Alphen aan den Rijn: Kluwer Law International, 2011), 299.

10 Krista Nadakavukaren Schefer, *International Investment Law: Text, Cases and Materials*, 1st ed. (Cheltenham: Edward Elgar Publishing, 2013), 167. Salacuse refers to expropriation as *"the most dramatic way"* in which governments can change the conditions for foreign investments, see Jeswald W. Salacuse, *The Law of Investment Treaties*, 1st ed., Oxford International Law Library (Oxford: Oxford University Press, 2010), 286.

11 E.g. the Italy–Bangladesh BIT, article 9(1).

12 See e.g. *Tecmed v Mexico*, Award, 29 May 2003.

international investment law could have been chosen. For example another route for exploring the right to regulate could be to expand the case-study to other material standards of protection, e.g. the fair and equitable treatment (FET) standard. Another option would have been to examine public policies invoked as the ground for circumstances precluding wrongfulness under the laws of state responsibility.[13] These considerations, however, fall outside the scope of this research. Hence, there is ample opportunity for further research on other aspects of the preservation of policy space in international investment law.

From the national perspective of the researcher (University of Copenhagen, Denmark) international investment law and investment arbitration is a fairly novel topic within academia besides a few – though significant – contributions by Spiermann.[14] Within the Nordic countries the subject is still in its rise. From an international point of view, however, this research finds itself in the middle of the fire.

3. Foreign investments, the context, the risks and the law

This initial chapter explains the need for an international investment law regime, the legal framework protecting foreign investments and its current challenges when it comes to host states' right to regulate.

3.1. Foreign investment and social and economic growth

This research is concerned with foreign direct investment. Foreign direct investment refers here to an investment made to acquire lasting interest in enterprises operating outside the economy of the investor, in which the investor's purpose is to gain an effective voice in the management of the enterprise. Foreign direct investment can be made in several ways, for example as the direct investment into production in a country by a company in another country, through the buying of a company in the target state, by setting up a subsidiary or by expanding operations of an existing business in that state through a joint venture with a local company. Foreign direct investment may for example involve the setting up of a manufacturing plant, the extraction of natural resources such as oil, gas and minerals or the construction of a major facility like an airport. Foreign investment is generally considered a prerequisite for social and economic growth,[15] as governments in states hosting foreign investments become concerned about foreign

---

13 See Andrea K. Bjorklund, "Emergency Exceptions: State of Necessity and Force Majeure," in *The Oxford Handbook of International Investment Law*, ed. Peter Muchlinski, Federico Ortino, and Christoph Schreuer (Oxford: Oxford University Press, 2008), 459–523.

14 Professor Ole Spiermann has dealt with aspects of international investment law and arbitration, see e.g. Ole Spiermann, "International voldgift under Danmarks bilaterale investeringsoverenskomster," *Juristen* 9 (2003): 325–40; Ole Spiermann, "Individual Rights, State Interests, and the Power to Waive ICSID Jurisdiction under Bilateral Investment Treaties," *Arbitration International* 20, no. 2 (2004): 179–211.

15 Jose E. Alvarez and Karl P. Sauvant, *The Evolving International Investment Regime: Expectations, Realities, Options*, 1st ed. (Oxford: Oxford University Press, 2011), 43.

influence on national policies, the local economy, security aspects and indigenous culture foreign investment is given political overtones.[16]

A basic presumption is that the furtherance of economic growth possesses an underlying social dimension since economic progression give rise to higher expectations of an improved standard of living, such as better health standards and labour rights. Foreign investment may have significant positive influence on the local community by contributing to the local welfare, for instance by creating new job opportunities, related industries and infrastructure. In addition, foreign investment may have the potential to address pressing global challenges, such as poverty alleviation and climate change. The negative aspects can be manifold, such as social dumping, degradation of the environment and violations of human rights. The foundation for this research is thus the premise that foreign investment may have significant social, political, and environmental impact. However, the interrelation between economic and social objectives in protection of foreign investments as yet remains less clear.

3.2. The concept of political risk

When companies look towards new markets abroad they face a variety of risks, which they have to consider before making the decision whether to invest or not. Businesses investing abroad expose themselves to the possibility that their investments will turn out not to be fruitful. One of the clear risks associated with investments includes the actual *business risks,* which covers, for example the risk that a product or service will not get in touch with the market or is subsequently overthrown by another product or service. Moreover, business risks involve the risk that a potential purchaser of the product or service abroad turns out to be unwilling or unable to pay for it. The prospect of success contains an inherent aspect of uncertainty. The existence of a business risk is thus inescapable.

Political risk plays a pivotal role in the perceived threat to corporate investments abroad, particularly in emerging markets. Political risk is here perceived as the link of commercial activity, including profitability, owing to politically determined considerations rather than competition and market-related circumstances. The concept of political risk covers 1) the risk of unrest and disturbances, including armed conflicts and 2) the risk of changes in the laws or administration of the laws of the state, i.e. the risk of onerous regulation.

In terms of unrest and disturbances, the presence of armed groups and civil disorder may constitute essential political uncertainty and instability. The risk that governments are being overthrown may be a serious risk. With some conflicts taking place for decades, the uncertainty itself may become what is most certain.[17]

---

16 Salacuse, *The Law of Investment Treaties,* 29–30; Muthucumaraswamy Sornarajah, *The Settlement of Foreign Investment Disputes,* 1st ed. (The Hague: Kluwer Law International, 2000), 5.

17 Examples of long-term conflicts are for instance the conflict between Sri Lanka and the Tamil Tigers (LTTE) and the conflict in Colombia between the government and the Fuerzas Armadas Revolucionarias de Colombia (FARC).

Other conflicts arise more abruptly or emerge unexpectedly, such as the domino effect testified by the Arab Spring.[18] It is likely that the presence of armed groups may trigger governmental activities, but for the concept of political risk the determining factor lies with the state hosting the investment.

This research deals with the second aspect of political risk, i.e. the risk of onerous regulation, which is a key risk to investors. This risk covers the likelihood of changes to the operation and profitability of the investment as a result of the policy or administration, which impacts on the existence and/or an investor's ownership of the investment, on the continuous operation of the investment as well as on the possibility of transfer of returns. In their exercise of regulatory power states frequently change their laws and regulate in response to changing economic circumstances, and these changes are likely to make certain activities less profitable or even uneconomic to continue. Political risk can thus be negatively delimited from actual business risk and is then associated with *governmental action*, i.e. a deliberate mechanism, a state acting in its sovereign capacity. Hence, political risk can be mentioned as a factor of varying importance to the risk profile of the investment. However, the political risk is not a matter of whether the state will impose new regulations or not but rather to what extent these actions will affect the investment. In international investment law, the element of risk forms part of the notion of a protected investment.[19]

3.3. Conceptualizing the 'right to regulate'

From a conceptual perspective, the *right to regulate* is an affirmation of states' authority to act as sovereigns on behalf of the will of the people. Some could explain this by the analytical construct of a 'social contract' between a state and its people, a 'contract' that ensures that they all gain security in return for subjecting themselves to an absolute sovereign.[20] The right to regulate thus covers the authority of states to adopt regulation, i.e. to make deliberate changes (e.g. through legislation and administrative orders). As will be shown below in Chapter 2 the right to regulate is the affirmation of the sovereign right for states to choose their political, social and economic priorities – within certain limits –

---

18 The findings of a foreign investor survey undertaken in 2011 by the World Bank's Multilateral Investment Guarantee Agency (MIGA) found that the turmoil did have a significant impact on corporate investors' investment intentions concerning the Middle East and North Africa, see also Paul Antony Barbour, Nathan M. Jensen, and Daniel Villar, "The Arab Spring: How Soon Will Foreign Investors Return?," *Columbia FDI Perspectives*, no. 67 (7 May 2012), <http://ccsi.columbia.edu/files/2014/01/FDI_67.pdf>.
19 Rudolf Dolzer and Christoph Schreuer, *Principles of International Investment Law*, 2nd ed. (Oxford: Oxford University Press, 2012), 60.
20 For Thomas Hobbes, the social contract was a necessity to avoid the state of nature, i.e. "a war of every man against every man". According to John Locke, however, the state of nature was not linked with chaos and horror but rather an "Eden before the Fall". Yet, a significant flaw in this state of nature was, according to Locke, the protection of property. Consequently, man renounced the idyllic state of nature and by contract gave up part of his liberty to a sovereign. See further in Freeman, *Lloyd's Introduction to Jurisprudence*, 105–12.

through the adoption of legislation and administrative practices without violating international rules protecting foreign investments. The scope to which states may regulate without violating international law, the regulatory space of manoeuvre, is also referred to as the *public policy space* of host states, the *regulatory scope of manoeuvre* or in connection with expropriation, the *police power* of the host state. This research also covers interferences with administrative rights necessary for the operation of the investment, e.g. the withdrawal of a licence or cancellation of a permit for violation of the conditions attached hereto.[21]

3.4. Increasing social welfare regulation enhances political risk

In some states, human rights concerns have accelerated regulation, negatively affecting the value of foreign investments. States may for example seek to advance the level of development through the promotion of human rights. Moreover, states are obliged to protect against human rights abuses within their territory and/or jurisdiction by third parties, including business enterprises. This requires that states take appropriate steps to prevent, investigate, punish and redress human rights abuse through effective policies, legislation, regulations and adjudication.[22] Commitments to human rights treaties generate a duty to advance human rights, which can be fulfilled through the adoption of laws and regulation.[23] In addition to what states are required to do under the human rights regime, states may – more generally – seek to adopt *social welfare regulation*. Social welfare regulation is here positively defined as regulation imposed to promote development considerations in the community interest beyond the duty to regulate under the human rights regime. Social welfare regulation is also referred to here as *bona fide* regulation, if generally applied.

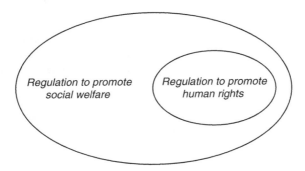

Figure 1.1 Social welfare regulation as a broader concept encompassing human rights regulation

---

21 Muthucumaraswamy Sornarajah, *The International Law on Foreign Investment*, 3rd ed. (Cambridge: Cambridge University Press, 2010), 16, 402–3. In many instances, the definition of an investment in an international investment agreement covers administrative rights, including licences and permits.

22 This is dealt with below in Chapter 4.

23 Chapter 4 analyses this duty to regulate under the human rights regime.

As a consequence of states' duty to regulate under the human rights regime and adoption of social welfare regulation the probability that investors are met by onerous regulation is likely to increase. Hence a growing risk of governmental interference with the investment generates the need for foreign investors to address this risk.

3.5. The need for addressing political risk

Political risk is particularly evident for long-term investments projects. As the time horizon of an investment prolongs, the political risk factor becomes increasingly important to address. International research points to the presence of political risk as being a major risk and obstacle to companies' investments in emerging markets.[24] It even seems to be a greater barrier than the scope for funding the investment and lack of macroeconomic stability.[25] The risk becomes even more apparent taking into account the fact that long-term foreign investment often involves substantial capital flows. As a consequence of increased regulation, in particular triggered by obligations to regulate to promote human rights, to safeguard the environment and to enhance development concerns, corporations are more and more concerned with how they can control or influence public policies. If not, investors may face regulation that negatively affects the investment. Ultimately, the regulation may result in investors challenging the measures in investment arbitration. These types of disputes have increased.[26]

As a risk-mitigating tool, states may negotiate international investment agreements (IIAs), such as bilateral investment treaties (BITs).

3.6. The general legal framework of protection of foreign investments

The vast majority of IIAs are formulated with the aim of protecting investors and their investments, and to attract capital that can contribute to economic growth and development in the host states.[27] Modern IIAs can generally be divided into

---

24 Multilateral Investment Guarantee Agency (MIGA), "World Investment and Political Risk. The Global Environment" (2009), available at: <http://www.oecd.org/investment/global forum/44235652.pdf>.

25 *Ibid.*

26 Sornarajah, *The International Law on Foreign Investment*, 77.

27 However, it is debated whether BITs in fact push forward foreign investment flows. See e.g. James Xiaoning Zhan, "The Spread of Bits and Their Changing Face," *ICSID Review* 24, no. 2 (2009): 339–46; Kenneth J. Vandevelde, "Investment Liberalization and Economic Development: The Role of Bilateral Investment Treaties," *Columbia Journal of Transnational Law* 36, no. 3 (1998): 524–5; Gus Van Harten, "Five Justifications for Investment Treaties: A Critical Discussion," *Trade, Law and Development* 2, no. 1 (2010): 19–58; Lauge Skovgaard Poulsen, "The Importance of Bits for Foreign Direct Investment and Political Risk Insurance: Revisiting the Evidence," in *Yearbook on International Investment Law & Policy*, ed. Karl P. Sauvant (Oxford: Oxford University Press, 2010), 539–74.

multilateral treaties and bilateral treaties. Multilateral treaties are for example treaties regulating investments in a specific geographical area, e.g. the North American Free Trade Agreement (NAFTA).[28] Multilateral treaties may also cover certain types of investments, e.g. the Energy Charter Treaty (ECT), which concerns, among other things, investment in the energy sector. Investment chapters may also be inserted into both multilateral and bilateral Free Trade Agreements (FTAs).

Bilateral investment treaties (BITs) have been negotiated since 1959 between two states for the mutual promotion and protection of foreign investments. Traditionally, BITs were concluded between a developed and a developing country. Some states adopted model treaty texts (model BITs) as a basis for negotiation. Even though the model BITs changed over time, the BITs concluded resembled each other in their purpose and content.[29]

Today, close to 2,850 BITs have come into existence[30] and to a large extent they rely on the same standards of protection covering: (i) full protection and security; (ii) fair and equitable treatment; (iii) prompt and effective compensation in the event of expropriation or similar measures; (iv) compensation for loss caused by war or insurrections; (v) guarantees of free transfers of funds; (vi) non-discrimination and most-favoured-nation treatment. This catalogue of rights encompasses the most common obligations for the host state to protect foreign investments, whereas BITs rarely impose obligations of any significance on the capital-exporting state. Furthermore, the vast majority of BITs includes an access to settlement of disputes by international arbitration, most frequently with the opportunity to settle claims at the Centre for Settlement of Investment Disputes (ICSID). The majority of IIAs allow for investor–state dispute settlement and thus the regime is enforced by private investors through ad hoc arbitration systems. Today, developing countries remain most often the state party involved in ICSID investment disputes, where South America makes up 29% of all cases (many of them against Argentina following the financial crisis), Sub-Saharan Africa 16%, Eastern Europe and Central Asia 24 % in contrast to Western Europe limited to only 2%.[31]

In Europe after the entering into force of the Lisbon Treaty in December 2009, EU member states can no longer conclude new BITs without the permission of the EU Commission. The EU Commission engaged in FTA negotiations with, for example, India, Singapore and Canada before the Lisbon Treaty was

---

28 Trade and investment agreement between the USA, Canada and Mexico.
29 Campbell McLachlan, Laurence Shore, and Matthew Weiniger, *International Investment Arbitration: Substantive Principles*, ed. Loukas A. Mistelis and Clive M. Schmitthoff, 1st ed., Oxford International Arbitration Series (Oxford: Oxford University Press, 2007), 26; Kenneth J. Vandevelde, *Bilateral Investment Treaties: History, Policy, and Interpretation*, 1st ed. (Oxford: Oxford University Press, 2010), 196.
30 All current BITs can be found on the webpage of United Nations Conference on Trade and Development (UNCTAD).
31 The ICSID Case-load Statistics, July 2013, see <https://icsid.worldbank.org>.

concluded. With the Lisbon Treaty in force the Commission requested that the EU Council should permit to broaden their mandate to include negotiations on investment protection. Since investment is now part of the EU's common commercial policy, the European Commission may thus legislate on investment. The Comprehensive Economic and Trade Agreement (CETA) between the EU and Canada has been negotiated so far, and the Transatlantic Trade and Investment Partnership agreement (TTIP) is currently at issue.

The European Convention on Human Rights (ECHR) contains provisions in its First Protocol on protection of private property rights. However, this convention does obviously not have investment protection as its primary purpose.

3.7. Insurances against political risk

In addition to treaty-based investment protection, investors may on their own initiative mitigate political risk by taking out an *insurance policy*. The Multilateral Investment Guarantee Agency (MIGA) offers Political Risk Insurances (PRI) for foreign private investments into projects in developing countries. MIGA can provide assurances for various types of non-commercial risks, including against expropriation, which covers losses that arise from nationalizations and confiscations as well as limited coverage for indirect expropriations.[32]

Another option that might be available for investors is to seek the support of national export credit agencies (ECAs) available in the home state. The ECA typically provides trade financing to national companies for their international activities, including insurances to companies in order to promote exports. These insurances may cover aspects of both commercial as well as political risks. ECAs may thereby remove the risk from the exporter. In general, ECAs (partly) cover the risks that regular private insurance companies exempt as situations of *force majeure*.[33]

It thus follows that there is (also) an opportunity to address political risks by taking out insurances.

3.8. Some remarks on investment protection under the WTO regime

From a legal perspective, trade and investment are in principle two separate things. There are, however, weighty reasons to attach some importance to the international trade regime. The drafting of a multilateral agreement covering

---

32 MIGA, for types of coverage, see <https://www.miga.org/investment-guarantees/overview/types-of-coverage/>.
33 See for example Denmark's export credit agency, <http://www.ekf.dk/en/Pages/default.aspx>.

investments has previously been a vital ambition under the World Trade Organization (WTO) and investment protection is included in many Free Trade Agreements (FTAs) today.

Within the WTO there are three main areas of work covering both trade and investment:[34]

- a Working Group established in 1996, which conducts analytical work on the relationship between trade and investment;
- the Agreement on Trade-Related Investment Measures (TRIMs Agreement);
- the General Agreement on Trade in Services (GATS Agreement) addresses foreign investment in services as one of four modes of supply of services.

At the 2001 Doha Ministerial Conference, the ministers recognized *"the case for constructing a multilateral framework to secure transparent, stable and predictable conditions for long-term cross-border investment, particularly facing foreign direct investment"*.[35]

Though a multilateral agreement was not concluded within the WTO framework, reminiscence hereof remains. This can for example be illustrated on the treaty-negotiating level where some states have chosen a WTO approach to narrow investment protection. Canada, for example, has opted for a list of general exceptions from BIT/FTA protections inspired by those contained in article XX of the GATT.[36]

The interaction of the trade and investment law regime may become a pertinent issue when private investors address trade issues that in principle should be handled by the WTO. Trade law and investment law contain similar aspects, and the analyses that are carried out by corporations in the early phase making the decision to trade or invest in the first place is likely to be close to identical. Yet, there are significant differences between trade law and investment law. An important observation is that many investors' rights do not exist in the trade law regime. Within the trade law regime there is no 'fair and equitable treatment' standard, no guarantee of 'full protection and security' and no equivalent to the 'umbrella clause' contained in many BITs. In addition hereto, there is no equivalent to the property protection contained in IIAs, which provides that 'prompt, adequate and effective' compensation must be paid for expropriations.

---

34 WTO, Trade and Investment. See further in Friedl Weiss, "Trade and Investment," in *The Oxford Handbook of International Investment Law*, ed. Peter Muchlinski, Federico Ortino, and Christoph Schreuer (Oxford: Oxford University Press, 2008), 183–223.
35 Doha Ministerial Declaration, adopted on 14 November 2001.
36 Further on regulation of investment in the trade regime see Petros C. Mavroidis, "Regulation of Investment in the Trade Régime: From ITO to WTO," in *Regulation of Foreign Investment: Challenges to International Harmonization*, ed. Zdenek Drabek and Petros Mavroidis, World Scientific Studies in International Economics (Singapore: World Scientific Publishing, 2013), 13–55.

Finally, there is no right under the trade law regime for private parties to challenge trade-restrictive measures or to claim compensation. No such private remedy is available under the trade law regime.[37]

Some investment tribunals have, nevertheless, referred to WTO case law when interpreting investment protection treaties. Contracting states to an IIA do have the opportunity to agree on interpretative guidance in IIAs and refer arbitral tribunals to WTO jurisprudence. However, drawing on WTO jurisprudence should be carried out with caution, since the substantive protection within these two legal regimes is fundamentally different.[38] From a theoretical perspective trade and investment should therefore be treated separately.[39] The potential for investment tribunals in 'borrowing' WTO arguments will therefore not be further addressed here.

3.9. Foreign investment in the era of globalization

From the beginning of the 1990s, globalization has increasingly been a theme on the global agenda.[40] Due to its sheer quantity foreign direct investment is an essential factor or conceivably 'the principal engine' under globalization. As globalization has generated more accessible ways of communication the attention given to human rights has increased, in particular to economic, social and cultural rights as well as development considerations.[41] Technological improvements have provided new channels for faster communication distributing information about natural disasters, insurrections or other conflicts with a tremendous speed. Reports are made directly from the battlefield, not only by journalists but also by the involved parties to the conflict through the use of social media. Information about major environmental catastrophes, such as the BP Deepwater Horizon accident, the Fukushima nuclear crisis or the collapse of the eight-storey commercial building and garment factory in Bangladesh has not passed the public unattended. Together with these new channels of fast communication, debates have arisen as to whether or when the international community is expected to respond to atrocities and take action against the responsible. 'Moral responsibility' with

---

37 See further in Michael J. Trebilcock and Robert Howse, *The Regulation of International Trade*, 3rd ed. (London: Routledge, 2005).
38 In this direction see Thomas W. Wälde, "Interpreting Investment Treaties," in *International Investment Law for the 21st Century: Essays in Honour of Christoph Schreuer*, ed. Christina Binder, Ursula Kriebaum, August Reinisch, and Stephan Wittich (Oxford: Oxford University Press, 2009), 772.
39 Further on the duality of the two systems, see Dolzer and Schreuer, *Principles of International Investment Law*, 19, 204–6.
40 Paul R. Viotti and Mark V. Kauppi, *International Relations Theory*, 5th ed. (Harlow: Pearson, 2011), 71–2.
41 This is confirmed by the adoption of the Optional Protocol to the International Covenant on Economic, Social and Cultural Rights (OP ICESCR) by the UN General Assembly in December 2008, which provides the Committee (the monitoring treaty-body of the ICESCR) with competence to consider individual complaints.

tremendous economic repercussions could in principle be imputed to corporations at a very early stage and way before initiation of legal proceedings.

These various specific incidents seem to give rise to discussions of more general international themes with potential implications for foreign investments and the need for international regulation. The financial crisis is one example. The collapses of banks and financial institutions have received tremendous global attention, which have triggered debates about designating regulations intended for the global scale, global governance, for issues that affect the international society as a whole. Climate change is another more general theme. The melting of ice in the Arctic area has for example led to new opportunities for investment in natural resources, not accessible just a few years ago. The interest of the international society is thus not limited to international common concerns as for example terrorism and global warming that transcends national borders and affects all human beings. The international society is *also* concerned with issues, which basically are national affairs. The point here is that international concern – the public interests of the international society – now extends beyond matters that are international to these national affairs. When governmental actions are fundamentally in opposition to the values of the international society as a whole, it may not (yet) automatically trigger international action, but at least states cannot be sure it will *not*. Globalization is thus to a degree enhancing integration of an international borderless society and a uniform culture. A consequence of globalization and the responses hereto is that regulating foreign investments is no longer purely a national concern.

The global BIT regime has evolved over time from European states negotiating BITs with developing countries, most commonly based on model BITs, which they presented to potential treaty partners as the basis for negotiation, to today's BIT regime, where developing countries have concluded BITs among themselves. Today, Western countries encounter the reciprocity of the BIT regime with developing countries such as India and China increasingly investing in European states. With a society in transformation, both on the national and the global level, the BIT regime has to respond to the changing context. Public policies should therefore be reflected in the BIT regime affecting the normative legal framework protecting foreign investment.[42] On this basis, the international investment regime is in a state of transition. In order to respond to the realities of today, reflection upon the legal framework that regulates foreign investment is needed.

4. The crisis of international investment law

The international investment law regime is in a 'state of crisis', a crisis that becomes visible in investment arbitrations. This crisis can be viewed from various

---

42 This transition is described in Alvarez and Sauvant, *The Evolving International Investment Regime.* See also more recent World Investment Reports (WIR) by UNCTAD describing policy trends and the emergence of a broader development policy agenda, e.g. WIR 2012, "Towards a New Generation of Investment Policies."

perspectives and labelled in numerous ways, e.g. as a legitimacy crisis or a sovereignty crisis.[43]

4.1. The legitimacy crisis of international investment law

The global network of BITs creates a number of systemic and substantive challenges. At the systemic level, with more than 2,800 treaties, numerous negotiations and multiple dispute settlements mechanisms, the sphere of BITs has become too large for states to control, too complicated for companies to benefit from, and too complex for stakeholders in general to monitor.[44] At the substantive level, standards of protection are often broad and vaguely formulated for example requiring states to provide 'full protection and security', 'fair and equitable treatment' or compensation for 'indirect expropriations.' The vaguely formulated standards generate much uncertainty with regards to interpretation of the content and scope of the obligations enshrined. In particular, it is unclear how much discretion should be allowed for states to make other priorities and what weight should be given to other international commitments.

As legal uncertainties become visible in the application of the law, controversies relating to international investment law have appeared in investment arbitrations with debates about the 'legitimacy of the system.'[45] The legitimacy of the international investment regime is challenged from various sides. In legal terms, legitimacy is typically associated with 1) impartiality, 2) certainty and 3) accountability and investment arbitration is claimed to lack in each of these areas.

In terms of the impartiality arbitrators are claimed to be too investor-friendly with pro-investor interpretations that tend to prioritize investment protection over the right for states to regulate.[46] Only investors may initiate arbitration

---

43 In 2010, a group of academics from various countries published a statement on the international investment regime expressing fundamental concerns. The statement can be found at <http://www.osgoode.yorku.ca/public-statement-international-investment-regime-31-august-2010/>.

44 See the critiques of the investment regime by José E. Alvarez, Professor of International Law, New York University School of Law, UN Audiovisual Library, Lecture Series, International Economic Law, Foreign Investment, <http://www.un.org/law/avl/>. See also the statement by Supachai Panitchpakdi, Secretary-General of UNCTAD at the UNCTAD World Investment Forum 2012, WIF 2012 Ministerial roundtable, Doha, 22 April 2012.

45 See e.g. Stephan W. Schill, "Enhancing International Investment Law's Legitimacy: Conceptual and Methodological Foundations of a New Public Law Approach," *Virginia Journal of International Law* 52, no. 1 (2011): 57–102; Stephan W. Schill, "W(h)ither Fragmentation? On the Literature and Sociology of International Investment Law," *European Journal of International Law* 22, no. 3 (2011): 894–7; Mark C. Weidemaier, "Toward a Theory of Precedent in Arbitration," *William and Mary Law Review* 51, no. 5 (2010): 1895–958; Tai-Heng Chen, "Precedent and Control in Investment Treaty Arbitration," *Fordham International Law Journal* 30, no. 4 (2007): 1014–49; Susan D. Franck, "The Legitimacy Crisis in Investment Treaty Arbitration: Privatizing Public International Law through Inconsistent Decisions," *Fordham Law Review* 73, no. 4 (2005): 1521–625.

46 See the Public Statement, "Pro-investor interpretations of investment treaties."

proceedings, and this alone could make the tribunals favour investors' interests because the tribunals depend on investors for employment. Arbitral tribunals are convened on a case-by-case basis but are claimed to have interpreted the same standards of protection inconsistently.[47] The arbitration process by definition lacks transparency, which is problematic in some cases involving key public policies. Weak accountability mechanisms for arbitrators do not allow for rectification. There is no appeals system to correct mistakes. The unpredictability of the law is thereby exacerbated by the weakness of accountability mechanisms.[48]

These concerns all presuppose the existence of 'a system' or 'a legal regime.' Yet, there is no such formal system established. BITs are not identical and arbitral practice appears to lack coherence due to the very nature of arbitration. International law does not generally support the *stare decisis* doctrine. Hence, fragmentation of the law is a risk and a reality. Yet, there are considerable reasons for perceiving international investment arbitration as a system.[49] So, to the extent that investment arbitration could be perceived as 'a system' the legitimacy seems to lack.

Above all, the 'legitimacy crisis' is largely a result of the recognition that BITs are not political statements 'signalling a state's good will to promote and protect foreign investment', but legally binding obligations under international law that are implemented by a powerful enforcement mechanism in the form of investment treaty arbitration.[50]

4.2. The sovereignty crisis of international investment law

A fundamental concern linked with the legitimacy concerns is the question of how states can create a legitimate system that binds them to their commitments pursuant to an IIA without overly impinging on their sovereignty. These concerns are intrinsically associated with the right for states to act in their sovereign capacity, i.e. the right to regulate. There appears to be a growing concern that states' policy space is vastly diminished.[51] In particular, there is a concern that BITs can interfere with states' sustainable development strategies and prevent them from implementing policies that address the environmental and social impact of

---

47 Controversies relate inter alia to the interpretation of umbrella clauses, the scope of indirect expropriations, the interpretation of the MFN clause. See also Muthucumaraswamy Sornarajah, "Starting Anew in International Investment Law," *Columbia FDI Perspectives*, no. 74 (16 July 2012), available at <http://ccsi.columbia.edu/files/2014/01/FDI_74.pdf>.

48 Jose E. Alvarez, "Part III: Critiques of the Investment Regime," *UN Audiovisual Library of International Law*, available at: <http://legal.un.org/avl/lectureseries.html>.

49 See below section 5.

50 Schill, "W(h)ither Fragmentation?," 896.

51 Anna Joubin-Bret, Marie-Estelle Rey, and Jörg Weber, "International Investment Law and Development," in *Sustainable Development in World Investment Law*, ed. Marie-Claire Cordonier Segger, Markus W. Gehring, and Andrew Paul Newcombe, Global Trade Law Series (Alphen aan den Rijn: Kluwer Law International, 2011), 15–31.

investments. This is referred to as 'the sovereignty crisis of international investment law.' This criticism has also been referred to as 'the public law challenge' of international investment law,[52] since investment treaty arbitration is viewed as a threat to public law values, such as democracy and the rule of law.[53] In the main, the critics argue, it is not democratically legitimate to confine cases testing public policies of national reforms to three international arbitrators in a closed forum. These concerns have been raised not only by academics but also by civil society, including NGOs seeking to promote the rule of law, transparency and insight into investment arbitrations.[54]

In addition to these considerations, human rights concerns add a further perspective. Sometimes, states wish to regulate to promote human rights. This becomes visible in investment arbitrations where states have sought to justify non-compliance with BITs on the basis that compliance interferes with measures necessary for realizing their legal obligations under human rights law, i.e. the obligations to respect, protect and fulfil human rights.[55] It is thus questionable whether states did foresee that such guarantees could limit their ability to fulfil human rights. Investment arbitrators are continuously confronted with human rights questions, which they have to address. Consequently, human rights and international investment law can no longer be viewed as two distinct branches of international law.

Some critics have expressed the sovereignty crisis by claiming that the current system of international investment law is not *balanced*. This imbalance is caused by the asymmetrical structure of BITs, which impose numerous obligations on states hosting foreign investments whereas they rarely impose any obligations on investors.[56] However, in opposition hereto, it has also been argued that tribunals 'have done a good job' in balancing rights and obligations and that these concerns simply have not been reflected in the final results of the cases.[57] Yet,

---

52 Stephan Schill, "The Public Law Challenge: Killing or Rethinking International Investment Law?," *Columbia FDI Perspectives*, no. 58 (30 January 2012), available at <http://ccsi. columbia.edu/files/2014/01/FDI_58.pdf>.

53 *Ibid*. See also Gus van Harten, *Investment Treaty Arbitration and Public Law*, ed. Catherine Redgewell, Dan Sarooshi, and Stefan Talmon, 1st ed., Oxford Monographs in International Law (Oxford: Oxford University Press, 2007); David Schneiderman, *Constitutionalizing Economic Globalization: Investment Rules and Democracy's Promise* (Cambridge: Cambridge University Press, 2008).

54 For the latter, see below Chapter 4, section 9.2.2: Human rights arguments by third parties.

55 Ashfaq Khalfan, "International Investment Law and Human Rights," in *Sustainable Development in World Investment Law*, ed. Marie-Claire Cordonier Segger, Markus W. Gehring, and Andrew Paul Newcombe, Global Trade Law Series (Alphen aan den Rijn: Kluwer Law International, 2011), 53.

56 The Statement "Pro-investor interpretations of investment treaties"; Patrick Dumberry and Gabrielle Dumas-Aubin, "How to Impose Human Rights Obligations on Corporations under Investment Treaties? Pragmatic Guidelines for the Amendment of Bits," in *Yearbook on International Investment Law & Policy 2011–2012*, ed. Karl P. Sauvant (Oxford: Oxford University Press, 2010), 569.

57 See the blog of Professor Andrew Newcombe, 3 September 2010 on the Kluwer Arbitration Blog, available at: <http://kluwerarbitrationblog.com/>.

the illustrative cases in this research demonstrate fundamental imperfections, i.e. imbalances (from a policy perspective) and fragmentations of the law (from a legal perspective).

These various challenges have led some states to reassess their investment treaty policies, to return to domestic law and domestic courts[58] or even to withdraw from the ICSID Convention.[59] Other states have tried to respond to these concerns by drafting new IIAs that include mechanisms that retain their right to regulate investment in the public interest.

4.3. The stability–flexibility dilemma

Taken together, the legitimacy crisis and the sovereignty crisis may be characterized as a stability–flexibility dilemma, which incorporates the tensions between these two anti-poles; ensuring a solid investment climate (stability) and retaining regulatory space of manoeuvre (flexibility).

Economic and regulatory stability is vital for the investor in its decision whether to engage in a long-term investment or not. Though the element of risk is inherent in every investment project, stability is an essential factor that the investor seeks to control due to the fact that investment projects oftentimes involve substantial capital flows. Hence, the interest of the investor is to maintain stability. Stability is not only a concern for the investor but also a key component for states to attract foreign investments. Stability is vital, not only in terms of legal stability, but also stability in the broader sense, on the political level. An essential point in this regard is that legal stability is not necessarily obtained by upholding the legal framework as it is in a context that changes.

States need flexibility in the form of a regulatory space of manoeuvre to promote social welfare and development and to live up to international human rights commitments. A level of flexibility in the legal framework is a central element to ensure a smooth and sustainable system providing enough leeway for states to develop by ensuring that investment protection can be adapted to national or regional policies.[60] Indeed, states may change their policies or want to respond to changing circumstances in the society and the public interest. Moreover, flexibility in the legal framework is in the interest of the investor to ensure that the project can be adapted to the context in which it operates and to respond to unanticipated events. Developments and unforeseen circumstances may thus entail the consequences that a fixed legal framework may become unbalanced. In short, both investors and host states need stability and flexibility.

---

58 Australia has issued a trade policy statement announcing that it would not include ISDS clauses in future IIAs.

59 Bolivia, Ecuador and Venezuela have denounced the ICSID Convention by a withdrawal pursuant to article 71 of the Convention.

60 See also Peter Muchlinski, "Policy Issues," in *The Oxford Handbook of International Investment Law*, ed. Peter Muchlinski, Federico Ortino, and Christoph Schreuer (Oxford: Oxford University Press, 2008), 5.

The stability–flexibility dilemma is intensified by the long-term nature of foreign investment projects. How and to what extent flexibility should be incorporated into the legal framework is, however, a contentious issue.

The stability–flexibility dilemma was articulated by an arbitral tribunal in the investment dispute, *Saluka v Czech Republic*,[61] where the tribunal was tasked with the determination of how to delimit compensable from non-compensable regulation:[62]

> "... *international law has yet to identify in a comprehensive and definitive fashion precisely what regulations are considered 'permissible' and 'commonly accepted' as falling within the police or regulatory power of States and, thus, non-compensable. In other words, it has yet to draw a bright and easily distinguishable line between non-compensable regulations on the one hand and, on the other, measures that have the effect of depriving foreign investors of their investment and are thus unlawful and compensable in international law.*"

Research carried out in relation to international investment law and the right to regulate encapsulates the fundamental dilemma between creating a stable legal environment that encourages foreign investors to invest, and flexibility so that states are not discouraged or barred from exercising their right to regulate. The crisis of international law thus calls for solutions to the stability–flexibility dilemma so that investors and investments enjoy legal protection against interferences that may occur. The legal protection that the investor can get is not a protection against interferences as such but in the form of a right to compensation for such interferences. At the same time, states may regulate but there is a need for distinguishing between types of regulation and the aim fulfilled. It is therefore disputed whether states should thus be liable to compensate investors for interferences caused by their commitments to human rights treaties or when they seek to enhance general social welfare and development.

Various suggestions have been made for accommodating these tension of the stability–flexibility dilemma in terms of improving the current international investment law regime, including suggestions to improve transparency and establishing an appeal system.[63] Moreover, it has been suggested that states should be able to raise counterclaims against investors.[64] On the theoretical level, novel arguments relating to the existence of a global administrative law

---

61 *Saluka v Czech Republic*, Partial Award, 17 March 2006.
62 *Ibid.*, para. 263.
63 Marie-Claire Cordonier Segger and Avidan Kent, "Promoting Sustainable Investment through International Law," in *Sustainable Development in World Investment Law*, ed. Marie-Claire Cordonier Segger, Markus W. Gehring, and Andrew Paul Newcombe, Global Trade Law Series (Alphen aan den Rijn: Kluwer Law International, 2011), 771–92.
64 Jean E. Kalicki, "Counterclaims by States in Investment Arbitration," *Investment Treaty News*, 14 January 2013, available at: <https://www.iisd.org/itn/2013/01/14/counterclaims-by-states-in-investment-arbitration-2/>.

and standards of global governance have been presented.[65] For example it has been suggested to draw upon WTO law, EU law and human rights to develop general principles of public law applicable as a recognized source of international law.[66] These suggestions confirm the notion of coherence as a guiding principle of international law.

All in all, there is a need to establish rules that more concretely address the stability–flexibility dilemma. These rules could be established at the contractual level between a host state and a concrete investor. This research, however, seeks to address the stability–flexibility dilemma from an international law perspective.

In terms of balancing investment protection with public policy concern, critics may put forward whether this is actually a *legal* problem. The answer to this question is that it is not purely a legal problem, but it can be addressed from a legal perspective. Two reasons support this view: Legal instruments such as BITs reveal that states consider this balancing of investment protection with their right to regulate. Secondly, in the end it becomes a legal problem when arbitrators are assigned to taking into account diverging interests, i.e. balancing investment protection with other international obligations.

5. International law as an evolving system

Various branches of general international law, including international investment law, can be referred to as 'specialized', 'subordinate' or 'self-contained' regimes.[67] These expressions are used to emphasize that each regime comes with its own principles, its own form of expertise and its own ethos, which is not necessarily identical with the ethos of the neighbouring specializations. Developments within these specialized areas alongside developments in general international law have led to an increasing fragmentation of international law.

Yet, international law needs order. Order is necessary to ensure a just and stable existence.[68] International law is here perceived as an element that binds members of the international community together in their adherence to recognized common values and standards. On the whole, states feel obliged to obey the rules of international law as a 'common frame of reference'.[69] The necessity to act in accordance with international rules is founded in the desire among states for ensuring stability and predictability.[70] On the basis of this desire of an international order, the idea of coherence transpires.

---

65 See generally, Stephan W. Schill, *International Investment Law and Comparative Public Law*, 1st ed. (Oxford: Oxford University Press, 2010).

66 Schill, "The Public Law Challenge," 186.

67 The ILC Report, *Fragmentation of International Law*, at 14, para. 15.

68 Malcolm N. Shaw, *International Law*, 6th ed. (Cambridge: Cambridge University Press, 2008), 1–7.

69 *Ibid.*

70 *Ibid.*

Treaties are often 'bargains' or 'package-deals' to the detriment of coherence. Still, the fundamental prerequisite for international law is to consider it as a system,[71] and in this system of international law there can never be a complete separation between law and policy.[72]

This research is about the explained stability–flexibility dilemma addressed from a theoretical and principled point of view. From a legal perspective, the flexibility dilemma can be characterized as a problem of the collision of the two regimes, international investment law and human rights.[73] Each legal regime consists of legal norms (rules, standards and principles) as well as its specific expertise, and interest, its ethos, and the collision thus concerns both law and policy. Resolving such conflict is thus the challenge.

There is no general basis in international law for attaching supremacy to one legal regime (e.g. the human rights regime) over another (e.g. the international investment law regime). The only recognized supremacy in international law is the supremacy of the UN Charter[74] and norms of *jus cogens*.[75] It therefore appears useful to develop an approach to the law that aims at unifying these two legal regimes.

The task of resolving this collision of legal regimes was initially taken up by the International Law Commission, which published a report on the Fragmentation of International Law in 2006 (the ILC Report).[76] The problem of colliding legal regimes has also been addressed in international law practice by the International Court of Justice (the ICJ). Through a 'borrowing process' in quite a few cases, the ICJ has borrowed concepts and findings from human rights bodies, with the aim of enhancing coherence.[77] This research builds on the work of the ILC on Fragmentation of International law.[78] The essence hereof is that the VCLT can work

---

71 Further on international law as a system, see e.g. Ralf Michaels and Joost H.B. Pauwelyn, "Conflict of Norms or Conflict of Laws? Different Techniques in the Fragmentation of International Law," in *Multi-Sourced Equivalent Norms in International Law*, ed. Tomer Broude and Yuval Shany, Studies in International Law (Oxford: Hart Publishing, 2011), 19–44.

72 Shaw, *International Law*, 11.

73 See also Jörg Kammerhofer, "The Theory of Norm Conflict Solutions in International Investment Law," in *Sustainable Development in World Investment Law*, ed. Marie-Claire Cordonier, Markus W. Gehring, and Andrew Newcombe, Global Trade Law Series (Alphen ann den Rijn: Kluwer Law International, 2011), 85.

74 VCLT article 30 (1) referring to article 103 of the UN Charter.

75 VCLT article 53. See also Shaw, *International Law*, 125.

76 The ILC report.

77 This 'borrowing process' is largely facilitated by the fact that a significant number of ICJ judges are former members of international human rights bodies; see further in Menno T. Kamminga, "Final Report on the Impact of International Human Rights Law on General International Law," in *The Impact of Human Rights Law on General International Law*, ed. Menno T. Kamminga and Martin Scheinin (Oxford: Oxford University Press, 2009), 3–4.

78 The ILC report.

as a legal tool, 'the glue', having a binding force on international law.[79] Moreover, the human rights regime may offer further guidance useful for enhancing coherence. Chapter 2 explains the theoretical foundations for enhancing coherence of the two legal regimes, the unification of international investment law.

79 The VCLT has been ratified by most states; but while some states have not ratified the VCLT it is nevertheless recognized as a restatement of customary law and thereby binding upon non-parties.

2 General international law, investment protection and the right to regulate

1. Aim

Chapter 2 embraces two essential aims. Firstly, a central objective of this part is to explain the stability–flexibility dilemma from a general international law perspective. Chapter 2 therefore explores the right for states to act in their sovereign capacity, i.e. the right to regulate under general international law (the flexibility aspect) vis-à-vis the boundaries of this right owing to states' obligations to protect foreign investors and their investments know under the concept of protection of aliens and their property (the stability aspect). The rules relating to the protection of aliens and their property, founded in customary international law, will be explained here in order to establish 'the law behind' the international investment law regime, i.e. the rules that were developed before the expansion of BITs.

The second aim of this part is to show how the paradigm of general international law may provide a theoretical framework, which is useful for developing solutions to the stability–flexibility dilemma of international investment law. For this purpose, rules of treaty interpretation are explained, but in addition hereto efforts are made to establish a theoretical basis for adjudicators, providing a more balanced approach to the stability–flexibility dilemma in practice. In this regard, this research embarks on the work of the ILC concerning Fragmentation of International Law[1] supplemented by considerations of *gravitational pull*.[2]

This part begins by explaining international investment law as a specialized regime of general international law encompassing central aspects of both public and private law.

1 The ILC report.
2 These considerations are expressed in academic literature by Bruno Simma and Theodore Kill. Simma is an experienced international law professor, who served as a judge on the International Court of Justice from 2003 to 2012 and before that at the International Law Commission. Kill, the student of Simma, served as a trainee in 2008–2009 at the International Court of Justice, and is now an Adjunct Professor of Law at George Mason University, Law School, Michigan.

2. International investment law as a special branch of general investment law

The term 'general international law' refers to the classical rules governing the relation between states also known as 'public international law' or just 'international law'. The body of international law covers customary norms, such as the laws of state responsibility and treaty interpretation, general principles of law such as the duty for states to act in good faith as well as commitments laid down by states in treaty obligations. 'International investment law' can be referred to as a special branch of general international law containing the rules governing a specific area of law, i.e. the protection of foreign investments. As a specialized system the specific characteristics of international investment law come into play, such as the various interests in the three-part relation of the host state–investor–home state. One of the specific characteristics of this branch of law is the public–private relation. Displaying the international investment law regime from a purely international law perspective would fail seriously for neglecting the private law character. The public–private law character of international investment law is therefore dealt with below.

2.1. *The public–private dichotomy*

The increasing porosity of the public–private divide is a central fact in economic relations.[3] Whereas private investors obviously seek to profit from the investment, the incentive for host states in attracting foreign investments is to enhance (economic) development. Beyond that, foreign investments are generally perceived beneficial to the interests of the community, i.e. the public interest. Also the long-term and large-scale nature of investment projects enhances the public interest at stake. Furthermore, many states subject foreign investments to prior screening and conditions to ensure that foreign investments do not work to the detriment of the interests of the state hosting the investment. The community interest in the investment thus becomes apparent already at the entry level.

In some types of investment projects the public interest is quite obvious, for example if the project concerns infrastructure, e.g. the building of highways or utility services, e.g. electricity or water. In other cases the public interest may seem less apparent but nevertheless be present, e.g. with regards to investments in an extractive project creating new job opportunities and related industries. Both private and public interest are present and the legal regime of international investment law thus has to embrace that. While both public and private interests are at issue, it is not always clear who will be responsible for serving the public interest. This role was originally bestowed upon states, but as private corporations today often perform public tasks, the perception of the public–private divide has been blurred in several ways.

---

3 David Kinley, *Civilising Globalisation: Human Rights and the Global Economy*, 1st ed. (Cambridge: Cambridge University Press, 2009), 152.

The blurring of the public–private divide is particularly evidenced by global movements towards privatizations of public utilities ranging from water and power, through telecommunications and banking to security, and the growth of public–private partnerships (PPP). These partnerships have blossomed with regards to investment projects creating utilities and infrastructure. For example, foreign investors are assigned to supply public services such as providing drinkable water or electricity, managing hazardous waste or ensuring public transportation.[4] Privatization of public utility might potentially constitute a threat to the interests of the public when investment projects are 'out of the hands' of the state.

Besides the blurring of public and private interests, another noteworthy aspect of the public–private dichotomy concerns the balance of power, especially negotiating power. This is not a legal aspect as such, but it may clearly entail legal consequences when agreements are negotiated, both on the international law level between states as well as in terms of the contracts negotiated between states and investors.

IIAs such as BITs establish the host state–investor–home state relation linking the public and the private, and as a special character of the international investment law regime the whole body of law covers both public and private legal agreements.

Finally, the public–private divide is blurred in investment arbitration as expressed by Schill *"by a division of epistemic communities"*[5] with those joining from the field of private commercial law and commercial arbitration and those coming from the public international law sphere and inter-state dispute settlement. This is deemed to result in *"veritable culture clashes"*.[6]

In sum, there appears to be a blurring of the public–private dichotomy, which becomes visible in several ways both in terms of interests, power relations, the legal framework and dispute resolution.

2.2. Types of foreign investment contracts

Host states and investors often negotiate investment contracts.[7] Such contracts are typically confidential, at least for a given period of time.[8] Model agreements may be publicly available and thereby provide an opportunity for public scrutiny.

---

4 Dolzer and Schreuer, *Principles of International Investment Law*, 80; Pierre-Marie Dupuy, "Unification Rather Than Fragmentation of International Law? The Case of International Investment Law and Human Rights Law," in *Human Rights in International Investment Law and Arbitration*, ed. Pierre-Marie Dupuy, Ernst-Ulrich Petersmann, and Francesco Francioni, International Economic Law Series (Oxford: Oxford University Press, 2009), 45.
5 Schill, "W(h)ither Fragmentation?," 888.
6 *Ibid.*
7 Dolzer and Schreuer, *Principles of International Investment Law*, 79; Jorge Daniel Taillant and Jonathan Bonnitcha, "International Investment Law and Human Rights," in *Sustainable Development in World Investment Law*, ed. Marie-Claire Cordonier Segger, Markus W. Gehring, and Andrew Paul Newcombe, Global Trade Law Series (Alphen aan den Rijn: Kluwer Law International, 2011), 62.
8 Usually until after the project has terminated.

Still, model agreements only lay down the basis for negotiation and thus do not reveal what is actually negotiated. The contracts allocate the terms and conditions on which the parties agreed, including provisions on the applicable law and the choice of forum for dispute resolution.[9] In many cases specific provisions address *force majeure*, good faith and changed circumstances. There are many types of contracts, which could be made in connection with foreign investment, and oftentimes a cluster of contracts will be necessary to cover a particular project.

The Joint Venture Agreement is a common type of agreement in foreign investment transactions, partly dictated by the fact that many laws of developing states require entry of foreign investment through joint ventures with local business partners. The use of joint ventures may thus be preferred in order to ensure that there is a factual integration of the foreign investment into the local economy.

Build, Operate and Own (BOO) agreements or Build, Operate and Transfer (BOT) agreements are typically being used for utilities or infrastructure projects, such as the building of highways, ports, mass transit systems, power plants, water supply systems and industrial areas.[10] Other types of contracts common for the construction of large facilities by a foreign company are so-called Turnkey contracts or 'design-and-build' contracts.[11]

Concession agreements are commonly used in the extractive industry.[12] The early law on foreign investment was largely created on the basis of concessions given to large foreign oil companies and the disputes that arose from them.

Production Sharing agreements or Profit-Sharing agreements are a common type of contract signed between a state and a resource extraction company (or group of companies) concerning how much of the resource extracted from the country each will receive. These widely replace the old concessions agreements.[13]

Many investment projects are thus founded on a contractual basis.

2.3. Internationalization of contracts

Regulatory measures may touch upon both treaty obligations as well as the underlying contracts. The relation between the treaty (a BIT) and the underlying contractual commitments therefore needs further attention. There is a continuous debate between those who believe BIT claims should be insulated from contractual claims and those who want to relate contract claims and BIT claims.[14] The connection between treaty and contract affects the scope of the right to

---

9 Dolzer and Schreuer, *Principles of International Investment Law*, 80.

10 *Ibid.*

11 For example used for the construction of an airport or a transport system. See Sornarajah, *The Settlement of Foreign Investment Disputes*, 43. See also Nicholas Dennys, Mark Raeside, and Robert Clay, *Hudson's Building and Engineering Contracts*, 12th ed. (London: Sweet & Maxwell, 2010), 495.

12 Sornarajah, *The Settlement of Foreign Investment Disputes*, 44–5.

13 *Ibid.* See also Dolzer and Schreuer, *Principles of International Investment Law*, 80.

14 James Crawford, "Treaty and Contract in Investment Arbitration," *Arbitration International* 24, no. 3 (2008): 351.

regulate. Hence, the treaty–contract relation is relevant to determine whether there are mechanisms that potentially may limit the right to regulate in the form of contractual commitments (e.g. stabilization clauses) or in the form of treaty standards (umbrella clauses).

Historically, international law was thought to be the most appropriate system for protection of foreign investments as established in concession agreements between the foreign investor and the state or a state company. The reason for this was that the law of the host state would not provide sufficient protection, since it could easily be changed by the host state. This concern remains today. Investors may also fear a lack of impartiality of national legal systems, practices of corruption, or simply just remain hesitant toward the credibility of national legal systems. As emphasized by Dolzer and Schreuer *"an independent judiciary cannot be taken for granted"* in many countries, and *"executive interventions in court proceeding are likely to influence the outcome"*, particularly where large amounts of money are at stake. The domestic courts of the investor's home state are usually not a viable alternative either, since they would often lack territorial jurisdiction over investments taking in foreign countries. Furthermore, rules of state immunity would constitute an obstacle to using domestic courts. For these reasons, investors have sought for ways to protect themselves from attempts by the state party to cancel or modify the contract without their consent. Foreign investors thus historically turned to international law for settlement of investment disputes as an additional assurance of the enforceability of their contracts. It is necessary to understand that the genesis of foreign investment arbitration lies in arbitration, which arose from foreign investment contracts, which was not backed up by treaties but prior to the negotiation of investment treaties.[15]

The initial view promoted by foreign investors was that a taking in violation of a foreign investment contract was illegal.[16] Today, the removal of the foreign investment transaction from the sphere of host state's law to international scrutiny has been referred to as the *internationalization of contracts.*[17] Internationalization of contracts may take place in many ways, for example on the basis of contractual clauses referring to the applicability of international law, clauses where the parties consent to international dispute settlement or stabilization clauses in the contract interfering with state sovereignty.[18] On the treaty level, internationalization may materialize in investment treaties (such as BITs) where protection of contractual commitments is included in the definition of a foreign investment.[19] Treaties may also contain an umbrella clause that might expand the treaty protection to contractual commitments undertaken by the host state.

---

15 Sornarajah, *The Settlement of Foreign Investment Disputes*, 277; Dolzer and Schreuer, *Principles of International Investment Law*, 235.
16 *Anglo-Iranian Oil Company case (United Kingdom v Iran)*, 22 July 1952; Sornarajah, *The Settlement of Foreign Investment Disputes*, 277.
17 Sornarajah, *The Settlement of Foreign Investment Disputes*, 289.
18 *Ibid.*, 294. See also Salacuse, *The Law of Investment Treaties*, 61.
19 The majority of modern IIAs define protected investments broadly and explicitly include contractual rights in the definition; see Stanimir Alexandrov, "Breach of Treaty Claims and

2.4. Treaty and contract – jurisdiction and merits

The relation between contract and treaty appears initially in an investment dispute as an issue of jurisdiction. When a dispute arises between the host state and the investor in terms of interference with the investment, there may in principle be two parallel ways for the investor to pursue its claim. The first level is the contractual level where the contract between state and investor contains a dispute settlement clause referring disputes to national courts (in the host state) or arbitration (e.g. at the International Chamber of Commerce). The existence of an international investment agreement, e.g. a BIT may then offer a second level of protection providing a direct access for investors to initiate international investment arbitration, for example at the ICSID for alleged breaches of the BIT by the state hosting the investment.

In order to decide whether there is a breach of an international obligation, the arbitrators will have to know exactly what the state has committed to in an international investment agreement, e.g. a BIT. The investment contract between the investor and the host state constitutes a part of the facts for this determination.[20] As a main rule, the breach of a contract is not identical with the breach of an *international* obligation.[21] The latter requires 'something more' internationalizing the claim, e.g. a stabilization clause (in the contract) or an umbrella clause (in the treaty).[22]

There are basically two parallel ways to pursue a claim for a regulatory action by the state. Whereas a *commercial dispute* concerns an assessment of which party has violated the contractual agreement and is obligated to reimburse the other party under the applicable law, the main purpose of an *investment dispute* is to review the host state's exercise of its sovereign powers and to review the legitimacy of its laws against parameters of international law.[23]

The 'treaty–contract' relation is particularly relevant in its material aspect for the determination of a breach of an international obligation owed to the state. The existence of an investment contract is not a precondition for initiating an investment claim on the basis of a BIT, but if there is a contract, it has an impact on the determination of the commitments made by the host state vis-à-vis the investor, for example if the contract serves as an additional guarantee accorded the

---

Breach of Contract Claims: Is It Still Unknown Territory?," in *Arbitration Under International Investment Agreements: A Guide to the Key Issues*, ed. Katia Yannaca-Small (Oxford: Oxford University Press, 2010), 325.

20 Ole Spiermann, "Applicable Law," in *The Oxford Handbook of International Investment Law*, ed. Peter Muchlinski, Federico Ortino, and Christoph Schreuer (Oxford: Oxford University Press, 2008), 111.

21 For expropriation of contractual rights see also Dolzer and Schreuer, *Principles of International Investment Law*, 126–9.

22 This is dealt with below in Chapter 5.

23 See also Giuditta Cordero Moss, "Soft Law Codifications in the Area of Commercial Law," in *International Investment Law and Soft Law*, ed. Andrea K. Bjorklund and August Reinisch (Cheltenham: Edward Elgar Publishing, 2012), 109–12.

investor in the form of a stabilization clause.[24] As explained in more detail below, the contract may also have implications for the expectations of the investor.[25]

3. Corporate actors with influence on the international investment law regime

From its inception, international law has been concerned with regulating the relationship between *states*. Historically, states have been the primary bearers of rights and obligations. Contrariwise, individuals or companies did not possess legal personality. If individuals or companies acquired a role in international affairs it was most commonly as 'beneficiaries' of treaties of commerce and navigation or of treaties concerning the treatment of foreigners.[26]

The traditional perception has, however, been increasingly challenged, since it has been claimed not to reflect today's reality of international law.[27] Post World War II other interests in the international community have given rise to discussions of the potential for new subjects of international law. The objects for such debates have mainly been international organizations, insurgents, national liberation movements, individuals and transnational corporations.[28]

With regards to transnational corporations, elements such as the capacity to influence decision-making processes and power balances vis-à-vis a government or local community have strengthened the role of corporations as 'participants' in international law. Corporations may for example play a pivotal role in decision-making processes as well as the enactment of (or reluctance towards) new laws and regulation. Changes in balance of power may constitute an added element for the perception of corporations as candidates as subjects of international law. The economic resources of corporations are greater than that of many states. Their ability to affect political events, policies and legislators may therefore be substantial. Corporations can be powerful and thereby play a predominant role in forming public policies, either directly or more indirectly by their mere presence or expressed interest in market access. It thus follows that corporations may have a strong impact with regards to forming the law. Moreover, an increased focus on companies, especially transnational, as actors with social responsibility,[29] has carried wood to the fire of the discussion of corporations as subjects of international law.[30]

---

24 See Chapter 5, stabilization clauses, section 8.5.1.
25 See Chapter 5, legitimate expectations, section 8.
26 James Crawford, *Brownlie's Principles of Public International Law*, 8th ed. (Oxford: Oxford University Press, 2012), 57; Shaw, *International Law*, 195; Antonio Cassese, *International Law*, 2nd ed. (Oxford: Oxford University Press, 2004), 143.
27 See Cassese, *International Law*, 134–50: The Reasons Behind the Emergence of New International Subjects.
28 Shaw, *International Law*, 46–7.
29 See below Chapter 3.
30 Andrew Clapham, *Human Rights Obligations of Non-State Actors*, 1st ed., Collected Courses of the Academy of European Law (Oxford: Oxford University Press, 2006), 4; Sornarajah, *The Settlement of Foreign Investment Disputes*, 9; Shaw, *International Law*, 250; Karsten

Following this development, various actors like corporations, business associations and NGOs exert influence on the international investment law regime. These actors may seek to influence BIT negotiations through lobbying or by pointing out side effects of the rules, social consequences for developing states liable to compensate foreign investors. Moreover, they may seek to shed light on other international commitments undertaken by states hosting foreign direct investments.

Corporations can thereby be characterized as influential actors of today's international investment law regime. An increasing role for parties – other than states – in decision-making processes has stirred the traditional perception of international law. Though not arguing that corporations are (potential) subjects of international law, the predominant role of corporations makes it reasonable to say that corporations constitute key *participants* of international law. In the same vein, states have gradually lost their predominant role as law-makers in international law. This development triggers new perceptions of rights and responsibility under the investment law regime.

4. The nature and scope of the right to regulate in general international law

In general international law the right to regulate is an inherent right of state sovereignty. However, there are limitations to this sovereign right since states are bound to accept the sovereign equality of other states.

4.1. *International sovereignty and the right to regulate*

As national sovereigns, states have the authority to act within their territory. Such actions are not subject to the control of other states. Essential elements of the concept of sovereignty are 'sovereignty over territory' and 'jurisdictional sovereignty'. Sovereignty over territory is usually linked with the state's power freely to use and dispose the territory and the right that no other state can intrude in the state's territory. Jurisdictional sovereignty normally manifests itself in three fundamental forms: *jurisdiction to prescribe* (i.e. the power to enact legal commands such as laws); *jurisdiction to adjudicate* (the power to settle legal disputes); *jurisdiction to enforce* (the power to ensure through coercive means that legal commands and entitlements are complied with).[31] This means that the concept of sovereignty allows states to make decisions as to the choice of a political, economic, social and cultural system, and the formulation of foreign policy.[32]

Nowrot, "Transnational Corporations as Steering Subjects in International Economic Law: Two Competing Visions of the Future," *Indiana Journal of Global Legal Studies* 18, no. 2 (2011): 803–42.

31 On the concept of sovereignty see in particular Cassese, *International Law*, 49–53.

32 See Charter of Economic Rights and Duties of States (UNGA resolution 3281 (XXIX)), 1974, article 1. This principle was also laid down in *Paramilitary Activities in and Against Nicaragua*, Judgment, 27 June 1986, ICJ Reports, at 108, para. 205.

States have the right to choose their forms of organization of their foreign economic relations, and to enter into bilateral and multilateral arrangements.[33] In addition, states haves the right to choose their ends and means, i.e. the model of its development.[34] Hence, it is within the sovereign power of states to perform activities that are deemed necessary or beneficial to their population. One may therefore conclude that deciding on the priorities of the state, in terms of political attention to some issues to the detriment of other issues (i.e. policy issues) as well as allocating economic resources to some individuals, companies or projects at the expense of others, is an essential part of the concept of national or internal sovereignty. At the same time, the right to respect for life and property of the state's nationals is equally considered integral parts of state sovereignty.[35] It can therefore be said that the concept of sovereignty in principle covers both the notion of regulation as well as investment protection.

From a national perspective, states may decide if, or to what extent, they may provide investment protection as well as whether they want to regulate. For example, in an investment context, the Charter of Economic Rights and Duties of States adopted by the UN General Assembly in 1974 mentions the right to regulate foreign investment in its article 2(2)(a):

> *"Each State has the right:*
> *To regulate and exercise authority over foreign investment within its national jurisdiction in accordance with its laws and regulations and in conformity with its national objectives and priorities. No State shall be compelled to grant preferential treatment to foreign investment."*

Pursuant to article 2(2)(b) of the Charter of Economic Rights and Duties of States each state has the right:

> *"To regulate and supervise the activities of transnational corporations within its national jurisdiction and take measures to ensure that such activities comply with its laws, rules and regulations and conform with its economic and social policies. Transnational corporations shall not intervene in the internal affairs of a host State. . . ."*

The Charter thus emphasizes the right for states freely to admit or reject foreign investments as well as to regulate foreign investment according to their own economic objectives.[36] Accordingly, the right to regulate is an expression of state sovereignty.

---

33 Charter of Economic Rights and Duties of States (UNGA resolution 3281 (XXIX)), 1974, article 4.
34 *Ibid.*, article 7.
35 Cassese, *International Law*, 51–2. See also Georges Abi-Saab, "Permanent Sovereignty Over Natural Resources and Economic Activities," in *International Law: Achievements and Prospects*, ed. Mohammed Bedjaoui (Dordrecht: Martinus Nijhoff Publishers, 1991), 599.
36 Abi-Saab, "Permanent Sovereignty over Natural Resources and Economic Activities," 605.

4.2. The bindingness as the essence of international state sovereignty

Historically, international law has been tolerating a freedom for states to regulate, rather than explicitly providing for such a right. The case of *S.S. Lotus*[37] from 1927 is a classic example in this regard, where state measures (in this case, Turkey exercising jurisdiction) were permitted, as long as they did not contravene an explicit prohibition. The Permanent Court of International Justice held that restrictions on sovereignty were not to be presumed.[38] Sometimes, the right to regulate is implied in general international law where states are allowed discretion in interpretation of international legal obligations (written or unwritten).

The sovereign right to regulate does, however, not give states unlimited or omnipotent power. Limitations to this right exist in the coexistence of states or in cooperation between states.[39]

In international law governing international relations, states coexist among other states. This fact entails in itself a limitation to sovereignty. The concept of sovereignty is an integral part of the principle of equality of states protecting territorial and political integrity respectively. According to article 2 of the UN Charter the organization of the United Nations is based on the principle of sovereign equality of all its member states. So, while states have to coexist with other states, they are also bound to respect the sovereignty of other states. In other words, states have motives for accepting legal limitations on their own conduct. The sphere of liberty by states is thereby delimited by the sphere of liberty of others. To determine which international issues limit states' right to regulate in practice is more controversial. However, some fundamental principles have been expressed.

The first fundamental principles, to which states were to abide, were enunciated in the UN Charter in 1945. These principles were: *self-determination of peoples, peaceful settlement of disputes, prohibition of the threat or use of force*. Though applicable only to the members of the UN, which at that time were a more limited group of states,[40] these principles could be perceived as the root of such issues that are international in character. The UN Charter has subsequently been updated and supplemented by international agreements, most importantly the 1970 UN Declaration on Friendly Relations expressing seven basic principles by

---

37 *S.S. Lotus* (*France v Turkey*), Judgment, Permanent Courts of International Justice, 7 September 1927. The case concerned a collision on the high seas between a French steamer and a Turkish steamer. Eight Turkish people drowned. The issue at dispute presented before the Permanent Court of International Justice was whether Turkey was able to exercise jurisdiction. France claimed jurisdiction contending that the state whose flag the vessel flew had exclusive jurisdiction.

38 *S.S. Lotus* (*France v Turkey*), at III, 18.

39 See further in Ole Spiermann, *International Legal Argument in the Permanent Court of International Justice: The Rise of the International Judiciary*, ed. James Crawford and John S. Bell, 1st ed., Cambridge Studies in International and Comparative Law (Cambridge: Cambridge University Press, 2010), 48–9, 394.

40 At that time 51 members, whereas today the UN has 193 member states.

which states were to abide by adding the principles of *sovereign equality of states*, the *prohibition of intervention in other states' affairs*, the *duty to cooperate* and *good faith* to the already existing three principles.[41] The seven principles were adopted by consensus and their application was extended to *all* states.

1970 UN Declaration on Friendly Relations:

> *"The principles of the Charter which are embodied in this Declaration constitute basic principles of international law, and consequently appeals to all States to be guided by these principles in their international conduct and to develop their mutual relations on the basis of the strict observance of these principles."*

Besides limitations on sovereignty based on the coexistence of states, states can make voluntary commitments that restrict state sovereignty. Such commitments could be explicitly laid down in agreements, such as treaties. And these commitments must be kept by states pursuant to the principle of *pacta sunt servanda*.[42] Engaging in such international commitments may sometimes be motivated by an expression of public will. In order to be elected, political candidates identify and seek to expand public desires of certain values. These values could for instance relate to the protection of the environment or human rights.

A famous example of the limitations on state sovereignty is the case of the *S.S. Wimbledon* from 1923.[43] The Permanent Court of International Justice (PCIJ) made it clear that the right of entering into international engagement *"is an attribute of state sovereignty"*.[44] So in essence, the ability to make a binding commitment is fundamentally what makes a state a state, or expressed as a dictum; *"the possibility of limiting conduct of tomorrow is an act of authority carried out today"*.[45] A state may not invoke the provision of its internal law as justification for its failure to perform a treaty.[46]

As international law develops, it may be that further international principles and issues could be added. In sum, states are free to do what they like as national

---

41 Cassese, *International Law*, 47.
42 The principle is codified in the VCLT article 26. It can also be found in the UN Charter article 2(2) whereby all member states shall fulfil in good faith the obligations assumed by them in accordance with the Charter.
43 *S.S. Wimbledon*; *United Kingdom, France, Italy, Japan v Germany*, (ser. A) No. 1, PCIJ, 28 June 1923. The case concerned the English steamship *S.S. Wimbledon* chartered by a French company. The ship was not allowed by Germany to pass through the German Kiel Canal carrying ammunition loaded in Greece for the Poland naval base. The vessel was delayed for several days and then forced to sail north of Denmark. Germany contended the transit of the vessel claiming that it was allowed to deny passage due to its right to remain a neutral power. However, Germany had earlier restricted its own powers through the Treaty of Versailles laying down a duty to allow the passage.
44 *Ibid.*, at IV The Law, para. 35.
45 See also Jan Paulsson, "A State's Power to Make Meaningful Promises to Foreigners," *UN Audiovisual Library of International Law*, available at: <http://www.un.org/law/avl/>.
46 The VCLT article 27.

sovereigns in terms of making political, economic and social prioritizations. As international sovereigns, states have to abide by 'certain rules of the game', especially respecting the sovereign equality of other states[47] (rules founded in the coexistence of states) as well as particular commitments the state may have entered into.

The bindingness of commitments made by states is put into effect through international adjudication. States cannot be a judge to controversies as to whether it has transgressed legal limits. International adjudication is therefore in the interests of the states to give force to the bindingness of their commitments. In this regard, the task for international tribunals is not to decide on national public policies. Rather, they should give effect to the commitments made by states. International tribunals are thereby valuable tools for states to enable states to make reliable promises.

4.3. Lifting treaty obligations on the basis of the principle of rebus sic stantibus

As now explained, the right for states to make binding commitments is an expression of state sovereignty. Yet, it appears that there is a very narrow exception to the principle of *pacta sunt servanda* expressed by the principle of *rebus sic stantibus*. According to the principle of *rebus sic stantibus* a fundamental change of circumstances may serve as a basis for terminating or withdrawing from a treaty.[48] Yet, the change of circumstances must be unforeseen at the time of the conclusion of the treaty and constitute an essential basis of the consent of the parties to be bound by the treaty.[49] Moreover, the effect of the change must be radically to transform the extent of the obligation.[50] If the fundamental change is the result of a breach by the party invoking it either of an obligation under the treaty or of any other international obligation owed to any other party to the treaty, the said fundamental change may not be invoked as a ground for termination or withdrawal.[51] The principle of *rebus sic stantibus* should be applied only in exceptional cases.[52]

When a dispute occurs, it may be that a state realizes that the world has changed to such an extent that it no longer wants to uphold the commitments it has voluntarily made for example in a BIT. Market prices may have changed the economic equilibrium substantially disfavouring the host state. Hence, the state may want to impose regulation as a measure of damage control. The question as

---

47 See also Cassese, *International Law*, 46.
48 VCLT by article 62.
49 VCLT article 62(1)(a). See also *Fisheries Jurisdiction* (*United Kingdom and Northern Ireland v Iceland*), ICJ Judgment of 2 February 1973; *Gabíkovo-Nagymaros Project* (*Hungary v Slovakia*), ICJ Judgment of 25 September 1997, para. 104, pp. 64f.
50 VCLT article 62(1)(b).
51 VCLT article 62(2)(b).
52 Shaw, *International Law*, 950–2.

to whether binding commitments made in BITs can be lifted on the basis of the principle of *rebus sic stantibus* may therefore occur as an issue of – in the view of host states – fundamental change of circumstances. Chapter 5 explains why this concept cannot generally be relied on by host states in their request for adopting new regulation without compensating investors protected by BIT standards.

5. Respecting the sovereign equality of other states

As a necessary corollary to state sovereignty, states have responsibility to respect the sovereign equality of other states.[53] The following explains the basic rules of state responsibility and the enforcement of the rules through diplomatic protection.

5.1. The fundamental rules of state responsibility

In international law a state is identified with its nationals. A state mistreating a national of another state is therefore considered mistreating the other state (the home state, or state of nationality). This may give rise to state responsibility and the requirement for reparation.[54] For states to be responsible for having committed an international wrongful act there should be 1) a breach of an international obligation, 2) which can be attributed to the state and 3) there should be no circumstances precluding wrongfulness.

The ILC has considered the general topic of state responsibility, and in 2001 the commission adopted the Draft Articles on Responsibility of States for Internationally Wrongful Acts. The ILC Draft Articles are considered to enjoy widespread, though not universal, support, with some provisions reflecting customary international law.[55] The ILC Draft Articles convey the secondary rules of state responsibility, which means the general conditions under international law for the state to be considered responsible for wrongful acts or omissions, and the legal consequences hereof. The Draft Articles thus do not attempt to define the content of the international obligations, the breach of which gives rise to responsibility, i.e. the primary rules.

The breach of an international obligation can be a violation of an obligation, which is either written (a treaty obligation) or unwritten (customary international law or a general principle applicable within the international legal order). State responsibility can thus arise from breaches of bilateral obligations or of obligations owed to some states or the international community as a whole. It may

---

53 In the *Spanish Zone of Morocco* Judge Huber emphasized that responsibility is the necessary corollary of a right, see *Spanish Zone of Morocco Claims*, General Decisions (Principles of State Responsibility), R.I.A.A, 1925, p. 641.

54 The obligation for states to make reparations to injuries can be traced back the work of Hugo Grotius in 1625 in his *De jure belli ac pacis* (*On the Law of War and Peace*).

55 Martin Dixon and Robert McCorquodale, *Cases and Materials on International Law*, 4th ed. (Oxford: Oxford University Press, 2003), 404.

involve relatively minor infringements as well as the most serious breaches of obligations under peremptory norms of general international law. Severity of the breach and the peremptory character of the obligation can affect the consequences but not the mere question of an international wrongful act as such. In this regard a contractual breach could in principle be as much an international wrongful act as an armed attack against another state. An breach of an international obligation may consist of one or more actions or omissions or a combination of both.[56]

The breach of an international obligation is explained in articles 12–19 of the Draft Articles. Interferences may take various forms and be applied for various reasons. For example, the interference may be direct in the form of a physical loss (e.g. nationalizations) or in the form of destruction (e.g. a local armed group may have bombed the facilities or taken employees as hostages) or more indirectly in the form of interferences with the value of the investment, including expectations of future gains (e.g. the state adopts new tariff regulation or environmental standards, which ban the use of a certain chemical that forces the company to find new ways of production). This research concerns the latter, i.e. the interferences with the value of the investment.

The violation must be due to conduct attributable to a state.[57] Article 4–11 of the Draft Articles deal with attribution. This requirement is generally not disputed for acts carried out by the state or state officials. A state is responsible for all actions of its officials and organs, including when the state exercises legislative, executive, and judicial or any other functions.[58] The question of attribution is controversial in international law, as well as in international investment law.[59]

---

56 In an investment context, state responsibility caused by the failure to protect has typically been invoked in cases of infringement of the full protection and security standard, see for example *Amco Asia Corporation and Others v The Republic of Indonesia*, ICSID Award, 20 November 1984 and *Wena Hotels v Egypt,* ICSID Award, 8 December 2002.

57 These requirements can be found in the leading cases: *Spanish Zone of Morocco* claims, General Decisions (Principles of State Responsibility) (1923), 641; Case concerning the *Factory of Chorzow,* PCIJ, Series A, no. 17 (1929), 29. Further on state responsibility see for example Shaw, *International Law*, 774–843; Cassese, *International Law*, 243–77; James Crawford and Simon Olleson, "The Nature and Forms of International Responsibility," in *International Law*, ed. Malcolm D. Evans (Oxford: Oxford University Press, 2003), 445–72.

58 ILC Draft articles on Responsibility of States for Internationally Wrongful Acts, 2001, article 4.

59 In investment disputes two general standards of attribution can be found, the 'Neer standard' and the 'ELSI standard'. In the *Neer* case from 1926, a case concerning the murder of an American citizen in Mexico, the issue for the US–Mexican Claims Commission was whether the failures of the Mexican authorities to investigate and initiate legal claims against the culprits were sufficient to give rise to an international delinquency so as to engage the responsibility of Mexico on the level of international law towards the US. The Commission laid down a very high threshold of attribution by imposing a requirement that the acts should amount to "an outrage", "to bad faith," or "to wilful neglect of duty" (at 61–2). The *ELSI* case from 1989 concerned the temporary requisition by a local major of an industrial

However, in terms of this research on the right to regulate, it requires less attention. This is due to the fact that the requirement of attribution would in principle always be fulfilled for regulatory measures since it is only the state that can adopt new laws and regulation.

In addition, state responsibility requires the absence of circumstances precluding wrongfulness. The circumstances precluding wrongfulness for a breach of an international obligation attributable to the state are enunciated in article 20–27 of the Draft Articles. For the matter of investment protection the circumstances precluding wrongfulness most commonly invoked are *force majeure* (article 23) and necessity (article 25). For example, necessity has been invoked by Argentina in relation with its financial crisis in 2000–2001, which led to numerous claims against the country for the adoption of economic reforms. As a consequence of state responsibility the injured state may under the concept of counter-measures demand for full reparation pursuant to article 31 of the Draft Articles. Pursuant to article 34 and 36 of the Draft Articles reparation may take the form of compensation.

As stated above, the rights of each state limit the rights of other states. Because the state *is* sovereign and coexists with other states, it can therefore invoke responsibility of other states.

5.2. Enforcing state responsibility through diplomatic protection

General international law allows for the enforcement of state responsibility through 'diplomatic protection' or 'diplomatic espousal', which is a means for a state to take action against another state on behalf of its own national, whose rights and interest have been injured by another state. Diplomatic protection may be carried out as consular action, negotiations with the other state, through political and economic pressure, by initiating judicial or arbitral proceedings or other forms of peaceful dispute settlement. As stated by the PCIJ in the *Mavrommatis* case:[60] *"By taking up the case of one of its subjects and by resorting to diplomatic action or international judicial proceedings on his behalf, a State is in reality asserting its own rights – its right to ensure, in the person of its subjects, respect for the rules of international law."*[61] By exercising diplomatic protection a state enforces its own right, and this is purely a political procedure. Thus, it is a right for the home state, not for the injured part, i.e. the investor.[62]

---

plant belonging to an Italian company owned by American shareholders. In this case the ICJ relied on a lower threshold for attribution referring to a criteria of "arbitrariness" (at 128).

60 *Mavrommatis Jerusalem Concessions (Greece v UK)*, PCIJ, Judgment, 26 March 1925.

61 *Ibid.*, at 12. This fundamental principle was later confirmed in the *Serbian Loans* case, see *Payment of Various Serbian Loans Issued in France (France v the Former Yugoslavia)*, PCIJ, Judgment, 12 July 1929, at 17.

62 In 2006 the ILC adopted its Draft Articles on Diplomatic Protection. These articles largely codify existing customary international law on the protection of nationals abroad by means of diplomatic protection.

From the investor's perspective relying on diplomatic espousal involves essential drawbacks. Firstly, the injured, i.e. the investor, must be a national of the state exercising diplomatic protection.[63] Secondly, the investor is required to exhaust all domestic remedies provided that there is a prospect of effective redress in the host state.[64] Hence, there are exceptions to this requirement, for example if the national courts are so corrupt that they cannot be expected to grant justice.[65]

A contentious issue concerning the nationality requirement is the protection of shareholding interests. In the case of *Barcelona Traction*[66] several judges expressed the opinion that shareholders had an independent right to protection under international law but there were fundamental differences concerning the precise nature of that right. A pertinent question was whether shareholders should be regarded as having a secondary right of protection, which could be activated only if the national state of the company had failed to act on its behalf. The majority, however, rejected this, arguing that a secondary right could only come into existence once the primary right had been extinguished, and the failure of a state to exercise a primary right did not necessarily distinguish it.[67] Thus, the home state of the company enjoys the discretion freely to decide if it wishes to exercise diplomatic protection as well as the method and the extent of protection. Unencumbered by the desire of the investor, the home state may also decide to settle a claim.

From the perspective of the home state, exercising diplomatic protection may involve major disadvantages, and the state may therefore choose to be reserved on this. In practice, the political inconvenience can be so significant that it outweighs the interest of the state advancing the alleged wrongful act against its national. For investors, relying on diplomatic protection remains a right for the host state upon its scrutiny, where the prospect of success of the home state negotiating compensation for an injury or pursuing a legal claim on behalf of the investor might be little. Today, recourse to diplomatic protection is made mainly in cases where treaty regimes do not exist or have proved inoperative.

BITs typically allow corporations to bring claims directly against the host state. Through the use of BITs the home state is relieved of political inconveniences that might have been the consequence of following the route of diplomatic protection on behalf of its national. At the same time, enforcement of the alleged wrongful act is handled in legal proceedings that in principle neither burdens nor involves the home state of the investor.

---

63 The ILC Draft Articles on Diplomatic Protection, articles 9–13 concerning nationality of legal persons. The nationality requirement can usually be achieved if the headquarter of the company is domiciled in the home state or the company is incorporated under the laws of the home state. Another possibility for fulfilling this requirement might be where a company is under effective control of the company or government of a third state.
64 The ILC Draft Articles on Diplomatic Protection, article 14.
65 See also The ILC Draft Articles on Diplomatic Protection, article 15.
66 *Barcelona Traction, Light and Power Company, Ltd,* Judgment (second phase), 5 February 1970, at 3, para. 96.
67 *Ibid.*

6. Protection of aliens and their property in general international law

Neither the conclusion of BITs nor the consent to international investment arbitration composes a general renouncement of state sovereignty. What *does* place considerable limitations upon state sovereignty is the material protection concerning the treatment to be accorded to aliens, a material protection found either in treaty provisions or in norms of customary international law.

The following explains the basic rules of investment protection under the general international law paradigm, i.e. the minimum standard of treatment. The content of the minimum standard refers to three important concepts: the full protection and security standard (FPS standard), the fair and equitable treatment standard (FET) and the concept of expropriation. All three concepts are recognized as forming part of the customary international law minimum standard of treatment, and all three concepts are almost always contained in BITs. Being customary norms, the minimum standard of treatment is also applicable if no BIT exists. The more contentious aspects of these concepts concern the actual content and scope of the protection and whether BITs enhance the level of protection. The three essential aspects of the minimum standard of treatment are explained below.

6.1. The Full Protection and Security (FPS) standard

The FPS standard obliges states to take active measures to protect foreign investments from adverse effects stemming from actions of the host state, its organs or from third parties. The standard primarily protects against various types of physical violence, e.g. the destruction of an investment or the invasion of the premises of the investment or failure to respond to disturbances like demonstrations or protests against a corporation.[68] Thus, an interference with the FPS standard is not a case of expropriation but one of loss and damage to property. In the *Tehran Hostage* case[69] the ICJ found a violation by Iran to grant 'constant protection and security' to the American nationals, both as a treaty obligation (the 1955 Treaty of Amity, Economic Relations and Consular Rights between Iran and the United States) and under general international law.[70]

In BITs, the FPS standard is one of the non-contingent standards of protection, which is either referred to as the obligation to grant 'full protection and

68 See for example the *Case Concerning United States Diplomatic and Consular Staff in Tehran* (*United States of America v Iran*), ICJ, Judgment of 24 May 1980; *AAPL v Sri Lanka*, Award, 27 June 1990 paras 45–6 and 78–9; *Wena Hotels v Egypt*, Award, 8 December 2000, para. 84; *AMT v Zaire*, Award, 21 February 1997, paras 6.02–6.03; *Tecmed v Mexico*, Award, 29 May 2003, paras 175–7.
69 *Case Concerning United States Diplomatic and Consular Staff in Tehran* (*United States of America v. Iran*), ICJ, Judgment of 24 May 1980.
70 *Ibid.*, para. 62 at 31.

security' or 'constant protection and security'.[71] Though broad, the standard does not provide an absolute protection of the investment. In contrast to FET, the FPS standard is typically not concerned with the process of decision-making by the organs of the host state. Rather, it is concerned with failures by the state to protect the investor's property from actual damage caused by state officials or by actions of others where the state has failed to exercise due diligence.[72]

6.2. The Fair and Equitable Treatment (FET) standard

The FET standard is also rooted in customary international law. Like the FPS standard it is vaguely formulated and a precise definition of the scope of the FET does not exist. However, cases seem generally to fall into two broad categories, where the first set of cases are concerned with the treatment of investors by courts of the host state and the second with administrative decision-making.[73]

Arbitral practice has given content to the standard for it to cover denial of justice, the breach of the standard in the course of the host state's judicial process, review of administrative action, or breach of the standard in the investor's treatment by the executive.[74] Cases where arbitrators have found a breach of the FET standard are typically concerned with the grant or withholding of licences for investments, or a fundamental change in the law affecting the investment climate. Onerous regulation may thus also interfere with the FET standard. In investment disputes tribunals typically assess the treatment accorded to investors by reference to 1) legitimate expectations[75] and 2) due process.[76] It is debated whether the FET standard referred to in BITs merely reflects the international minimum standard as contained in customary international law, or whether the standard offers an autonomous standard that is additional to general international law.[77]

---

71 See further in Dolzer and Schreuer, *Principles of International Investment Law*, 166; Mclachlan et al., *International Investment Arbitration*, 247–50; Schefer, *International Investment Law*, 311–27.

72 See inter alia *AMT v (the former) Zaire*, ICSID Award, 21 February 1997 and *Wena Hotels v Egypt*, ICSID Award, 8 December 2000.

73 Mclachlan et al., *International Investment Arbitration*, 226.

74 See e.g. *Mondev International Ltd. v United States of America*, ICSID Award, 11 October 2002 and *Loewen Group, Inc. and Raymond L. Loewen v United States of America*, ICSID Award, 26 June 2003. See also Mclachlan et al., *International Investment Arbitration*, 229–33.

75 The concept of legitimate expectations in the context of cases of indirect expropriation is dealt with below in Chapter 5.

76 Mclachlan et al., *International Investment Arbitration*, 234.

77 Some arbitral tribunals have interpreted the FET and FPS standards in BITs as higher standards than required by international law by emphasizing the purpose of the standards *"to set the floor, nor a ceiling"*, see e.g. *Azurix v Argentina*, ICSID Award, 14 July 2006, para. 361. In NAFTA practice the question has been resolved by the NAFTA Commission, which has adopted a binding interpretation on NAFTA article 1105(1) explicitly stating that the obligation to provide FET does not require treatment in addition to or beyond that which is required by customary international law.

6.3. Evolving international protection of property

Protection of private property is a fundamental right in general international law. Property protection is embodied in international law as a core value, which can be retrieved in other areas of international law, e.g. with regards to state recognition of pre-existing private property claims in territory that no state has previously claimed (occupation of *terra nullius* vis-à-vis the right of indigenous peoples), and the principle that 'acquired rights' survive state succession and must be respected by the successor state.[78] The right to protection of property, however, is not absolute and numerous examples of the recognition of nationalizations or expropriations can be found in international law. Expropriation is usually perceived as a coercive measure by individual administrative measures whereas nationalizations are large-scale takings based on an executive legislative act. An expropriation thus typically targets a specific business.[79]

Protection of property against expropriation has historically evolved through three key phases: the colonial era;[80] through the wave of Friendship, Commerce and Navigation (FCN) treaties; and through the BIT regime. Parallel to the developments in the BIT regime protection of property rights grew out of the human rights regime.[81]

Throughout the colonial era, the concept of property protection was retroactively applied by requiring states to return property already taken, and these rules of property protection were applicable only for expropriations that occurred during hostilities.[82] According to the customary law study carried out by the International Commission of the Red Cross/Crescent (ICRC), there are fundamental customary norms protecting property against destruction and seizure in international armed conflicts,[83] and in non-international armed conflicts.[84] Rules concerning protection of property under the international humanitarian law regime are not absolute either, since the protection may be denied if required by imperative military necessity.[85]

---

78 Private property rights do not elapse automatically as a consequence of the legal title of territory being transferred. See further in Shaw, *International Law*, 1001–4.
79 Expropriation refers to a governmental taking or modification of an individual's property rights, whereas nationalization refers to an act where an industry is brought under governmental control or ownership; see Bryan A. Garner, *Black's Law Dictionary*, 7th ed. (Minnesota: West Group, 1999). For the distinction between confiscations, expropriations and nationalizations see also Sornarajah, *The International Law on Foreign Investment*, 364–7.
80 Kenneth Vandevelde delimits this phase from 1820–1944, see Vandevelde, *Bilateral Investment Treaties*, 19ff.
81 For property protection as a human right see below Chapter 4, section 5.
82 Vandevelde, *Bilateral Investment Treaties*, 19–38, 282.
83 I.e. a conflict between two states.
84 Such as an armed conflict between a rebel group and the host government. For the rules of international humanitarian law relating to protection of property see in particular rule 49–52 at <http://www.icrc.org/eng/assets/files/other/customary-law-rules.pdf> and <http://www.icrc.org/eng/resources/documents/publication/pcustom.htm>.
85 Jean-Marie Henckaerts and Louise Doswald-Beck, *Customary International Humanitarian Law*, ed. International Committee of the Red Cross, 1st ed., 2 vols., vol. 1, Customary

Political and economic ties throughout the 19th century led to FCN treaties, which contained a variety of provisions on seizure of property.[86] Property protection was extended to provisions with prospective, rather than retrospective, protection, applicable not only during hostilities but also in times of peace. The FCN treaties also addressed other matters, including consular rights and the freedom of navigation.[87]

Historically, protection of property in international law was linked with the state's obligations to respect the sovereignty of peoples and nations over their natural wealth and resources. The articulation of the principle of *permanent sovereignty over natural resources* as a fundamental principle in international law emerged in the 1950s during the process of decolonization as a basic constituent of the right to self-determination and an inherent element of state sovereignty. The most significant statement regarding permanent sovereignty over natural resources can be found in the UN General Assembly resolution 1803 (XVII) of 14 December 1962, 'Permanent sovereignty over natural resources'. The principle of permanent sovereignty over natural resources was later developed in the Charter of Economic Rights and Duties of States from 1974, which established the new international economic order, explicitly linking economic growth and social development.[88] A fundamental principle governing economic relations among states, articulated in the Charter, is the obligation to act in good faith[89] by respecting international obligations, including human rights.[90] Moreover, states should strive towards promoting international social justice[91] and international cooperation for development.[92] The Charter also stresses the right for states to regulate and to supervise the activities of transnational corporations so as to ensure that they conform to economic and social policies of the state.[93]

International Humanitarian Law (Cambridge: Cambridge University Press, 2005), rule 51(c). Yet, the protection of property against pillage provides an absolute protection, see rule 52.

86 Vandevelde, *Bilateral Investment Treaties*, 20–31, 282.

87 J. Romesh Weeramantry, *Treaty Interpretation in Investment Arbitration*, ed. Loukas A. Mistelis, 1st ed., Oxford International Arbitration Series (Oxford: Oxford University Press, 2012), 10.

88 Several references are given in the *preamble*, such as *"international co-operation in solving international problems in the economic and social fields"*; *"promote the establishment of the new international economic order. . . irrespective of their economic and social systems"*; *"The promotion by the entire international community of the economic and social progress of all countries"*; *"the need to establish and maintain a just and equitable economic and social order"*. In the operational part of the treaty, article 7 for instance states that every state *"has the primary responsibility to promote the economic, social and cultural development of its people."* Another example is article 9 declaring that all states *"have the responsibility to co-operate in the economic, social, cultural, scientific and technological fields for the promotion of economic and social progress."*

89 The Charter of Economic Rights and Duties of States, Chapter I, Principle j.

90 *Ibid.*, Principle j and k.

91 *Ibid.*, Principle m.

92 *Ibid.*, Principle n.

93 The Charter of Economic Rights and Duties of States, Chapter II, article 2(2)(b).

Neither the 1803 resolution nor the Charter lay down an absolute protection of property. Nationalizations, expropriations or requisitioning are thus implicitly recognized, i.e. in paragraph 4 of the 1803 resolution and in article 2(2)(c) of the Charter of Economic Rights and Duties of States if based on "grounds or reasons of public utility, security or national interest"[94] and conditioned upon payment of 'appropriate compensation'.[95] Both instruments envisage the possibility of disputes arising either out of the act of nationalization or expropriation itself, or from compensation, i.e. the financial consequences of the act.[96] Yet, these legal instruments do not elaborate further on the concept of expropriations and which measures may be considered expropriatory acts. The key aspects of these two instruments, which should be highlighted here are: 1) that the protection of property was linked with economic and social development; and 2) that the objectives of international economic law were not pursued at the expense of other international commitments, including human rights.

6.4. Protection of aliens and their property

The way property has been protected in general international law has mainly been by laying down conditions for expropriation. This entails first and foremost a duty to compensate foreigners for deprivation of property rights. The *Chorzòw Factory*[97] case from 1928 is an often-quoted case in this regard.

The dispute concerned the taking by Poland of the Chorzòw Factory, which was built when the territory was part of the German Reich. Since the German factory, however, was privately owned, it could only be taken pursuant to the conditions for expropriation, including compensation to prior owners.

In this case, the PCIJ pronounced on the obligation to pay compensation by stating that *"reparation must, as far as possible, wipe out all the consequences of the illegal act and re-establish the situation which would, in all probability, have existed if that act had not been committed."*[98]

In some instances, the duty to pay compensation has been extended to contractual takings. Though the mere breach of a contract does not trigger state responsibility, there are precedents reinforcing the duty to pay compensation for a breach of contract. The *Norwegian Shipowners' Claim*[99] from 1922 is an important precedent in this regard.[100] The tribunal awarded compensation

---

94 UNGA resolution 1803 (XVII), para. 4. The Charter of Economic Rights and Duties of States is silent on this subject.

95 *Ibid.*, article 2(2)(c).

96 Abi-Saab, "Permanent Sovereignty over Natural Resources and Economic Activities," 609.

97 *Factory of Chorzòw*, ICJ, Judgment, 13 September 1928.

98 *Ibid.*, p. 47.

99 *Norway v United States of America*, PCA, Award, 13 October 1922.

100 The dispute arose from a series of legislative and administrative measures by the United States during World War I in preparation for United States' participation in the war, including the seizure of ships built in American shipyards, even those that were built to the order

to the Norwegian government finding that the United States *"took both in fact and in law, the contracts under which the ships in question were being or were to be constructed"*.[101] Practice seems to require some element, beyond the mere breach of contract, i.e. a sovereign act, which could constitute a confiscatory taking or a fundamental denial of justice.[102] Protection of contractual rights has also been referred to under the concept of protection of 'acquired rights'. According to this notion, a taking of rights acquired, transmitted, and defined by a contract is considered as much a wrong as a taking or destruction of tangible property. The taking of acquired rights entitles the victim to compensation.[103]

As an additional perspective on the concept of protection of property and expropriations in international law, it is worthwhile to mention an old but significant study by Isi Foighel from 1957 concerning nationalizations. In this study, Foighel emphasizes the difference between foreigners and nationals in terms of the need for protection of property against governmental interferences. Foighel makes two remarkable claims, yet which prove to be highly relevant: 1) the existence of 'emotional views' against state measures interfering with private property rights and 2) the need for a balance of interest, the latter, however, is only implied by Foighel. With regards to 'emotional views' Foighel argues that interference carried out by a foreign state is more severe than interference by one's own government. In terms of nationalization of foreign property, Foighel articulates *"that a person will feel stronger sense of injury if his property is taken away by a foreign government [. . .] than if a corresponding loss was occasioned by this own government"*.[104] Accordingly, a foreigner will feel stronger against interferences with private property rights than a national, who can participate in the democratic procedure of electing a government. As admitted by Foighel these *"basically emotional views, even if they lack rational foundation [. . .] must be included as a factor of importance when attempting to assess the weight that can be attached to the protests of states against the measures of nationalization undertaken by foreign*

---

of foreign nationals. The legislation also provided for the cancellations of existing contracts for the building of ships, which were taken over by the American governmental entity, the Fleet Corporation. A number of shipbuilding orders made on the part of Norwegian nationals were affected by the measures.

101 *Norway v United States of America*, PCA, Award, 13 October 1922, para. 326. See also Vandevelde, *Bilateral Investment Treaties*, 283; Ivar Alvik, *Contracting With Sovereignty: State Contracts and International Arbitration*, 1st ed., vol. 31, Studies in International Law (Oxford: Hart Publishing, 2011), 216; Crawford, *Principles of Public International Law*, 547.

102 See for example *Jalapa Railroad and Power Co. (US v Mexico)*, the American–Mexican Claims Commission, reported in M. Whiteman, ed., "Digest of International Law," vol. 8, 1948, 8. See also Crawford, *Principles of Public International Law*, 548.

103 Crawford, *Principles of Public International Law*, 534–5.

104 Isi Foighel, *Nationalization: A Study in the Protection of Alien Property in International Law*, 1st ed. (Copenhagen: Nyt Nordisk Forlag, 1957), 30.

states".[105] In his reference to a weight of the protests against state interferences, Foighel thus seems ahead of his time by implicitly promoting the view that there should be a balance of interest.

6.4.1. The standard of compensation

The standard of compensation for deprivations of property rights has been subject to some debate in general international law. In a famous study of law from 1868 by the Argentine jurist Carlos Calvo, Calvo published what was referred to as the *Calvo Doctrine*. According to this doctrine jurisdiction in international investment disputes lies with the country in which the investment is located. The Calvo Doctrine thus suggests that compensation is to be decided by the host state and, as long as there is equality between nationals and foreigners and thus no discrimination, there cannot be any claim in international law. Hence, the Calvo Doctrine does not recognize an international minimum standard of treatment for alien property.[106]

The United States has been a forceful protagonist of an international minimum standard for the treatment of property of foreigners and opposed the Calvo Doctrine according to which compensation should be determined by the host state. The United States on the contrary attached significant importance to what is known as the *Hull Formula*, a rule named after its creator Cordell Hull. Hull was an American politician, who served as a Secretary of State during World War II. Before that, in 1938 Hull engaged in a famous dialogue with the Mexican Foreign Minister concerning the failure of Mexico to compensate Americans who lost farmlands during Mexican nationalization reforms in the late 1920s. Throughout the 1930s Mexico expropriated 17 foreign oil companies.[107] Facing a claim for compensation from the United States, Mexico contended that foreign investors were only to be treated as nationals and could not be granted a better protection under international law than what was afforded to nationals. However, Secretary Hull insisted, 'prompt, adequate and effective' compensation to be paid, i.e. the Hull Formula.[108] The Hull Formula has subsequently been adopted in the majority of BITs.

---

105 *Ibid.*, at 31.

106 It also denies the right of foreign nationals to seek diplomatic protection from their national state by requiring that the foreign national submit to the jurisdiction of domestic courts. See also Dolzer and Schreuer, *Principles of International Investment Law*, 1–2.

107 Vandevelde, *Bilateral Investment Treaties*, 283; See also Dolzer and Schreuer, *Principles of International Investment Law*, 2; Thomas W. Wälde and Borzu Sabahi, "Compensation, Damages, and Valuation," in *The Oxford Handbook of International Investment Law*, ed. Peter Muchlinski, Federico Ortino, and Christoph Schreuer (Oxford: Oxford University Press, 2008), 1068–9.

108 Vandevelde, *Bilateral Investment Treaties*, 284; Wälde and Sabahi "Compensation, Damages and Valuation," 1068–9.

6.5. *Preliminary conclusion*

The minimum standard of treatment covers protection of individuals as well as foreign companies. The minimum standard goes beyond protection of tangible property against physical destruction to the protection of acquired rights, including protection of contractual rights against governmental interferences. Yet, the obligation to protect foreigners and their property is not absolute. States may decide on economic and political priorities and thereby exercise their right to regulate. On this basis, there is a general recognition that not all interferences trigger the duty to compensate. Yet, general international law does not pronounce further on the threshold as to when compensation should be paid. Customary international law, however, does not project a static photograph of the minimum standard of treatment of aliens.[109] Accordingly, the minimum standard of treatment of aliens and their property is not frozen in time and it may further develop.

7. General international law as a legal paradigm with steering effect on the paradigm of international investment law

The following will show that general international law is useful for solving the stability–flexibility dilemma and enhancing a more coherent approach to international investment law.

The VCLT serves as the main tool for interpreting BITs. The VCLT was adopted in 1969 and entered into force in 1980. Pursuant to article 4 of the convention the formal scope of application is limited to treaties, which are concluded by states after the entry into force of the convention. However, since it largely codifies customary law,[110] the principles enshrined in the VCLT are technically applicable as customary norms even to earlier concluded BITs or BITs concluded between parties that are not state parties to the VCLT.

7.1. *References to general international law in BITs*

General international law is a part of the BIT regime. Many BITs contain clear references to general international law. The French Model BIT contains for example in article 4 a specific reference to general principles of international:

> "*Chacune des Parties contractantes s'engage à assurer, sur son territoire et dans sa zone maritime, un traitement juste et équitable, conformément aux principes du Droit international, aux investissements des investisseurs de l'autre*

---

109 See also *ADF Group Inc. v United States*, ICSID, Final Award, 9 January 2003, para. 179.
110 See *Danube Dam (Gabcíkovo-Nagymaros Project) (Hungary v Slovakia)*, ICJ, 1977, para. 46 and para. 99. See also, Weeramantry, *Treaty Interpretation in Investment Arbitration*, 6; Cassese, *International Law*, 179.

Partie et à faire en sorte que l'exercice du droit ainsi reconnu ne soit entravé ni en droit, ni en fait."

The Italian Model BIT is another example. This model BIT contains a clear reference to general international law since it explicitly requires that expropriation and compensation should *"conform to the principles of international law."*[111]

Apart from model texts, references to general international law can also be found in concrete treaties, e.g. in the BIT between France and Haiti, which refers to general principles of international law in article 3:

"Chacune des Parties contractantes s'engage à assurer sur son territoire et dans sa zone maritime un traitement juste et équitable, conformément à sa législation, dans le respect des principes du droit international, aux investissements des nationaux et société de l'autre Partie et à faire en sorte que l'exercice du droit ainsi reconnu ne soit entravé ni en droit ni en fait."

Another example is the BIT between Canada and the Philippines, which refers to principles of international law in article II by stating:

"Each Contracting Party shall accord investments or returns of investors of the other Contracting Party [. . .] (a) fair and equitable treatment in accordance with principles of international law."

The BIT between Sweden and Mexico also contains a reference to general international law in article 2(3), which states:

"Investments by investors of Contracting Parties shall at all times be accorded fair and equitable treatment in accordance with the relevant international standards under International Law."

In the BIT between the United Stated and Poland the parties refer to international law as the lower limit for treatment of foreign investment in article II:

"Investments shall at all times be accorded fair and equitable treatment, shall enjoy full protection and security and shall in no case be accorded treatment less than that required by international law."

Accordingly, international law is here considered the minimum standard of treatment. The BIT between the United States and Poland also refers to international law in article XII(1)(b), which requires that *"[t]his Treaty shall not derogate from international legal obligations."* This is indeed a broad restriction, since it may cover all sorts of international obligations stemming from the paradigm of

---

111 Italian Model BIT, 2003, article V(5).

general international law as well as other special branches of law, including human rights law.

In sum, references to general international law occur in various ways in BITs. Though oftentimes linked with the FET standard references to general international law are also made with regards to the international minimum standard of which treatment of foreign investors and their investments cannot go below. Even for BITs with no explicit references to general international law, the general international law paradigm still applies, in particular the rules relating to interpretation of treaties. This is because no treaty can exist in isolation of general international law. The fundamental rules of interpretation of treaties found in the VCLT would therefore be applicable directly or as customary norms.

7.2. *The use of general international law in investment arbitration*

In investment disputes, general international law is referred to on a regular basis, especially with regards to providing the sources of law or rules of treaty interpretation. Moreover, the general rules of state responsibility have been referred to, for instance the rules on circumstances precluding wrongfulness like the concept of necessity or *force majeure*. More specifically, investment tribunals refer to e.g. the VCLT as a tool for interpreting IIAs like BITs, to early case-law by the PCIJ, to case-law by the Iran–US Claims tribunal or to the ICJ. Moreover, investment tribunals have alluded to the positive presumption that parties refer to general principles of international law for questions, which the treaty (e.g. the BIT) does not itself resolve in express terms. So, general international law is widely part of investment arbitration.

The general principles of international law serve various functions in investment arbitration. A key function is that general principles of international law are used to 'fill the gap' and thereby avoiding a *non liquet* when a treaty is silent on a specific matter. Another function of the general principles of international law is that they are used to choose between two or more conflicting interpretations of a treaty or customary rule.[112] In addition hereto, it could be argued that general principles of international law provide presumptions of treaty interpretation. In the case of *SGS v Philippines* the tribunal considered the approach adopted by another tribunal in *SGS v Pakistan* and found that the reliance on general principles of international law as a means to generate a general presumption against the broad interpretation of the umbrella clause was unjustified.[113] The interesting point here, however, is that the tribunal did not reject as such that general international law can lay down presumptions of interpretation.

---

112 See further on the use of general principles of international law in Cassese, *International Law*, 188–9.

113 *SGS v Philippines*, ICSID Decision on Objections to Jurisdiction, 29 January 2004, para. 122.

Three key functions of general international law in investment arbitrations are significant:

- the *gap-filler function*, most importantly by providing customary norms of substantive protection of aliens and their property and the sovereign right to regulate. These rules are useful when IIAs are silent on a matter. These rules are explained above;[114]
- the function of *providing rules for interpretation* of treaty rules, such as BITs and other international commitments.[115] This will be dealt with below;
- the function of creating presumptions of interpretation through what will be referred to as a *'gravitational pull'*. This is also further explained below.

The following addresses the latter two functions.

7.3. General international law as a tool for interpreting BITs

A key function of the general international law regime is that it serves as a tool for the interpretation of BITs. As with interpretation of other treaties in international law, the starting point should be found in the VCLT.

For ICSID claims the Convention of the Settlement of Investment Disputes between States and Nationals of Other States from 1965 (the ICSID Convention) is essential. The ICSID Convention offers a procedural framework pursuant to which investment disputes may be resolved, but it does not contain much guidance on the interpretation of IIAs. In cases where an ICSID claim is based on a BIT, the BIT together with other rules of general international law would usually be considered the primary sources of the applicable legal rules. Contractual or statutory interpretation rules or others national laws or techniques for interpreting documents are typically deemed less important. To the extent that there may be inconsistencies between national law and public international law, the latter will prevail. The absence of (other) rules guiding the interpretations of BITs thereby reinforces the importance of the VCLT. This perception is confirmed in a study of references to the VCLT by foreign investment tribunals, which shows an increase over time in references to the VCLT.[116] The VCLT is thus crucial for interpreting BITs whereas it is not applicable to investment contracts between private investors and states, unless the parties have agreed so.

114 Chapter 2, section 6.
115 The difference between gap-filling and interpretation is that gap-filling is concerned with filling out a legal lacuna through the use of rules that are not articulated in the treaty, e.g. by referring to customary law or other treaty obligation. Conversely, interpretation is based on the rule already articulated in the treaty and does not rely on rules 'outside' of the treaty. However, the line between gap-filling and interpretation is more theoretical than of practical relevance.
116 Weeramantry, *Treaty Interpretation in Investment Arbitration*, 26.

7.3.1. *Approaches to treaty interpretation*

Three approaches to treaty interpretation are particularly relevant for the interpretation of BITs. The first approach focuses on the *actual text* of the agreement and emphasizes the analysis of the words used. This legal method of interpretation aims at an objective method of interpretation. This approach, however, is oftentimes not likely to bring the arbitrators far due to the vaguely formulated standards of protection. Another approach is to attach significant importance to the *intentions* of the parties adopting the BIT, which is thus the more subjective approach. However, for those who are tasked with interpreting BITs (in practice; the arbitrators) the initial intentions of the parties can be difficult to deduce. Arbitrators rarely have significant information concerning the intentions of the parties at the time of the negotiation. Furthermore, it may be questionable how much weight should be given to such intentions several years, perhaps decades, after the treaty has been negotiated. A third approach adopts a wider perspective and emphasizes the *object and purpose* of the treaty (the teleological approach). The teleological approach takes into account all aspects of the agreement from the words employed to the intention of parties and the aims of the particular treaty.[117]

Each of these approaches to treaty interpretation tends to confer the primacy on one particular aspect of treaty interpretation, if not to the exclusion then to the subordinate of the others. These three approaches may produce the same result in practice. Yet, they are also capable of leading to radically divergent results.

Turning to the VCLT, article 31 reflects customary law[118] and embraces a more integrated approach to interpretation of treaties:

> *"A treaty shall be interpreted in good faith in accordance with the ordinary meaning to be given to the terms of the treaty in their context and in the light of its object and purpose."*

Article 31 thereby lay down the criteria of 1) good faith, 2) ordinary meaning, 3) context and 4) object and purpose.

The criterion of good faith forms part of the broader international principle of *pacta sunt servanda*, described as *"one of the basic principles governing the creation and performance of legal obligations"*.[119] According to practice in investment

---

117 Shaw, *International Law*, 932–8; Crawford, *Principles of Public International Law*, 378–84; Malgosia Fitzmaurice, "The Practical Working of the Law of Treaties," in *International Law*, ed. Malcolm D. Evans (Oxford: Oxford University Press, 2003), 280–1.

118 *Territorial Dispute (Libyan Arab Jamahiriya/Chad)*, ICJ, Judgment, 3 February 1994, para. 41. See also Casesse, *International Law*, 179.

119 Enshrined in the VCLT article 26 and described in Weeramantry, *Treaty Interpretation in Investment Arbitration*, 45. See also *Nuclear Test case (New Zealand v France)*, ICJ, Judgment, 20 December 1974, para 49, p. 473.

disputes, conduct that violates the principle of good faith need not be intentional, manifestly damaging or fraudulent.[120]

The interpretation of treaties in accordance with its ordinary meaning is basically the point of departure when interpreting BITs. Furthermore, one may assume that the ordinary meaning of the BIT is most likely to reflect the intentions of the parties. It is argued that arbitral tribunals so far appear to have favoured an emphasis on a textual interpretation.[121] However, this does not necessarily mean that it is always considered the most important or decisive element in the VCLT.[122]

The third criterion mentioned in article 31(1) requires an interpretation to take into consideration the context of the terms subject to interpretation. The context of a treaty is set out in some detail in article 31(2) and embraces any instrument of relevance to the conclusion of the treaty, as well as a treaty's preamble and annexes. Legal scholars have highlighted the importance of this criterion by stressing that there is *"no such thing as an abstract ordinary meaning of a phrase, divorced from the place which that phrase occupies in the text to be interpreted"*.[123] In investment arbitration, tribunals have frequently paid significant attention to the context. At the same time, however, the context alone has usually not been determinative of an interpretation.[124]

The fourth element mentioned in article 31(1) of the VCLT is the criterion of taking into account the object and purpose of a treaty. In principle, object and purpose are two criteria, but practice has employed a unitary concept rather than two terms having distinct meanings and functions.[125] Tribunals in investment arbitration have generally refrained from using this criterion to reach an outcome that contradicts or displaces the textual meaning of a treaty.[126] In order to deduce the object and purpose of the parties, the starting point would be the BIT itself. The preamble of the BIT, which is obviously an integral part of the treaty, has on a number of occasions assisted tribunals to elucidate the aim and intentions of the parties.[127]

Article 31(1) does not articulate any priority in relation to the four criteria, but none of these elements can be excluded completely. The absence of an order has

120 *Tecmed v Mexico*, ICSID, Award, 29 May 2003, para. 71.
121 Weeramantry, *Treaty Interpretation in Investment Arbitration*, 49.
122 *Aguas del Tunari S.A. v Bolivia*, ICSID, Decision on Jurisdiction, 21 October 2005, para. 226.
123 Ian McTaggart Sinclair, *The Vienna Convention on the Law of Treaties*, 2nd ed., Melland Schill Monographs in International Law (Manchester: Manchester University Press, 1973), 121.
124 Weeramantry, *Treaty Interpretation in Investment Arbitration*, 67; Fitzmaurice, "The Practical Working of the Law of Treaties," 186–8.
125 Weeramantry, *Treaty Interpretation in Investment Arbitration*, 68.
126 *Ibid.*
127 *Ibid.*, at 71 and 77. See also Fitzmaurice, "The Practical Working of the Law of Treaties," 189–90.

been confirmed in arbitral practice.[128] All these elements would therefore have to be taken into consideration but it is left with the interpreter to assess their relative value and weight.

The VCLT itself does not provide guidance for adjudicators concerning when to choose a broad or a narrow interpretation or when to decide if an interpretation is 'balanced'. Arbitrators may therefore face dilemmas when attempting to give effect to one or more criteria at the risk of allowing detriment to others. So, though the VCLT does not state an order of importance between the four criteria, the weight that should be granted to the last criterion (object and purpose) is particularly controversial. Whereas some scholars maintain that *"great weight was attributed to the purpose pursued by contracting parties, as laid down in the text of the treaty"*,[129] others perceive the object and purpose as a subordinate criterion.[130] The latter view can also be found in treaty practice in investment disputes.[131]

Finally, another important principle enshrined in the VCLT is the *principle of effectiveness* (or *effect utile*), according to which a treaty must be interpreted as to enable its provisions to be 'effective and useful', i.e. to have the appropriate effect.[132] Cassese contends that the principle of effectiveness is intended to expand the normative scope of the treaties, to the detriment of the old principle whereby, in case of doubt, limitations of sovereignty were to be strictly interpreted.[133] In terms of the interpretation of BITs, the principle of effectiveness is relevant as to interpret the substantive provisions so as to grant effective rights to investors. This, does not entail, however, that investors have unlimited rights.

7.3.2. Relevance of preambles

Preambles to treaties are generally perceived as introductory statements expressing the purpose and underlying goals of the treaty. Although preambles do not usually contain provisions or dispositions of substance, it is nevertheless generally accepted that they are relevant and important as guides to the manner in which the treaty should be interpreted.[134] By constituting an essential element of the context of the treaty,[135] the function of the preambles is 'to drag' the interpretation

---

128 See for instance *Aguas del Tunari S.A. v Bolivia*, ICSID, Decision on Respondent's Objections to Jurisdiction, 21 October 2005, para. 91.
129 Cassese, *International Law*, 179.
130 Weeramantry, *Treaty Interpretation in Investment Arbitration*, 68, 75; Sinclair, *The Vienna Convention on the Law of Treaties*, 130.
131 See e.g. *Feldman v Mexico*, ICSID, Interim Decision on Preliminary Jurisdictional Issues, 6 December 2000, para. 35.
132 Cassese, *International Law*, 179; Dapo Akande, "International Organizations," in *International Law*, ed. Malcolm D. Evans (Oxford: Oxford University Press, 2003), 280–1.
133 *Ibid.*, at 178–80.
134 See also the *Beagle Channel* arbitration between Argentina and Chile, 51 ILR 93, 1977, para. 19.
135 Cf. the VCLT article 31(2).

of the substantive parts in the direction which aligns the most with the goals of the treaty.

Most commonly, preambles in BITs contain only limited, if any, guidance on the object and purpose of the BIT. Historically, the object and purpose of BITs has been to promote and protect foreign investors and their investments (the traditional approach). The policy goals, which can be found in this type of preamble, typically refer to protection and promotion of mutual economic development or equivalent formulations.

> Example of a preamble drafted on the basis of the traditional approach:
>
> **(India–Greece BIT 2008)**
>
> > *"- desiring to intensify investment flows to the mutual benefit of both States on a long term basis,*
> > *- having as their objective to create favourable conditions for investments by investors of either Contracting Party in the territory of the other Contracting Party,*
> > *- recognizing that the promotion and protection of investments, on the basis of this Agreement, will stimulate the business initiative in this field."*

> Example of a preamble drafted on the basis of the traditional approach:
>
> **(German Model BIT 2008)**
>
> > *"- desiring to intensify economic co-operation between the two States,*
> > *- intending to create favourable conditions for investments by investors of either State in the territory of the other State,*
> > *- recognizing that the encouragement and contractual protection of such investments are apt to stimulate private business initiative and to increase the prosperity of both nations."*

Some of the more recently drafted BITs, however, contain an alternative approach.[136]

7.3.3. Interpreting silence

When IIAs are silent on a matter it is the task for the interpreters to decide whether they consider that, if the parties to a treaty had wanted the matter in

---

136 This is further explained below in Chapter 3, section 7.

question covered, they would have provided for it or, conversely, they would explicitly exclude it if this had been their intent.

Treaty silence on matters, which could have been included, generates uncertainty. In practice, when faced with silence, arbitrators are often reluctant to imply terms in a treaty. For instance, in the *Methanex* case, the tribunal held, since the parties did not incorporate a non-discrimination requirement in a provision in which they might have done so, *"it would be wrong for a tribunal to pretend that they had"*.[137] A pertinent question is if such an approach should be applied when it comes to silence on policy issues. Silence on policy matters is not to be confused with an instance of textual ambiguity or lacuna, which more directly invites a tribunal to contemplate law-making.

The approach to silence on policy goals of the treaty is relevant in terms of assessing which policy considerations can or should be taken into account when interpreting a BIT. Obviously, a BIT is placed in a societal context even when the treaty itself does not refer to policy issues.

The BIT between United Kingdom and Uganda is an example of this approach, where policy goals apart from investment promotion and protection are not mentioned:

United Kingdom–Uganda BIT, *preamble*:

"Desiring to create favourable conditions for greater investment by nationals and companies of one State in the territory of the other State;

Recognising that the encouragement and reciprocal protection of such investments will be conducive to the stimulation of individual business initiative and will increase prosperity in both States."

Another evidence of the traditional approach to investment protection with no references to other policy concerns than promotion and protection of investments is found in the BIT between Germany and Venezuela:

Germany–Venezuela BIT, *preamble*:

"In dem Wunsch, die wirtschaftliche Zusammenarbeit zwischen beiden Staaten zu vertiefen,

In dem Bestreben, günstige Bedingungen für Kapitalanlagen von Staatsangehörigen oder Gesellschaften des einen Staates im Hoheitsgebiet des anderen Staates zu schaffen,

In der Erkenntnis, daß eine Förderung und ein vertraglicher Schutz dieser Kapitalanlagen geeignet sind, die private wirtschaftliche Initiative zu beleben und den Wohlstand beider Völker zu mehren . . . "

---

137 *Methanex Corporation v. United States*, UNCITRAL, Final Award, Part IV, Chapter C, para. 16.

The question would then be whether *other* policy concerns that are not mentioned could be taken into account.

When BITs contain no references to policy considerations at all or only refer to economic concerns, it remains questionable whether the states actually intended that the substantive parts should be interpreted in the light of other (social and environmental) policy concerns not explicitly mentioned. Accordingly, silence on policy considerations in BITs leads to reluctance among arbitrators to include such concerns. However, this does not necessarily mean that the state parties did not intend to promote investment protection in accordance with other social objectives. In many cases, states may simply not have taken these concerns into account, either because they did not have these concerns at the time of negotiating the BIT, or because they did not observe the linkage between investment promotion and protection and other public interests. Moreover, it might be that states simply were not able to foresee the consequences of concluding a BIT.

In the *Tokios* case[138] the tribunal expressed the view that *"it is not for tribunals to impose limits on the scope of BITs not found in the text, much less limits nowhere evident from the negotiating history"*.[139] This perception, however, concerns an assessment of the jurisdictional scope of the BIT, not the interpretation of the substantive standards of treatment. One can therefore not infer from this view alone that there cannot be other elements limiting the substantial scope of the investment protection, including public policies linked with other international commitments.

When BITs are silent on policy matters, support may be found by asserting other international commitments legally binding upon the state parties. Moreover, the methodology proposed below suggests an obligation for arbitrators to take into account broader societal aspects, including social welfare policies.

7.4. *Adjudicating investment disputes towards a jurisprudence constante*

There is no *stare decisis* doctrine in general international law and thus no binding precedent.[140] In principle decisions are binding only *inter partes*. This is stated for the ICJ in article 59 of the ICJ Statute, whereas for ICSID awards, this is stated in article 53(1) of the ICSID Convention.[141] Even though there is no formal system of investment treaty arbitration as such, evidence of systems or patterns occurs moving toward a more consistent practice in many areas.

138 *Tokios Tokelés v Ukraine*, ICSID, Decision on Jurisdiction, 29 April 2004.
139 *Ibid.*, para. 36.
140 Jan Paulsson, "The Role of Precedent in Investment Arbitration," in *Arbitration Under International Investment Agreements: A Guide to the Key Issues*, ed. Katia Yannaca-Small (Oxford: Oxford University Press, 2010), 699.
141 With regards to the ICSID Convention, it may, however, be contended that article 53(1) is directed at the *res judicata* effect of awards (no appeal) rather than at their impact as precedents in later cases.

From a general international law perspective, it is widely recognized that international tribunals can rely on judicial decisions as a source of law. This is stated in the ICJ Statute article 38(1)(d),[142] and the ICJ has even relied on not only previous judgments but also on arbitral decisions as a basis for authority.[143]

Arbitral practice in investment disputes displays the formation of a *de facto* doctrine of precedent or a movement towards a *jurisprudence constante*.[144] This is because the treaty provisions contain such vague substantive language that the content is unclear. Therefore, it is inevitable that arbitral decisions as they accumulate will help 'to flesh out' the normative content of treaty standards.

From a more principled-based perspective, this movement toward a *jurisprudence constante* is a key element in the promotion of international justice and the rule of law. As expressed by Sir Hersch Lauterpacht:[145]

> *"It is in the interest of international justice that its continuity should not be confined to the jurisprudence of the Court itself. International arbitral law has produced a body of precedent, which is full of instruction and authority. Numerous arbitral awards have made a distinct contribution to international law by reason of their scope, their elaboration, and the conscientiousness with which they have examined the issue before them."*

Precedents enhance the predictability of investment arbitration and are necessary because of the need for consistency. According to Sureda, consistency is determined *"not only by the weight that precedents may be given but also by the values or policies that they reflect"*.[146] In addition, a more consistent arbitral practice enhances the legitimacy of the system. For that reason, the question should rather be whether there is cause not to follow the reasons and conclusions of earlier cases. So, arbitrators could be said to face at least an informal pressure to review, explain and often harmonize the treaty and customary international law provisions that they apply and interpret.

---

142 Though article 38 of the ICJ Statute is technically an instruction to the ICJ concerning the sources of law, the provision has generally been recognized as laying down the general sources of international law. See also Shaw, *International Law*, 109–12.

143 Arbitrations such as the *Alabama Claims Arbitration* (*United States v United Kingdom*), and the *Island of Palmas* (*United States v the Netherlands*) have frequently been cited.

144 Christoph H. Schreuer and Matthew M. Weiniger, "A Doctrine of Precedent?," in *The Oxford Handbook of International Investment Law*, ed. Peter Muchlinski, Federico Ortino, and Christoph Schreuer (Oxford: Oxford University Press, 2008), 1189–95. See also Jan Paulsson, "The Role of Precedent in Investment Arbitration," 712.

145 Hersch Lauterpacht, *The Development of International Law by the International Court*, Reis. ed., Grotius Classic Reprint Series (Cambridge: Cambridge University Press, 2011), 17–18.

146 Andrés Rigo Sureda, "Precedent in Investment Treaty Arbitration," in *International Investment Law for the 21st Century: Essays in Honour of Christoph Schreuer*, ed. Christina Binder, Ursula Kriebaum, August Reinisch, and Stephan Wittich (Oxford: Oxford University Press, 2009), 839.

Indeed, there is a fine line between a formal doctrine of precedent and the more persuasive role, which is here suggested for arbitral decisions. The fact that most ICSID arbitral decisions are published on the Internet allows access to former decisions by the arbitrators as well as both parties to the dispute and others. The movement toward a *jurisprudence constante* is thus a significant contribution to the unification of international investment law, which shall be further addressed below.

7.5. *Unification of international investment law*

The proliferation of international law is not a new concern. According to Crawford for example *"international law has always been diverse, has always had the capacity to fragment"*.[147] Still, the stability–flexibility dilemma displays the need for an international investment law regime, which on the one hand ensures investors a stable legal environment but at the same time allows for flexibility for states to carry out its policies. In the attempt to approach the question of the scope of the right to regulate, a more principled approach needs to be developed.

As highlighted by Dupuy, the parallel development of the human rights regime and the international investment law regime should not be deemed as substantiating the fragmentation of international law. Rather, it should be substantiated that the two legal regimes *"belong to the same legal order"*.[148] As established, BITs as well as arbitral practice do refer to general international law. It thus seems plausible to draw further on general international law to establish a theoretical framework to develop a method to resolve some of these fundamental legal issues covered by the stability–flexibility dilemma, including the issue of colliding legal regimes. As held by Sureda *"the search for consistency and predictability goes hand in hand with shared values. The lack of those will hamper a jurisprudence constante."*[149] There is therefore a need for a broader unification approach to international law that embraces legal norms, policies and values.

7.5.1. *The principle of systematic integration*

The question as to what extent international investment law should be interpreted in accordance with other branches of international law was a fundamental question for the ILC in the Commission's work relating to the Fragmentation of International Law.[150] The solution proposed by the ILC was based on the VCLT

---

147 James Crawford, "Continuity and Discontinuity in International Dispute Settlement," in *International Investment Law for the 21st Century: Essays in Honour of Christoph Schreue,* ed. Christina Binder, Ursula Kriebaum, August Reinisch, and Stephan Wittich (Oxford: Oxford University Press, 2009), 817.
148 Dupuy, "Unification Rather than Fragmentation of International Law?," 61.
149 Sureda, "Precedent in Investment Arbitration," 842.
150 ILC, "Fragmentation of International Law: Difficulties Arising from the Diversification and Expansion of International Law. Report of the Study Group of the international Law Commission," *op. cit.*

and founded in *the principle of systemic integration*.[151] The VCLT article 31(3)(c) was perceived as an expression of this principle:[152]

> *"There shall be taken into account, together with the context:*
> *. . . (c) any relevant rules of international law applicable in the relations between the parties."*

The principle of systemic integration goes further than merely restating the applicability of general international law. It points to "the need to take into account the normative environment more widely".[153]

Adopting an approach of systemic integration means that interpretation is founded on two basic presumptions:[154]

> *Presumption no. 1 (positive presumption):*
>
> *Parties to a treaty are taken to refer to general principles of international law for all questions, which the treaty does not itself resolve in express terms or in a different way.*
>
> *Presumption no. 2 (negative presumption):*
>
> *In entering into treaty obligations, the parties intend not to act inconsistently with generally recognized principles of international law or with previous treaty obligations toward third states.*

Systemic integration attaches further importance to customary norms and general principles of law and thus requires more than a harmonizing approach to treaty interpretation. So, the VCLT article 31(3)(c) requires that the interpretation of treaties take into account any relevant rule of international law applicable in the relations between the parties. Hence, the VCLT article 31(3)(c) does provide a legal basis for arbitrators to take into account human rights obligations binding upon the state party, for instance by interpreting a BIT in accordance with other human rights treaties. This latter element is a central point of this research.

7.5.2. *External rules with gravitational pull*

Simma and Kill have dealt with the question as to what extent international investment law should be interpreted in accordance with other branches of international law. They adopt the term 'external rules' of international law for the

151 *Ibid.*, paras 410–80.
152 *Ibid.*, paras 413, 208.
153 *Ibid.*, paras 415, 209.
154 *Ibid.*, paras 465, 234.

rules that are perceived as part of the general international law paradigm.[155] They build upon a theory of external rules constituting the steering wheel of specialized systems of international law. At the same time, they acknowledge that external rules themselves are not fixed but an evolving body of law.[156]

Based on the practice of the ICJ, Simma and Kill articulate two important observations of the use of external rules. *Firstly*, external rules in general international law are used to define the meaning in a specific treaty, i.e. a treaty belonging to the special branch of international law.[157] *Secondly*, the ICJ has employed a presumption that treaties are intended to produce effects in accordance with existing rules of international law. External rules thereby enhance a process of coherence.[158] It is this latter observation that is subject to further consideration in the following.

7.5.3. Examples of the presumption of harmonizing effects

There are significant examples in international law demonstrating that treaties produce harmonizing effects. In the *Indian Passage* case[159] from 1957 the ICJ held that it is a rule of interpretation that a treaty text, in principle, should be interpreted *"as producing and as intended to produce effects in accordance with existing law and not in violation of it"*.[160]

In the *ELSI* case[161] from 1989 the ICJ had to decide whether an important principle of customary international law (the requirement to exhaust local remedies before initiating an international claim) had been tacitly dispensed with. The ICJ found itself *"unable to accept that an important principle of customary international law should be held to have been tacitly dispensed with, in the absence of any words making clear an intention to do so"*.[162]

In the *Oil Platforms* case[163] from 2003 Iran had instituted proceedings against the United States concerning a dispute arising out of the attack by several warships of the United States Navy in the 1980s and destruction of three offshore

---

155 Bruno Simma and Theodore Kill, "Harmonizing Investment Protection and International Human Rights: First Steps Towards a Methodology?," in *International Investment Law for the 21st Century: Essays in Honour of Christoph Schreue*, ed. Christina Binder, Ursula Kriebaum, August Reinisch, and Stephan Wittich (Oxford: Oxford University Press, 2009), 678–707.

156 *Ibid.*, 678–707.

157 *Ibid.*, 682–91. Simma and Kill relies on a study of the practice of the ICJ by looking to external rules of international law as interpretative aids.

158 *Ibid.*

159 *Right of Passage Over Indian Territory (Portugal v India)*, Preliminary Objections, Judgments, 26 November 1957, ICJ Reports (1957).

160 *Ibid.*, para. 142.

161 *Elettronica Sicula S.p.A. (ELSI) (United States v Italy)*, Judgment 20 July 1989, ICJ Reports (1989).

162 *Ibid.*, para. 50.

163 *Oil Platforms Case (Iran v United States)*, ICJ, Judgment, 6 November 2003.

oil production complexes, owned and operated for commercial purposes by the National Iranian Oil Company. The ICJ made an express reference to the VCLT article 31(3)(c) and stressed that an interpretation of a treaty must take into account any relevant rules of international law applicable in the relations between the parties.[164] The United States had argued that its 1955 Treaty of Amity, Economic relations, and Consular Rights with Iran governed the circumstances under which a state party to the treaty could resort to the use of force without violating the treaty or general international law. In this regard, the ICJ stressed that *"the application of the relevant rules of international law [. . .] forms an integral part of the task of interpretation entrusted to the Court"*.[165] The ICJ thus employed the presumption that the 1955 Treaty of Amity, Economic relations, and Consular Rights was not intended to produce results that diverged with international law on the use of force.

7.5.4. Human rights exerting a 'gravitational pull' on IIAs

The two distinct functions of a) defining the meaning of an explicit treaty term and b) presuming that the effects are intended to be in accordance with existing rules of international law, have been referred to by Simma and Kill as the *clarification* of meaning of the terms employed in the treaty, and the *qualification* of treaty rules by external factors.[166]

Clarification is merely explanatory. This means that external rules can clarify the scope and content of other legal rules. The prerequisite is the existence of uncertainty. Otherwise, clarification of a rule would not be relevant.

Qualification, however, is an approach that goes one step further by implicitly containing an assessment of the legal norm encompassed in a treaty under a special branch of international law with the normative content of another treaty norm found in another branch of international law. In other words, the qualification test requires an assessment of how a legal norm in one of the paradigms of international law (e.g. international investment law) should be interpreted in order to achieve a result with another paradigm of international law (e.g. human rights), which is most coherent. So, the qualification of a rule articulated in a BIT could be dependent on the normative content of a human rights norm. This presumption is thus employed to resolve issues of interpretation that relate to the broader normative content of the treaty, rather than to the meaning of a specific term.

By applying this presumption or qualification test to the investment law regime, human rights treaties might be perceived as the external factor, the normative rules, producing effects on the normative rules of international investment law

---

164 *Ibid.*, paras 39 and 41.
165 *Ibid.*, para. 41.
166 Simma and Kill, "Harmonizing Investment Protection and International Human Right," 683, at note 23.

contained in BITs. Simma and Kill explain this as *"external rules exerting a sort of gravitational pull on the treaty rule that will result in a treaty interpretation that more closely coheres with the external rule"*.[167]

An approach to the law as encompassing external rules with a gravitational pull on specialized systems of international law appears convincing. Yet, this approach also contains some weaknesses. It may be that two states by concluding a BIT expressly intended to contract out of the 'default' rules of general international law. In this case, an interpreter should not bring back these rules into the case, unless the states have negotiated rules contrary to customary norms with the status of *jus cogens*. This is also highlighted by Simma and Kill stating that states, *"do not have a completely free hand in the legal ordering of their relations"*.[168]

So, Simma and Kill notice that where the parties "do not appear to" have intended to alter existing rules of international law an interpreter is justified in adopting an interpretation that coheres with those previously existing rules.[169] The question is then when do the parties "appear to" have intended to alter existing rules? Does such a meaning require explicit support either in the treaty itself, annexes or preparatory work? What is the likelihood that the parties did not implicitly – through the mere negotiation of a BIT – seek to alter existing rules of international law? As mentioned, investment tribunals have made reference to a positive presumption that parties refer to general principles of international law for questions that the BIT in question does not resolve. Human rights commitments may also be an implied limitation as to what a state can actually engage in under the international investment law regime. Chapter 4 analyses the positive international human rights obligations, which may impose limits to investment protection.

7.5.5. *Policy concerns exerting a 'gravitational pull' on IIAs*

In addition to norms with the status of *jus cogens* that impose a limit to what obligations states can validly commit to, there may also be other norms that can impose a limitation to what states can agree to. It is here suggested that norms, not having a legally binding character, nevertheless may exert 'gravitational pull' on the international investment law regime. It is thus suggested that policy concerns (which potentially can evolve into legal norms) may have a steering effect on the interpretation of BITs. In this way, a BIT should be interpreted so as to be presumed to have legal effect in accordance with key policy concerns.

A more holistic approach to international investment law includes norm coherence as well as policy coherence. Policy coherence is thus an additional aim to legal coherence. The challenge is, however, that these policy concerns are neither easily discernible nor exhaustively defined since they are evolving as societal

---

167 *Ibid.*, 683.
168 *Ibid.*, 690.
169 *Ibid.*

expectations and needs change. Yet, some key policy concerns can be deduced from views expressed by key actors of international law mentioned earlier. Chapter 3 of this research serves this purpose.

7.6. *State of the art: A theory of gravitational pull*

The principle of systemic integration, as set out by the ILC, focuses on 'taking into account' other rules of international law in the more narrow sense and thus not the broader principles or considerations.[170] The approach by Simma and Kill centralizes on 'a gravitational pull' that may generate rules of presumption. These approaches appear valuable and are not mutually exclusive. Yet, these approaches could be taken a step further in a methodology, that relies on a combination of legal coherence and policy coherence.

This research thus relies on a broader unification approach to the law. Unification is here perceived as an aim, a means to enhance coherence and not as a goal as such. A completely coherent system of international law is perceived as a theoretical achievement, which in practice hardly is a viable goal due to the proliferation of norms of international law. However, this does not undermine the importance of applying a unified approach to the law, an approach that goes further than a reconciliation of two legal systems by the lowest common denominator.

To respond to the dynamism of international law a unification approach allows taking into account continuous developments. *Unification* also appears to be slightly different than *harmonizing*. Harmonization as an approach to treaty interpretation is carried out through a balanced and proportionate interpretation, where one treaty is interpreted in a harmonized manner to achieve the most coherent effect. Harmonization may be a step toward unification of two or more (opposing) legal regimes.

A unification approach is an elaboration of the systemic integrationist approach. A unification approach to the law adds key policy concerns as contextual elements that should be taken into account when interpreting treaties.

Another aspect, which could be considered, is the *consequential aspect* highlighted by Brownlie in his Separate Opinion in *CME v Czech Republic*.[171] In his Separate Opinion, Brownlie analyses the preamble of the Netherlands–Czech Republic BIT. With regards to the criteria relevant for determining compensation, Brownlie highlights the effects upon the value of the investment as a relevant, though not sole, criterion.[172] He points to 'just compensation' as the standard of compensation embraced in the Netherlands–Czech Republic BIT as being a deliberate choice by the state parties in contrast to for example the United States

---

170 ILC, "Fragmentation of International Law: Difficulties arising from the Diversification and expansion of International Law. Report of the Study Group of the international Law Commission", *op. cit.*, para. 425, p. 214.

171 Separate Opinion on the issues at the quantum phases of *CME v Czech Republic* by Ian Brownlie, C.B.E., Q.C., 14 March 2003.

172 *Ibid.*, para. 21.

of America–Czech Republic BIT, which refers explicitly to the 'fair market value' of the expropriated investment.[173] Brownlie then articulates that the generally international recognized standard of compensation does not necessarily follow the *Hull Formula*.[174] While being cautious about explicitly stating what is then to be considered the generally recognized standard, Brownlie relies on the 'appropriate compensation' standard as explicitly stated in the UN General Assembly Resolution 1803 (XVII),[175] and the Charter of Economic Rights and Duties of States.[176] He then suggests that the amount of compensation might be modified by a general legitimate expectation standard and the actual conditions. These expectations are varying from case to case according to the facts and the legal framework, but generally he considers that:[177]

> "1) *The host state is not accepting a risk, which will have consequences of paying compensation at a level, which would cause catastrophic economic consequences for the host State and its population.*
>
> 2) *An investment is carrying the expectation that it will be profitable, but only on a basis of reasonable expectations.*
>
> 3) *Explicit indications of the investor's expectation of profitability will provide a primary criterion of what is a reasonable rate of return."*

Hence, Brownlie seems to add decisive weight to the object and purpose of the BIT. Moreover, he adds a consequential aspect requiring that the BIT should be interpreted in a consequential manner, i.e. with consideration to the consequences to ensure avoidance of potential 'catastrophic economic consequences'. The interpretation of an expropriation standard of compensation, so as to enhance its effects in coherence with other international obligations, calls for a balanced standard in which elements such as potential 'catastrophic economic consequences' could be taken into consideration in a proportionality test.

A somewhat weak point to the aspect of avoiding catastrophic economic consequences is the question, which naturally arises, relating to how to determine what should be considered 'catastrophic economic consequences'. In this regard, it should be stated that these consequences must be large-scale and fundamental for the general population in terms of standard of living and the enjoyment of fundamental human rights, such as an economic crisis reaching a threshold of a state of emergency situation. Other elements that may add to the 'catastrophic economic consequences' are for instance the long-term nature of a concrete investment project and the privatization of essential public services or functions.

---

173 Article III(1).
174 Separate Opinion on the issues at the quantum phases of *CME v Czech Republic* by Ian Brownlie, C.B.E., Q.C., 14 March 2003, para. 31.
175 UNGA Resolution 1803 (XVII), 14 December 1962.
176 Charter of Economic Rights and Duties of States (UNGA Resolution 3281 (XXIX)), 1974.
177 Separate Opinion on the issues at the quantum phases of *CME v Czech Republic* by Ian Brownlie, C.B.E., Q.C., 14 March 2003, para. 58.

Claims against states for sovereign debt restructuring, like the claims for compensation against Argentina, and likely claims against Greece, would then in sum not require the state to compensate beyond a level that would have 'catastrophic economic consequences'. Hence, this approach lays down an inherent limitation or bar for compensation claims based on regulatory takings for social welfare purposes.

In sum, this theoretical approach can be articulated as *a theory of gravitational pull* that enhances legal coherence and policy coherence between the two legal regimes; international investment law and human rights law:

The theory of gravitational pull:

BITs should be interpreted in a harmonizing manner with human rights obligations.

The interpretation should be based on the positive presumption that general principles of law apply and the negative presumption against inconsistencies.

The interpretation must take into account the particular context of the case as well as inherent limitations to treaty standards such as avoiding catastrophic economic consequences for the host state and its population.

The gravitational pull theory would then require the following:

1) an identification of relevant legal norms;
2) an identification of key policy concerns;[178]
3) a balanced approach to interpretation;[179]
4) an identification of possible limitations to treaty standards.[180]

8. Preliminary conclusions

States have lost their monopoly as a political actor in the international system, as new actors have proved gradually more influential in the law-making process. Changing roles of actors of international law has the potential to enhance the need for adapting the international investment law regime. This part explained the right to regulate in general international law as an expression of states' sovereignty. Under the concept of the right to regulate in general international law, states are free to decide on their economic and social policies while respecting the sovereign rights of other states. Even though BITs largely govern the international investment law regime, general international law is still relevant as an

---

178 See below Chapter 3.
179 See below Chapter 5 section 9.
180 See below Chapter 5 section 8.

underlying body of law. In this part a unification approach to international investment law is laid down to ensure greater legal and policy coherence.[181] Chapter 2 has thus shown that the paradigm of general international law serves not only a gap-filler function in international investment law but also the basis for further advancing a principled theoretical framework. Most importantly, Chapter 2 has established a theoretical framework in which the general international law paradigm can work as an all-embracing legal paradigm having a steering effect, or a gravitational pull, on IIAs such as BITs. This framework is based on the approach to treaty interpretation encompassing a presumption that the effects of a particular treaty are presumed in coherence with existing rules of international law as well as a consequential aspect embracing an impact assessment.

---

181 See also Federico Ortino, "The Social Dimension of International Investment Agreements: Drafting a New Bit/Mit Model?," *International Law FORUM du droit International 7*, no. 4 (2005): 245.

3 The context of international investment law

From policy to legal norms

1. Introduction

This part focuses on key policy aspects of the international investment law regime, where discussions of regulatory flexibility originally occurred in the context of the 1994 North American Free Trade Agreement (NAFTA). The outcome of multilateral efforts to negotiate an international investment treaty is addressed, and it is explained how fragmentation has served as an engine under the BIT regime. Also, central areas of consensus are spelled out. Key policy trends are identified explaining their potential impact on fragmentation or unification of the international investment law regime. The final part, Chapter 3, addresses two possible ways for enhancing policy coherence.

2. Regulatory chill

Policy consistence is beneficial for both states and investors. Inconsistent policies create uncertainty as to the stability of the legal environment. Policy coherence fertilizes legal stability and adds clarity to the distinction between compensable and non-compensable regulation. States pay remarkable interest in attracting foreign investment, so even changing governments have an interest in maintaining a general level of policy coherence, though newly elected governments may sometimes want to change core policies to keep promises articulated in an election campaign. From the investment law perspective states may fear that raising social standards will deter new investments or lead to industrial flight. In other words, states may have valid reasons for believing that regulatory measures may impede on protected foreign investments and trigger adjudication.

The mere threat of a lawsuit may have a chilling effect on states' desire to regulate, i.e. 'a regulatory chill'.[1] Examples of such regulatory chill cover areas like health and the environment.[2]

---

1 Report of the Special Representative of the Secretary-General, John Ruggie, on the issue of human rights and transnational corporations and other business enterprises to the UN Human Rights Council, 11th session, 22 April 2009, para. 30. See A/HRC/11/13. See also Stephanie Leinhardt, "Some Thoughts on Foreign Investors' Responsibilities to Respect Human Rights," *Transnational Dispute Management (TDM)* 10, no. 1 (2013): 6ff.
2 Kyla Tienhaara, *The Expropriation of Environmental Governance: Protecting Foreign Investors at the Expense of Public Policy*, 1st ed. (Cambridge: Cambridge University Press, 2009), 25. The case of *Ethyl Corporation v Canada* addressed below is one example in this regard.

Empirically, the regulatory chill is, however, rather difficult to verify due to the fact that evidence is needed for what has *not* happened. A concrete example of the regulatory chill in a BIT context is the case of the Indonesian mining companies.[3]

In 1999 Indonesia passed a number of reform laws, including an act on Forestry, which prohibited open-cast mining in protected forest areas for environmental concerns. The measure affected about 150 mining companies with operations and/or undeveloped mining exploration contracts in these areas. A group of foreign-owned mining companies threatened to initiate international arbitration against Indonesia, alleging expropriation.

In this case, foreign investors could have made a claim under the UK–Indonesia BIT or the Australia–Indonesia BIT. In response to this threat, Indonesia retreated from the ban, first by exempting several of the companies from the ban and promising to assess the situation of other affected companies. Subsequently the government decided to repeal the ban.[4] While most BITs impose a duty for states to compensate investors for indirect expropriations through formulations such as *"tantamount to expropriation"*[5] without explaining when regulatory measures may fall within the ambit of such measures, the regulatory chill is a relevant concern. Besides that, a potential regulatory chill might also occur later on with regards to enforcement of arbitral awards. There may be situations where governments decide not to challenge an award and pay damages because they fear that a challenge might have a negative impact on the general investment climate.[6]

3. The NAFTA experience

Though BIT negotiations commenced with the BIT between Germany and Pakistan in 1959, discussions of leaving room for regulatory flexibility did not transpire in Europe, but in North America. In the examination of policy concerns that may influence the interpretation of BITs it is not only relevant to turn to the NAFTA; it is simply necessary to understand how policy discussions on the right to regulate evolved. The prospect of challenging regulation as an interference with an investment materialized for the first time in NAFTA claims by the

---

3 Ryan Suda, "The Effect of Bilateral Investment Treaties on Human Rights Enforcement and Realization," in *Transnational Corporations and Human Rights*, ed. Olivier De Schutter, Studies in International Law (Oxford: Hart Publishing, 2006), 100f; Kyla Tienhaara, "What You Don't Know Can Hurt You: Investor–State Disputes and the Protection of the Environment in Developing Countries," *Global Environmental Politics* 6, no. 4 (2006): 73–100.
4 Suda, "The Effect of Bilateral Investment Treaties on Human Rights Enforcement and Realization," 100; Tienhaara, "What You Don't Know Can Hurt You," 90.
5 See below Chapter 5 section 30.3.
6 Prabhash Ranjan and Deepak Raju, "The Enigma of Enforceability of Investment Treaty Arbitration Awards in India," *Asian Journal of Comparative Law* 6, no. 1 (2011): 25.

end of the 1990s, where the implementation of Chapter 11 of the NAFTA led to unanticipated disputes brought against United States and Canada, two developed countries.[7]

Chapter 11 is basically a BIT in a FTA. It permits investors from one of the NAFTA countries (United States, Canada and Mexico) to make claims against another NAFTA member hosting the investment, including for regulatory actions.[8] No NAFTA tribunal is competent to recommend that a government should change its laws, regulations or policies, but it may award the investor compensation when regulatory measures are deemed to cross the line from being a regulatory interference to a regulatory expropriation (an indirect expropriation).

In its origin, the NAFTA was perceived as a means to protect investors from the United States and Canada against the Mexican judiciary by providing a mechanism for them to discard Mexican courts.[9] However, as it turned out due to the reciprocal nature of the treaty, it also provided an access for investors to challenge regulation by Canadian and American authorities.

The case, *Ethyl Corporation v Canada*, which was initiated three years after the conclusion of the NAFTA in 1997, came to illustrate this point.

The dispute concerned a Canadian ban on import of the fuel additive, methylcyclopentadienyl manganese tricarbonyl (MMT). Canada considered MMT to be a dangerous toxin because the manganese in MMT emissions were said to pose a significant public health risk for humans. However, this claim could not be sufficiently verified scientifically. Ethyl Corporation, the maker of MMT, challenged this ban under the NAFTA. Ethyl argued that the ban was a violation of rules enshrined in the NAFTA requiring national treatment for foreign investors, because it banned imports, but not local production.

In a jurisdictional award, the arbitral tribunal found that it had jurisdiction to assess the claim.[10] Following the arbitral decision, however, Canada repealed the MMT ban and paid a significant amount in settlement of the claims. In addition to that Canada even took the unprecedented step of issuing a statement that MMT was neither a risk to the environment nor the public health.[11]

---

7 Roberto Echandi, "What Do Developing Countries Expect from the International Investment Regime?," in *The Evolving International Investment Regime: Expectations, Realities, Options*, ed. Jose E. Alvarez and Karl P. Sauvant (Oxford: Oxford University Press, 2011), 16.

8 More generally on the NAFTA, see Dolzer and Schreuer, *Principles of International Investment Law*, 15–17; Sornarajah, *The International Law on Foreign Investment*, 253f; Andreas F. Lowenfeld, *International Economic Law*, ed. John Jackson, 2nd ed., International Economic Law Series (Oxford: Oxford University Press, 2008), 475–85; Jennifer A. Heindl, "Toward a History of NAFTA's Chapter Eleven," *Berkeley Journal of International Law* 24, no. 2 (2006): 672.

9 See further in Heindl, "Toward a History of NAFTA's Chapter Eleven."

10 *Ethyl Corporation v Canada*, NAFTA, Award on Jurisdiction, 24 June 1998.

11 See Timothy Ross Wilson, "Trade Rules: Ethyl Corporation v. Canada (NAFTA Chapter 11) Part 1: Claim and Award on Jurisdiction?," *Law and Business Review of the Americas* 6, no. 1 (2000): 52–71; Timothy Ross Wilson, "Trade Rules: Ethyl Corporation v. Canada (NAFTA

Another case concerning an investment claim over regulatory action against Canada was the case of *S.D. Myers v Canada*.[12]

S.D. Myers was an American corporation, which had an investment in Canada. One of the core business activities of the American corporation was the treatment of Polychlorinated biphenyl (PCB), an environmentally hazardous chemical compound used mainly in electrical equipment. Due to a Canadian order prohibiting the export of PCB waste to the United States, S.D. Myers and its Canadian investment was precluded from carrying out the business they intended. The purpose of the imposed export ban was, according to Canada, to protect the environment, because Canada believed that PCB should be handled in Canada by Canadians. The export prohibition was in effect for approximately 16 months.

The arbitral tribunal ruled in favour of Canada and did not find Canada liable to compensate the American investor for the regulatory action. The reason for this was mainly based on the temporary character of the measure, whereas the tribunal did not rule out that regulatory conduct could be the subject of a legitimate complaint.[13]

The first investment claim decided against the United States based on the NAFTA was the *Methanex* case initiated in 1999.[14]

The Canadian investor, Methanex, was a major producer of methanol, a key component in MTBE (methyl tertiary butyl ether) used to increase oxygen content and act as an octane enhancer in unleaded gasoline. In March 1999 the State of California ordered a ban on the use of the fuel additive MTBE. Methanex was the world largest producer of methanol but had never produced or sold MTBE. Methanex initiated international arbitration against the United States and claimed that the banning of the fuel additive was a disguised discriminatory preference for ethanol producers. The United States argued that the banning of MTBE was necessary to prevent contamination of drinking water supplies, since the use of MTBE was posing a significant risk to human health and safety.

The arbitral tribunal decided to dismiss all claims put forward by Methanex,[15] but the case attracted significant attention from environmental organizations, which claimed that the BIT in reality was a freezing of the right to regulate by the United States.[16]

The early NAFTA claims are noteworthy since they demonstrate the first tensions between investment protection and legitimate regulatory measures. The

---

Chapter 11) Part 2: Are Fears Founded?," *Law and Business Review of the Americas* 6, no. 2 (2000): 205–42.

12 *S.D. Myers v Canada*, NAFTA, Partial Award, 2000.

13 *Ibid.*, para. 281.

14 *Methanex Corporation v United States of America*, UNCITRAL, 3 August 2005.

15 *Ibid.* The final award can be found at <http://www.state.gov/documents/organization/51052.pdf>.

16 See further on the webpage of the International Institute for Sustainable Development, IISD, available at <http://www.iisd.org/investment/dispute/methanex_background.asp>.

issues they raised with regards to the interaction between investor protection and environmental protection or protection of public health led to general discussion of states' right to regulate. These discussions had implications for the BIT negotiations of USA and Canada and led to remarkable changes in BIT negotiations around the world.[17]

3.1. Changes in North American investment policy following the NAFTA experience

Changes in American investment policy are essential to the rest of the world since the United States is both a major capital exporter and importer. Long before the *Methanex* case was initiated, the United States had a BIT programme in place. In 1977 the United States initiated a model BIT programme, and the United States was the first state to declare its investment policy globally with the earliest model BIT drafted four years later in 1981.[18] This was the way the United States communicated internationally how BITs should be adopted and the message was clear, strongly emphasizing that investors should be awarded prompt, adequate and effective compensation for interferences amounting to expropriation (the Hull Formula). In the first phase of the American BIT programme the United States primarily engaged in BIT negotiations with less developed states with no former FCN treaty relation in place.[19] Due to the fact that investment flows were primarily going one way only, the goal was to impose investment protection on foreign investments' host states through the adoption of BITs with countries that would not impose a threat by bringing claims against the United States. The reasons hereof were that either they did not have any significant investments in the United States or, if they had, they were not likely to spend resources to initiate legal proceedings against the United States.

The American Model BIT was subsequently revised with minor changes. When the United States later faced lawsuits from Canadian investors, however, it provided the necessary understanding of the reciprocity of the NAFTA. Canadian investments constitute a significant source of investment in the United States, and the United States thus had to make a shift in its BIT programme. Triggered by the NAFTA experience, the 2004 Model BIT was drafted, a model based on an extensive revision of the earlier model with numerous changes and the length of the model more than tripled. In the 2004 version safeguards against regulatory

---

17 Though not in Europe.

18 For a complete history of the investment policy programme, see Kenneth J. Vandevelde, *US International Investment Agreements*, 1st ed. (Oxford: Oxford University Press, 2009), chapters 2 and 3.

19 E.g. with Egypt, Panama, Cameroon, Morocco, Congo, Bangladesh, Haiti, Senegal, Turkey and Grenada; see Vandevelde, *US International Investment Agreements*, 94. However, one may sometimes question the reality of a negotiation process due to imbalances of negotiating power. For example, the United States negotiated a BIT with Grenada three years after invading the country.

expropriation claims were adopted in a side agreement in the form of an annex to the treaty.[20] With regards to expropriation claims, Annex B, article 4(b) of the 2004 American Model BIT stated:

> *"Except in rare circumstances, non-discriminatory regulatory actions by a Party that are designed and applied to protect legitimate public welfare objectives, such as public health, safety and the environment, do not constitute indirect expropriations."*

The 2004 American Model BIT was – in contrast to many European model BITs – more protective to maintaining host states' regulatory space of manoeuvre, where regulatory measures to protect health, safety and the environment only exceptionally would trigger claims of compensation for indirect expropriations.[21]

Again in Spring 2012 a revised version of the United States' model (2012 American Model BIT) was released as an outcome of a more than three-year process with input from a variety of actors, including the United States' Congress, companies, business associations, labour groups, NGOs, and academics. The process to reach the 2012 version demonstrates two essential aspects: Firstly, it shows the presence of significant public interest in foreign investment policy. Secondly, it allows time for hearing a broad range of stakeholders demonstrates substantial commitment to reach a more balanced approach to rights and obligations.[22]

The final result, however, was perhaps less significant. Proposals to expand transparency concerns and public participation provisions relating to investment arbitration were discarded in favour of retaining the language found in the 2004 American Model BIT. Likewise, with regards to the substantive investment protections, the 2012 version contains almost no changes to the core substantive protections. A requested – but dismissed – change was to limit the scope of conduct considered to be an indirect expropriation by removing the reference to "except in rare circumstances" in Annex B of the treaty. This would have been a further step in broadening the scope, or lifting the threshold, for regulatory measures not amounting to indirect expropriation. In the end, the wide participation did not reflect far-reaching changes since the drafters chose to maintain the approach laid down in the 2004 Model BIT for expropriation claims. BIT

---

20 Rainer Geiger, "Multilateral Approaches to Investment: The Way Forward," in *The Evolving International Investment Regime: Expectations, Realities, Options*, ed. Jose E. Alvarez and Karl P. Sauvant (Oxford: Oxford University Press, 2011), 155; Vandevelde, *US International Investment Agreements*, 105–7.

21 In addition to this annex, the material standards of protection were clarified such as the minimum standard and the FET standard, which was linked with customary international law.

22 See press release from Washington, DC, 20 April 2012, which refers to the 2012 US Model BIT's *"particular [. . .] carefully calibrated balance"* between investor protection and public interest, an approach which already follow from the previous version, the 2004 US Model BIT, available at: <http://www.state.gov/r/pa/prs/ps/2012/04/188198.htm>.

negotiations between the United States and China may add further to the discussions on states' right to regulate, e.g. by providing more elaborate provisions on compensable vs. non-compensable regulation. The negotiations of an investment agreement between these two countries are particularly interesting due to the fact that both states are now major capital importers and exporters and thus seek to ensure their own policy space while not undermining protection of their own investors. A treaty text between these two countries may thus potentially serve as a template for future investment protection treaties.

The NAFTA experience also had implications for Canada's negotiations of investment protection treaties, for example with the EU, where Canada has been a strong proponent of the preservation of policy space in the Comprehensive Economic and Trade Agreement (CETA) from 2014. Indeed, the NAFTA experience had implications subsequently negotiated BITs since the reciprocal nature of investment treaties became clear.

4. Lack of a multilateral treaty enhancing the BIT regime

In international investment law there is neither a single unified treaty text on protection of foreign investments nor an overarching institution. However, there have been several attempts to form a multilateral treaty. The lack of a multilateral treaty may add to further fragmentation. Yet, the various proposals for a multilateral treaty do have some value in terms of establishing areas of consensus vs. issues subject to disagreement. The multilateral negotiations are addressed below, first from a general perspective and then subsequently with a focus on the protection of investments against (indirect) expropriations.

4.1. Fragmentation in negotiations

Even long before the WTO came into being in 1995, multilateral trade and investment negotiations took place.[23] Already in 1948 efforts were made to create an international trade organization that would embrace both trade and investment through the *Havana Charter*. However, with no prospect of success the charter never came into force. Proposals for the negotiation of a multilateral investment agreement have been made from time to time since the end of World War I. One of the most significant early efforts was launched by groups of European business people and lawyers, under the leadership of Hermann Abs, the chairperson of the Deutsche Bank in Germany, and Lord Shawcross, former Attorney-General of the United Kingdom. They published the 1959 *Abs–Shawcross Draft Convention on Investments Abroad*, but it was regarded as too ambitious.

---

23 The WTO system was developed through a series of trade negotiations under the General Agreement on Tariffs and Trade (GATT). The last round – the 1986–94 Uruguay Round – led to the establishment of the WTO.

Multilateral efforts continued and in 1961 Professor Louis Sohn and Richard Baxter of Harvard Law School proposed the *Draft Convention on the International Responsibility of States for Injuries to Aliens*, known as the *Harvard Draft Convention*. The convention largely codified customary law. Nevertheless, it was not adopted.[24]

Subsequently, institutional attempts to draft a multilateral treaty were made under the auspices of the OECD. In 1967, the OECD prepared the *Draft Convention on the Protection of Foreign Property* (the OECD Draft Convention) although this was not adopted either.[25] The most recent initiative by the OECD was the negotiations on the *Multilateral Agreement on Investment* (MAI Draft Convention), for which the OECD Investment Committee began the preparatory work in 1992. The negotiations set out in 1995 to provide high standards for the liberalization of investment regimes and investment protection. The MAI Draft Convention was founded on three pillars: investment liberalization, investment protection and dispute settlement.[26] The negotiations, however, were challenged massively from non-state actors, including trade unions, environmental organizations and other public interest groups, which inter alia argued that the interpretation of the indirect expropriation standard would effectively nullify many regulatory acts of governments.[27] When the negotiations were terminated in 1998 there were several standing issues in the MAI Draft Convention, including the core tensions between investment protection and states' right to regulate.[28] Nevertheless, there were some areas of consensus, including the basic recognition of states' right to regulate.[29]

Since neither the OECD nor the WTO succeed in the negotiations of a multilateral investment treaty, the negotiations of BITs gained importance. The

---

24 Lowenfeld, *International Economic Law*, 23–6; Andrew Newcombe and Lluís Paradell, *Law and Practice of Investment Treaties: Standards of Treatment*, 1st ed. (Austin: Kluwer Law International, 2009), 21–2; Vandevelde, *Bilateral Investment Treaties*, 196; Chester Brown, *Commentaries on Selected Model Investment Treaties*, ed. Philip Alston and Vaughan Lowe, 1st ed., Oxford Commentaries on International Law (Oxford: Oxford University Press, 2013), 6–8.

25 Newcombe and Paradell, Law and Practice of Investment Treaties: Standards of Treatment, 30; Vandevelde, *Bilateral Investment Treaties*, 69f. The text of the OECD Draft Convention on the Protection of Foreign Property, including the explanatory notes can be found at <http://www.oecd.org/investment/internationalinvestmentagreements/39286571.pdf>.

26 Petros C. Mavroidis, "All Clear on the Investment Front: A Plea for a Restatement?," in *The Evolving International Investment Regime: Expectations, Realities, Options*, ed. Jose E. Alvarez and Karl P. Sauvant (Oxford: Oxford University Press, 2011), 97–8.

27 UNCTAD, "Lessons from the MAI" (1999): 17, available at <http://unctad.org/en/docs/psiteiitm22.en.pdf>. See also Mavroidis, "All Clear on the Investment Front," 98.

28 Stephan W. Schill, *The Multilateralization of International Investment Law*, ed. Lorand Bartels, Thomas Cottier, and William Davey, 1st ed., Cambridge International Trade and Economic Law (Cambridge: Cambridge University Press, 2009), 63; UNCTAD, "Lessons from the MAI" (1999): Executive Summary.

29 Geiger, "Multilateral Approaches to Investment: The Way Forward," 158.

disappointments on the multilateral level thus served as an engine under the BIT regime. One may question whether consensus among states has grown since the late 1990s. This is doubtful, due to new policy issues that have been added to the debate, such as the need for ensuring sustainable development and issues of corporate social responsibility.[30] New multilateral negotiations therefore run the risk of further polarizing the debate concerning the right to regulate. Also, it is questionable in which forum new multilateral negotiations could take place. Owing to earlier resistance towards adopting a multilateral agreement, legitimacy and political support appears to lack to embark once more on this assignment within OECD or the WTO. The UNCTAD has not yet been accepted as a negotiating forum for binding agreements.[31]

4.2. Areas of consensus on regulatory measures and law of expropriation

Notwithstanding the shelving of the negotiations of a multilateral agreement on trade and investment, the various multilateral proposals did contribute to the development of significant aspects of the right to regulate and the law on expropriation. These aspects concern mainly the articulation of further requirements for lawful expropriations and an acknowledgment of protection of general regulatory measures.

According to the customary norm of protection of aliens and their property, the minimum standard laid down a requirement for states to compensate foreigners for expropriation of their property. However, conditions hereof were later spelled out. The Abs–Shawcross Draft Convention made a contribution in this regard. In addition to the requirement to compensate for expropriations, the Abs–Shawcross Draft Convention enunciated a requirement of non-discrimination in article III. Furthermore, expropriation should not be contrary to undertakings given by the expropriatory party. Accordingly, the Abs–Shawcross Draft Convention acknowledged that there might be situations where states have provided foreigners with an additional guarantee not to expropriate.

While imposing no requirement of expropriations to be for a public purpose the Draft Convention did require that expropriation should be under due process of law.[32] As a noteworthy novel feature, the Abs–Shawcross Convention provided for a direct investor–state arbitration mechanism.

A particular aspect of the Harvard Draft Convention is that it recognizes a concept of non-compensable takings in its article 10(5):

> *"An uncompensated taking of an alien property or a deprivation of the use or enjoyment of property of an alien which results from the execution of the tax*

---

30 These policy trends are explained below.
31 Geiger, "Multilateral Approaches to Investment: The Way Forward," 161.
32 Vandevelde, *Bilateral Investment Treaties*, 285.

laws; from a general change in the value of currency; from the action of compe-
tent authorities of the State in the maintenance of public order, health or moral-
ity; or from the valued exercise of belligerent rights; or is otherwise incidental to
the normal operation of the laws of the State, shall not be considered wrongful,
provided:

a)   *it is not a clear and discriminatory violation of the law of the State*
     concerned;
b)   *it is not the result of a violation of Articles 6 to 8 of this Convention;*
c)   *it is not an unreasonable departure from the principles of justice recognized*
     by the principal legal systems of the world; and
d)   *it is not an abuse of the powers specified in this paragraph for the purpose of*
     depriving an alien of his property."

As examples of a taking of property *"arising out of the action of [the] competent*
authorities of the state in [the] maintenance of public order, health and morality"
the explanatory notes refers to confiscation of goods, which have been smuggled
into a country and the seizure of such articles as narcotics, liquor, obscene materials, firearms, and gambling devices that are unlawfully in a person's possession.[33]
The regulatory space of manoeuvre is thus limited to more imminent security
concerns or protection of morals.

Article 3 of the OECD Draft Convention articulates the four requirements of expropriation (public purpose, non-discrimination, due process and
compensation):

Article 3:

"No Party shall take any measures depriving, directly or indirectly, of his prop-
erty a national of another Party unless the following conditions are complied
with:

(i)   *The measures are taken in the public interest and under due process of*
       law;
(ii)   *The measures are not discriminatory or contrary to any undertaking*
       which the former Party may have given;
(iii) *The measures are accompanied by provision for the payment of just com-*
       pensation. Such compensation shall represent the genuine value of the
       property affected, shall be paid without undue delay, and shall be trans-
       ferable to the extent necessary to make it effective for the national entitled
       thereto."

33 Louis B. Sohn and Richard Baxter, *Convention on the International Responsibility of States for*
   Injuries to Aliens (Preliminary Draft With Explanatory Notes), 1st ed. (Cambridge: Harvard
   Law School, 1959), 71.

In addition to these conditions for expropriation, the OECD Draft Convention is notable for imposing a fifth condition in article 3, i.e. that the taking of property is not *"contrary to any undertaking which the former Party may have given"*. Yet, it was not human rights obligations the drafters had in mind at that time of writing. The explanatory notes explain this:[34]

> *". . . where an undertaking by a Party exists not to expropriate certain property at all or during a specified period, that engagement must be respected. Thus, measures of deprivation of these two types are prohibited absolutely."*

According to the OECD Draft Convention, property protection could thus be extended to an absolute protection on the basis of a specific commitment made by the state, i.e. commitments in terms of stabilization clauses on a contractual basis.

The focus was thus primarily to establish legal stability for foreign investors. A guarantee by host states would then constitute an additional element adding further certainty and stability for investors.

A notable aspect from the OECD Draft Convention is the distinction between 'full reparation' and 'just compensation'. Whereas article 3 refers to 'just compensation', the explanatory notes states that in cases where state parties have specifically undertaken not to expropriate, there is *"a duty of the Party to make 'full reparation' rather than pay 'just compensation'"*.[35] This indicates that under certain circumstances (where states have made explicit commitments), the duty to compensate is extended from *"the genuine value at the moment of the taking"*[36] to full compensation, which then in principle may include the capitalization of further expectations of the investor such as future income.

Accordingly, the additional fifth condition (that measures are not contrary to an undertaking given by a state party) could be interpreted as an element that should be taken into account in the determination of the standard of compensation, rather than as a criterion for whether the state may expropriate or not.

A noteworthy aspect in the explanatory notes to the OECD Draft Convention is the general recognition of states' right to regulate:[37]

> *"Article 3 acknowledges, by implication, the sovereign right of a State, under international law, to deprive owners, including aliens, of property which is within its territory in the pursuit of its political, social or economic ends. To deny such a right would be attempt to interfere with its powers to regulate – by virtue of its independence and autonomy, equally recognised by international law – its political and social existence. The right is reconciled with the obligation of the State to respect and protect the property of aliens by the existing requirements*

---

34 OECD Draft Convention with explanatory notes, para. 6, p. 20.
35 *Ibid.*, para. 8, p. 21.
36 *Ibid.* According to the explanatory notes this is what is meant by 'just compensation'.
37 *Ibid.*, para. 1, p. 18.

for its exercise – before all, the requirement to pay the alien compensation if his property is taken."

The following explanatory elaborates on the concept of 'taking', which seems to be decisive as to whether the investor should be compensated. In this regard, the explanatory note implies that general and lawful regulatory measures should not be considered a taking. However, regulatory measures that result in a loss carried out with the intent of wrongfully depriving the investor of the essence of its rights fall within the scope of a taking.[38]

In terms of expropriation, article 2 of the later OECD initiative, the MAI Draft Convention sought to reinforce the four generally accepted criteria for expropriation (public purpose, non-discrimination, due process and compensation):[39]

Article 2:

"A Contracting Party shall not expropriate or nationalise directly or indirectly an investment in its territory of an investor of another Contracting Party or take any measure or measures having equivalent effect (hereinafter referred to as 'expropriation') except:

a)   *for a purpose which is in the public interest,*
b)   *on a non-discriminatory basis,*
c)   *in accordance with due process of law, and*
d)   *accompanied by payment of prompt, adequate and effective compensation."*

The concept of indirect takings under expropriation provisions had been consistently followed in BITs, and it was therefore thought to be a rather settled issue. However, it faced strong opposition in the MAI negotiations, especially after the NAFTA experience explained above.[40]

On the right to regulate with the aim of promoting environmental concerns and other key social welfare interests, the MAI Draft Convention followed the NAFTA example.[41] According to the commentaries to the final text of the agreement, most delegations believed that the MAI should address regulatory measures in the interest of the environment and labour rights. There was some controversy as to whether the reference should be given as environmental or labour 'measures', 'standards' or 'laws', but still, there was consensus that these

---

38 *Ibid.*, para. 3(a), p. 18.
39 The DRAFT MAI negotiating text can be found on the webpage of the OECD.
40 UNCTAD, "Lessons from the MAI" (1999): 18. The paper lay down the factors determinative for discontinuing the negotiations: UNCTAD Series on issues in international investment agreements, available at <http://unctad.org/en/Docs/psiteiitm22.en.pdf>.
41 See further in Geiger, "Multilateral Approaches to Investment: The Way Forward," 157–60.

issues had to be addressed somehow in the text.[42] Whether the text should refer to other matters as well (such as health and safety) was less clear. With respect to property protection against expropriations, the right to regulate and the calculation of compensation for expropriations were key issues.[43]

More controversial was the question about dispute settlement in the context of general regulatory activity, a question that related to larger outstanding questions about the scope and application of the MAI. Of delegations indicating a position, the views were highly diverging. Some held the opinion that investor–state dispute settlement should not be available to challenge binding labour and environment provisions, while others extended this view by declaring that state-to-state dispute settlement should not be available either. Others expressed a view in favour of the dispute mechanisms.[44]

All in all, when examining the commentaries to the negotiations there are noteworthy areas of consensus. First and foremost, there was agreement on the objective of protecting general non-discriminatory regulation. There was also consensus that this is a broader issue, not just relevant to labour and environmental regulation.

5. Notable trends in international investment policy

The following explains essential policy trends of the international investment law regime that are relevant as contextual elements for interpretation of BITs. Whether these trends may contribute positively to harmonization or add to further fragmentation is not easily determinable though predictions hereof are subsequently articulated.

5.1. Increased governmental role in the economy

A key policy trend is the involvement of governments in the economy. Governments have gradually become more steering and regulating, thereby moving away from a 'hands-off approach' to economic growth and development, which previously prevailed.[45] State-owned enterprises (SOEs) are becoming important players of the investment regime as well as sovereign wealth funds (SWFs). Today, the magnitude in investments by SWFs has grown remarkably, in particular as a result of revenues from extraction of natural resources.[46]

---

42 See The Commentaries to the final text of the agreement considered in the course of the MAI negotiations, pp. 25f.

43 Calculation of compensation, see The Commentaries *op. cit.*, pp. 30–3. See also UNCTAD, "Lessons from the MAI," 18.

44 The Commentaries *op. cit.*, p. 6.

45 UNCTAD, "WIR 2012" (2012): 100; R. Dolzer and C. Schreuer, *Principles of International Investment Law*, 87, available online at: <http://unctad.org/en/PublicationsLibrary/wir2012_embargoed_en.pdf>.

46 Geiger, "Multilateral Approaches to Investment: The Way Forward," 154. See also Victoria Barbary and Bernardo Bortolotti, "Sovereign Wealth Funds and Political Risk: New

In some countries, investments by foreign SWFs have been a source of concern due to security reasons or foreign immunity issues.[47] With an increased governmental role in foreign economies, foreign states may also become responsible for key public functions. At the same time the choices made by SOEs do not always correspond to those that would be made by private commercial entities. Still, this trend may constitute a factor contributing to the unification of the international investment law regime, since governments in principle are in a better position of having more knowledge about the whole panoply of international obligations entered into, particularly the human rights obligations of the state.

5.2. Sustainable development

The international investment law regime has grown out of the desire to enhance economic growth. Over the years, however, the pursuance of non-economic interests like protection of the environment and promotion of social welfare has been increasingly linked with foreign investments. Today, a greater connectivity appears between economic and non-economic goals demonstrating that these interests are not intrinsically opposed.[48] Sustainable development was originally defined in the Brundtland Report as development "that meets the needs of the present without compromising the ability for future generations to meet their own needs".[49] The concept of sustainable development, founded on the three key pillars, has long become part of the international investment law regime.[50]

Figure 3.1 The three key aspects of sustainable development

Challenges in the Regulation of Foreign Investment," in *Regulation of Foreign Investment: Challenges to International Harmonization*, ed. Zdenek Drabek and Petros Mavroidis, World Scientific Studies in International Economics (Singapore: World Scientific Publishing, 2013), 307–39.

47 Under the doctrine of foreign state immunity, a state is not subject to the full range of rules applicable in the other state, since the doctrine bars domestic courts from adjudicating or enforcing certain claims against foreign states. See further in David Gaukrodger, "Foreign State Immunity and Foreign Government Controlled Investors," in *OECD Working Papers on International Investment 2010/2* (Paris: OECD, 2010), available at <http://papers.ssrn.com/sol3/papers.cfm?abstract_id=1629251>.

48 The heavy volume "Sustainable Development in World Investment Law" from 2011 in itself manifests this connectivity, see Marie-Claire Cordonier, Markus W. Gehring, and Andrew Newcombe, *Sustainable Development in World Investment Law*, 1st ed., Global Trade Law Series (Alphen aan den Rijn: Kluwer Law International, 2011).

49 Report of the World Commission on Environment and Development, "Our Common Future" (The Brundtland Report), 1987.

50 See UNCTAD, "WIR 2012," 89–105.

Though sustainable development traditionally has not been reflected in IIAs, the sustainable development dimension of foreign investment is perceived to be crucial.[51] In 2005 the Canadian international research institute, the International Institute for Sustainable Development (IISD) published a Model Investment Agreement. This Model text is interesting as it proposes rights and obligations for investors, home states and host states and claims to be *"a model consistent with the goals and requirements of sustainable development and the global economy of the 21st century"*.[52] The model may serve as a template for the negotiation of more balanced investment treaties.

In 2012, the UNCTAD launched its Investment Policy Framework for Sustainable Development as a response to the transitions of the international investment regime, including discussions about a lack of or need for a sustainable development dimension of IIAs.[53] It is not a model treaty but a guide for national and international investment policy making. In essence, the framework addresses the stability–flexibility dilemma[54] on a policy level by providing guidance to governments. Governments can then choose the policy options that best suit their states' levels of development and respective policy objectives. Among these policy options the framework identifies the options that could be particularly supportive of sustainable development. On this basis it may serve as a point of reference for future negotiations of IIAs, including BITs. Also, a new generation of BITs contains explicit references to sustainable development.[55]

In principle, the concept of sustainable development may add to the unification of the international investment law regime, because it encompasses both investment protection (through the economic development dimension) and human rights (through the social development dimension).

5.3. *Social responsible investments and green growth*

The focus on sustainable development objectives has also led to new types of investments with an increasing emphasis on the promotion of 'social responsible investments' or 'ethical investing' as well as 'low-carbon investment' or so-called 'green investments'.[56] Though the definition of the term 'social responsible investment' is a broad and sometimes controversial term, it appears that social

---

51 Geiger, "Multilateral Approaches to Investment: The Way Forward," 155.
52 The Model Investment Agreement can be found at the webpage if the IISD. See <http://www.iisd.org/publications/pub.aspx?pno=686>.
53 E. Tuerk and F. Rojid, *Investment Treaty News*, 30 October 2012 and the IPFSD, pp. 3–9. The Framework is considered a 'living document' designed to be further developed. For this purpose, UNCTAD created a discussion platform in an online forum that provides investment stakeholders and the international community with an opportunity to discuss views. See <http://investmentpolicyhub.unctad.org/>.
54 See above Chapter 1, section 2.3.
55 See below section 7.
56 See for example G. Inderst, C. Kaminker, and F. Stewart, "Defining and Measuring Green Investments: Implications for Institutional Investors Asset Allocations," *OECD Working*

responsible investors include certain common elements in their investment decision processes.

In addition to considerations of financial or business risk, a social responsible investor typically devotes attention to a combination of ethical, religious, social and environmental concerns.[57]

Under the umbrella of the UN, social responsible investment is an approach to investment *"that explicitly acknowledges the relevance to the investor of environmental, social and governance (ESG) factors, and the long-term health and stability of the market as a whole"*.[58] In the initial phase, a screening process may for example systematically exclude objectionable investments according to decision rules established beforehand. A common decision rule in this regard is to exclude companies involved in weapon production, tobacco, alcohol, or gambling. Investors can express their commitment to ESG issues through the voluntary commitment to the Principles for Responsible Investment (PRI), which were launched in 2006 at the New York Stock Exchange.[59] If an investor has committed to the PRI, it may be supportive of an argument that general non-discriminatory regulation within ESG issues should be presumed non-compensable.

5.4. Corporate Social Responsibility (CSR)

Corporations are increasingly called upon to demonstrate corporate social responsibility (CSR). The very heart of CSR concerns the question of what business is for.[60] Though CSR is a contested concept in itself,[61] the CSR construct can be said to describe the relationship between business and the larger society. The assertion by Milton Friedman that 'the only social responsibility of business is to increase profits'[62] has been replaced by the so-called Triple Bottom Line, consisting of the three Ps: people, planet and profit.[63]

Papers on Finance, Insurance and Private Pensions, no. 24 (August 2012), available at <http://www.oecd-ilibrary.org/environment/towards-a-green-investment-policy-framework_5k8zth7s6s6d-en>; OECD, "Towards a Green Investment Policy Framework," Report, 2012.

57 Andrew Crane, Abagail McWilliams, Dirk Matten, Jeremy Moon, and Donald S. Siegel, *The Oxford Handbook of Corporate Social Responsibility*, 1st ed., Oxford Handbooks in Business and Management (Oxford: Oxford University Press, 2008), 250.

58 Briefing Note about the UN Principles for Responsible Investments, p. 1.

59 See <http://www.unpri.org/about-pri/about-pri/>.

60 Crane et al., *The Oxford Handbook of Corporate Social Responsibility*, 3f.

61 It is widely acknowledged within the literature on CSR that there is a distinct lack of consensus or even broad agreement about how to define the concept of CSR; see Jeanette Brejning, *Corporate Social Responsibility and the Welfare State: The Historical and Contemporary Role of CSR in the Mixed Economy of Welfare*, 1st ed. (Burlington: Ashgate Publishing, 2012), 30.

62 Milton Friedman, *Capitalism and Freedom: Fortieth Anniversary Edition*, 1st ed. (Chicago: University of Chicago Press, 2002), 133.

63 Crane et al., *The Oxford Handbook of Corporate Social Responsibility*, 81, 556f.

CSR has evolved from a social policy of philanthropy throughout the 1990s to an economic policy of today where corporations perceive CSR as part of the companies' competitive strategy. Today, the concept of CSR is largely seen as a voluntary commitment by corporations to take social responsibility in various areas of the business activity from considerations of which countries to engage in, the selection and employment of staff, the choice of sub-contractors and suppliers, the selection of production ways and channels of distribution. Though CSR is largely linked with responsibility and not liability in the strict legal sense, the consequences of refraining from making business decisions in a socially responsible way may be too costly for companies.[64]

Discussions on CSR have also led to several international attempts to attach human rights responsibility to corporations. The UN Sub-Commission on the Promotion and Protection of Human Rights drafted the *Norms on the Responsibilities of Transnational Corporations and Other Business Enterprises With Regard to Human Rights* (the UN Draft Norms) in 2003, but the initiative was deemed too immature and did not obtain the necessary support from the international business sector. The norms developed remain in draft form and are therefore not legally binding.[65] Yet, they demonstrate consensus in terms of a need for and willingness to address corporate behaviour in the society. The matter of linking corporations with human rights has subsequently been addressed in other ways. Codes of conduct are for example proliferating.

Codes of conduct are adopted by corporations – sometimes together with NGOs – with the intention to regulate the corporate business activity internally as well as communicating the CSR commitments externally. Codes of conduct are typically associated with non-binding rules adopted on a voluntary basis as guidelines for the operations of corporations; but codes of conduct are also adopted for international organizations and NGOs.[66]

On the international level the UN has adopted the Global Compact. The UN Global Compact is an initiative for businesses that are committed to aligning their operations and strategies with ten universally accepted principles in the areas of human rights, labour, environment and anti-corruption.[67] More recent international collaborations have sought to enhance corporations' commitments to

---

64 Peter Muchlinski, "Regulating Multinationals: Foreign Investment, Development and the Balance of Corporate and Home Country Rights and Responsibilities in a Globalizing World," in *The Evolving International Investment Regime: Expectations, Realities, Options*, ed. Jose E. Alvarez and Karl P. Sauvant (Oxford: Oxford University Press, 2011), 41.

65 Leinhardt, "Some Thoughts on Foreign Investors' Responsibilities to Respect Human Rights," 2.

66 August Reinisch, "The Changing International Legal Framework for Dealing with Non-State Actors," in *Non-State Actors and Human Rights*, ed. Philip Alston, Collected Courses of the Academy of European Law (Oxford: Oxford University Press, 2005), 43–9.

67 When joining the Global Compact, companies commit to issue an annual Communication on Progress (COP), a public disclosure to stakeholders (e.g. investors, consumers, civil society and Governments) on progress made in implementing the ten principles of the UN Global Compact, and in supporting broad UN development goals.

the Global Compact.[68] The Global Compact has later been supplemented by the Guiding Principles on Business and Human Rights proposed by UN Special Representative John Ruggie and endorsed by the UN Human Rights Council in 2011. The Guiding Principles are founded on a six-year long process of research and consultations with the participation of a variety of actors including governments, businesses, NGOs and IGOs. The Guiding Principles rest on three pillars: the state duty to protect human rights; the corporate responsibility to respect human rights; and access to remedy.[69] The second pillar of the UN Guiding Principles explains how companies should respect human rights, and reduce the risk of causing or contributing to human rights violations. In this way the Guiding Principles may constitute a yardstick for stakeholders to assess businesses' respect for human rights. The Guiding Principles have subsequently served as the basis for a revision in 2011 of the OECD Guidelines for Multinational Enterprises (OECD Guidelines).

The OECD Guidelines is another voluntary initiative consisting of principles of responsible business conduct in areas such as employment and industrial relations, human rights, environment, information disclosure, combating bribery, consumer interests, science and technology, competition, and taxation.[70] The OECD Guidelines seek to control business behaviour *"that might otherwise escape oversight because no single jurisdiction clearly has authority over some of the activities engaged in by multinational corporations"*.[71]

International instruments with a more thematic focus have also been adopted. One example is the ILO Tripartite Declaration of Principles concerning Multinational Enterprises and Social Policy focusing on labour rights.[72] At the regional level too, codes of conduct have been drafted, in particular in the framework of the EU. Moreover, standardization systems have been developed, providing corporations with a seal of approval for their social welfare considerations. The International Organization for Standardization is one of the most productive institutions of voluntary international

---

68 A coalition of 34 institutional investors managing approximately US$3.3 trillion in assets was in March 2013 encouraging 1,900 companies, located in 44 countries, to consider joining the UN Global Compact. See further at the webpage of the UN Global Compact, The News Archive, 27 March 2013.

69 See also Daniel Augenstein and David Kinley, "When Human Rights 'Responsibilities' Become 'Duties': The Extra-Territorial Obligations of States That Bind Corporations," in *Human Rights Obligations of Business: Beyond the Corporate Responsibility to Respect?*, ed. Surya Deva and David Bilchitz (Cambridge: Cambridge University Press, 2013), Chapter 11.

70 See further in Jarrod Hepburn and Vuyelwa Kuuya, "Corporate Social Responsibility and Investment Treaties," in *Sustainable Development in World Investment Law*, ed. Marie-Claire Cordonier, Markus W. Gehring, and Andrew Newcombe, Global Trade Law Series (Alphen aan den Rijn: Kluwer Law International, 2011), 592–4.

71 Andrea K. Bjorklund, "Assessing the Effectiveness of Soft Law Instruments in International Investment Law," in *International Investment Law and Soft Law*, ed. Andrea K. Bjorklund and August Reinisch (Cheltenham: Edward Elgar Publishing, 2012), 56.

72 See <http://www.ilo.org/empent/Publications/WCMS_094386/lang--en/index.htm>.

standards. For example, the ISO 26000 provides guidance on how businesses and organizations can operate in a socially responsible way with key elements such as ethical behaviour and transparency as core elements to contribute to the welfare of society.[73]

5.5. *Transparency*

Transparency is a fundamental value in a democratic society and a mechanism to enhance credibility in public institutions and decision-making. Transparency is a way to ensure awareness of the law and that it is applied on a non-discriminatory basis. Though there is an increasing focus on the promotion of transparency in international investment law, transparency is not a new item on the investment policy agenda. Already in 1976 the members at that time committed to the OECD Declaration and Decisions on International Investment and Multinational Enterprises agreeing to *"provide an open and transparent environment for international investment"* and *"to encourage the positive contribution multinational enterprises can make to economic and social progress".*[74]

Transparency may also benefit the investor by fostering of a more predictable investment climate, in which investors can clearly assess the conditions and rules applying to their investments. Hence, transparency is also closely related to the protection of the investor's legitimate expectations.[75] The degree of secrecy varies depending on the applicable arbitration rules designated in the investment treaty or contract. The most frequently referred to are the rules under the ICSID and the UNCITRAL.[76] Amendments of the ICSID Rules have improved public access to information and the scope for public participation in investment dispute proceedings.[77] Furthermore, many ICSID awards are published on the ICSID website.[78] The UNCITRAL Arbitration Rules, on the other hand, do not provide for a public record of the dispute. A working group under the United Nations Commission on International Trade Law (UNCITRAL) has agreed on rules to bring greater transparency to treaty-based investment arbitrations conducted under the UNCITRAL Arbitration Rules.[79]

---

73 See <http://www.iso.org/iso/home.htm>.
74 See <http://www.oecd.org/daf/inv/investment-policy/oecddeclarationanddecisions.htm>.
75 *Ibid.*, p. 149.
76 Nathalie Bernasconi-Osterwalder, "Transparency and Amicus Curiae in ICSID Arbitrations," in *Sustainable Development in World Investment Law*, ed. Marie-Claire Cordonier Segger, Markus W. Gehring, and Andrew Paul Newcombe, Global Trade Law Series (Alphen aan den Rijn: Kluwer Law International, 2011), 194.
77 See ICSID Arbitration rule 37(2) for the test for the tribunal to apply in exercising its discretion of whether to accept a third party intervention in the form of an *amicus brief.*
78 As a minimum, information on the registration of all requests for conciliation or arbitration and the date and method of the termination of each proceeding is published.
79 The work of the Working Group II, 2000 to present: Arbitration and Conciliation is available at: <http://www.uncitral.org/uncitral/en/commission/working_groups/2Arbitration.html>.

The lack of transparency and public participation in investment arbitrations is increasingly raised as a matter of concern.[80] Arbitration is fundamentally conditioned on the confidentiality between the parties. This fundamental condition, however, does not really seem plausible for investment disputes where the state is party to the dispute. At least not in cases involving regulatory interferences.[81]

Most BITs do not address transparency concerns.[82] Increasing transparency may positively add to the unification of international investment law since (opposing) rights and obligations become more clear and comprehensible.

5.6. *Enforcing social responsibility through quasi-judicial mechanisms and social reporting*

A major point of critique when it comes to the concept of CSR concerns the fact that it relies on voluntariness and soft law instruments that are not legally binding in the strict sense but impose 'moral duties' on corporations. In essence, the problem with the nature of social responsibility is largely confined to the question of the (lack of) enforcement mechanisms. From the international perspective, two examples of CSR enforcement measures are worth highlighting. Under the framework of the OECD, the OECD has imposed an obligation for adhering states to establish a National Contact Point to address non-compliance with the OECD Guidelines.[83] Another initiative introduced in an attempt 'to give teeth' to voluntary CSR commitments is the establishment of reporting procedures, known as social reporting or social auditing. Corporations committing to the UN Global Compact are required to report on CSR under the Communication on Progress (COP).[84] The reports are published on the webpage of the UN Global Compact.[85] If the company fails to submit a report it will be labelled 'non-communicating'. Companies, who remain non-communicating for 12 consecutive months will be expelled from the Global Compact.

---

80 Bernasconi-Osterwalder, "Transparency and Amicus Curiae in ICSID Arbitrations," 191.
81 Howard Mann, "Civil Society Perspectives: What Do Key Stakeholders Expect from the International Investment Regime?," in *The Evolving International Investment Regime: Expectations, Realities, Options*, ed. Jose E. Alvarez and Karl P. Sauvant (Oxford: Oxford University Press, 2011), 23, 26; Dolzer and Schreuer, *Principles of International Investment Law*, 286–8.
82 UNCTAD, "Bilateral Investment Treaties 1995–2006: Trends in Investment Rulemaking" (2007): 77, available at <http://unctad.org/en/docs/iteiia20065_en.pdf>.
83 See further <http://www.oecd.org/daf/inv/mne/ncps.htm>.
84 See further <https://www.unglobalcompact.org/>.
85 COPs are made publicly available through the Global Compact website at the moment they are submitted by the participant. Any interested party can access a company's COP through the 'Participant Search' browser on the website, <http://www.unglobalcompact.org/participants/search>.

Some states such as the United States, United Kingdom, France, South Africa and Denmark have introduced national legislative steps to compel corporations to report on their CSR policies.[86] Denmark has been among the first countries to introduce a model on CSR reporting, which actually combines the voluntary aspect with binding legal requirements.[87]

Danish businesses are free to choose whether or not they wish to engage in CSR and have a CSR policy or not. However, from 2009, large businesses[88] in Denmark have been required to account for their work on CSR. Pursuant to a statutory requirement businesses in Denmark must then take a position on CSR in their annual reports.[89] This means that if the corporation chooses not to have a CSR policy, it must state this in its annual report. There is no requirement to state the reasons therefor. If the corporation on the contrary decides to have a CSR policy, it is required to report on its CSR policy.

Various initiatives have transpired in the area of social reporting. The Global Reporting Initiative (GRI) is a notable example in this regard. GRI has developed a comprehensive Sustainability Reporting Framework, which is widely used around the world. The Sustainability Reporting Framework enables all organizations to measure and report on their economic, environmental, and social and governance areas of performance, i.e. the aforementioned sustainable development issues under the umbrella of the Triple Bottom Line.[90]

CSR enforcement mechanisms are largely morally confined and not legal in the strict sense. Yet, the value hereof should not be underestimated in terms of the impact CSR reporting and the communication hereof may have on other essential business elements such as competitiveness and the reputation of the business. So, whereas governments navigate in the realm of public policy, CSR is used to designate a voluntary corporate activity, a private policy. Private policy may potentially have a greater impact than public policy, both in the negative and positive sense. Increasing self-regulation may reduce the need for regulation by the state within this area. Also corporate self-regulation may be complementary to state regulation or it may work as a substitute in fragile states refraining from regulating. The concept of CSR, involving business' self-regulation, is thus

---

86 Hepburn and Kuuya, "Corporate Social Responsibility and Investment Treaties," 594f.
87 If a business has acceded to the UN Global Compact or the Principles for Responsible Investment (PRI) and publishes the associated progress report, the business is exempt from having to prepare a separate report on CSR.
88 I.e. businesses that exceed at least two of the following three size limits: 1) total assets/liabilities of DKK 143 million; 2) net revenue of DKK 286 million or 3) an average of 250 full-time employees.
89 The Danish Parliament (Folketinget) adopted the proposed "Act Amending the Danish Financial Statements Act (Accounting for CSR in large businesses)" on 16 December 2008. An unofficial translation into English is available at: <http://csrgov.dk/file/319999/proposal_report_on_social_resp_december_2008.pdf>.
90 Further information on the Global Reporting Initiative is available at <https://www.global reporting.org>.

relevant since it might have implications toward the 'right to regulate' under investment protection treaties.

6. Rebalancing – imposing social responsibility on investors

The increase in soft law instruments could have a positive impact on a unification process of international investment law. Soft law instruments are created for multiple reasons, but one of the reasons is that there is a lack of agreement on what the 'hard law', i.e. the legally binding norms, should be.[91] In some instances, however, soft law may be desirable for the very reason it is 'soft'. For example, governments may sometimes participate in non-binding cooperative arrangements when they would not adopt hard law obligations, where participation or even less – a consensus outcome – would otherwise have been inconceivable. Hence, the process itself may generate legitimacy. The Guiding Principles by John Ruggie is an important example in this regard. The large number of inclusive stakeholder consultations contributed to a widespread positive response. In the end the international approval was evidenced by the consensus adoption of the Guiding Principles in the UN Human Rights Council in June 2011.[92]

According to Bjorklund, three main functions of soft law are particularly relevant in an international investment law context. Firstly, soft law instruments may constitute emergent hard law with the potential of developing into customary international law if not formalized in a legally binding instrument.[93] Yet, as highlighted by Bjorklund, expecting that all soft law instruments should eventually become hard law in order to serve useful purposes would be expecting too much.[94] Still, soft law instruments might strongly influence the behaviour of decision-makers without their effect being of a legally binding nature. Secondly, soft law might serve as a gap-filler in hard law,[95] which is particularly relevant due to the often very vaguely formulated investment protection standards.[96] Thirdly, soft law might also be intended to describe and possibly influence the development of hard law, for example the drafting of treaties.[97] In this way, soft law may push forward new directions of the law, thereby contributing to the development of international investment law.

---

91 Bjorklund, "Assessing the Effectiveness of Soft Law Instruments in International Investment Law," 58.
92 See further at <http://www.business-humanrights.org/SpecialRepPortal/Home/Protect-Respect-Remedy-Framework/GuidingPrinciples>.
93 Bjorklund, "Assessing the Effectiveness of Soft Law Instruments in International Investment Law," 70–1.
94 *Ibid.*, 55.
95 *Ibid.*, 71–7.
96 See also F. Ortino concerning the desirability of 'rules' instead of 'standards' in IIAs in Federico Ortino, "Refining the Content and Role of Investment 'Rules' and 'Standards': A New Approach to International Investment Treaty Making," *ICSID Review* 28, no. 1 (2013): 152–68.
97 Bjorklund, "Assessing the Effectiveness of Soft Law Instruments in International Investment Law," 77–9.

As mentioned, BITs rarely impose any (soft law) obligations on investors. The Norwegian Draft Model BIT from 2008, which later was shelved but reoccurred in a revised version again in 2015, attempts to impose social responsibility. The 2008 Draft Model BIT contained several explicit references to CSR. The preamble *"emphasizing the importance of CSR"* underlines CSR as a key policy priority. Moreover, the suggested article 32 with the title; *"corporate social responsibility"* states:

> *"The Parties agree to encourage investors to conduct their investment activities in compliance with the OECD Guidelines for Multinational Enterprises and to participate in the United Nations Global Compact."*

With this approach where state parties should just 'encourage' responsible business conduct, CSR remains a voluntary concept.

References to responsible business conduct in BITs today are still very rare, and in the few instances where they occur, they serve as policy commitments by states rather than legally binding commitments. The preambular text of the BIT between Austria and Tajikistan from December 2010 is so atypical and remarkable for its references to responsible corporate business conduct, anti-corruption, and protection of environment, human rights and labour right that it deserves to be fully cited:

> *"[. . .] EXPRESSING their belief that responsible corporate behaviour, as incorporated in the OECD Guidelines for Multinational Enterprises, can contribute to mutual confidence between enterprises and host countries;*
>
> *EMPHASISING the necessity for all governments and civil actors alike to adhere to UN and OECD anti-corruption efforts, most notably the UN Convention against Corruption (2003);*
>
> *TAKING NOTE OF the principles of the UN Global Compact;*
>
> *ACKNOWLEDGING that investment agreements and multilateral agreements on the protection of environment, human rights or labour rights are meant to foster global sustainable development and that any possible inconsistencies there should be resolved without relaxation of standards of protection."*

Though this approach, which largely follows the Austrian Model BIT, is more elaborate, it does not appear to go any further than emphasizing the importance of social and environmental responsibility in the moral sense. CSR thus remains a voluntary concept, which at best should oblige governments to encourage investors to implement CSR guidelines combined with a social reporting mechanism.

States may choose to incorporate social responsibility in IIAs. A question that occurs then is the question of the legal implication of a 'hardening of soft law'. For example, the BIT between Austria and Tajikistan, which refers to the UN Global Compact in the preamble, could hardly be considered as imposing legally binding obligations on investors. In this way, the reference to the soft law instruments in the preambular text rather works as a 'comply-or-explain' approach.[98] In legal terms this is *an encouragement* to states *to encourage* their own investors to commit to the UN Global Compact. Another example of an obligation for state parties to encourage the adoption of voluntary CSR measures is the Joint Declaration concerning Guidelines to Investors attached to the 2002 Chile–EU Association Agreement.[99] According to this declaration, the two parties remind their multinational enterprises of their recommendation to observe the OECD Guidelines for Multinational Enterprises, wherever they operate. No binding legal obligation can be deduced from this declaration, neither with regards to enterprises nor concerning states giving rise to state responsibility in case of failure to encourage. Yet, it demonstrates the desire among some states to encourage responsible business behaviour and employ a more balanced and coherent approach balancing legitimate welfare regulation with investment protection.

Clearly, there are conceptual difficulties in blending binding legal instruments (BITs) with voluntary guidelines since it is unclear to what extent the soft law instruments should be complied with. When expressed in a preamble, the soft law instruments remain guidelines. If the reference is articulated in the substantive parts of the BIT, however, it could arguably enhance further 'hardening of the soft law', but this is controversial. Even when not specifically mentioned in a BIT, the investor may still voluntarily commit to the various legal instruments on corporate conduct based on an acknowledgement that foreign investment has social, political and environmental effects. Adherence to a CSR policy may thereby assist corporations in managing these wider effects involved in foreign investment, particularly in weakly governed zones.[100]

Soft law norms allow states to work towards convergence and harmonization. Therefore, soft law instruments could potentially be of significant value to the international investment law regime in terms of enhancing greater policy coherence. Eventually, soft law may harden once normative positions and rationalistic preferences have moved sufficiently to make a binding commitment politically acceptable.[101] Even if there is no basis for agreement on legally binding commitments, soft law may still guide conduct in a stabilizing and useful manner. Hence, soft law may have a positive impact on a unification process of international investment law.

---

98 E.g. in an annual account or COP report, and thus not in an investment claim as such.

99 *Agreement Establishing an Association Between the European Community and Its Member States, of the One Part, and the Republic of Chile, of the Other Part*, 30 December 2002.

100 See also Hepburn and Kuuya, "Corporate Social Responsibility and Investment Treaties," 597f. See also Ortino, "The Social Dimension of International Investment Agreements," 243–50.

101 See also Pierre-Marie Dupuy, Ernst-Ulrich Petersmann, and Francesco Francioni, *Human Rights in International Investment Law and Arbitration* (Oxford: Oxford University Press, 2009), 87.

7. Rebalancing – policy objectives in preambles

Apart from imposing social responsibility on investors, states may also seek to balance rights and obligations on the treaty level. One way to do this is to include social and environmental policy objectives in BITs. The examination of BITs demonstrates that this method has been resorted to by some states in more recently negotiated BITs.

A key observation is that preambles of BITs post year 2000 have become more elaborate than in the earlier BIT phase. Hence, preambles appear increasingly relevant to the interpretation of the substantive parts of the treaty. In a number of investment disputes, tribunals have relied on preambles to cast light on the object and purpose of the treaty.[102] A strong political message stated in the preamble to a treaty may indeed have an impact on the normative content of the substantive investment protection. For instance, depending on the strength of the language, public policy concerns referred to in the preamble of a BIT may have an impact on the legitimate expectations of the investor.

The examination of BITs shows that BIT preambles to a large extent can be divided into two categories, which could be referred to as 1) *the traditional approach* 2) or *the balanced approach*.

Founded in the liberal investment regime, BITs with preambles following the traditional approach contain the key policy objective; to promote and protect investment. This approach typically encompasses references to the following components:

1) favourable conditions for investment;
2) a correlation between foreign investment on the one side and further investments, flow of capital and transfer of technology on the other side;
3) an outcome of the agreement perceived favourable to the economy of the states and/or economic development;
4) the reciporcity or mutal recognition of rights and obligations.

The phrases used are for instance:

Examples of component number 1)

> *"Desiring to create favourable conditions for investments . . . "* (Denmark–Egypt BIT 1996)
> *"Intending to create favourable conditions for investments. . . "* (Germany–Zimbabwe BIT 1995)

---

102 E.g. *SGS v Philippines*, ICSID, jurisdiction, 29 January 2004, para. 116; *Tecmed v Mexico*, ICSID award, 29 May 2003, para. 156; *Bayindir v Pakistan*, ICSID, Jurisdiction, 14 November 2005, para. 137; *Metalclad v Mexico*, ICSID Award, 30 August 2000, para. 71.

> *"Desiring to create favourable conditions for greater investments . . . "* (United Kingdom–Burundi BIT 1990)
>
> *"Dans l'intention de créer et de maintenir des conditions favorables aux investissements des investisseurs. . . "* (Switzerland–Cambodia BIT 1996)
>
> *"Con el proposito de crear condiciones favorables para las inversions"* (Chile–Argentina BIT 1991)

Examples of component number 2)

> *"Recognizing that the encouragement and contractual protection of such investments are apt to stimulate private business initiative. . . "* (Germany–Zimbabwe BIT 1995)
>
> *"Will be conducive to the stimulation of individual business initiative"* (United Kingdom–Burundi BIT 1990)
>
> *"Teniendo en cuenta que el mantenimiento de un clima satisfactorio para las inversiones, en conformidad con las leyes del país receptor, es la mayor manera de establecer y conservar un adecuado flujo internacional de capitals"* (Brazil–Venezuela BIT 1995)[103]

Examples of component number 3)

> *". . . to increase the prosperity of both nations"* (Germany–Zimbabwe BIT 1995)
>
> *". . . will increase prosperity in both states"* (United Kingdom–Burundi BIT 1990)
>
> *". . . will stimulate [. . .] the economic development of the Contracting Parties"* (Gambia–Netherland BIT 2002)

Examples of component number 4)

> *"Recognizing [. . .] a fair and equitable treatment of investments on a reciprocal basis. . . "* (Denmark–Egypt BIT 1999)
>
> *"Recognizing [. . .] the encouragement and reciprocal agreement. . . "* (United Kingdom–Burundi BIT 1990)
>
> *"Desiring to intensify economic co-operation between both countries"* (Spain–Namibia BIT 2003)
>
> *"Recognizing that a fair and equitable treatment of investments on a reciprocal basis. . . "* (Russia–Sweden BIT 1995)

Some of the more recent BITs depart from this traditional approach adopting the balanced approach.[104] The balanced approach to preambles refers to preambles

---

103 According to the UNCTAD database as of 1 June 2013 none of the Brazilian BITs are in force.

104 In a study by UNCTAD of "Bilateral Investment Treaties 1995–2006: Trends in Investment Rulemaking" the UNCTAD refers to this second category of preambles by referring

that add further policy concerns to that of investment promotion and protection. This is done for example by underlining that the economic goals must not be pursued at the expense of other public interests, such as health, safety, environment and labour.

Example of a preamble drafted on the basis of a balanced approach:

(United States of America Model BIT 2012)

"Desiring to promote greater economic cooperation between them with respect to investment by nationals and enterprises of one Party in the territory of the other Party;

Recognizing that agreement on the treatment to be accorded such investment will stimulate the flow of private capital and the economic development of the Parties;

Agreeing that a stable framework for investment will maximize effective utilization of economic resources and improve living standards;

Recognizing the importance of providing effective means of asserting claims and enforcing rights with respect to investment under national law as well as through international arbitration;

Desiring to achieve these objectives in a manner consistent with the protection of health, safety, and the environment, and the promotion of internationally recognized labor rights;

Having resolved to conclude a Treaty concerning the encouragement and reciprocal protection of investment;"

Canada and the United States have particularly shown a strong commitment to enunciating public policy in the preamble.

Though it is rarely the case, some states may choose to adopt a BIT without a preamble at all.[105] However, this does not mean that an investment claim initiated on the basis of such a BIT exists isolated from its policy context. Arbitrators would still be able to take into account the specific policy context. The gravitational pull theory would oblige arbitrators to do so. Still, attaching (some) importance to silence by state parties on policy prioritizations is obviously challenging.

When the negotiating parties explicitly decide to deviate from the traditional approach – by adopting the balanced approach – the interpreter, i.e. the

---

to 'non-traditional preambles'. Since the number of these 'non-traditional preambles' may evolve and (in the long run) become the preferred approach the term 'non-traditional preambles' appears unsuitable. 'Non-traditional' is not appropriate for what may become conventional. Therefore, it is more convenient to use the term of 'a balanced approach', which refers to the content of the second category of preambles. The UNCTAD study is primarily a descriptive study of a number of BITs.

105 See for example the BIT between Switzerland and Bangladesh from 1995.

adjudicator, is specifically required to attach determinative importance to these preambles. Hence, when the states have decided to elaborate further on the object and purpose of the BIT, it means that they intended particular importance to be granted to these objectives when interpreting the substantive parts. In other words, interpreters must naturally attach higher importance to objectives being explicitly stated in the preamble than to objectives not written in the BIT. There are thus preambles, which could be considered 'of particular relevance' for the interpretation of the substantive parts of the treaty. In line with annexes or other agreements or instruments accepted by the parties in connection with the conclusion, preambles are considered part of the contextual elements.[106]

A pertinent question is to determine the legal implications of the insertion of several objectives into a preamble. To what extent should such objectives have an impact on the interpretation of the substantive parts of the BIT? How do these purposes relate? How should they be prioritized? These questions are especially challenging where the various purposes seem to drag the treaty interpretation in different directions. As a main rule, an interpretation of the treaty requires all purposes to be taken into account on an equal footing, which in other words requires the adjudicator to adopt a balanced approach.

BITs with references to non-economic policy concerns demonstrate the desire among some states to negotiate new BITs containing language that explicitly calls for investment policies in coherence with public policies aimed at promoting development within these areas. To conclude, the preamble of a BIT is of key importance for interpreting the substantive parts of the treaty, in particular where it seems to deviate from the more common traditional approach, for example by elaborating further on the object and purpose of the treaty. Preambles containing various policy objectives may thus call for a balanced approach to interpretation,[107] and BITs may thereby enhance both legal and policy coherence.

8. Preliminary conclusions

In Chapter 2 the theoretical approach of the unification of international investment law was laid down. In this regard, determinative importance was attached to the need for striving for legal coherence as well as policy coherence. For the purpose of the latter, Chapter 3 has now outlined the policy context of the international investment law regime.

Whereas some policy concerns may add to further fragmentation of international law other trends may be beneficial to a more holistic approach. Some policy trends may thereby contribute positively to the unification by offering contextual elements for a harmonized approach to interpretation. However, it is not easy to determine on a general basis whether policy trends may 'drag the law' in a particular direction. As to the right to regulate and the concept of expropriation,

---

106 VCLT article 31(2).
107 The implications of 'a balanced approach to interpretation' is further explained in Chapter 5.

the multilateral negotiations do reveal essential aspects of consensus, particularly with regards to laying down the conditions for expropriations: public purpose, non-discrimination, due process and compensation. The multilateral negotiations also showed a general acknowledgement of the need to protect general non-discriminatory regulation, which should not be deemed compensable. Furthermore, there was consensus that this is a broader issue, not just relevant to labour and environmental regulation.

On the national level, policy making is moving from an era of liberalization to an era of regulation.[108] On an international level, the increase in self-regulation is particularly striking, especially with regards to the expansion of soft law instruments. It also occurs that various trends are closely interlinked. For example, a social responsible investor may commit to social reporting on CSR policies in order to promote transparency. The key policy trends identified are not relevant only as contextual elements but also because they may potentially function as catalysts for the expanding intersections between the two legal regimes – international investment law and human rights. For example, CSR standards may eventually evolve into hard law norms.

It appears that there are various opportunities for enhancing policy coherence. This could for example be done by requiring or encouraging investors to comply with various soft law instruments. On the treaty level, there is ample opportunity to enhance policy coherence by including references to other non-economic policy objectives in BITs.

108 UNCTAD, "WIR 2012," Chapter 3.

4 Human rights in the international investment law regime
The duty to regulate

1. Introduction

Chapter 4 deals with intersections of the human rights regime and the international investment law regime. While considering investment liberalization from the perspective of the promotion and protection of human rights, a new dimension is brought forward to the discussion of the right to regulate, i.e. the duty to regulate.[1] The following explains what this duty to regulate entails from the investment law perspective. The focus is therefore the implementation of human rights through regulatory measures potentially constituting an impediment to the (value of the) investment. Related human rights aspects are dealt with to demonstrate the complexity of legal research in the cross-cutting area of international investment law and human rights.

2. The human rights regime as another specialized branch of international law

While international investment law is one specialized legal paradigm under the overall umbrella of general international law, other specialized or subordinated legal regimes can be identified, for example the rules relating to the laws of wars, i.e. international humanitarian law, international refugee law, the law of the sea etc.

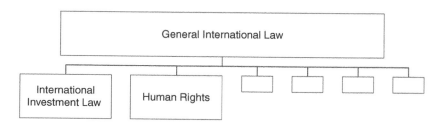

Figure 4.1 General international law as the overarching steering paradigm of the specialized systems of international law.

---

1 UN High Commission for Human Rights, "Human Rights, Trade and Investment," Report, 2 July 2009, para. 31.

As will be shown, the human rights paradigm contains rules obliging states to protect and promote human rights thereby generating an obligation to regulate foreign investment. In addition, investments are protected under the human rights regime through the concept of protection of property rights. The human rights regime is thus particularly interesting since it protects investments while also obliging states to regulate. As a specialized system, however, the human rights regime manages its own rules, its own principles and values, its own ethos. The human rights paradigm is primarily concerned with the protection of the individual. Another distinctive feature of the human rights regime is the presence of rules with a particular legal status such as *jus cogens* norms with obligations *erga omnes*.[2] At the same time, the human rights regime is not a separate legal paradigm discernible from general international law.

Another particular aspect of the human rights regime is the special universal character of human rights norms. In principle, all human rights are universal, indivisible, and interrelated.[3] The international community must therefore treat human rights globally 'in a fair and equal manner', on 'the same footing', and 'with the same emphasis'.[4] The universality of human rights seems to embrace diverging perceptions. It may refer to an absolute concept of universal norms, however allowing room for national discretion. Alternatively, universality of human rights could be perceived as a relative concept referring to uniformity of standards across various contexts as opposed to openness to contextual diversity. The universality of international human rights norms is thereby the 'centralizing tendency'.[5] This perception is beneficial to this research, and the universality of human rights is thus perceived through the lenses of this centralizing tendency.

The legal paradigm of international investment law consists of layers of general international law, of general standards of international economic law, and of distinct rules peculiar to its domain. Still, the investment law regime is not a closed legal circuit, but must interact with other regimes of international law. It is here contended that rules within the human rights paradigm should be added to this list to avoid (further) fragmentation of international law.

3. Human rights altering the concept of sovereignty

As explained in Chapter 2, the right to regulate is an inherent part of state sovereignty. In Chapter 2, sovereignty was explained as an external autonomous right for states to engage and commit themselves to the international community.[6]

---

2 *Erga omnes* obligations are generally perceived as obligations with a superior status, Shaw, *International Law*, 260, 275. Cassese distinguishes between *erga omnes* obligations and the correlative *erga omnes* rights; see Cassese, *International Law*, 64.
3 The World Conference on Human Rights in Vienna, 1993, The Vienna Declaration and Programme of Action, article 5.
4 *Ibid.*
5 See also Eva Brems, *Human Rights: Universality and Diversity*, 1st ed., vol. 66, International Studies in Human Rights (Nijhoff: Brill Nijhof, 2001), 14.
6 See above Chapter 2, section 4.1 and 4.2.

Yet, another aspect of state sovereignty has grown out of the human rights regime. After World War II the increasing focus on human rights protection of individuals had an impact on the prevailing understanding of the concept of sovereignty. The Universal Declaration of Human Rights (UDHR) from 1948 provides in article 21(3):

> *"The **will of the people** shall be the basis of the authority of government; this will shall be expressed in periodic and genuine elections which shall be by universal and equal suffrage and shall be held by secret vote or by equivalent free voting procedures."* (Emphasis added)

International law thus explicitly linked the concept of sovereignty with 'the will of the people' in an international constitutive document.[7]

This approach was later reaffirmed in other human rights instruments, including in article 1 common to the two fundamental human rights conventions, the International Covenant on Civil and Political Rights (ICCPR) and the International Covenant on Economic, Social and Cultural Rights (ICESCR).

In the same vein, resolutions by the UN General Assembly have linked the exercise of 'full permanent sovereignty' with the right to regulate. For example, the Charter of Economic Rights and Duties of States (UNGA resolution 3281 (XXIX)) 1974 lay down the principle of permanent sovereignty in article 2(1):

> *"Every State has and shall freely exercise full permanent sovereignty, including possession, use and disposal, over all its wealth, natural resources and economic activities."*

The principle of permanent sovereignty is then further elaborated on stressing a right for states to exercise authority over foreign investment.[8] Subsequently, the Charter emphasizes the right for states *"to regulate and supervise the activities of transnational corporations within its national jurisdiction and take measures to ensure that such activities comply with its laws, rules and regulations and conform with its economic and social policies".*[9] Moreover, transnational corporations *"shall not intervene in the internal affairs of a host State".*[10]

What becomes visible here is an alternative concept of state sovereignty, where the will of the people is instrumental to control foreign investments. So, whereas Chapter 2 dealt with an *external autonomous* concept of sovereignty, i.e. the capacity for states to make international commitments, a concept of *internal absolute alienability* has later evolved.[11] This latter perception of sovereignty placed

---

7 See also Michael W. Reisman, "Sovereignty and Human Rights in Contemporary International Law," *American Journal of International Law* 84, no. 4 (1990): 868.
8 UNGA resolution 3281 (XXIX), 1974, article 2(2)(1).
9 *Ibid.*, article 2(2)(2).
10 *Ibid.*
11 Alvik, *Contracting With Sovereignty*, 240–4.

the will of the population at the forefront of which a government is expected to exercise power. As expressed by Reisman: *"[T]he sovereignty of the Sovereign, became the sovereignty of the people: popular sovereignty."*[12] Consequently, the central aspect of this perception of sovereignty is the public interest, and the state is considered a servant or the guardian of the interests of its population. This view appears to be shared by Shaw, who states that the conception of the role of the state in the society has changed so as to emphasize the responsibility of the government towards its citizens. These changes are evidenced by the significant growth of social welfare legislation.[13] The human rights regime thereby adds a further perspective to the concept of sovereignty.

4. A human rights discourse in international adjudication

The human rights regime has gradually been given a more predominant role in general international law thereby having an impact on other specialized systems of general international law. The following clarifies how human rights exert influence on the international investment law regime, but before that it is convenient to explain how human rights have had an impact on general international law.

On the one hand the human rights regime may be perceived as a specialized paradigm originally stemming from the overall paradigm of general international law. As part of general international law the human rights paradigm must follow principles and rules under this overall umbrella. These principles and rules include rules concerning interpretation of treaties, basic principles and generic understandings of concepts such as 'state', 'sovereignty', 'stare decisis' and 'res judicata'. These concepts are fundamentally the same, notwithstanding whether an international court faces human rights issues or matters relating to other areas of international law, e.g. territorial disputes.

The question as to the impact of human rights on general international law is answered on the basis of the jurisprudence of the International Court of Justice (ICJ), which, like the arbitral tribunals, was not established with the primary objective of resolving human rights issues. It appears that the ICJ has moved from an early phase marked by a certain restraint to decide on human rights questions, to a greater degree of readiness to engage in human rights considerations. Since international human rights treaties generally have their own dispute settlement procedure,[14] the ICJ has dealt with human rights issues in disputes

12 Reisman, "Sovereignty and Human Rights in Contemporary International Law," 867.
13 Shaw, *International Law*, 55.
14 See e.g. the treaty-body system under the thematic human rights conventions such as the Human Rights Committee monitoring the International Covenant on Civil and Political Rights (ICCPR), whereas regional human rights treaties have adopted various forms of disputes settlement procedures such as the European Court of Human Rights (ECtHR) monitoring the European Convention of Human Rights (ECHR).

that at the inception did not concern human rights but nevertheless raised such issues.[15]

The establishment of the UN was in itself a particular accelerator for human rights entering general international law. The UN Charter expresses this common *"reaffirmation of faith in fundamental human rights"*.[16] *"Promoting and encouraging respect for human rights and for fundamental freedoms"* was articulated in article 1 of the UN Charter as being a fundamental purpose of the UN. From the outset, human rights were thus a cornerstone of international cooperation.

In the jurisprudence of the former Permanent Court of International Justice (PCIJ), the predecessor of the ICJ, human rights questions were addressed only with hesitation and restraint. In the early jurisprudence of the PCIJ in contentious cases, limitations on sovereignty were not to be presumed, and treaty provisions stipulating such limitations were to be interpreted restrictively. Human rights considerations appeared more or less incidentally in cases concerning issues that either had nothing to do with human rights, or where human rights considerations played a subordinate role. Human rights considerations were largely referred to by the court more or less like an *obiter dictum*, and as in the words of Simma *"not necessarily in an entirely positive, fully welcoming sense"*.[17]

In the *Corfu Channel* case[18] (*United Kingdom of Great Britain and Northern Ireland v Albania*) from 1949, the ICJ touched peripherally upon human rights concerns.

The case arose from incidents in 1946 where British destroyer ships struck mines in Albanian waters in the Corfu Channel and suffered damages, including loss of life. 45 British sailors died and 42 were wounded by the mines placed in Albanian waters, which was regarded as safe territory. The ICJ was requested to determine whether Albania was responsible for the explosions and liable to pay compensation. Albania did not notify or warn the British warships of the existence of the minefield and the danger they were approaching.

The loss of human life was a significant part of the dispute. The ICJ here stressed the duty of the parties to clear their territorial sea of mines:

> *"The obligations incumbent upon the Albanian authorities consisted in notifying, for the benefit of shipping in general, the existence of a minefield in*

15 Sandy Ghandhi, "Human Rights and the International Court of Justice the Ahmadou Sadio Diallo Case," *Human Rights Law Review* 11, no. 3 (2011): 527f.

16 The UN Charter, *Preamble*.

17 Bruno Simma, "Mainstreaming Human Rights: The Contribution of the International Court of Justice," *Journal of International Dispute Settlement* 3, no. 1 (2012): 4, 3–12. The reason for this may be found in the reluctance by the ICJ judges toward undertaking a more legislative role. On the legislative role of the ICJ judges see Shiv Bedi, *The Development of Human Rights Law by the Judges of the International Court of Justice*, 1st ed., Studies in International Law (Oxford: Hart Publishing, 2007), 29–32.

18 *Corfu Channel (United Kingdom of Great Britain and Northern Ireland v Albania)*, Judgment, 9 April 1949, p. 22.

Albanian territorial waters and in warning the approaching British warships of the imminent danger to which the minefield exposed them. Such obligations are based, not on the Hague Convention of 1907, No. VTII, which is applicable in time of war, but on certain general and well-recognized principles, namely: **elementary considerations of humanity,** *even more exacting in peace than in war [. . .]."* (Emphasis added)

The basis of this obligation was thus found in "certain general and well-recognized principles", including "elementary considerations of humanity", which indirectly points to human rights considerations. The ICJ appealed to common human values, such as human dignity and respect for the human right to life.[19]

Another example of peripheral human rights considerations by the ICJ is the later *Barcelona Traction* case.[20]

The claim arose out of the restrictions by the Franco ruling on foreigners doing business in Spain. The claim concerned the adjudication in bankruptcy of Barcelona Traction, a company incorporated in Canada. A central aspect of the case concerned the claim by Belgium on behalf of the Belgium minority shareholders for reparation for damage.

At the outset of the discussion relating to the conditions for diplomatic protection of shareholders, the ICJ introduced a new category of obligations by referring to "obligations *erga omnes*":[21]

"When a State admits into its territory foreign investments or foreign nationals, whether natural or juristic persons, it is bound to extend to them the protection of the law and assumes obligations concerning the treatment to be afforded them. These obligations, however, are neither absolute nor unqualified. In particular, an essential distinction should be drawn between the **obligations of a State towards the international community as a whole,** *and those arising vis-à-vis another State in the field of diplomatic protection. By their very nature the former are the concern of all States. In view of the importance of the rights involved, all States can be held to have a legal interest in their protection; they are obligations* **erga omnes.***"* (Emphasis added)

The ICJ thus made an important contribution to the development of human rights law by drawing this fundamental distinction between a state's obligations towards another state and its obligations towards the international community as a whole.

---

19 See also Bedi, *The Development of Human Rights Law*, 105–7.
20 *Barcelona Traction, Light and Power Company, Limited (Belgium v Spain)*, Judgment, 5 February 1970.
21 *Barcelona Traction, Light and Power Company, Limited (Belgium v Spain)*, Judgment, 5 February 1970, para. 33 at p. 33.

In the following paragraph the ICJ elaborated further upon these obligations *erga omnes* by referring to "genocide" and "principles and rules that concern the basic rights of the human person":[22]

> *"Such obligations derive, for example, in contemporary international law, from the outlawing of acts of aggression, and of genocide, as also from the principles and rules concerning the basic rights of the human person, including protection from slavery and racial discrimination. Some of the corresponding rights of protection have entered into the body of general international law (Reservations to the Convention on the Prevention and Punishment of the Crime of Genocide, Advisory Opinion, I.C.J. Reports 1951, p. 23); others are conferred by international instruments of a universal or quasi-universal character."*

In subsequent ICJ judgments and advisory opinions human rights considerations have taken up slightly more space, though such considerations have come up more on an incidental basis than as lengthy human rights discussions. The two advisory opinions, by which the ICJ confirmed the immunities of United Nations' Special Rapporteurs in the field of human rights, the *Mazilu* case[23] (1989) and the *Cumaraswamy* case[24] (1999), are examples hereof.

A later development shows how the ICJ to a greater extent was engaged in human rights considerations, particularly in terms of the development of the concept of self-determination of peoples. Examples in this regard are the decisions and advisory opinions on *South West Africa*[25] containing substantive

---

22 *Barcelona Traction, Light and Power Company, Limited (Belgium v Spain)*, Judgment, 5 February 1970, para. 34 at p. 33. See also Bedi, *The Development of Human Rights Law*, 155–60.

23 *Applicability of Article VI, Section 22, of the Convention on the Privileges and Immunities of the United Nations*, Advisory Opinion, 13 June 1989. Mazilu was elected by the Commission on Human Rights, a subsidiary organ of the Economic and Social Council, to serve as a member of the Sub-commission on Prevention of Discrimination and Protection of Minorities. Mazilu was called upon to prepare a report on the issue of youth and human rights but was kept in detention for three years in Romania, for his critical report on human rights in Romania made in his capacity as the UN Special Rapporteur on human rights and youth. The Advisory Opinion concerned whether Mazilu enjoyed the privileges and immunities of the UN and whether there had been a breach thereof.

24 *Difference Relating to Immunity from Legal Process of a Special Rapporteur of the Commission on Human Rights*, Advisory Opinion, 29 April 1999. Cumaraswamy, a Malaysian jurist, was appointed Special Rapporteur on the Independence of Judges and Lawyers by the UN Commission on Human Rights. Cumaraswamy claimed that he was entitled to immunity from legal process of every kind for the words spoken by him during an interview published in an article. In its Advisory Opinion the ICJ held that the Government of Malaysia should have informed the Malaysian courts of dealing with the question of immunity as a preliminary issue to be expeditiously decided.

25 South West Africa cases (1960–66), see Bedi, *The Development of Human Rights Law*, 109–56.

conclusions for the anti-apartheid and wider human rights community[26] as well as the more recent advisory opinions concerning the *Wall*[27] (2004) and the *Kosovo Declaration of Independence*[28] (2010), where the ICJ was explicitly requested to assess human rights considerations, including the right of peoples to self-determination.[29]

Another more recent case is the *Diallo* case[30] (*Guinea v Democratic Republic of Congo*) from 2010, where the ICJ deliberately prioritized considerations of physical human rights violations over property infringements, despite the fact that the claimant in the original claim made the reverse prioritization.

The case arose from the mistreatment of a Guinean businessman, Diallo, in the Democratic Republic of Congo (DRC). The mistreatment of Diallo was directed at his person as well as at his companies. He was illegally arrested and detained and his two companies were expropriated.

In Guinea's original application, allegations of violations by the DRC relating to international economic law and the protection of property enjoyed priority over the claimed violations against the person of Diallo. While declining jurisdiction over the company and shareholders' claims in 2007 the ICJ decided on the aspects of the case relating to the human rights violations against the person of Diallo. The ICJ found that the Democratic Republic of Congo had violated fundamental human rights in the International Covenant on Civil and Political Rights (ICCPR)[31] and the regional human rights convention, the African Charter on Human and Peoples' Rights (ACHPR)[32] such as the right to liberty and security of person and freedom from arbitrary detention. Accordingly, the case was transformed in substance into a human rights protection case.[33] As phrased by Simma: *"From now on, the human rights aspects rose like a phoenix from the ashes of the case"*.[34]

The only contentious cases the ICJ can hear according to its mandate are legal disputes between states.[35] In addition, the ICJ issues the mentioned advisory opinions on legal questions if asked by the General Assembly or Security Council or by another UN organ or specialized agency authorized by the General Assembly.[36] Though there are no limits in terms of which types of legal

---

26 Simma, "Mainstreaming Human Rights," 6.

27 *Legal Consequences of the Construction of a Wall in the Occupied Palestinian Territory*, Advisory Opinion, 9 July 2004.

28 *Accordance With International Law of the Unilateral Declaration of Independence in Respect of Kosovo*, Advisory Opinion, 22 July 2010.

29 Simma, "Mainstreaming Human Rights," 6.

30 *Ahmadou Sadio Diallo* (*Guinea v Democratic Republic of Congo*), Judgment, 30 November 2010.

31 Article 9.

32 Article 6.

33 Ghandhi, "Human Rights and the International Court of Justice," 528.

34 Simma, "Mainstreaming Human Rights," 14.

35 ICJ Statute, article 34(1).

36 ICJ Statute, article 65(1).

inter-state disputes the ICJ can deal with, the majority of cases concerns disputes over land frontiers and maritime boundaries. Yet, it is striking that despite the fact that the ICJ is not a specialized human rights institution, it has made some important contributions to human rights processes through significant case-law and advisory opinions. It also appears that the ICJ is increasingly tasked with considering human rights issues.[37] In response hereto, the ICJ has gradually become more open to decide on human rights questions. The reason therefor can be manifold, but may in any event be an outright expression of an increasing human rights attention in international law, not only by states, but also by individuals and in particular NGOs and IGOs. The ICJ, in the role as the guard of general international law, but faced with human rights issues, demonstrates how human rights enter more and more other areas of international law. The ICJ is thus *"paving the way for the acceptance of human rights arguments"* more generally.[38]

Correspondingly, investment tribunals increasingly face human rights questions, which will entail consequence of the legal protection of foreign investments. For example, the minimum standard of treatment of investors and their investments may potentially be influenced by the human rights regime. Accordingly, the rules on treatment of foreigners in general have to a large extent been absorbed by rules on human rights. It is therefore likely that an increased dissemination of human rights considerations in the general international law paradigm may impact upon other specialized branches of international law such as the international investment law regime.

5. Investment protection as the human right to protection of property

Human rights are typically associated with the protection of the human person. Yet, some human rights are relevant for legal entities as well. Corporate investors enjoy human rights protection, such as the right to a fair trial, the right to privacy, the right to freedom of expression as well as property rights.[39] At the same time, states may seek to limit this protection through regulatory means to promote human rights. This particular issue is part of the overall stability–flexibility dilemma concerning investment protection and the right to regulate.

To understand this field of tension, an account of private investors' human right to protection of property is required. This follows below. Subsequently, the duty to regulate under the human rights regime is explained. Afterwards, further attention is given to the role of corporations in terms of more recent developments and efforts to enhance human rights obligations of corporations.

---

37 Simma, "Mainstreaming Human Rights," 12.
38 *Ibid.*, 21.
39 *Sunday Times v United Kingdom*, ECtHR, 26 April 1979.

5.1. *The human rights protection of property*

Despite differences in legal traditions, political and cultural backgrounds, states perceive property protection as a core value of their society. Property rights enjoy protection under most constitutions. For example the German *Grundgesetz für die Bundesrepublik Deutschland* (1949) contains protection of property rights in article 14. The *Constitution of the United States* encompasses property protection in the Bill of Rights in Amendment V. The *Constitution of the Republic of South Africa* (1996) contains the Bill of Rights in its Chapter 2, where article 25 contains the fundamental rules of property protection. Property protection can also be found for instance in the *Constitution of the United Arab Emirates* (1971) in article 21; the *Constitution of the Republic of Argentina* (1994) section 17; the Danish *Grundlov* (1953) section 73; the Norwegian *Grunnlov* (1814) section 105; the *Constitution of Gambia* (1997) section 22; the *Constitution of India* (1949) article 300A; the *French Constitution* (1958) article 34; the *Russian Constitution* (1993) articles 34, 35 and 44; and the *Spanish Constitution* (1978) section 33.[40]

As previously stated, human rights are largely concerned with protection of the individual person.[41] The nature of property rights as human rights may appear somewhat different as it is connected with the possession of something else detached from the physical person of the individual. Yet, this does not affect the legal status of property rights vis-à-vis other human rights. There is no assumption that property rights take lower (or higher) priority than other human rights.[42]

Protection of property rights is laid down in various international law instruments. The Universal Declaration of Human Rights (UDHR) stipulates e.g. in article 17 that:

1) Everyone has the right to own property alone as well as in association with others.
2) No one shall be arbitrarily deprived of his property.

The protection of property is broad though not unlimited. It is subject to limitations for the purpose of securing respect for *"the rights and freedoms of others"* and of meeting the *"just requirements of morality, public order and the general welfare in a democratic society"* as well as by its location by other social, economic and cultural rights.[43] The International Covenant on Civil and Political Rights

---

40 Most constitutions can be found in the database of the University of Richmond, see <http://confinder.richmond.edu/>.
41 E.g. the right to life, protection from torture and inhuman treatment etc.
42 For the nature of property rights see also Jeff Waincymer, "Balancing Property Rights and Human Rights in Expropriation," in *Human Rights in International Investment Law and Arbitration*, ed. Pierre-Marie Dupuy, Ernst-Ulrich Petersmann, and Francesco Francioni, International Economic Law Series (Oxford: Oxford University Press, 2009), 277–84.
43 See UDHR article 29; Stephen Andrew James, *Universal Human Rights: Origins and Development*, 1st ed. (New York: LFB Scholarly Publishing, 2007), 147.

(ICCPR) and the International Covenant on Economic, Social and Cultural Rights (ICESCR) subsequently turned the Universal Declaration into legally binding commitments, but quite strikingly none of the instruments made any reference to property rights.

Other international instruments deal with aspects of property protection such as the Convention on Elimination of Discrimination Against Women (CEDAW), which in article 16 sets out equal rights of spouses to enjoyment and disposition of property. The Convention on Protection of Migrant Workers (CMW) recognizes in article 15 the right to property and the right to adequate compensation in case of expropriation with regard to migrant workers and their families.

Regional human rights conventions also refer to the protection of property. The 1948 American Declaration on the Rights and Duties of Man states in article XXIII:

> *"Every person has a right to own such private property as meets the essential needs of decent living and helps to maintain the dignity of the individual and of the home."*

Although the declaration is not formally a legally binding treaty, it has been a legal source for the jurisprudence of both the Inter-American Court of Human Rights and the Inter-American Commission on Human Rights. It is now largely superseded in the current practice of the inter-American human rights system by the more elaborate provisions of the American Convention on Human Rights, encompassing the right to protection of property in article 21.

The African Charter on Human and Peoples' Rights (ACHPR) guarantees property protection in article 14, which states:

> *"The right to property shall be guaranteed. It may only be encroached upon in the interest of public need or in the general interest of the community and in accordance with the provisions of appropriate laws."*

In Europe, the human right to protection of property is provided for in Protocol 1 article 1 of the ECHR, which states:

> *"Every natural or legal person is entitled to the peaceful enjoyment of his possessions.*
> *No one shall be deprived of his possessions. . . "*

Likewise, the EU Charter of Fundamental Rights, which came into force with the Treaty of Lisbon on 1 December 2009, contains property protection in its article 17.[44]

---

44 See <http://www.eucharter.org/>.

In an international investment law context there are two fundamental reasons for focusing on the ECHR as it has been interpreted by the ECtHR. Firstly, in the course of time, the ECtHR has developed a well-established practice in terms of interpreting human rights, including protection of property. This is not to say that other human rights institutions are irrelevant. However, the regional system of the ECHR is by far the most advanced.[45] Secondly, the jurisprudence of the ECtHR is particularly interesting since arbitral practice in several cases has chosen to rely on precedents from the ECtHR.[46]

5.2. The protection of property under the ECHR Protocol 1 article 1

Human rights under the ECHR and its Protocols have been interpreted in a teleological and flexible manner.[47] As a basic principle the ECHR should be understood as *"a living instrument to be interpreted in the light of present-day conditions"*.[48] The object and purpose of the convention concerning the primary protection of individuals requires that the ECHR should be interpreted so as *"to make its safeguards practical and effective"*.[49] Moreover, it has been established by the ECtHR that the provisions should be interpreted *"as far as possible in harmony with other principles of international law"*.[50]

Protection of property was left out in the main convention of the ECHR from 1950,[51] but subsequently in 1952 it found its way into Protocol 1 article 1, which states:

> *"Every natural or legal person is entitled to the peaceful enjoyment of his possessions. No one shall be deprived of his possessions except in the public interest and subject to the conditions provided for by law and by the general principles of international law.*
>
> *The preceding provisions shall not, however, in any way impair the right of a State to enforce such laws as it deems necessary to control the use of property in accordance with the general interest or to secure the payment of taxes or other contributions or penalties."*

Investors, including corporations, have the right to enjoyment of possession under the ECHR and the entitlement of initiating proceedings as 'victims' of

---

45 Cassese, *International Law*, 389.
46 See e.g. *Tecmed v Mexico*, Award, 29 May 2003; *Siemens v Argentina*, Award, 6 February 2007.
47 *Tyrer v United Kingdom*, no. 5856/72, 25 April 1978.
48 See e.g. *Selmouni v France*, no. 25803/94, 28 July 1999, para. 101.
49 *Soering v United Kingdom*, no. 14038/88, 7 July 1989.
50 *Al-Adsani v United Kingdom*, no. 35763/97, 21 November 2001, para. 60.
51 It was extremely difficult to reach an agreement on a formulation of the right to property, see David J. Harris, Michael O'Boyle, and Colin Warbrick, *Law of the European Convention on Human Rights*, 2nd ed. (Oxford: Oxford University Press, 2009), 655.

interferences.[52] Applicants can also be accepted victims of legislation as such.[53] Legal entities, including investors may thus have legal standing within the human rights regime of the ECHR. In terms of the protection of property this is explicitly stated with the reference to the entitlement of *"every legal person"*. The article thus has a commercial character and has been used extensively by corporations in the advancement of business interests.[54]

5.2.1. Protected property

Protocol 1 article 1 refers to *"the peaceful enjoyment of possessions"*, which in substance is guaranteeing the right of property.[55] The article does not guarantee the right to acquire possessions.[56] Rather existing possessions are protected. The term 'possessions' has an autonomous meaning and should be understood in a broad sense.[57] Practice supports a broad notion of 'possessions' and has included physical property,[58] company shares,[59] and contractual rights having an economic value,[60] for example intellectual property rights such as patents,[61] copyrights[62] or goodwill.[63] Acquired rights of economic value of the individual interest are protected,[64] whereas general expectations do not have the degree of concreteness to bring them within the scope of 'possessions' under Protocol 1

---

52 Corporations along with shareholders, trade unions, churches and NGOs have all been accepted as 'victim' pursuant to the admissibility criteria specified in article 34 of the ECHR. In terms of shareholder, the Commission has considered that an individual who held a substantial majority shareholding in a company could, under certain circumstances, claim to be a victim of measures directed against the company, see *Kaplan v United Kingdom*, Commission's Report, 17 July 1980. At the same time, the Commission has held that the question of whether a shareholder may claim to be a victim of measures affecting a company cannot be determined on the sole criterion of whether the shareholder retains the majority of company shares, see *Agrotexim Hellas S.A. and others v Greece*, no. 14807/80, 12 February 1992. See further in Iain Cameron, *An Introduction to the European Convention on Human Rights*, 5th ed. (Uppsala: Iustus Forlag, 2006), 56.
53 See e.g. *Norris v Ireland*, no. 10581/83, 26 October 1988.
54 Robin C.A. White and Clare Ovey, *The European Convention on Human Rights*, 5th ed. (Oxford: Oxford University Press, 2010), 477.
55 *Marckx v Belgium*, no. 6833/74, 13 June 1979, para. 63.
56 *Ibid.*, para. 50.
57 White and Ovey, *The European Convention on Human Rights*, 481.
58 E.g. *Wiggins v United Kingdom*, no. 7456/76, 8 February 1978.
59 E.g. *Bramelid and Malmström v Sweden*, no. 8588/79 and 8589/79, 12 October 1982.
60 E.g. *Beyeler v Italy*, no. 33202/96, 5 January 2000.
61 E.g. *Smith Kline and French Laboratoires v Netherlands*, no. 12633/87, 4 October 1990.
62 E.g. *Melnychuk v Ukraine*, no. 28743/03, 5 July 2005.
63 E.g. *Van Marle and Others v Netherlands*, no. 8543/79 8674/79 8675/79 8685/79, 26 June 1986.
64 Harris et al., *Law of the European Convention on Human Rights*, 657; Pieter van Dijk, Fried van Hoof, Arjen Van Rijn, Leo Zwaak, Cees Flinterman, and Aalt Willem Heringa, *Theory and Practice of the European Convention on Human Rights*, 4th ed. (Antwerpen: Intersentia, 2006), 866.

article 1. More concrete and legitimate expectations may fall within the ambit of protection.[65]

It is worth noticing that there are potentially remarkable differences in the conception of 'protected property' within the legal regime of human rights vis-à-vis the international investment law regime.[66]

5.2.2. Interference with property rights

Protection of property rights is not an absolute right under Protocol 1 article 1. The state may interfere with property in various ways, such as in the form of deprivations, control of use or by imposing measures that effectively limit the enjoyment of property rights.

Back in 1982, in the case of *Sporrong Lönnroth v Sweden*[67] the ECtHR pointed out that Protocol 1 article 1 contains three distinct rules:

1. The first rule is the general rule laying down the principle of peaceful enjoyment of property.
2. The second rule covers deprivation of possessions subject to certain conditions.
3. The third rule recognizes that states are entitled, amongst other things, to control the use of property in accordance with the general interest, by enforcing such laws, as they deem necessary for the purpose.[68]

In *James and Others v United Kingdom*[69] the ECtHR pronounced on the relationship between the three rules: *"The three rules are not, however, 'distinct' in the sense of being unconnected. The second and third rules are concerned with particular instances of interference with the right to peaceful enjoyment of property and should therefore be construed in the light of the general principle enunciated in the first rule."*[70]

Interferences may occur as expropriations *de jure* (i.e. a formal taking of the legal title) or *de facto* (i.e. without a taking of the legal title), which are considered deprivations of property. Deprivations are allowed if *"in the public interest"*, *"subject to the conditions provided for by law"* and by *"the general principles of international law"*.[71]

---

65 *Pudas v Sweden*, no. 10426/83, 27 October 1987. The expectations of the investor is dealt with in Chapter 5.
66 E.g. with regards to rules as to shareholder standing, the protection of intangible property and the role played by national law in defining what is 'property'; see Timothy G. Nelson, "Human Rights Law and BIT Protection: Areas of Convergence," *Transnational Dispute Management (TDM)* 10, no. 1 (2011): 30.
67 *Sporrong and Lönnroth v Sweden*, no. 7151/75; 7152/75, 23 September 1982.
68 *Ibid.*, para. 61.
69 *James and Others v United Kingdom*, no. 8793/79, 21 February 1986.
70 *Ibid.*, para. 37.
71 Protocol 1 article 1(1).

The characterization of a public purpose as a legitimate aim is primarily for the state. Where interference involves the implementation of social and economic policies by a legislative measure (i.e. regulation) it will be presumed that the interference has a legitimate aim. This means that the onus of proof lies with the applicant claiming to be a victim of an interference to demonstrate that the state's judgment is *"manifestly without reasonable foundation"*.[72]

The requirement of lawfulness derives from the rule of law. This means that the state must have a basis in national law for its interference. The law concerned must be *"accessible, precise and foreseeable"*. Where the applicant is a company the ECtHR will expect the company to obtain specialist advice on the requirements of domestic law.[73]

The third condition, requiring that the deprivation should be in accordance with the *"general principles of international law"*, has created most difficulties of interpretation. Controversies have primarily concerned whether the duty to pay compensation were to be extended to the state's own nationals.[74]

Other types of interferences that are not *de facto* or a *de jure* expropriation may, nevertheless, be as serious as a denial of the enjoyment of the possessions. The fact that a measure does not come within the exceptions to property protection enunciated under the second or third rule does not mean that there has been an interference with the peaceful enjoyment of possessions. The case of *Sporrong Lönnroth v Sweden*[75] is a leading precedent in this regard.

The Swedish government had granted the Stockholm City Council an expropriation permit for redevelopment purposes of property owned by Sporrong and Lönnroth. Moreover constraints with regards to construction and renovation of the properties were imposed upon Sporrong and Lönnroth. The expropriation permits lasted for 23 and eight years respectively, but the local authorities never exercised their power of formal expropriation. Sporrong and Lönnroth challenged the restrictions since they were *de facto* barred from selling their property at a reasonable price. Besides that they could not undertake necessary renovations either.

The pertinent issue in this case was whether the expropriation permits and prohibition of construction for a lengthy period of time amounted to a violation of the property rights of the applicants, irrespective of the fact that no express expropriation actually occurred. The ECtHR agreed that it had to ascertain whether the situation amounted to a *de facto* expropriation as argued by the applicants; but it did not find that this was the case. The ECtHR attached decisive

---

72 *James and Others v United Kingdom*, no. 8793/79, 21 February 1986, para. 46. See also Harris et al., *Law of the European Convention on Human Rights*, 668.

73 *Carbonara and Ventura v Italy*, no. 24638/94, 30 May 2000, para. 64 referring to *Hentrich v France*, no. 13616/88, 22 September 1994, para. 42. See also Harris et al., *Law of the European Convention on Human Rights*, 670.

74 Dijk et al., *Theory and Practice of the European Convention on Human Rights*, 885–7; Francis G. Jacobs and Robin C.A. White, *The European Convention on Human Rights*, 2nd ed. (London: Clarendon Press, 1996), 255f.

75 *Sporrong and Lönnroth v Sweden*, no. 7151/75; 7152/75, 23 September 1982.

importance to the fact that the right to the enjoyment of possession did not disappear so as to be assimilated to a deprivation of possessions. The applicants were still able to continue to utilize their possessions and the possibility of selling subsisted.[76] The ECtHR also held that it was not a situation of control of use either.[77] The ECtHR then turned to the first sentence of the first paragraph of article 1 and found that for the purpose of this provision it had *"to determine whether a fair balance was struck between the demands of the general interest of the community and the requirements of the protection of the individual's fundamental rights"*.[78] When there is no denial or deprivation, the measure is thus to be assessed under the requirements articulated in rule no. 3 referred to as the 'fair balance test'.

The fair balance test was spelled out in 1986 in *James and others v United Kingdom*,[79] where the ECtHR held that measures of interference must *"strike a fair balance between the interests of the community and the applicant's rights"*.[80] To satisfy the fair balance test, a state must show that the burden, which falls upon the private part, is not excessive or disproportionate.

It may be formally necessary to determine whether an interference is a deprivation of property or an extensive control of the use of property. In principle these two forms of interferences are governed by different provisions, but in a number of cases the ECtHR has not specified the relevant sentence into which interference falls. Today, it appears that identification of the type of interference is less important to the outcome of a case in the process involved in the application of the test of fair balance.[81] Furthermore, the complexity of the factual and legal position may prevent classification in a precise category.[82] Hence, the ECtHR nowadays reviews both the lawfulness and legitimate purpose of the measure as well as the proportionality. This assessment extends to the question of whether the measure was taken on a non-discriminatory basis, and whether it was in fact used for a purpose other than that for which it was conferred.[83] The fair balance test is perhaps the most remarkable aspect of the determination of whether an interference amounts to a violation of Protocol 1 article 1.

5.2.3. *The duty to pay compensation*

The duty to pay compensation follows implicitly with the requirement that deprivations must be in accordance with *"general principles of international law"*.

---

76 *Ibid.*, para. 63.
77 *Ibid.*, para. 64.
78 *Ibid.*, paras 69 and 73.
79 *James and Others v United Kingdom*, no. 8793/79, 21 February 1986.
80 *Ibid.*, para. 59.
81 Harris et al., *Law of the European Convention on Human Rights*, 668, 679; Dijk et al., *Theory and Practice of the European Convention on Human Rights*, 875.
82 *Beyeler v Italy*, no. 33202/96, 5 January 2000, para. 106.
83 *Fredin v Sweden*, no. 12033/86, 18 February 1991, para. 50.

Since the rules of customary international law lay down a duty to compensate *foreigners* for deprivation of their property, measures taken by a state with respect to the property of its *own* nationals are therefore in principle not subject to these general principles of international law.[84]

The duty to pay compensation also constitutes an element in the fair balance test.[85] This means that a taking of property without payment of an amount reasonably related to its value will normally constitute a disproportionate interference. Yet, *"legitimate objectives of public interest may call for less than reimbursement of the full market value"*.[86] So, Protocol 1 article 1 does not guarantee a right to full compensation. The amount is within the state's margin of appreciation.[87] While the ECtHR has stated that there must be a reasonable relation between the amount paid and the market value of the property, the state is entitled to take other factors into account, such as economic reforms and social justice, and thereby decide for an amount of compensation lower than the market value.[88]

Whereas the previously mentioned *Hull formula*[89] in general international law calls for *"prompt, adequate and effective compensation"* the human right regime thus leaves the amount of compensation within state discretion. The state may decide a lower amount as appropriate compensation.

Some support for this approach is also found in general international law. Most importantly, the UN General Assembly resolution 1803 (XVII) of 14 December 1962, 'Permanent sovereignty over natural resources' endorses a flexible standard in item 4 by referring to *"appropriate compensation"* and thereby indicating a lower standard than the *"prompt, adequate, effective compensation"* standard.

A flexible standard allows taking into account broader societal aspects, like the public interest and rationale behind the measure. A flexible standard thereby encourages a more justice-based standard or, as some critics of the current investment law regime has urged for, a more balanced approach.

---

84 In *Lithgow v United Kingdom* the ECtHR found that the general principles of international law are not applicable to a taking by a state of the property of its own nationals (para. 119). Yet compensation terms were considered material to the assessment whether a fair balance had been struck between the various interests at stake (para. 120); see *Lithgow and Others v United Kingdom*, no. 9006/80 9262/81 9263/81 9265/81 9266/81 9313/81 9405/81, 8 July 1986. Since article 1 of the ECHR, however, extends protection to everyone within the jurisdiction of the state and article 14 explicitly prohibits discrimination on grounds of national origin, Protocol 1 article 1 appears to cover nationals as well. Accordingly, there is a duty for state to provide compensation for expropriations or *de facto* expropriations not only for foreigners but also for nationals.

85 Harris et al., *Law of the European Convention on Human Rights*, 680; Dijk et al., *Theory and Practice of the European Convention on Human Rights*, 876, 881.

86 *Holy Monasteries v Greece*, no. 13092/87; 13984/88, 9 December 1994, para. 71.

87 Cameron, *An Introduction to the European Convention on Human Rights*, 135. See also Harris et al., *Law of the European Convention on Human Rights*, 680–6.

88 Cameron, *An Introduction to the European Convention on Human Rights*, 135. See also Nelson, "Human Rights Law and BIT Protection," 33–4, 36–7.

89 See above Chapter 2, section 6.4.1.

5.2.4. *A regulatory prerogative in the ECHR*

Though not explicitly, the mentioned third rule of Protocol 1 article 1 implies that the duty to compensate is not applicable to normal regulation. When evaluating forms of restrictions on the right to property national authorities have been given 'a wide margin of appreciation' in assessing the need and specific measure to impinge on the right to property.[90]

Regulatory restrictions imposed on the right to property must be scrutinized by reference to three justificatory criteria:[91]

i)   lawfulness of the enforcement measure;
ii) legitimate aim in the general interest; and
iii) proportionality of the means to the legitimate aim.

A specific measure should not only be *necessary* but also *proportionate*.

Though often invoked by claimants, the ECtHR has persistently rejected that a state should apply the *'least restrictive measures'* or *'the less onerous measures'*.[92] The ECtHR has thus rejected a strict necessity test, but will assess whether the measure imposed is *'reasonable'* and *'suited'* to achieve the legitimate aim.[93] States are thereby given a larger margin of appreciation for control measures that are less intrusive than for deprivation of property.[94] In general, the jurisprudence on the right to property discloses a lax standard of proportionality. States are given a wide margin of appreciation in planning and implementing social and economic policy, since the member states are in a better position to assess social and economic needs.[95] Though not establishing a hierarchy of norms, the ECtHR seems to support that it will sometimes be necessary to balance between conflicting interests, usually between those of the individual against those of the community.[96]

The express recognition of a regulatory prerogative may thus in a given case establish a broader exemption from obligations to compensate than what is

---

90 In Spring 2013, the Council of Europe's decision-making body, the Committee of Ministers, adopted the Protocol No. 15 amending the ECHR. Notable in this regard is the inclusion of a specific reference to the doctrine of the margin of appreciation in the preamble of the treaty. On the margin of appreciation see White and Ovey, *The European Convention on Human Rights*, 78–81.

91 *Sporrong and Lönnroth v Sweden*, Commission's Report, 8 October 1980, para. 105.

92 *James and Others v United Kingdom*, no. 8793/79, 21 February 1986; *Tre Taktörer Aktiebolag v Sweden*, no. 10873/84, 7 July 1989.

93 *Mellacher and Others v Austria*, no. 10522/83 11011/84 11070/84, 19 December 1989, para. 53.

94 See also Jonas Christoffersen, *Fair Balance, Proportionality, Subsidiarity and Primarity in the European Convention on Human Rights*, 1st ed. (Leiden: Martinus Nijhoff Publishers, 2009), 121f.

95 Cameron, *An Introduction to the European Convention on Human Rights*, 134.

96 White and Ovey, *The European Convention on Human Rights*, 8.

supported by customary international law or by IIAs that do not contain this limitation.[97] In the investment law context, the jurisprudence by the ECtHR may serve as a source of inspiration providing useful analytical tools, especially in terms of a balance of interests in a fair balance test and the adoption of the principle of proportionality.

6. The duty to regulate and state obligations under the human rights regime

Striving for development is a primary goal for most states, though the model for this may vary largely. One thing is what a state *can* do as a sovereign to promote social welfare or to enhance human rights protection. Another thing is what a state is *required* to do under what will be explained as the duty to protect human rights.

The following deals with this duty to protect human rights.

6.1. The 'duty to regulate' to protect second and third generation rights

Human rights can be assigned to three categories, relating to the order in which they came into existence.[98]

First generation rights are generally perceived as being the civil and political rights of individuals such as the right to life, freedom of speech, or the right to a fair trial. The primary international legal instrument in this regard is the International Covenant on Civil and Political Rights (ICCPR).

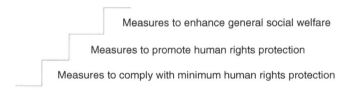

Measures to enhance general social welfare

Measures to promote human rights protection

Measures to comply with minimum human rights protection

Figure 4.2 States may step-by-step enhance the level of human rights implementation.

---

97 See also Jr. Jack Coe and Noah Rubins, "Regulatory Expropriation and the Tecmed Case: Context and Contributions," in *International Investment Law and Arbitration: Leading Cases from the ICSID, NAFTA, Bilateral Treaties and Customary International Law*, ed. Tod Weiler (London: Cameron May, 2005), 609–11.

98 The theory on the generation of human rights was initially proposed in 1979 by the Czech jurist Karel Vasak at the International Institute of Human Rights in Strasbourg. Though disputed his theory seems to serve well for clarification purpose in this context. See further on the generation of rights in Theodor Meron, "On a Hierarchy in International Human Rights," *American Journal of International Law* 80, no. 1 (1986): 1–23. With regards to protection of collective rights of groups and individuals, see also Shaw, *International Law*, 281–302.

Second generation rights evolved post-World War II and are fundamentally economic, social or cultural in nature. These rights cover for instance the right to work, housing, health and social security. The key international legal instrument in this regard is the International Covenant on Economic, Social and Cultural Rights (ICESCR).

The *third generation rights* are largely collective in their nature such as the right to a healthy environment, the right to natural resources, the right to self-determination and the right to development.

Delimiting civil and political rights from economic social and cultural rights is historically linked with East–West tensions. Whereas the market economies of the West tended to attach greater importance to civil and political rights, the centrally planned economies of the East highlighted the significance of economic, social and cultural rights. Hence, the two separate Covenants were negotiated. As these tensions diminished, the third generation rights grew out of North–South frictions.

From the international investment law perspective – in the context of the right to regulate – the human rights, which seem to intersect with investment protection, are primarily second or third generation rights. In other words, parallel to the development of the BIT regime, new human rights norms – economic, social, cultural or collective in their nature – came into being.

6.2. The 'respect, protect, fulfil' framework

By becoming parties to international human rights treaties, states assume obligations to respect, to protect and to fulfil human rights. Taken together these duties are referred to as the 'respect, protect, fulfil' framework.[99]

The obligation to *respect* requires that the state refrain from interfering with the enjoyment of human rights. This is the *direct* responsibility of states. States may thus not engage in a practice or activity that denies or limits human rights arbitrarily or unreasonably.[100]

The obligation to *protect* requires states to protect individuals and groups against human rights abuses. This may also be referred to as the *indirect* responsibility of states. This obligation requires states to prevent interferences by third

---

99 The framework was proposed by Eide in the 1980s as the Rapporteur to the then UN Sub-Commission on Prevention of Discrimination and Protection of Minorities. Eide originally conveyed four 'layers' of state obligations, which could be discerned as an obligation to respect, protect, ensure and promote. Later this was revised to become the tripartite division of the human rights obligations of states. See further in Olivier De Schutter, *International Human Rights Law: Cases, Materials, Commentary*, 1st ed. (Cambridge: Cambridge University Press, 2010), 242–56. See also the Maastricht Guidelines on Violations of Economic, Social and Cultural Rights from 1997, para. 6. The Guidelines are later referred to as a tool providing guidance on the interpretation of economic, social and cultural rights.

100 See also, Report by the Committee on Economic, Social and Cultural Rights, 38th and 39th session, 2007, E/2008/22 and E/C.12/2007/3, para. 44.

parties. Third parties include individuals, groups, corporations and other entities as well as agents acting under their authority.[101] The duty to protect obliges states to exercise due diligence to prevent private persons, including corporations, to violate human rights. The duty to protect has been recognized in Principle 1 of the Guiding Principles on Business and Human Rights.[102]

The obligation to *fulfil* means that states must take positive action to facilitate the enjoyment of basic human rights. States must thus adopt appropriate measures, which basically means that states must regulate, i.e. the duty to regulate. This could be done for instance through the adoption of legislation and the creation of institutions to realize the right. Introducing new regulations to promote human rights is an important aspect of states' duty to fulfil human rights.[103] An essential conceptual understanding of human rights thus lies within the fact that there are no distinctions between rights as such, whereas the useful distinctions relate to the duties.[104]

6.3. State obligations pursuant to the UN International Covenant on Civil and Political Rights (ICCPR)

The 1966 International Covenant on Civil and Political Rights (ICCPR) is a legally binding multilateral treaty, which enjoys widespread recognition.[105] The ICCPR focuses largely on protection of the physical integrity of the human person and freedoms and liberties such as the right to life,[106] freedom from torture[107] and slavery,[108] prohibition or arbitrary arrest and detention,[109] prohibition of the use of imprisonment as a punishment for breach of contract,[110] the right to privacy,[111] freedom of expression,[112] and provisions assuring the right to freedom of association and the right to form and join trade unions.[113]

---

101 *Ibid.*, para. 45.
102 See above, Chapter 3, section 14.7. The Human Rights Council has endorsed the Guiding Principles, Resolution 17/4, 16 June 2011. See also Patrick Dumberry and Gabrielle Dumas-Aubin, "When and How Allegations of Human Rights Violations Can Be Raised in Investor–State Arbitration," *The Journal of World Investment & Trade* 13, no. 3 (2012): 349–72.
103 UN High Commission for Human Rights, "Human Rights, Trade and Investment," 2 July 2009, para. 31.
104 In this regards, De Schutter refers to the political philosopher, Henry Shue, see Schutter, *International Human Rights Law*, 242.
105 There are 167 state parties as of 11 March 2013, see the UN Treaty Collection Database for data ratifications.
106 ICCPR article 6.
107 ICCPR article 7.
108 ICCPR article 8.
109 ICCPR article 9.
110 ICCPR article 11.
111 ICCPR article 17.
112 ICCPR article 19.
113 ICCPR article 21.

The rights enshrined should be implemented pursuant to article 2 of the ICCPR reflecting the 'respect, protect, fulfil' framework:

> "*1. Each State Party to the present Covenant undertakes to respect and to ensure to all individuals within its territory and subject to its jurisdiction the rights recognized in the present Covenant, without distinction of any kind, such as race, colour, sex, language, religion, political or other opinion, national or social origin, property, birth or other status.*
>
> *2. Where not already provided for by existing legislative or other measures, each State Party to the present Covenant undertakes to take the necessary steps, in accordance with its constitutional processes and with the provisions of the present Covenant, to adopt such laws or other measures as may be necessary to give effect to the rights recognized in the present Covenant.*
>
> *3. Each State Party to the present Covenant undertakes:*
>
> *(a) To ensure that any person whose rights or freedoms as herein recognized are violated shall have an effective remedy, notwithstanding that the violation has been committed by persons acting in an official capacity;*
>
> *(b) To ensure that any person claiming such a remedy shall have his right thereto determined by competent judicial, administrative or legislative authorities, or by any other competent authority provided for by the legal system of the State, and to develop the possibilities of judicial remedy;*
>
> *(c) To ensure that the competent authorities shall enforce such remedies when granted.*"

The Human Rights Committee (HRC) oversees the implementation of the ICCPR. In its General Comment no. 31 the HRC explains the nature of the general legal obligations imposed on states parties.[114] It follows from the commentary that the legal obligations under article 2(1) are both negative and positive in nature. The negative obligation requires state parties to refrain from violation of the rights recognized by the treaty. The ICCPR expresses this negative obligation with the reference to the initial core obligation *"to respect"* the rights contained.[115] The positive obligation incumbent on state parties is the obligation *"to ensure"* treaty rights. This obligation requires that state parties ensure that individuals are protected by the state, not just against violations of treaty rights by its agents, but also against acts committed by private persons or entities that would impair the enjoyment of treaty rights.[116] According to the HRC, the positive obligation to ensure treaty rights contains a due diligence obligation, which means that state parties have an obligation to prevent, punish, investigate and redress the harm

---

114 General Comments by the Human Rights Committee can be found at the webpage of the Office of the UN High Commissioner for Human Rights.

115 Human Rights Committee, General Comment no. 31, 2004, para. 5.

116 *Ibid.*, para. 8.

caused by acts by private persons or entities.[117] Both positive and negative obligations have immediate effect for all state parties.[118]

The requirement pursuant to article 2(2) *"to take steps"* to give effect to rights of the ICCPR is absolute and of immediate effect.[119] Failure to comply with this obligation cannot be justified by reference to political, social, cultural or economic considerations within the state, not even severe economic crisis. The ICCPR contains a non-discrimination aspect in implementing the rights.[120]

Whereas few rights in the ICCPR are absolute,[121] many substantive human rights can be subject to limitations. Yet, any restrictions have to be permissible under the relevant provisions of the treaty. In this regard, the HRC has emphasized that where such restrictions are made, states must demonstrate their necessity and only take measures that are proportionate to the pursuance of legitimate aims. Restrictions may in no way impair the essence of a treaty right.[122] Reservations to article 2 are incompatible with the ICCPR in the light of its objects and purposes.[123]

6.3.1. Civil and political rights in an international investment law context

The question that now arises is how human rights claims of infringements of the ICCPR come up in an international investment law context.

In most cases investment claims are initiated by corporations. In a smaller number of claims, however, individual business persons bring claims that may involve not only strictly economic issues but also on occasion more traditional international claims for mistreatment of aliens, such as allegations of false imprisonment, harassment and physical abuses, including serious contentions such as allegations of torture.[124] In the modern era, it is relatively rare that investment treaties are used as a path to initiate claims for the protection of civil and political rights of individual aliens. In an investment context, today, it is more likely that claims of infringements of the rights enshrined in the ICCPR would transpire as claims against foreign investors for malpractice or mistreatment neglected by the host state than claims of ill-treatment of the investor.

---

117 *Ibid.*, para. 8.
118 *Ibid.*, para. 5.
119 Human Rights Committee, General Comment no 31, 2004, para. 14.
120 Article 2(1).
121 E.g. ICCPR article 11 concerning the freedom from imprisonment for inability to fulfil a contractual obligation.
122 Human Rights Committee, General Comment no. 31, 2004, para. 5.
123 Human Rights Committee, General Comment no. 24, 1994, para. 9.
124 These types of claims still occur, see e.g. *Trinh Vinh Binh v Vietnam*, Award, 1 March 2007, UNCITRAL procedural rules based on the Netherlands–Vietnam BIT from 2005.

6.4. State obligations pursuant to the UN International Covenant on Economic, Social and Cultural Rights (ICESCR)

Like the ICCPR, the 1966 International Covenant on Economic, Social and Cultural Rights (ICESCR) is a legally binding multilateral treaty enjoying widespread recognition.[125] The catalogue of binding commitments cover aspects as diverse as labour rights,[126] social security,[127] health,[128] housing[129] and education,[130] cultural life[131] and general standard of living.[132]

The focus of the following is the implementation of the ICESCR, i.e. state obligations under the treaty, and thus not the scope or interpretation of specific rights in the ICESCR. Substantial guidance for interpretation of the treaty is found in the General Comments by the treaty body to the ICESCR, the Committee on Economic, Social and Cultural Rights (CESCR).[133] Other basic legal interpretative sources on economic, social and cultural rights are the *Limburg Principles on the Implementation of the ICESCR* from 1987[134] and the *Maastricht Guidelines on Violations of Economic, Social and Cultural Rights* from 1997.[135]

When it comes to second-generation rights, i.e. the economic, social and cultural rights, the link between law and policy becomes particularly evident. On the one hand, states have legal duties to implement economic, social and cultural rights. On the other hand, states may choose to go beyond that. Whereas the former is a legal obligation, the latter is a policy choice.

The enjoyment of economic, social and cultural rights seems to receive significant attention on the international agenda. These rights are subject to much debate e.g. within the UN Human Rights Council and the Human Rights Council has adopted a number of resolutions on these issues.[136]

6.4.1. ICESCR article 2

The obligations of member states to implement the rights under the ICESCR are laid down in article 2. Guidance for interpretation is provided for in General Comment no. 3.

---

125 164 state parties as of 17 August 2015, see the UN Treaty Collection Database for data ratifications.
126 ICESCR article 6, 7 and 8.
127 ICESCR article 9.
128 ICESCR article 12.
129 ICESCR article 11.
130 ICESCR article 13 and 14.
131 ICESCR article 15.
132 ICESCR article 11.
133 The CESCR was established under ECOSOC Resolution 1985/17 of 28 May 1985. General Comments by the Committee on Economic, Social and Cultural Rights can be found at the webpage of the Office of the UN High Commissioner for Human Rights.
134 Available at <http://www.escr-net.org/docs/i/425445>.
135 Available at <http://www1.umn.edu/humanrts/instree/Maastrichtguidelines_.html>.
136 Available at <http://www.ohchr.org/en/hrbodies/hrc/pages/hrcindex.aspx>.

"*Article 2*

1   *Each State Party to the present Covenant undertakes to take steps, individually and through international assistance and co-operation, especially economic and technical, to the maximum of its available resources, with a view to achieving progressively the full realization of the rights recognized in the present Covenant by all appropriate means, including particularly the adoption of legislative measures.*

2   *The States Parties to the present Covenant undertake to guarantee that the rights enunciated in the present Covenant will be exercised without discrimination of any kind as to race, colour, sex, language, religion, political or other opinion, national or social origin, property, birth or other status.*

3   *Developing countries, with due regard to human rights and their national economy, may determine to what extent they would guarantee the economic rights recognized in the present Covenant to non-nationals.*"

The core obligation for states is *"to take steps"* to the maximum of their available resources. This obligation conveys an obligation of conduct, a duty to take action. According to the CESCR the undertaking *"to take steps"* is not dependent on a particular government or economic system.[137] Yet, it is a requirement that it is a democratic system and that all human rights are respected.[138] A democratic government, however, does not in itself suffice. The concept of progressive realization acknowledges the fact that full realization of all economic, social and cultural right will generally not be able to be achieved in a short period of time. In principle, the full realization of all economic, social and cultural rights is hypothetical, or an ideal for states to strive for, because even in the most dedicated and well-resourced state there may always be room for improvement. On this particular aspect, the obligations differ fundamentally from the nature of the state obligations contained in article 2 of the ICCPR, which – as explained – embodies an immediate obligation to respect and ensure all of the relevant rights, i.e. an obligation of result. Conversely, *"progressive realization"* means realization over time.[139] This flexible device reflects reality. Though the nature of the state obligations in the two covenants largely differ, it does not, however, make it less an obligation for the state to implement the rights.

The means that should be used in order to satisfy the obligation *"to take steps"*, are referred to in article 2 (1) as being *"all appropriate means, including*

---

137 See also the Limburg Principles, 1987, Principle 6, according to which *"the achievement of economic, social and cultural rights may be realized in a variety of political settings [. . .]. Successes and failures have been registered in both market and non-market economies, in both centralized and decentralized political structures."*

138 Committee on Economic, Social and Cultural Rights, General Comment no. 3, 1990, para. 8.

139 See also Theo van Boven, "Categories of Rights," in *International Human Rights Law*, ed. Sangeeta Shah, Sandesh Sivakumaran, and Daniel Moeckli (Oxford: Oxford University Press, 2010), 174.

particularly the adoption of legislative measures".[140] In this regard, the General Comment no. 3 mentions that in some instances (e.g. to combat discrimination) and in some fields (e.g. health, education, protection of children and mothers), legislation is highly desirable or even indispensable.[141] Yet, the CESCR does not elaborate further on the rationale behind legislative measure being indispensable in some areas, except that in the absence of legislative measures, *"it may be difficult"* to implement the rights. At the same time, the examples given are not an exhaustive list. The General Comment thus leaves open whether there might be other areas where legislative measures are indispensable.[142]

Accordingly, states are obliged to regulate through the adoption of legislative measures to ensure the progressive full realization of economic, social and cultural rights. The adoption of legislative measures, however, is by no means exhaustive of the state obligation.[143] In addition to legislation, judicial remedies (on the national level) should be considered in order to make rights effective and justiciable, i.e. that rights can be invoked. Other appropriate measures include for example administrative, financial, educational and social measures.[144]

6.4.2. ICESCR and obligations of immediate effect – the duty to make certain policy prioritizations

As mentioned earlier, all human rights are universal, indivisible and interdependent and interrelated,[145] notwithstanding whether they are civil, political or economic, social or cultural in their nature. In that sense, all human rights are interlinked. There is also a material connection between the two types of rights – civil and political rights – vis-à-vis economic, social and cultural rights. As explained by Van Boven, the interlinkage between civil and political rights and economic, social and cultural rights can be found in an indirect protection of economic, social and cultural rights through the protection of civil and political rights. For example, while invoking the right to life, the right to health, food and water is implicit. Likewise, the right to freedom from forced or compulsory labour indirectly protects the right to work and to fair conditions of work.[146] The main difference between these two types of rights lies within the way they should be implemented. Whereas the state obligations in the area of civil and political rights are obligations of result, state obligations to implement economic, social and cultural rights are obligations of conduct.

---

140 See also the Limburg Principles, Principle 17 and 18.
141 Committee on Economic, Social and Cultural Rights, General Comment no. 3, 1990, para. 3.
142 *Ibid.*, para. 4.
143 *Ibid.*
144 *Ibid.*, para. 7.
145 Vienna Declaration and Programme of Action, adopted by the World Conference on Human Rights, 25 June 1993.
146 Boven, "Categories of Rights," 178–81.

While the ICESCR provides for progressive realization and acknowledges the constraints due to the limits of available resources, it also imposes obligations of immediate effect. First and foremost, it is an immediate obligation to undertake to guarantee that relevant rights will be exercised without discrimination.[147] Second, it is an obligation with immediate effect to undertake to take steps,[148] and this obligation is not qualified or limited by other considerations.[149] So, the pivotal point here is that while acknowledging that the full realization of the relevant rights may be achieved progressively, steps towards that goal must be taken immediately after the treaty has entered into force for that particular state.[150] The obligation, which has immediate effect here, is thus the obligation to act. Such steps must be as deliberate, concrete and targeted as possible.[151] These obligations of immediate effect ensure that the striving nature of the obligations contained in the ICESCR does not deprive the obligation of all meaningful content. Thirdly, it may added that many of the economic, social and cultural rights contain a minimum core obligation to ensure the satisfaction of the very least minimum essential levels of each of the rights incumbent on state parties.[152] Hence, the requirement to provide minimum protection is also an aspect of the obligations having immediate effect. An assessment as to whether a state has discharged its minimum core obligations must always take into account resource constraints applying within the country concerned.[153] Resource constraints are no excuse for not providing the minimum protection required. For instance, the ability to develop strategies and programmes for their promotion is not eliminated by resource constraints.[154] Hence, an assessment of whether the state has spent its resources with a sufficiently high prioritization of promoting economic, social and cultural rights becomes an assessment of whether the state has made economic, social and cultural rights a priority. Since an issue of prioritizations is a matter of state policy one may consider whether it can be an international legal norm to make certain policy prioritizations. The ICESCR thus seems to suggest this.

6.4.3. Enforcement of economic, social and cultural rights

In 2008 the Optional Protocol to the International Covenant on Economic, Social and Cultural Rights was adopted, providing the CESCR with

---

147 ICESCR article 2(2).
148 ICESCR article 2(1). See also the Limburg Principles, Principle 21 and 22.
149 See also General Comment no. 3, paras 1 and 2; Boven, "Categories of Rights," 175.
150 General Comment no. 3, para. 2.
151 *Ibid.* See also the Limburg Principles, 1987, Principle 8.
152 See also the Maastricht Guidelines on Violations of Economic, Social and Cultural Rights para. 9.
153 Cf. the formulation *"to its maximum available resources"*.
154 General Comment no. 3, paras 11 and 12.

competence to receive and consider communications.[155] According to article 2 of the Optional Protocol, claims can be submitted by individuals, or groups of individuals, under the jurisdiction of a state party, claiming to be victims of a violation of any of the economic, social and cultural rights set forth in the ICESCR by that state party.

Though the CESCR may consider individual claims involving parties to the Optional Protocol, the basis for decision-making is less clear. It follows from article 8 of the Optional Protocol that when examining communications, the CESCR shall consider the 'reasonableness' of the steps taken by the state party. Reasonableness as a criterion contains an inherent weakness due to its vagueness. In the assessment of the reasonableness of the steps taken, the CESCR shall bear in mind that the state party may adopt a range of possible policy measures for the implementation of the rights set forth in the ICESCR. The Optional Protocol thus supports that states are granted a wide margin of discretion in terms of realizing the economic, social and cultural rights encompassed in the treaty.

It is a mistake to assume that large-scale investments by multinational enterprises in developing countries are incompatible with the principles of the ICESCR per se, but there is a risk that globalization and increasing competition for investments may downgrade prioritization of human rights, in particular economic, social and cultural rights.[156] The corporate sector may have an impact on the implementation of the rights under the ICESCR, and this issue has been addressed by the CESCR in the series of General Comments on the various rights enshrined in the treaty.[157]

For example, with regards to the *right to water*, the CESCR has focused on the steps that states have to take to protect the right to water, where water services are operated or controlled by third parties:

> *"The obligation to protect requires State parties to prevent third parties from interfering in any way with the enjoyment of the right to water. Third parties include individuals, groups, corporations and other entities as well as agents acting under their authority. The obligation includes, inter alia, adopting the necessary and effective legislative and other measures to restrain, for example, third parties from denying equal access to adequate water; and polluting and inequitably extracting from water resources, including natural sources, wells and other water distribution systems."*[158] (Emphasis added)

---

155 In addition to the Committee on Economic, Social and Cultural rights, other committees with competence can consider individual communications involving issues related to economic, social and cultural rights in the context of its treaty.

156 Committee on Economic, Social and Cultural Rights, Statement, *Globalization and Economic, Social and Cultural Rights*, 11 May 1998, para. 3.

157 See also Committee on Economic, Social and Cultural Rights, Statement, *On the Obligations of States Parties Regarding the Corporate Sector and Economic, Social and Cultural Rights*, 12 July 2011.

158 General Comment no. 15, 2002, para. 23.

And

> *"Where water services (such as piped water networks, water tankers, access to rivers and wells) are operated or controlled by third parties, States parties must prevent them from compromising equal, affordable, and physical access to sufficient, safe and acceptable water. To prevent such abuses an effective regulatory system must be established, in conformity with the Covenant and this General Comment, which includes independent monitoring, genuine public participation and imposition of penalties for non-compliance."*[159] (Emphasis added).

A considerable number of investment disputes have occurred in the water and sanitation sector, in particular against Argentina.[160] For example, an investment dispute arose out of a major investment in the water utility of the municipality of Buenos Aires in Argentina by a consortium of foreign investors.[161] Together with local investors, the foreign companies created a local entity, Aguas Argentinas S.A., which entered into a 30-year contract to manage the water and sewage concession. In the face of the Argentine financial crisis, the public authorities froze the water prices charged to consumers. The investor argued that it was contractually entitled to modifications of tariff rates in the event of inflation or currency devaluation, so as to maintain the economic equilibrium of the project. In March 2006, the Argentine government terminated the concession alleging technical failures by Aguas Argentinas S.A. By this time, the foreign investors had already initiated international arbitration alleging that Argentina violated standards of protections in BITs signed with the investors' home countries – France, Spain and the United Kingdom.[162]

Apart from states' obligation to ensure that corporations refrain from interfering, the CESCR has also articulated corporate duties in terms of realizing

---

159 *Ibid.*, para. 24.
160 *Compañía de Aguas del Aconquija S.A. and Vivendi Universal v Argentina* (ICSID Case no. ARB/97/3); *Aguas Provinciales de Santa Fe, S.A., Suez, Sociedad General de Aguas de Barcelona, S.A. and Interagua Servicios Integrales de Agua, S.A. v Argentina* (Case no. ARB/03/17); *Aguas Cordobesas, S.A., Suez, and Sociedad General de Aguas de Barcelona, S.A. v Argentina* (Case no. ARB/03/18); *Aguas Argentinas, S.A., Suez, Sociedad General de Aguas de Barcelona, S.A. and Vivendi Universal, S.A. v Argentina* (Case no. ARB/03/19); *Azurix Corp. v Argentina* (ICSID Case no. ARB/01/12); *Azurix Corp. v Argentina* (ICSID Case no. ARB/03/30); *Impregilo S.p.A. Argentina* (ICSID Case no. ARB/07/17). The various decisions and awards can be found at the ICSID webpage under the case number.
161 Including Suez, Vivendi, Anglian Water Group and Aguas Barcelona.
162 See further concerning the water disputes in Luke Eric Peterson, "Human Rights and Bilateral Investment Treaties: Mapping the Role of Human Rights Law within Investor–State Arbitration" (Montreal: Rights & Democracy, 2009), 23.

economic, social and cultural rights. For example, with regards to the *right to food*, the CESCR has stated in General Comment no. 12 to article 11 that:

> *"Violations of the right to food can occur through the direct action of States or **other entities insufficiently regulated by States**. These include: [. . .] failure to regulate activities of individuals or groups so as to prevent them from violating the right to food of others, or the failure of a State to take into account its international legal obligations regarding the right to food when entering into agreements with other States or with international organizations."*[163] (Emphasis added)

And

> *"While only States are parties to the Covenant and are thus ultimately accountable for compliance with it, all members of society – individuals, families, local communities, non-governmental organizations, civil society organizations, as well **as the private business sector – have responsibilities in the realization** of the right to adequate food. The State should provide an environment that facilitates implementation of these responsibilities. The private business sector – national and transnational – should pursue its activities within the framework of a code of conduct conducive to respect of the right to adequate food, agreed upon jointly with the Government and civil society."*[164] (Emphasis added)

Accordingly, the CESCR here advocates that corporations have 'responsibilities'. Though the CESCR has given some importance to the responsibility of corporations in the full realization of economic, social and cultural rights, the primary responsibility of realizing the rights enshrined in the ICESCR lies with the state only. Where developing states have regularly raised issues relating to enforceability of social, cultural and economic rights, developed countries have proceeded more reluctantly. It remains quite difficult to deal with such claims legally. Rather the distribution of resources is a classical matter for political decision-making.

6.4.4. *A duty to make certain policy prioritizations*

The development of a state is largely measured by the standard of living, including the extent to which the people enjoy economic, social and cultural rights. The standard of public health and the educational system etc. is an essential parameter in this evaluation. The progressive realization of economic, social and cultural

---

163 General Comment no. 12, 1999, para. 19.
164 *Ibid.*, para. 20.

rights clearly has a direct bearing on a development progress,[165] and the adoption of regulation is an essential instrument in this regard. Another component that may positively contribute to the development of a state is foreign investment.

The nature of economic and social rights is somewhat controversial.[166] According to one view economic and social rights are not 'true rights' but should rather 'principles, aspirations or policy goals'.[167] Another point of view admits economic and social rights as 'rights', but perceives them as different in nature from civil and political rights.[168] As suggested by Cassese, a general distinction should be made between i) a core of fundamental values, which must be common to all nations, states and individuals and may not be derogated from and ii) other values, the application of which may need to take into account national conditions.[169] As norms of *jus cogens* clearly belong to the first category, it seems plausible also to include the core obligation of immediate effect under the ICESCR of the economic, social and cultural rights, referred to here as *'a duty to make certain prioritizations'*. The core obligations having immediate effect under the ICESCR explained here thus show that economic and social and cultural rights under the ICESCR are 'rights', but the extent to which they are enforced *beyond* the core duty to make certain prioritizations is a policy question.

The theoretical scope of the duty to regulate under the international investment law regime would therefore – as a minimum – allow for regulation falling within the ambit of the duty to make certain prioritizations. Measures imposed to implement this minimum obligation would thereby in principle not be compensable.

6.4.5. *Margin of discretion in judicial review*

From the human rights perspective, a pertinent question is to determine whether a state satisfies its commitments in terms of realizing economic, social and cultural rights. From the investment law perspective, the question is whether investment protection standards could be exempted or lowered for such regulatory measures.

---

165 Pius Langa, "Taking Dignity Seriously: Judicial Reflections on the Optional Protocol to the ICESCR," *Nordic Journal of Human Rights* 27, no. 1 (2009): 37f.

166 Urfan Khaliq and Robin Churchill, "The Protection of Economic and Social Rights: A Particular Challenge?," in *UN Human Rights Treaty Bodies: Law and Legitimacy*, ed. Helen Keller and Geir Ulfstein, Studies on Human Rights Conventions (Cambridge: Cambridge University Press, 2012), 199.

167 See for example Michael J. Dennis and David P. Stewart, "Justiciability of Economic, Social, and Cultural Rights: Should There Be an International Complaints Mechanism to Adjudicate the Rights to Food, Water, Housing, and Health?," *American Journal of International Law* 98, no. 3 (2004): 462–515.

168 See for example K. Tomasevski, "Human Rights and Poverty Reduction, Strengthening Pro-Poor Law: Legal Enforcement of Economic and Social Rights," *The Overseas Development Institute*, January 2005.

169 See also Antonio Cassese, "A Plea for a Global Community Grounded in a Core of Human Rights," in *Realizing Utopia: The Future of International Law*, ed. Antonio Cassese (Oxford: Oxford University Press, 2012), 139.

In terms of assessing the compliance with obligations *"to take steps" "by all appropriate means"* towards the progressive realization of economic, social and cultural rights, the CESCR will assess *"the appropriateness"* of the measure and whether it is *"adequate"* and *"reasonable"*.[170] As a tool for this assessment the CESCR will consider inter alia:

a) the extent to which the measures taken were deliberate, concrete and targeted towards the fulfilment of economic, social and cultural rights;
b) whether the state party exercised its discretion in a non-discriminatory and non-arbitrary manner;
c) whether the state party's decision (not) to allocate available resources is in accordance with international human rights standards;
d) where several policy options are available, whether the state party adopts the option that least restricts rights of the ICESCR;
e) the time frame in which the steps were taken;
f) whether the steps had taken into account the precarious situation of disadvantaged and marginalized individuals or groups and whether they were non-discriminatory, and whether they prioritized grave situations or situations of risk.[171]

These aspects provide some clarification to the aforementioned vague criterion of 'reasonableness'. A failure to take 'reasonable' steps would constitute a breach of obligations under the ICESCR, if it cannot be justified by the lack of resources. States thus have a margin of discretion to ensure the optimum use of resources and to adopt national policies and prioritize certain resource demands over others. This approach largely mirrors the margin of appreciation doctrine in the jurisprudence of the ECtHR, explained above.

The boundaries for such margin of appreciation are inherent as a core of minimum rights, i.e. a core that may evolve over time. In other words, the extent of a state's discretion in deciding its policy and budget priorities is limited by the human rights standards a state has committed itself to uphold. The minimum standard covers the obligations of immediate effect 1) to take steps; 2) not to discriminate; and 3) to ensure basic rights through e.g. the development of plans and strategies.[172] The obligation of progressive realization thus exists independently of a cutback in resources. It requires effective use of resources available.[173]

---

170 Report of the United Nations High Commissioner for Human Rights, 2007, para. 69. E/2007/82, available at: <http://www.ohchr.org/Documents/Issues/ESCR/E_2007_82_en.pdf>.

171 Report of the Committee on Economic, Social and Cultural Rights, 38th Session, 2007, *"An Evaluation of the Obligation to Take Steps to the 'maximum of available resources' Under and Optional Protocol to the Covenant,"* E/C.12/2007/1, para. 8.

172 Report of the United Nations High Commissioner for Human Rights, 2007, para. 72. E/2007/82, available at: <http://www.ohchr.org/Documents/Issues/ESCR/E_2007_82_en.pdf>.

173 See also Limburg Principles, 1987, Principle 23.

These legal obligations of immediate effect can in principle be assessed by an adjudicating body. In principle, an investment tribunal could assess the steps taken by a state to progressively realize economic, social and cultural right using the above-mentioned tool by the CESCR. Investment tribunals could thereby assess whether steps taken by the state are 'adequate' and 'reasonable' and, in the affirmative, such steps should be taken into account in the determination of the legitimacy of the investor's expectations. The last criterion (ensuring basic rights) might comprise most difficulties due to its more indeterminable character. The legal determination of what is to be considered the basic or minimum rights is a challenge, but in principle, the task should be feasible also for arbitral tribunals.

Assessment of regulatory measures beyond the minimum obligations is a different task. The CESCR does not prescribe the specific policy measures a state needs to take to respect, protect and fulfil human rights. The testing of the 'appropriateness' or 'reasonableness' beyond ensuring minimum rights is largely a policy issue outside legal or quasi-judicial review. National courts and international treaty-monitoring bodies, such as the CESCR, or arbitral tribunals, are thereby not competent to decide upon the reasonableness of national policies as such. Such determination would interfere with the prerogative and democratic mandate of national legislatures.[174] Policy prioritization by the state can thus only be subject to a limited review, to determine whether they comply with the duty to make certain minimum policy prioritizations.

6.4.6. Economic, social and cultural rights in an international investment law context

The issue of state obligations to promote and protect economic, social and cultural rights is a contentious issue particularly in the context of international investment law, where states have entered into other binding commitments. From the investment law perspective, the question is whether states can be released from investment protection (and thus the duty to compensate the investor) where they regulate to fulfil their duty to regulate. In the affirmative, the question is whether states may go even beyond what is required under the concept of the duty to regulate to protect and promote human rights, enhancing social welfare and raising standards of living exercising their right to regulate.

In investment arbitration, it may be an argument for the host state that it should not be required to compensate the investor, if the measure concerned is imposed to fulfil these minimum obligations of an immediate character. However, for arbitral tribunals the assessment of whether the state has acted to implement

---

174 See also Report of the United Nations High Commissioner for Human Rights, 2007, para. 70. E/2007/82, available at: <http://www.ohchr.org/Documents/Issues/ESCR/E_2007_82_en.pdf>. Yet, the Limburg Principles suggest that though the appropriateness of the means shall be determined by the state party, it shall be subject to review by the UN Economic and Social Council (ECOSOC), see Principle 20.

the minimum core obligation pursuant to the ICESCR is challenging, though not impossible. This is due to the current character of investment arbitrations where most arbitrators come from the private commercial field or as academics with general international law competencies and rarely with insights of human rights obligations. The CESCR, however, provides significant support for this assessment since the committee has determined that certain types of measures fall within this minimum duty to make certain prioritizations, e.g. the adoption of fundamental health regulation. Consequently, this type of regulation cannot at the same time require the state to compensate investors under a BIT.

7. Development in international investment law and investment arbitration

As earlier explained, the second generation rights, i.e. the economic, social and cultural rights are at the core when it comes to states' right to regulate. Apart from that third generation rights may increasingly become an issue in investment arbitration, in particular the right to development.

The international investment law regime rests on a principal presumption of development. Investment promotion is considered to enhance development of the state, and indeed the potential is there due to the fact that private foreign investment flows are typically much larger than development aid from states and international organizations.[175]

'The right to development' was initially articulated as a human right in the African Charter on Human and Peoples' Rights in 1981.[176] Subsequently, the right progressed from the regional human rights sphere to the international human rights sphere. In 1986 the UN General Assembly adopted a Declaration on the Right to Development.[177] Pursuant to the Declaration the *"right to development is an inalienable human right"* and everyone is *"entitled to participate in, contribute to, and enjoy economic, social, cultural and political development, in which all human rights and fundamental freedoms can be fully realized".*[178] The right to development has subsequently been reaffirmed in other international instruments.[179]

---

175 Christoph H. Schreuer and Ursula Kriebaum, "From Individual to Community Interest in International Investment Law," in *From Bilateralism to Community Interest: Essays in Honour of Bruno Simma*, ed. Ulrich Fastenrath et al. (Oxford: Oxford University Press, 2011), 1081.
176 African Charter on Human and Peoples' Rights, article 22.
177 The UN Declaration on the Right to Development, General Assembly, 4 December 1986. A/RES/41/128.
178 *Ibid.*, article 1.
179 See inter alia the 1992 Rio Declaration on Environment and Development, the 1993 Vienna Declaration and Programme of Action, the Millennium Declaration, the 2002 Monterrey Consensus, the 2005 World Summit Outcome Document and the 2007 Declaration on the Rights of Indigenous Peoples.

The human right to development encompasses all human rights – civil, political, economic, social and cultural – as well as other principles such as good governance, equality, non-discrimination, transparency and international cooperation.[180] At the World Conference on Human Rights the right to development was articulated in the same vein as the reaffirmation of the obligations of the international community to support *"countries committed to the process of democratization and economic reforms" "in order to succeed in their transition to democracy and economic development"*.[181] The human right to development is largely perceived as an issue of fundamental development to least developed states, though there is no legal basis for limiting the right to development to developing countries or transition economies only.

States' obligation to implement the right to development largely reaffirms the concept of state obligations under the ICESCR. Like the state obligations under the ICESCR, states have the duty *"to take steps, individually and collectively, to formulate international development policies with a view to facilitating the full realization of the right to development"*.[182] These 'steps' include *"the formulation, adoption and implementation of policy, legislative and other measures at the national and international levels"*.[183] Accordingly, this is an obligation of conduct having immediate effect.

The right to development could be perceived as an extension of states' duty to progressively realize economic, social and cultural rights. Accordingly, states' duty to enhance development, as explained above under the ICESCR, is extended with a right – for groups of individuals – to development. The human right to development thereby comprises a broader concept than the duty to regulate under the ICESCR.[184]

The issue of development is also addressed in the context of international investment law. The preamble to the ICSID Convention refers initially to *"the need for international cooperation and development and the role of private international investment therein"*. Historically BITs were entered into between a developed and a developing country. Through time, the BIT regime has changed significantly, and the contemporary BIT regime reveals a much more nuanced picture with for instance south–south agreements and agreements between European states and newly advanced economies such as the BRIC countries. Yet, the

---

180 Office of the High Commissioner for Human Rights, The Right to Development at Glance, see <http://www.ohchr.org/Documents/Issues/RtD/RTD_at_a_glance.pdf>.
181 Vienna Declaration and Programme of Action, adopted by the World Conference on Human Rights in Vienna, 25 June 1993, *op. cit.*, para. 9.
182 The UN Declaration on the Right to Development, General Assembly, 4 December 1986, article 4.
183 *Ibid.*, article 10.
184 This is demonstrated in article 2 of the UN Declaration on the Right to Development, which articulates that states have *"the right and the duty to formulate appropriate national development policies that aim at the constant improvement of the well-being of the entire population and of all individuals."*

aim of foreign investments contributing to development remains. In BIT practice development has typically come up as a reference in the preamble to the promotion of *"economic development"*,[185] to increase *"prosperity"*[186] or more recently *"sustainable development"*.[187] Furthermore, the discussion about the development dimension of international investment law has also had an impact on the controversial issue of a definition of protected investments.[188] When it comes to investment arbitration proceedings have traditionally been initiated against developing states or states that are less developed than the state of which the investor is a national (incorporated).

A pertinent question in investment arbitration is whether consideration should be accorded to the 'developing' nature of a host state. The question of relevance of the host state's level of development was touched upon in an investment dispute against India, *White Industries Australia Limited v India*.[189] The case concerned the protracted effort by an investor to enforce a commercial arbitral award in Indian courts. In the investment dispute India tried to invoke the status as a developing country as an excuse for not granting protection to investors, as they were required to under the BIT between Australia and India. Responding to the claim of a denial of justice India argued that the investor should *"take the conditions of the host state as it finds them"* and that India's judicial system had *"always been notoriously slow"*.[190] The point was that India claimed that the standards against which a state's conduct is to be measured should *"take into account the circumstances of the host state"*.[191] However, the tribunal did not comment directly as to whether this argument was taken into account.

The need for development may trigger social reforms thereby enhancing the adoption of regulatory measures. Yet, the level of development is less likely to constitute a justification for the denial of justice.[192] The status of development, however, could potentially become a legal criterion in the assessment of a breach of an expropriation standard under the necessity-criteria. The level of

---

185 United States Model BIT (2012); French Model BIT (2006); South Africa–The Netherlands BIT (1999); Turkey–Bulgaria BIT (1997).

186 German Model BIT (2008); Columbia Model BIT (2007); India Model BIT (2003); Italian Model BIT (2003); Denmark–Kuwait BIT (2001); Italy–Bosnia Herzegovina BIT (2005); Sweden–India BIT (2001); Russia–India BIT (1996); Italy–Bangladesh BIT (1994); Germany–Burundi BIT (1988).

187 E.g. Canada–Kuwait (2011); Canada–Jordan BIT (2009).

188 It is disputed whether economic development is a criterion under the definition of an investment pursuant to the ICSID Convention, see Dolzer and Schreuer, *Principles of International Investment Law*, 75; Sornarajah, *The International Law on Foreign Investment*, 10; Schreuer and Kriebaum, "From Individual to Community Interest in International Investment Law,"1082f.

189 *White Industries Australia Limited v India*, Award, UNCITRAL, 30 November 2011.

190 *Ibid.*, at 5.2.10, p. 60.

191 *Ibid.*, at 5.2.18, p. 62.

192 See further on the denial of justice to foreign nationals in human rights treaties vis-à-vis investment treaties in Nelson, "Human Rights Law and BIT Protection," 40–1.

development of the host state could thereby in principle constitute an element in a proportionality test. However, as explained earlier, while states cannot invoke resource constraints for not implementing the minimum core obligations under the ICESCR, resource constraints cannot either be invoked as an excuse for not providing – at least – the core protection to investors in the form of the minimum standard of treatment.

8. Corporate investors as complementary duty bearers?

As corporate actors enter the sphere of international relations, their rights and duties become more and more complex. Corporate investors are increasingly assessed on their human rights commitments. This development is part of the broader policy discussions concerning corporate social responsibility (CSR) as addressed earlier.[193]

8.1. Corporate human rights violations

Though the degree of corporate participation may vary broadly, human rights violations carried out or assisted by foreign corporations are a reality today. Examples hereof range from trade with conflict diamonds,[194] to toxic waste scandals[195] and shady labour practices.[196] Yet, when it comes to corporate liability for human rights abuses, the discussion is largely confined to international criminal law.

The issue of corporate liability for international crimes dates back to the birth of international criminal itself, the Nuremberg trials post-World War II.[197]

---

193 See above Chapter 3, section 5.4.
194 Fragile states, which have previously suffered from conflicts funded in part by diamonds, are for example Sierra Leone, Angola, Liberia, the Ivory Coast and the Democratic Republic of the Congo (DRC).
195 E.g. the multinational company, Trafigura, which was found guilty of exporting toxic waste, *BBC News*, 23 July 2010, <http://www.bbc.co.uk/news/world-africa-10735255>.
196 E.g. the claims against Nike for tolerating 'sweatshops', has made the company reassess their business ethics, *The Guardian*, 20 May 2001, <http://www.guardian.co.uk/world/2001/may/20/burhanwazir.theobserver>; *The Guardian*, 6 July 2012, <http://www.guardian.co.uk/environment/green-living-blog/2012/jul/06/activism-nike>.
197 See *United States v Krupp*, Trials of War Criminals before the Nuremberg Military Tribunals under Control Council no. 10, Judgment, 31 July 1948. The case involved Alfred Krupp and ten other officials of the Krupp industrial firm, who were convicted of charges relating to, inter alia, the use of slave labour. Another example is the case of *The United States of America v Carl Krauch et al. (I.G. Farben)*, 30 July 1948. This case involved directors and officers of the Farben corporate enterprise, who were committed inter alia for the commission of war crimes and crimes against humanity through participation in enslavement and forced labour of the civilian population of countries and territories occupied or controlled by Germany and the design and production of poisonous gas used in concentration camps of the German regime.

Though the International Criminal Court (ICC)[198] has no formal jurisdiction over corporations, corporate accountability was, however, actively discussed in the preparatory process of the Statute of the ICC. References to the prosecution of corporate entities were even inserted in the draft statute, but eventually the references were left out from the text of the final statute.[199] Nevertheless, these initiatives reflect a potential for holding companies accountable under the international criminal law regime.

At national level, the accountability mechanisms for corporate human rights violations are significantly diverse. Examples of corporations being held accountable for human rights abuses are rare.[200] Acts often appear to 'get relabelled' so what was once a human rights violation becomes a civil wrong, a tort or a breach of contract.[201]

Not every claim regarding corporate human rights violations or complicity in such violations constitute an international crime. For example, if the corporation is accused of denying political expression in the workplace, international law has not criminalized violations of freedom of expression as an international crime. So, neither the state nor the company has committed an international crime in this regard.[202] Hence, such a violation is rather considered an international tort, or delict, by the state.[203] Though this concept is short in terms of theoretical development, the issue is not purely theoretical. For example, the claims against Royal Dutch Petroleum in the *Kiobel* case[204] concerns complicity in international torts.

Activities carried out by corporations may also have a negative impact on the enjoyment of economic, social and cultural rights. Examples range from child

---

198 The ICC is a permanent international court established to investigate, prosecute and try individuals accused of committing the most serious crimes of concern to the international community as a whole, namely the crime of genocide, crimes against humanity, war crimes and the crime of aggression.

199 Clapham, *Human Rights Obligations of Non-State Actors*, 244–2.

200 The Dutch case of Frans Cornelis Adrianus van Anraat is one example. Van Anraat was a Dutch businessman, who sold raw materials for the production of chemical weapons to Iraq during the reign of Saddam Hussein. In May 2007, the Dutch appeal court sentenced Van Anraat to 17 years in prison for complicity to multiple war crimes by directly supplying thousands of tons of base materials for chemical weapons used by Saddam Hussein in the 1980s. The case is referred to in Antonio Cassese, *International Criminal Law*, 2nd ed. (Oxford: Oxford University Press, 2008), 143.

201 Andrew Clapham, "Non-State Actors," in *International Human Rights Law*, ed. Sangeeta Shah, Sandesh Sivakumaran, and Daniel Moeckli (Oxford: Oxford University Press, 2010), 565.

202 See also Clapham, *Human Rights Obligations of Non-State Actors*, 265; Clapham, *Human Rights Obligations of Non-State Actors*, 261.

203 *Ibid.*

204 In October 2011, the United States' Supreme Court agreed to hear the case of Esther Kiobel, a Nigerian national, who filed the lawsuit for her late husband, Dr Barinem Kiobel, and other Nigerians. They claimed that three international oil companies had arranged for the Nigerian government to use its military forces to put down resistance to the companies' drilling for oil in the Ogoni region of the Niger Delta in Nigeria.

labour and unsafe working conditions, restrictions on trade union rights and discrimination against female workers, to harmful impact on the right to health, the environment, the standard of living, the conditions for indigenous peoples and practices of corruption.[205] Though an investor may choose to structure its business through the establishment of a local subsidiary, this may not in itself free the investor from responsibility.

Corporations may indirectly be held accountable for human rights violations. As held by Reinisch there is a growing tendency *"to turn against accomplices"* in cases where the main perpetrator cannot be held accountable.[206] However, one should be cautious of expanding the scope of human rights accountability. Indeed, corporate complicity is a complex issue and the degree of 'culpability' of behaviour may diverge considerably. Clearly, there is a need for distinguishing between the degrees of culpability. For example, there are considerable differences between doing business in a state with a poor human rights record, not paying attention to environmental harm, to actively employing slave labour. Hence, it appears plausible to distinguish different categories of complicity, i.e. between actively assisting in human rights violations by others, benefiting from the opportunities created by human rights violations, or silence or inaction towards human rights violations.

Another pertinent question concerns to what extent investors can be liable for violations further down the supply chain. If a foreign investor were to be accountable for all actions for which it is responsible in the supply chain, corporations would be deterred from investing in states where they might be held responsible for acts of the state.

All in all, when considering human rights violations outside the sphere of international criminal law, violations by corporate actors are subject to domestic laws only. Discussions relating to the considerations of corporate responsibility for human rights violations is a parallel to the 'respect-aspect' of the state obligations under the 'respect, protect, fulfil' framework. As states are bound to respect human rights, corporations are called upon to respect human rights as well. However, to maintain that there is an international legal obligation for corporations in this respect is disputed, though such obligation is possibly emerging. The previously mentioned Ruggie Framework seems to suggest this.[207]

8.1.1. *The extraterritorial dimension of human rights*

Under international law accountability mechanisms are lacking when it comes to human rights violations by corporations. In practice, holding corporations

---

205 Committee on Economic, Social and Cultural Rights, "Statement on the Obligations of States Parties Regarding the Corporate Sector and Economic, Social and Cultural Rights", 12 July 2011, para. 1.
206 Reinisch, "The Changing International Legal Framework," 65.
207 Chapter 3, section 5.4.

accountable for human rights violations is typically left with the state hosting the investment. Relying on host states, however, may be doubtful and consequently the question of whether other states (such as the home state of the investor) can address human rights violations becomes relevant.

The question of third states' rights to exercise jurisdiction for human rights violations abroad has been dealt with in international criminal law under the concept of universal jurisdiction.[208]

Apart from matters subject to universal jurisdiction, which should not be further adressed here, a relevant issue is the question of extraterritoriality. When states undertake obligations in the area of human rights, they tend to consider that such obligations apply to individuals subject to their jurisdiction in their own territory. However, international bodies set up for scrutinizing compliance with human rights have increasingly interpreted human rights obligations as having – in addition – an extraterritorial scope.[209] Practice from human rights bodies[210] as well as the ICJ[211] confirms that human rights protection contains an extraterritorial dimension. This means that states are to respect human rights obligations not only in their own territory but also abroad, when they exercise authority, notwithstanding if the individuals subject to this authority or power have the nationality of the state or are foreigners.[212] Accordingly, human rights obligations of the investor's home state may extend to the territory in which the investor operates.

The concept of extraterritoriality is not just a theoretical idea but has become relevant in practice. The United States' Aliens Tort Claims Act (ATCA) is one example hereof.[213] The ATCA grants jurisdiction to United States' Federal Courts over *"any civil action by an alien for a tort only, committed in violation of the law of nations or a treaty of the United States"*. The ATCA thus serves as a legal basis of jurisdiction for American courts to hear claims against corporations for human rights abuses committed abroad. A number of oil companies have been accused of human rights violations, such as practising forced labour and playing a role in acts of torture and rape. Other claims under the ATCA relate to detention facilities run by private corporations. As stated by Clapham, the evolving law on the application of the ATCA may potentially affect not only the cases before the

---

208 Clapham, *Human Rights Obligations of Non-State Actors*, 237f; David Kinley, *Civilising Globalisation: Human Rights and the Global Economy*, 1st ed. (Cambridge: Cambridge University Press, 2009), 19; Dumberry and Dumas-Aubin, "When and How Allegations of Human Rights Violations Can Be Raised in Investor–State Arbitration," 353.

209 Cassese, *International Law*, 384f.

210 E.g. ECtHR, *Loizidou v Turkey*, Preliminary Objections, no. 15318/89, 23 March 1995, para. 57; The Inter-American Commission of Human Rights, *Coard et al. v United States*, 29 September 1999, para. 37.

211 ICJ, Advisory Opinion, *Legal Consequences of the Construction of a Wall*, 9 July 2004, para. 108–11.

212 Cassese, *International Law*, 386.

213 The United States' Aliens Tort Claims Act is one example, see Clapham, *Human Rights Obligations of Non-State Actors*, 252–4, 443–50. See also Reinisch, "The Changing International Legal Framework," 42–62.

courts but also the parameters of legal liability for companies more generally.[214] An example of an ATCA claim is the case of *Kiobel v Royal Dutch Petroleum*. In this case a class action suit was filed in the United States on behalf of Nigerian residents who protested against the environmental impacts of oil exploration in Nigeria. The Nigerians alleged that the subsidiary of the Dutch/British company, Shell, armed, financed, and conspired with Nigerian military forces to suppress the protests against the corporation. However, the case turned out somewhat discouragingly for the extraterritorial application of human rights, and the extra-territorial state duty to protect human rights abroad remains a contentious issue in international law.[215]

8.2. Corporate human rights compliance

The question of corporate human rights violations incorporates the retrospective view, where violations have occurred. When proactively addressing the avoidance of potential human rights violations, it becomes a matter of human rights compliance. Human rights compliance concerns the non-interference with human rights.

Human rights may be a topic of discussion at a shareholder meeting. Corporate behaviour and decision-making in areas relating to human rights often draw great attention from the media as well as from NGOs. Corporations may undertake a human rights due diligence before making the decision whether to invest or not. Human rights violations of non-state actors such as corporations may be the subject of litigation before national courts.[216] Moreover, corporate human rights compliance may be assessed in quasi-judicial processes.[217] Corporations are increasingly giving importance to human rights compliance. This aspect is caused by changes in corporate culture, regulatory frameworks, consumer attitude and social and political expectations.[218]

There are two predominant approaches for ensuring that corporations respect human rights obligations when doing business abroad. One approach is to impose obligations on states. Another approach involves the use of soft law instruments. The first approach focuses on the state's duty to protect, explained above under the 'respect, protect, fulfil' framework. The second approach that

---

214 Clapham, *Human Rights Obligations of Non-State Actors*, 252f.

215 See further in Ziad Haider, "Corporate Liability for Human Rights Abuses: Analyzing Kiobel & Alternatives to the Alien Tort Statute," *Georgetown Journal of International Law* 43, no. 4 (2012): 1361–90; Daniel Augenstein and David Kinley, "When Human Rights 'Responsibilities' Become 'Duties': The Extra-Territorial Obligations of States That Bind Corporations," in *Human Rights Obligations of Business: Beyond the Corporate Responsibility to Respect?*, ed. Surya Deva and David Bilchitz (Cambridge: Cambridge University Press, 2013), 271–94.

216 *Kiobel v Royal Dutch Petroleum*, op. cit.

217 See for example the Danish Mediation and Complaints-Handling Institution for Responsible Business Conduct, <http://www.businessconduct.dk/>.

218 Kinley, *Civilising Globalisation: Human Rights and the Global Economy*, 152.

has been developed in order to ensure corporate human rights compliance concerns the advancement of soft law instruments imposing moral obligations rather than strictly legal ones.[219] Numerous initiatives have been undertaken in the development of codes of conduct.[220] For instance, the OECD Guidelines for Multinational Enterprises establishes that corporations should *"respect human rights in every country in which they operate".*[221] Compliance should be ensured for example by having *"appropriate due diligence processes in place".* In this aspect, the OECD Guidelines implements the human rights due diligence obligation laid down in the Ruggie Framework, the *UN Guiding Principles on Business and Human Rights.*[222] Companies are thereby required to carry out risk-based human rights due diligence to identify, prevent and mitigate actual and potential adverse impacts and account for how these impacts are addressed. In essence, however, due diligence is a process-requirement and not a specific standard that companies have to live up to. It requires companies to know and describe the risk of adverse impacts and thus on that basis to take steps to address the risk. In the same manner, companies should also *"respect environmental*[223] *and labour standards".*[224] Corporate human rights compliance could be considered a parallel development to the 'protect' aspect under the 'respect, protect, fulfil' framework where states are duty bound to protect human rights.

8.3. *Corporate human rights promotion*

Next to the human rights agenda of corporate human rights compliance follow the tendencies of proactive human rights engagement by corporations. Corporations have capacity to create wealth, jobs and income. Corporations may thus positively contribute to the progressive realization of human rights by raising standards of living as key drivers of the global economy.

   Though international human rights treaties only bind states some human rights treaties are also directed at corporate activities. This is the case for the ICESCR, where the role of private parties is addressed in relation to the realization of the rights. It is stated that corporations can make positive contributions, for example with regards to the right to work by creating jobs, through hiring

---

219 See above, Chapter 3.
220 Dumberry and Dumas-Aubin, "When and How Allegations of Human Rights Violations Can Be Raised in Investor–State Arbitration," 351.
221 OECD Guidelines for Multinational Enterprises, IV Human Rights, p. 31.
222 The general principles are laid down in the UN Global Compact, which states in Principle 1: *"Businesses should support and respect the protection of internationally proclaimed human rights"* and Principle 2: *"make sure that they are not complicit in human rights abuses."* In the more elaborated *UN Guiding Principles on Business and Human Rights* Principle 17 the parameters for human rights due diligence is defined, while Principles 18–21 elaborate its essential components.
223 OECD Guidelines for Multinational Enterprises, IV Human Rights, p. 42.
224 *Ibid.,* p. 35.

policies and non-discriminatory access to work.[225] The ILO Conventions are also directed against corporate activities since the subject matter addresses all types of employers, in particular corporations. As mentioned, the corporate sector may contribute to the realization of economic, social and cultural rights in various ways.[226] Corporations may thereby attain the role as *"contributors to the establishment and maintenance of national social and economic order"*, as well as assuring *"international peace and stability"*.[227]

Various soft law instruments encourage corporations to promote human rights. For example, the OECD Guidelines for Multinational Enterprises contains human rights obligations, which goes beyond the mere compliance. According to these guidelines corporations should *"seek ways to prevent or mitigate adverse human rights impacts that are directly linked to their business operations, products or services by a business relationship, even if they do not contribute to those impacts"*.[228] Correspondingly, the environmental principles articulated in the UN Global Compact covers an obligation to promote environmental standards, since members should *"undertake initiatives to promote greater environmental responsibility"*[229] and *"encourage the development and diffusion of environmentally friendly technologies"*.[230] Arguably, the obligation to *"work against corruption in all its forms, including extortion and bribery"*[231] could be perceived as a duty extending beyond mere compliance to promotion of anti-corruption more generally. Proactive corporations may even be designated as 'agents of justice',[232] when they go beyond mere compliance with laws of the host state to the promotion of human rights.

This aspect concerning corporate human rights promotion is a parallel development to the 'fulfil' aspect of the 'respect, protect, fulfil' framework. Whereas states are obliged to fulfil human rights for example through regulatory measures, corporate human rights promotion is a concept that encourages corporations to develop human rights strategies, e.g. in the form of codes of conduct.

8.4. Privatizing the duty to regulate – a special case

A particular issue that calls for further attention is privatizations. Privatizations could be considered a special case when dealing with the intersections of the international investment law regime and the human right regime.

---

225 The Committee on Economic, Social and Cultural Rights has held in their General Comment to article 6 of the ICESCR that various private actors such as private enterprises – national and multinational – have a particular role in this regard, the Committee on Economic, Social and Cultural Rights, General Comment no. 18, 2005, para. 52.
226 Committee on Economic, Social and Cultural Rights, Statement, "Statement on the Obligations of States Parties Regarding the Corporate Sector and Economic, Social and Cultural Rights", 12 July 2011, para. 1.
227 Kinley, *Civilising Globalisation: Human Rights and the Global Economy*, 158.
228 OECD Guidelines for Multinational Enterprises, IV Human Rights, p. 31.
229 The UN Global Compact, Principle 8.
230 *Ibid.*, Principle 9.
231 *Ibid.*, Principle 10.
232 Onora O'Neill, "Agents of Justice," *Metaphilosophy* 32, no. 1–2 (2001): 180–95.

Foreign investors increasingly manage traditional public functions such as supplying public services, e.g. providing drinkable water or electricity, managing hazardous waste or ensuring infrastructure.[233] Privatization of central public functions generally shifts powers and responsibilities from governments to the market.[234] Yet, this does not hold true for human rights obligations. Privatizations could be considered a special case when it comes to human rights implementation. It may be that the privatized service does not correspond to the minimum level of human rights protection – e.g. to ensure access to a minimum quantity of water – either because the local people are not able to pay for it, or the quality is too poor. It may also be that human rights violations occur as a side-effect of the activity of the privatized service for example in the form of pollution of the environment.

In terms of civil and political rights, the positive obligations of state parties to ensure treaty rights of the ICCPR will only be fully satisfied if individuals are protected by the state.[235] With regards to economic, social and cultural rights, these rights sometimes protect access to essential services, i.e. the minimum standard. For example, the right to an adequate standard of living is protected in article 11 of the ICESCR, and the right to water is inherently linked to the right to adequate housing, food and the right to health in article 11 and 12 of the ICESCR. States are thereby obliged to ensure access to the necessary minimum supply for these services. The UN High Commissioner for Human Rights has noted in a report concerning 'Human Rights, Trade and Investment' in respect of privatization and the right to water that *"while promoting investment through private sector participation in the water and sanitation sector might be a possible strategy to upgrade the sector, there is concern that private sector participation might threaten the goal of basic service provision for all, particularly the poor, and transform water from being an essential life source to primarily an economic good".*[236] So, privatizations may sometimes constitute a threat to the public interest and negatively impede on human rights, but in other instances privatizations may be beneficial to human rights where foreign investors are instrumental to ensure development and fundamental societal services.

As public functions increasingly become privatized the question is whether this process alters the positive human rights obligation imposed on states. Privatizing essential public functions has sometimes led to the false assumption that the responsibility for the realization of economic, social and cultural rights

---

233 See also Ursula Kriebaum, "Privatizing Human Rights, the Interface Between International Investment Protection and Human Rights," in *The Law of International Relations – Liber Amicorum Hanspeter Neuhold*, ed. August Reinisch and Ursula Kriebaum (Utrecht: Eleven International Publishing, 2007), 165.

234 Augenstein and Kinley, "When Human Rights 'Responsibilities' Become 'Duties': The Extra-Territorial Obligations of States That Bind Corporations," 271–94.

235 Human Rights Committee, General Comment no. 31, 2004, para. 8.

236 UN High Commission for Human Rights, "Human Rights, Trade and Investment," 2 July 2009, para. 41.

automatically has been subcontracted to the foreign investor.[237] From a traditional international law perspective the state will remain responsible.[238] A massive growth in privatizations as well as public–private partnerships has, however, led to *"an increasing porosity of the public/private divide in economic relation"*, which may have an impact on the protection and promotion of human rights.[239] Indeed, the privatization of a number of functions, which traditionally have been assumed by the state, has blurred the distinction between the core state functions and the market.[240]

Corporations are significant depositories of assets and technology and a primary force for wealth creation and allocation.[241] Yet, the current international investment treaty regime does not provide for rules for situations where investors take on board the role as the public caretaker. 'Privatization of human rights' is not a way for states to escape their human rights responsibility under international law, but it may potentially generate a complementary 'duty bearer' of human rights protection.[242] From the international investment law perspective, privatizations could arguably be considered a special case, which calls for special rules addressing human rights issues where public utility or vital services are privatized.

9. Human rights in international investment law and investment arbitration

The following addresses substantial human rights issues in international investment law and investment arbitration focusing on BITs and ICSID arbitrations. The first part explains how human rights are referred to in BIT practice. The subsequent part explains how human rights come up in investment disputes.

9.1. Human rights in BITs

The primary aim of BITs is to promote economic growth. Yet, the economic dimension of BITs is not the only one, since there is an inherent social dimension of investment treaties.[243] In terms of the positive aspects, economic development through foreign investments may constitute an essential basis for fertilizing human rights protection and promotion. BITs may thus add to the positive development of human rights. The negative aspects of BITs for the realization of

---

237 Kriebaum, "Privatizing Human Rights," 166.
238 Clapham, *Human Rights Obligations of Non-State Actors*, 11.
239 Kinley, *Civilising Globalisation: Human Rights and the Global Economy*, 152f.
240 Schutter, *International Human Rights Law*, 248.
241 Salacuse, *The Law of Investment Treaties*, 23.
242 As explained by Reinisch the 'privatization' of human rights is here referred to not in the sense of *Drittwirkung* but *"as an allusion to the increased self-regulation instead of state regulation"*; see Reinisch, "The Changing International Legal Framework," 42–3.
243 Ortino addresses the interrelation between the economic and social dimensions of IIAs in Ortino, "The Social Dimension of International Investment Agreements," 243.

human rights are mainly twofold. Firstly, BITs can limit the capacity of states to impose human rights obligations on transnational corporations. Secondly, BITs can hinder states from progressively realizing second and third generation human rights. Regulation to promote and protect human rights is one of the positive societal aspects, which could be part of the investment equation.

General references to human rights are rare but examples can be found in BITs negotiated by Austria. For example, the BITs between Austria and Kazakhstan and Austria and Tajikistan both negotiated in 2010 refer to human rights in the preamble:[244]

> *"acknowledging that investment agreements and multilateral agreements on the protection of environment, human rights or labour rights are meant to foster global sustainable development and that any possible inconsistencies there should be resolved without relaxation of standards of protection."*

References to human rights concerns expressed as 'health', 'safety'/'security' and 'environment' often fall in the same vein. For example, in the Canadian Model BIT from 2004 health, safety and the environment has been singled out as policy concerns, which require further notice. In article 11 of the model BIT the parties recognize that *"it is inappropriate to encourage investment by relaxing domestic health, safety or environmental measures. . . "*. This provision has also found its way into recent BIT practice of Canada.[245] In the recently negotiated BIT between Canada and Benin from 2013 the contracting parties *"may adopt or enforce a measure necessary to protect human, animal or plant life or health"*.[246] Other states such as the United States, the Netherlands and Sweden, have followed the same approach in their model treaty texts with corresponding references to achieving investment promotion and protection without relaxing health, safety and environmental measures of general application.[247] This reference is also found in BITs by other states, for instance in the preambles of the BITs between Turkey and Nigeria (2011),[248] in recent BITs by Japan with Columbia (2011),[249]

---

244 The bilateral treaties entered into by Austria can be found at the webpage of the Ministry of Foreign Affairs, see <http://www.bmeia.gv.at/europa-aussenpolitik/voelkerrecht/staatsvertraege/bilaterale-staatsvertraege/>.

245 Canada–Benin BIT, 2013, article 15; Canada–China BIT, article 18(3), 2013; Canada–Slovakia BIT 2012, article II(4); Canada–Romania BIT, 2011, article II(5); Canada–Latvia BIT, 2011, article II(5); Canada–Jordan BIT, 2009, article 11. The bilateral Canadian Foreign Investment Promotion and Protection Agreements (FIPAs) can be found at the webpage at the Ministry of Foreign Affairs and International Trade to Canada, see <http://www.international.gc.ca/trade-agreements-accords-commerciaux/agr-acc/index.aspx?lang=eng>.

246 Canada–Benin BIT, 2013, article 20(1)(a)(i). See also the Canada–China BIT, 2012, article 33(2)(b); Canada–Slovakia BIT, 2012, article IX(1)(a).

247 See the preambles to the United States' Model BIT 2012, the Dutch Model BIT, 2004 and the Swedish Model BIT 2003.

248 Signed in 2011 but according to the UNCTAD database not yet in force.

249 Signed but not yet in force.

Uzbekistan (2009) and Peru (2009), and BITs by China with Guyana (2004) and with Trinidad and Tobago (2004).

References to 'health, safety and environment' are often linked with the expropriation clause for the purpose of distinguishing compensable from non-compensable regulation.[250] For example the Model BIT of Columbia from 2007 states that measures *"for public purposes or social interest or with objectives such as public health, safety and environment protection, do not constitute indirect expropriation".*[251] Another example is the BIT between Turkey and Nigeria from 2011, which states in article 7(2):[252]

> *"Non-discriminatory legal measures designed and applied to protect legitimate public welfare objectives such as health, safety and environment, do not constitute indirect expropriation."*

The right to health is an internationally recognized human right.[253] The right to health is often associated with the right to health care, but it also covers broader aspects such as safe drinking water and adequate sanitation, safe food, adequate nutrition and housing, healthy working and environmental conditions, health-related education and information. Health is sometimes singled out or referred to more indirectly.

For example, a reference to health is found in a BIT between the Czech Republic and India from 2011, where measures *"for the prevention of diseases and pest in animals and plants"* exceptionally may exempt investment protection.[254]

Sometimes measures to promote labour rights are added to the list of measures of general application, which should not be relaxed to the detriment of investment protection.[255] Labour rights are also sometimes singled out as a matter allowing for greater public scrutiny.[256] Human rights in the form of international labour rights are explicitly addressed and enhanced under the framework of the ILO.[257]

In terms of references to the environment and the links to human rights, it may be more controversial whether there is an internationally recognized human right to a clean environment as such. However, the protection of the environment is

---

250 This distinction in BITs and in arbitral practice is addressed below in Chapter 6.
251 Columbian Model 2007, article VI(2)(c). See correspondingly the US Model BIT 2012, article 4(b) or Austrian Model BIT 2008, article 7(4).
252 Signed in 2011 but according to the UNCTAD database not yet in force.
253 See for example the ICESCR article 12; the 1979 Convention on the Elimination of All Forms of Discrimination against Women (CEDAW) article 11(1)(f), article 12 and article 14(2)(b), the 1989 Convention on the Rights of the Child (CRC) article 24; the 2006 Convention on the Rights of Persons with Disabilities (CRPD) article 25.
254 Czech Republic–India BIT, 2011, article 12.
255 See e.g. the preambles to the United States' BIT 2012 or the Swedish Model BIT 2003.
256 E.g. US Model BIT, article 13(5) requires that each party provide the opportunities for public participation regarding labour matters.
257 See <http://www.ilo.org>.

in any case closely linked with the protection of other human rights, such as the right to water and the right to health. More generally, the many linkages between the protection of human rights and protection of the environment have long been recognized internationally. The 1972 United Nations Conference on the Human Environment declared that *"man's environment, the natural and the man-made, are essential to his well-being and to the enjoyment of basic human rights – even the right to life itself"*.[258] Research and seminars have been jointly organized by the United Nations Commission on Human Rights, the United Nations High Commissioner for Human Rights and the Executive Director of the United Nations Environment Programme.[259] The Convention on the Rights of the Child (1989) also refers to aspects of environmental protection in respect to the child's right to health. Article 24(2)(c) provides that states shall take appropriate measures to combat disease and malnutrition *"through the provision of adequate nutritious foods and clean drinking water, taking into consideration the dangers and risks of environmental pollution"*. The African Charter on Human and Peoples' Rights contains several provisions related to environmental rights. For example, article 24 states that *"all peoples shall have the right to a general satisfactory environment favourable to their development"*. Article 11 of the Additional Protocol to the American Convention on Human Rights in the area of Economic, Social and Cultural Rights (1988), concerning 'right to a healthy environment' proclaims that *"everyone shall have the right to live in a healthy environment and to have access to basic public services"*. In 2007 the UN General Assembly adopted the United Nations Declaration on the Rights of Indigenous Peoples. It is the first General Assembly Declaration on Human Rights, which recognizes the conservation and protection of the environment and resources as a human right. Article 29 of the Declaration states: *"Indigenous peoples have the right to the conservation and protection of the environment and the productive capacity of their lands or territories and resources. States shall establish and implement assistance programmes for indigenous peoples for such conservation and protection, without discrimination."* In sum, most human rights treaties were drafted and adopted before environmental protection became a matter of international concern. As a result, there are few references to environmental matters in international human rights instruments though environmental protection has gradually been perceived as a human right to a healthy environment.

More generally, the link between foreign investments and environmental protection is not a new topic. For decades, NGOs have accused MNEs of being responsible for pollution caused in particular in developing countries where environmental standards are loose. One argument has been that IIAs secure the export of highly polluting industries into the developing world.[260] Few, but some,

---

258 Declaration of the United Nations Conference on the Human Environment, Stockholm, 5–16 June 1972, see <http://www.unep.org/documents.Multilingual/Default.asp?DocumentID=97&ArticleID=1503&l=en>.
259 See further at <http://www.ohchr.org/EN/Issues/Pages/ListOfIssues.aspx>.
260 Sornarajah, *The International Law on Foreign Investment*, 225–7.

IIAs have been drafted to respond to this concern and this response has first and foremost been within the NAFTA context. This was earlier referred to as the NAFTA experience.[261] Article 1114(1) of NAFTA contains a provision, which requires arbitrators to pay attention to not to construe Chapter 11 to prevent a state party from adopting, maintaining, or enforcing any measures that it considers appropriate to ensure that the investment activity is undertaken *"in a manner sensitive to environmental concerns"*.[262] The Canadian model from 2004 contains several references to environmental protection, including the aforementioned specific provision in article 11 on investment and health, safety and the environment. Other states have singled out environmental considerations in specific provisions. For instance, the Columbia BIT from 2007 states in its article VIII on 'Investment and Environment':[263]

> *"Nothing in this Chapter shall be construed to prevent a Party from adopting, maintaining, or enforcing any measure that it considers appropriate to ensure that an investment activity in its territory is undertaken in accordance with the environmental law of the Party, provided that such measures are proportional to the objectives sought."*

The 2012 US Model BIT advances environmental concerns in its article 12 on 'Investment and Environment', which, apart from a general mutual recognition of each parties' respective environmental laws and policies, contains a rule on interpretation of environmental measures[264] and a right to request consultations with the other party with regards to environmental matters[265] as well as a confirmation by the parties to provide opportunities for public participation when deemed appropriate.[266]

All in all, states have highlighted environmental concerns by stating that the parties agree not to lower environmental standards to attract foreign investments.[267] However, in most IIAs, an environmental exception has not been spelt out.[268] On the contrary, the predominant BIT approach has been to disregard environmental concerns and emphasize the protection of foreign investments.

Safety/security concerns mentioned in BITs as exceptional measures could in principle cover a broad range of situations, which could be claimed to fall under the concept of an *ordre public* exemption. From a human rights perspective, however, this exemption is primarily linked with the safety and security of the individual human being rather than for instance an economic crisis.

261　See Chapter 3, section 3.
262　NAFTA, article 1114(1).
263　Columbia BIT, 2007, article VIII.
264　US Model BIT, 2012, article 12(5).
265　*Ibid.*, article 12(6).
266　*Ibid.*, article 12(7).
267　Canadian Model BIT, 2004, article 11.
268　See e.g. Model BITs of Germany, 2008; France, 2006; China 2003; Sweden 2003.

As mentioned, there are also broader societal interests, which are reflected in some BITs referring to for example sustainable development,[269] transparency[270] and corporate social responsibility.[271] In some instances explicit reference has been made to transparency, whereas other BITs demonstrate the parties' intentions to promote transparency without explicit reference hereto. The BIT between Japan and Uzbekistan exemplifies the latter by stating in article 7:

> *"Each Contracting Party shall promptly publish, or otherwise make publicly available, its laws, regulations, administrative procedures, administrative rulings of general application and international agreements as well as, in accordance with its laws and regulations, judicial decisions of general application, which pertain to or affect investment activities."*

Responsible corporate behaviour has also been referred to through references to the OECD Guidelines for Multinational Enterprises. The Austrian Model BIT from 2008 is an example in this regard. This model text also includes a reference to the principles of the UN Global Compact. Other more indirect references to the OECD Guidelines can also be found. For example, the state parties to the BIT between Austria and Mexico from 2001 declare to bear in mind *"the entry and the expansion of investments in their territory by investors of the other Contracting Party are subject to relevant instruments of the OECD in the field of international investments"*.

Though these references are not explicitly reproduced in human rights terminology (there is no internationally recognized right to sustainable development, to transparency or duty of corporate social responsibility), these concepts still strongly reflect fundamental human rights concerns. The right to development is a human right,[272] and transparency, in particular in terms of state obligations, can be considered an underlying or associated value in the enjoyment of fundamental human rights.

All in all, IIAs such as BITs have only in a few instances referred to human rights. If BITs refer to human rights, the references are typically drafted in permissive and encouraging terms, rather than expressly referring to human rights *obligations* for governments or investors.

Based on the BIT examination the following can be concluded:

- BITs rarely contain an explicit reference to 'human rights'.
- When references to regulatory measures to promote social welfare occur this is most frequently a reference to 'health, safety and the environment'.

---

269 E.g. Canada–China BIT, 2012, *preamble*; Austria–Kazakhstan BIT, 2010, *preamble*.
270 E.g. Canada–China BIT, 2012, article 17; Japan–Columbia, 2011 BIT, *preamble*; Austria–Kazakhstan BIT, 2010, article 6.
271 E.g. the preamble of the Austria–Tajikistan BIT, 2010 refers to *"responsible corporate behaviour, as incorporated in the OECD Guidelines for Multinational Enterprises"*.
272 See above Chapter 4, section 7.

- Sometimes the reference to 'labour or labour nights' is added.
- Some BITs contain explicit references to investment policy combined with sustainable development policies, transparency and corporate social responsibility.

9.2. Human rights in investment arbitration

Though investment arbitrations have taken place for more than 50 years, human rights have only more recently come up in the context of investment arbitration.

At the initial phase of an investment dispute the question is whether the tribunal will have jurisdiction over human right claims. The mere allegation of a human rights violation does not suffice to confer jurisdiction on an international investment arbitral tribunal. To determine whether an investment tribunal is competent to decide on human rights claims the clause that establishes jurisdiction is decisive. The exact formulation of the consent in the clause, conferring jurisdiction upon the tribunal, is decisive. Typically, it will be restricted to 'investment disputes' or 'to alleged violations of the substantive rights in the investment treaty'. However, consent to arbitration offered in BITs typically refers to 'any dispute'[273] concerning an investment.[274] This reference does not restrict a tribunal's jurisdiction to claims arising from the substantive standards of the BIT. Other formulations may narrow the scope of arbitral disputes.[275]

Another question is then whether human rights are part of the applicable law. As just explained above it is not impossible that human rights are explicitly referred to in BITs. Human rights may also be included in the parties' choice of law.[276] In addition hereto, human rights should – under a unified approach to the law – be taken into account when interpreting the substantive standards of the BIT. As mentioned above the legal basis hereof is the VCLT article 31(3)(c).[277]

9.2.1. Examples of human rights issues in the case-law of investment tribunals

The following examples of investment disputes illustrate how arbitral tribunals have dealt with human rights until now.

---

273 E.g. the Italian Model BIT (2003), article IX(1); French Model BIT (2008) article 7.
274 Dolzer and Schreuer, *Principles of International Investment Law*, 260.
275 German Model BIT (2008), article 9(1), which refers to *"disputes between the contracting states concerning the interpretation or application of this treaty"* thereby excluding pure contract claims. See also Dumberry and Dumas-Aubin, "When and How Allegations of Human Rights Violations Can Be Raised in Investor–State Arbitration," 358–60; Ursula Kriebaum, "Human Rights of the Population of the Host State in International Investment Arbitration," *The Journal of World Investment & Trade* 10, no. 5 (2009): 660f.
276 Clara Reiner and Christoph Schreuer, "Human Rights and International Investment Arbitration," in *Human Rights in International Investment Law and Arbitration*, ed. Pierre-Marie Dupuy, Ernst-Ulrich Petersmann, and Francesco Francioni, International Economic Law Series (Oxford: Oxford University Press, 2009), 84.
277 See above Chapter 2, section 7.5. See also Kriebaum, "Human Rights of the Population of the Host State," 661f.

1) 1989: *BILOUNE V GHANA*[278]

Biloune was a Syrian national and the principal shareholder of a corporation in Ghana. He was arrested by the authorities and deported from Ghana. Ghana effectively expropriated the assets of his corporation. Biloune initiated investment arbitration and claimed compensation for these acts, which he perceived as an interference with his investment. The tribunal emphasized that its competence was limited to commercial disputes arising under the contract between the parties only in respect of foreign investment, and that it lacked jurisdiction to address a claim of violation of human rights. The tribunal thus found that it had jurisdiction to settle the dispute regarding the alleged expropriation, but not with regard to the human rights violations.[279]

2) 2001: *LAUDER V CZECH REPUBLIC*[280]

The American national Ronald Steven Lauder invested in the private television broadcaster TV Nova in the Czech Republic through his German company, which was later succeeded by the Dutch company Central European Media (CME). Lauder claimed a breach of the BIT between Czech Republic and the United States through various actions by the Media Council. Since indirect expropriation was not defined in the BIT, the arbitrators looked to various secondary studies, as well as the jurisprudence of the ECHR for guidance as to how indirect or *de facto* expropriations are defined.[281]

3) 2002: *MONDEV V UNITED STATES OF AMERICA*[282]

The case arose out of a commercial real estate development contract concluded between the City of Boston, the Boston Redevelopment Authority (BRA) and the Massachusetts limited partnership owned by Mondev International Ltd., a company incorporated under the laws of Canada. The project concerned the construction of a department store, a retail mall, and a hotel in a designated area in downtown Boston.[283] Following a dispute between the parties, Mondev filed a suit in Massachusetts' courts against the two other contracting parties. The suit was dismissed. One of the reasons for this was a Massachusetts' statute granting the BRA immunity from suits for intentional torts.[284] Subsequently, Mondev brought a NAFTA claim. The NAFTA tribunal concluded that it had jurisdiction

---

278 *Biloune v Ghana*, Award, 27 October 1989.
279 The case is referred to in Reiner and Schreuer, "Human Rights and International Investment Arbitration," 99f. The award is not publicly available through the database of ITA law, but parts and summaries can be found at <http://www.ohchr.org/EN/Issues/Pages/ListOfIssues.aspx> and <http://www.biicl.org/files/3935_1990_biloune_v_ghana.pdf>.
280 *Ronald Lauder v Czech Republic*, Award, 3 September 2001.
281 *Ibid.*, paras 200–2. The tribunal referred to the Judgment by the ECtHR in *Mellacher and Others v Austria*, no. 10522/83 11011/84 11070/84, 19 December 1989.
282 *Mondev v United States of America*, Award, 11 October 2002.
283 *Ibid.*, the facts of the underlying dispute, see paras 37–40.
284 *Ibid.*, para. 1.

only with regard to the question of whether the conduct of the American courts in dismissing the claim constituted a breach of the NAFTA. Noteworthy is that the NAFTA tribunal turned to the case-law of the interpretation of ECHR article 6(1), right to fair trial, for determining whether the American court decisions concerning statutory immunities breached the minimum standard clause in NAFTA 1105(1). On the relevance of the jurisprudence of the ECtHR the tribunal explained:[285]

> *"These decisions concern the 'right to a court', an aspect of the human rights conferred on all persons by the major human rights conventions and interpreted by the European Court in an evolutionary way. They emanate from a different region, and are not concerned, as Article 1105(1) of NAFTA is concerned, specifically with investment protection. At most, they provide guidance by analogy as to the possible scope of NAFTA's guarantee of 'treatment in accordance with international law, including fair and equitable treatment and full protection and security'."*

Accordingly, the tribunal did not find the jurisprudence of the ECtHR irrelevant to the question of the scope of NAFTA protection. On the contrary, the tribunal appeared to be slightly open to comparative reviews of decisions of the ECtHR, which could thus potentially *"provide guidance by analogy"*.

4) 2003: *TECMED V MEXICO*[286]

The *Tecmed* case does not directly involve human rights law. Yet, the case is relevant due to the reference made by the tribunal to the jurisprudence of the ECtHR. The dispute concerned the decision by Mexico's environmental agency not to renew the permit of a Spanish investor to operate a landfill of hazardous waste. The decision was largely based on environmental concerns. In this case, the tribunal attached determinative importance to the 'vulnerability' of foreign investors. This vulnerability of foreign investors was based on the fact that foreign investors have either reduced or no participation in decision-making processes that affect them, mainly because they are not entitled to exercise political rights reserved to the nationals of host states.[287] In terms of investors bearing an excessive share of the burden involved in the realization of public objectives, the tribunal cited a judgment by the ECtHR, the case of *James and others v United Kingdom*:[288]

> *"Especially as regards a taking of property effected in the context of a social reform, there may well be good grounds for drawing a distinction between*

---

285 *Ibid.*, para. 144.
286 *Tecmed v Mexico*, Award, 29 May 2003.
287 *Ibid.*, para. 122.
288 *James and Others v United Kingdom*, ECtHR, Judgment, no. 8793/79, 21 February 1986, para. 63, cited in *Tecmed v Mexico*, Award, 29 May 2003, para. 122.

nationals and non-nationals as far as compensation is concerned. To begin with, non-nationals are more vulnerable to domestic legislation: unlike nationals, they will generally have played no part in the election or designation of its authors nor have been consulted on its adoption. Secondly, although a taking of property must always be effected in the public interest, different considerations may apply to nationals and non-nationals and there may well be legitimate reason for requiring nationals to bear a greater burden in the public interest than non-nationals."

The *Tecmed* case is thus another example of how tribunals have drawn on jurisprudence by the ECtHR.

5) 2006: *AZURIX V ARGENTINA*[289]

The *Tecmed* tribunal's reference to the ECtHR's decision in *James and others v United Kingdom* was later discussed in the *Azurix* case. Azurix was a company established in the United States, which invested in a utility system that distributed drinking water and treated sewerage water in Argentina's Province of Buenos Aires. Azurix initiated investment arbitration alleging that Argentina violated its BIT with the United States from 1991. Argentina raised the question of consistency between the BIT and international human rights law, and argued that the measures imposed were justified by the need to protect consumers' rights, including the human right to water. According to an expert opinion by Argentina the public interest at stake, the human rights of the people, were to prevail over the private interest of a service provider.[290] The tribunal, however, addressed this only briefly by noting that the matter *"had not been fully argued"* and that it *"failed to understand the incompatibility in the specifics of the instant case"*.[291] In the assessment of the question of whether the acts amounted to regulatory expropriation, the tribunal referred to the judgment by the ECtHR in *James and others v United Kingdom*[292] and concluded that the test of proportionality found in the jurisprudence of the ECtHR provided useful guidance for the arbitral tribunal.[293] The links between human rights and international investment law in this case were thus constructed as 1) a question of inconsistency and 2) a question of the relevance of the jurisprudence of the ECtHR.

6) 2007: *SIEMENS V ARGENTINA*[294]

Like the *Azurix* case, the links between human rights and international investment law were perceived in *Siemens v Argentina* as 1) a question of inconsistency

---

289 *Azurix v Argentina*, Award, 14 July 2006.
290 *Ibid.*, para. 254.
291 *Ibid.*, para. 261.
292 *Ibid.*, paras 311–12.
293 *Ibid.*, paras 311–12.
294 *Siemens v Argentina*, Award, 6 February 2007.

between the Germany–Argentina BIT and human rights and 2) a question of the relevance of jurisprudence by the ECtHR. The dispute arose from an investment made by Siemens, through a local subsidiary, in Argentina that won the bid for providing an integrated immigration control system, including the development of a national identification control system. Following disputes between the parties and the economic crisis of Argentina, Argentina terminated the contractual relationship. Argentina drew attention to human rights as part of the applicable law through its incorporation in the Constitution of Argentina, which recognized the *"right to property"* as well as the *"right of the state to regulate"* *"provided it is done by law and subject to principles of reasonableness and equality"*. Argentina put forward a *lex speciali*-argument on the basis of the Constitution stating that *"treaties rank above the law"* and *"treaties must conform to the principles of public law set by the Constitution"*.[295] Nevertheless, the arbitral tribunal held that *"the argument had not been developed by Argentina"* and the tribunal avoided further elaboration.[296] As to the relevance of the jurisprudence of the ECtHR, the tribunal did rely on the citation of ECtHR in *James and others v United Kingdom* articulated in the *Tecmed* case and considered the purpose and the proportionality of the measure vis-à-vis the interference with the investment.[297] Consequently, the tribunal more indirectly relied on jurisprudence by the ECtHR in the determination of compensation.

7) 2008: *BIWATER GAUFF V TANZANIA*[298]

This investment dispute was about a water-privatization project in Tanzania. In 2003, Tanzania obtained US$140 million in funding by the World Bank, African Development Bank and European Investment Bank for a comprehensive programme of repairing, updating, and expanding Dar es Salaam's water and sewerage infrastructure. Biwater Gauff (a joint venture of two European companies, one registered in the United Kingdom and one registered in Germany) successfully bid for the rights to develop the water and sewer system and formed another company, City Water, to operate the project. However, due to the mismanagement of the project, City Water failed to generate the expected income. Consequently, City Water was confronted with extreme financial and practical difficulties and could thus not live up to their contractual commitments. The Water Authority of Tanzania decided to begin the process to terminate the contract with City Water. Government officials deported City Water's senior management and appointed new management, entered City Water's offices, took control of the company's assets and informed City Water staff of the changes. Subsequently, an investment claim was initiated based on a UK–Tanzania BIT.

---

295 *Ibid.*, para. 74.
296 *Ibid.*, para. 79.
297 *Ibid.*, para. 354.
298 *Biwater Gauff (Tanzania) Ltd. v Tanzania*, Award, 24 July 2008.

In this case the government of Tanzania relied on jurisprudence by the ECtHR in claiming that it was entitled to a *"measure of appreciation"*.[299] In addition, Tanzania held that in case of a crisis it had *"more than a right"* to protect such services, but also a moral and possibly even a legal obligation to do so.[300] Tanzania thus invoked human rights considerations. The tribunal, however, did not really consider this point. Apparently, the arbitral tribunal did not find it necessary to consider the relevance of the jurisprudence by the ECtHR. However, human rights issues were taken into account under *amicus briefs* submissions by NGOs. In this regard, the tribunal held that contributions by NGOs with interests, expertise and perspectives on human rights issues *"provided a useful contribution to the proceedings"*.[301]

9.2.2. Human rights in key investment relationships

As a subject matter, human rights may potentially come up in these five key relationships:[302]

i) the home state and the host state;
ii) the host state and the investor;
iii) the host state and the individual/the community;
iv) the individual/the community and the investor;
v) the home state and the investor.

In terms of the relation between the home state and the host state, human rights might be an issue on the treaty-negotiating level when states negotiate IIAs such as BITs.

With regards to the host state–investor relation, human rights are practically non-existing in the underlying contractual relation, though there is a potential in this regard. For example, the host state may impose CSR reporting requirements. In investment arbitration, human rights may be invoked on both sides.

In the relation between host state and individuals/the community of the state, human rights may occur in various ways. The host state may be bound by general commitments to human rights treaties or at least by norms of customary international law. States seeking to promote and protect human rights may adopt general regulation for these purposes. States may also issue concrete orders to a particular investor to undertake certain arrangements, with the potential of interfering with

---

299 *Ibid.*, para. 434.
300 *Ibid.*, para. 434.
301 *Biwater Gauff (Tanzania) Ltd. v Tanzania*, Award, 24 July 2008, para. 359.
302 The role of the three actors (investor, host, and host state's population or representatives) is addressed by Kriebaum in Ursula Kriebaum, "Foreign Investments & Human Rights – The Actors and Their Different Roles," *Transnational Dispute Management (TDM)* 10, no. 1 (2013), available at <http://www.transnational-dispute-management.com/article.asp?key=1925>.

an investment and triggering the duty to compensate the investor. Furthermore, host states may invoke human rights as a defence in investment claims.

In the relationship between the individual/community and the investor, human rights might be an issue in terms of the form of obligations imposed on an investor in the national law of the host state, e.g. requirements relating to health, safety and working conditions for employees, or as voluntary commitments by the investor of corporate social responsibility.

In terms of the home state–investor relation, human rights may come up as a question of extraterritorial application of human rights encompassed in the national law of the host state,[303] or as the host state's enforcement of CSR commitments.[304]

HUMAN RIGHTS ARGUMENTS BY THE INVESTOR

When human rights issues have arisen in investment arbitrations it has most typically, at least to date, been in situations where human rights obligations of the host state have either been invoked by the investor or are used by arbitrators to help elucidate BIT obligations.[305] As explained, investors have claimed infringements of their investments with reference to the human right to protection of property.[306] Furthermore, investors have brought human rights arguments into play for their preferred interpretation of a given BIT obligation. Human rights analogies of due process and the conditions for expropriation are examples in this regard. More rarely, investors have argued that arbitrators in an ICSID claim had jurisdiction to examine whether human rights obligation found in other treaties such as the ECHR have been breached.[307]

---

303 See above Chapter 4, section 24.1.1.
304 See for example the recently established Danish Mediation and Complaints Handling Institution for Responsible Business Conduct, <http://www.businessconduct.dk/>.
305 Reiner and Schreuer, "Human Rights and International Investment Arbitration," 88. See also Peterson, "Human Rights and Bilateral Investment Treaties," 23.
306 See Chapter 4, section 21.
307 *Spyridon Roussalis v Romania*, Award, 7 December 2011. Article 10 of the Greece–Romania BIT provided that *"[i]f the provisions of law of either Contracting Party or obligations under international law existing at present or established hereafter between the Contracting Parties in addition to this Agreement, contain a regulation, whether general or specific, entitling investments by investors of the other Contracting Party to a treatment more favourable than is provided for by this Agreement, such regulation shall to the extent that it is more favourable, prevail over this Agreement"*. The tribunal did not exclude the possibility that international obligations of the contracting states could include obligations deriving from the ECHR and its Additional Protocol 1, but the issue was considered 'moot' in the present case and did not require decision by the tribunal, *"given the higher and more specific level of protection offered by the BIT to the investors compared to the more general protections offered to them by the human rights instruments"*. Consequently, article 10 of the BIT could not serve as an instrument for enlarging the protections available to the claimant from the Romanian state under the BIT: see para. 312.

Investors have also used human rights institutions, such as the ECtHR, to initiate claims of infringement of their human right to protection of property. Investors thus sometimes commence human rights claims before the ECtHR either as an alternative for, or in addition to, investment treaty claims initiated against a host government.[308]

HUMAN RIGHTS ARGUMENTS BY THE HOST STATE

In recent times, states hosting foreign investments have begun to invoke human rights obligations aiming to rebut allegations that they have mistreated a foreign investor. Apart from invoking human rights in the relation between a host state and an investor, human rights have also been invoked by host states on a more general basis as establishing an emergency situation or a state of necessity (*ordre public*) as a circumstance precluding wrongfulness. This was what the Argentine government did (in vain) in the mass claim situation by foreign investors in the wake of the 2000–2001 financial crisis. In the light of the global financial situation it is likely that other states, e.g. Greece, will face similar claims.

Drawing on the human rights concept of the margin of appreciation, host states have argued that tribunals should show restraint in assessing regulatory measures. Yet, tribunals have taken divergent positions in this regard. Some tribunals have plainly denied the application of a margin of appreciation doctrine. For example, the arbitral tribunal in *Siemens v Argentina* expressed the view that a margin of appreciation permitted in Protocol 1 of the ECHR was not to be accorded under the BIT in question.[309] In *Biwater Gauff v Tanzania*, the government of Tanzania claimed that the measures were within the margin of appreciation under international law.[310] However, the tribunal did not give its opinion on this view but referred to the acts as *"clearly the exercise of sovereign executive authority"*.[311] Other tribunals, however, have explicitly allowed for a margin of appreciation. In *Continental Casualty v Argentina* the American-based investor, Continental Casualty had initiated arbitration against Argentina under the United States–Argentina BIT, alleging that certain emergency measures taken in response to the financial crisis had violated standards of protection in the BIT. Continental Casualty owned one of Argentina's major insurance companies that provided workplace compensation insurance. In this case the tribunal held that the extreme social and economic crisis provided sufficient justification for the government's

---

308 See e.g. the case of the investors in the Russian Oil company, Yukos, who have pursued investment treaty claims (Permanent Court of Arbitration, UNCITRAL rules on the basis of the Energy Charter Treaty) as well as claims before the ECtHR (*Yukos v Russia*, no. 14902/04, 29 January 2009, where the ECtHR declared the case admissible and Final Judgment, no. 14902/04, 8 March 2012).

309 *Siemens v Argentina,* Award, 6 February 2007, para. 354. The BIT concerned was the BIT between Germany and Argentina.

310 *Biwater Gauff (Tanzania) Ltd. v Tanzania,* Award, 24 July 2008, para. 436.

311 *Ibid.*, para. 502.

acts.[312] In addition, the tribunal indicated that in applying emergency measures, states should be accorded a *"significant margin of appreciation"*.[313] Concerning the application of a margin of appreciation, the tribunal stated that a broader scope should be allowed in situations of emergency, including situations of financial crisis. In short, the tribunal concluded that *"a time of grave crisis is not the time for nice judgments, particularly when examined by others with the disadvantage of hindsight"*.[314] There is currently no general recognition by tribunals that such margin of appreciation should be allowed.

Human rights arguments may also be articulated by the host state as claims against the investor. As mentioned, the investor may be directly or indirectly involved in human rights violations. Yet, to date, states have not introduced (counter-) claims against investors for breaches of human rights. Instead, host states have relied on human rights considerations defensively to justify measures with adverse effects on the investment, arguing that their treatment of an investor was necessary to protect human rights commitments.[315]

It is argued that difference might be made to distinguish between normal times and times of economic and political turmoil.[316] However, the argument is less convincing when it comes to practical applicability. Sometimes economic and political turmoil emerge abruptly. On other occasions protracted conflicts, on-going tensions and instability for decades becomes the *de facto* 'normal times'. Anyhow, it may be difficult in practice to determine exactly when a state of economic and political turmoil occurred, especially when there is no official proclamation of a state of emergency.

For counterclaims, there may be a potential for host states, particularly if clauses on CSR is 'hardened' either in the contract between the host state and the investor or in the substantive parts of the investment protection treaty, i.e. in the BIT.

---

312 *Continental Casualty Company v Argentina*, Award, 5 September 2008, para 180. The tribunal held: *"It is impossible to deny, in the Tribunal's view, that a crisis that brought about the sudden and chaotic abandonment of the cardinal tenet of the country's economic life, such as the fixed convertibility rate which had been steadfastly recommended and supported for more than a decade by the IMF and the international community; the near collapse of the domestic economy; the soaring inflation; the leap in unemployment; the social hardships bringing down more than half of the population below the poverty line; the immediate threats to the health of young children, the sick and the most vulnerable members of the population, the widespread unrest and disorders; the real risk of insurrection and extreme political disturbances, the abrupt resignations of successive Presidents and the collapse of the Government, together with a partial breakdown of the political institutions and an extended vacuum of power; the resort to emergency legislation granting extraordinary legislative powers to the executive branch, that all of this, taken together, does not qualify as a situation where the maintenance of public order and the protection of essential security interest of Argentina as a state and as a country was vitally at stake."*

313 *Continental Casualty Company v Argentina*, Award, 5 September 2008, para. 181.

314 *Ibid.*

315 Kriebaum, "Foreign Investments & Human Rights – The Actors and Their Different Roles," 6–9; Reiner and Schreuer, "Human Rights and International Investment Arbitration," 89.

316 Taillant and Bonnitcha, "International Investment Law and Human Rights," 61.

HUMAN RIGHTS ARGUMENTS BY THIRD PARTIES

Human rights claims have not been limited to the two parties to the disputes. Third parties, who urge to have their voices heard, have filed so-called *amicus curia* submissions.[317] *Amicus curiae* submissions are representing the voice of the public and may sometimes be relevant to ensure that investment tribunals take into account the broader implications. Third party interventions may supplement arguments by the host states but may also bring new issues into the light. It may also be that host states – for several reasons – chose not to invoke human rights considerations, for example due to the fear of political reprisals, acknowledging obligations for themselves in other settings or due to complicity in human rights violations by the investor. Allowing third party interventions in investor–state disputes increases transparency, promotes accountability and enhances the perceived legitimacy of the system.

Pursuant to the ICSID Arbitration Rules, rule 37, a tribunal may – after consulting the parties[318] – allow a person or entity that is not a party to the dispute, for instance an NGO, to file a written submission regarding a matter within the scope of the dispute. For the determination of whether to admit *amici* interventions the tribunal should consider inter alia:[319]

- if the non-disputing party submission would assist the tribunal in the determination of a factual or legal issue related to the proceeding by bringing a perspective, particular knowledge or insight that is different from that of the disputing parties;
- whether the non-disputing party submission would address a matter within the scope of the dispute; and
- whether the non-disputing party has a significant interest in the proceeding.

The permission of *amici* interventions does not entitle the non-disputing party to any procedural rights and privilege.[320] Rather it is a specific and defined opportunity to make a particular submission.

---

317 *Amicus curia* means 'friend of the court'. At the international level *amicus curiae* submissions have been accepted in various courts such as the ECtHR, the European Court of Justice (ECJ) and within the WTO Dispute Settlement Body. See also Reiner and Schreuer, "Human Rights and International Investment Arbitration," 90–3; James Harrison, "Human Rights Arguments in "Amicus Curiae" Submissions: Promoting Social Justice?," in *Human Rights in International Investment Law and Arbitration*, ed. Pierre-Marie Dupuy, Ernst-Ulrich Petersmann, and Francesco Francioni, International Economic Law Series (Oxford: Oxford University Press, 2009), 396–421; Bernasconi-Osterwalder, "Transparency and Amicus Curiae in ICSID Arbitrations," 191–207.

318 Hence, it is not a precondition that the parties consent.

319 ICSID Arbitration Rules, rule 37(2).

320 *Biwater Gauff (Tanzania) Ltd. v Tanzania*, Procedural Order No. 5, 2 February 2007, para. 47.

In the aforementioned case of *Biwater Gauff v Tanzania*, the tribunal allowed the *amici* intervention of an NGO, which was able to support the tribunal *"with specialized interests and expertise in human rights, environmental and good governance issues"*.[321] Additionally, the tribunal stressed the public interest dimension of the dispute and the increase in transparency.[322]

In the case of *Piero Foresti, Laura de Carli and others v South Africa*[323] an ICSID tribunal for the first time granted *amicus* organizations access to the parties' documents despite the objections of a party.[324] The desirability of *amicus curiae* admissions may diverge depending on the issue at dispute[325] and the character of the third party concerned. An ICSID tribunal in 2012 for example adopted a very restrictive view on the *amicus curiae* admissions and held that the third party petitioners were *"not independent"* of, or *"neutral"* towards, the two disputing parties, and *"would not offer anything of relevance within the scope of the ICSID proceedings"*.[326] In cases where the measure claimed to be an interference with the investment is a general policy measure, there is likely to be weighty reasons for allowing *amici* interventions.

FUTURE DEVELOPMENTS?

If human rights have come up it has been an issue raised by one of the parties to the dispute or more recently by third parties in *amicus briefs* interventions highlighting public interest, but not *ex officio* by the arbitral tribunal. This is in line with the fundamental nature of arbitration, where the arbitrators largely rely on an adversarial system.[327] Due to the increasing developments in soft law

---

321 *Ibid.*, para. 20 and *Biwater Gauff (Tanzania) Ltd. v Tanzania*, Award, 24 July 2008, para. 359. See also Bernasconi-Osterwalder, "Transparency and Amicus Curiae in ICSID Arbitrations," 191–207.

322 Referring to *Suez, Sociedad General de Aguas de Barcelona, S.A. and Vivendi Universal, S.A. v Argentina*, Order in Response to a Petition by Five Non-Governmental Organizations for Permission to make an *amicus curiae* Submission, 12 February 2007, see *Biwater Gauff (Tanzania) Ltd. v Tanzania*, Procedural Order No. 5, 2007, para. 52.

323 *Piero Foresti, Laura de Carli and Others v South Africa*.

324 *Piero Foresti, Laura de Carli and Others v South Africa*, Letter Regarding Non-Disputing Parties, 5 October 2009. The tribunal acted under a slightly different framework as in the case of *Biwater Gauff v Tanzania* since the arbitration in *Piero Foresti, Laura de Carli and others v South Africa* was governed by the ICSID Additional Facility Rules. Yet, the wording of rule 41(3) of the ICSID Additional Facility Rules is identical to that of rule 37(2).

325 See further James Harrison, "Human Rights Arguments in 'Amicus Curiae' Submissions," 396–421.

326 *Bernhard von Pezold v Zimbabwe*, Procedural Order No. 2, 26 June 2012 and *Border Timbers Limited v Zimbabwe*, Procedural Order No. 2, 26 June 2012. The two identical tribunals denied admission of *amicus curiae* submissions of the European Center for Constitutional and Human Rights (ECCHR) and a group of indigenous communities in Zimbabwe in two joined cases brought by foreign investors against Zimbabwe, see also <http://www.ecchr.de/index.php/home_en.html>.

327 On adversarial approaches to litigation in civil procedure in general see John Anthony Jolowicz, *On Civil Procedure*, ed. James Crawford and John S. Bell, 1st ed., vol. 13,

instruments emphasizing a duty for investors to demonstrate human rights commitments, it is likely that investment arbitration have merely faced the first tentative beginnings of the enunciation of human rights arguments. Home states may increasingly take on board the task to enforce human rights extraterritorially through the investor's duty to respect human rights. The promotion of transparency in investment disputes and the associated willingness of (some) arbitrators to consider legal arguments from third parties in *amicus briefs* may give rise to a growing number of interventions by third parties bringing in human rights evidence or human rights legal argumentation into certain investment disputes.[328] By allowing *amici* submissions tribunals thus recognize and affirm the public interest in an investor–state dispute. Moreover, human rights concerns have gradually been inflicted directly upon arbitrators through institutional procedures to promote transparency.[329]

It is likely that the more recent developments, where human rights have paved their way into investment treaty arbitrations, show only the tip of the iceberg. Human rights arguments may potentially advance even further in future investor–state disputes, in particular as arguments for limiting investment protection and/or lowering compensation. The contextual elements and trends in policy-making highlighted in Chapter 3 support this view. In essence, foreign corporations investing in long-term projects are more and more considered having *"the highest level of responsibility to meet their duties and obligations as foreign investors, before seeking the protection of international law"*.[330] Foreign investor should therefore carry out human rights due diligence before initiating an investment claim for human rights related regulation. This view supports the unification perspective on international law. On the treaty level, contracting states may to a significant degree seek to include human rights references, directly or more indirectly, though this is currently not a general tendency.

The reservation by arbitrators toward engaging in human rights concerns is largely founded in the arbitral nature of the investment dispute settlement system. Yet, there are several ways for human rights arguments to enter investment dispute arbitration, even when not raised by the parties to the dispute. Human rights could be taken into account as part of the applicable law but also on the basis of more general theoretical considerations of a unification of international law.[331]

Cambridge Studies in International and Comparative Law (Cambridge: Cambridge University Press, 2000), 175–82.

328 See also UNCTAD, *Selected Recent Developments in IIA Arbitration and Human Rights*, IIA Monitor no. 2, 2009, UNCTAD/WEB/DIAE/IA/2009/7.

329 Under the UNCITRAL framework a working group has drafted a proposal of new UNCITRAL rules for greater transparency in investor–state disputes; see <http://www.uncitral.org/uncitral/en/commission/working_groups/2Arbitration.html>.

330 *Biwater Gauff (Tanzania) Ltd. v Tanzania*, Award, 24 July 2008, para. 380.

331 See further below, Chapter 5.

10. Preliminary conclusion

With the development of human rights post-World War II the concept of human rights also changed the perception of sovereignty by linking sovereignty with the will of the people, the community interests. Chapter 4 of this research has shown how investments are protected as the human rights to property protection. This part has also shown how the right to regulate sometimes may become a duty to regulate under the human rights regime concerning the obligations to implement human rights. In particular, it appears that under the ICESCR, states have a duty to make certain minimum policy prioritizations. Developments in the human rights regime have also led to new perceptions of the corporate actor, where corporations are bound by moral or non-legally binding obligations to demonstrate social responsibility, particularly on the basis of privatizations when tasked with core social functions such as providing facilities or fundamental services to the population. Human rights have as yet only been sporadically referred to in IIAs such as BITs. Nonetheless, practice in investment disputes shows that human rights issues do come up in investment arbitration. While human rights may be the basis for interfering with the investments of foreign investors, investments are also protected by the human rights regime in the form of protection of property.

The concept of human rights in international investment arbitration is a broad concept covering human rights on both sides of the disputes, raised by the parties to the dispute or by non-disputing parties. Human rights arguments are increasingly invoked by third parties, especially with regards to investment claims where the interference is based on regulatory measures. This tendency represents a more general concern by the international society that investment protection is detrimental to host states' ability to exercise their duty to regulate or – beyond that – to raise human rights standards.

5 The case-study of expropriation claims in international investment law and investment arbitration

1. Introduction

The primary aim of Chapter 5 is to provide clarification for defining the scope of the right to regulate. Chapter 5 will thus 'measure the regulatory space' of host states in order to determine whether there are some types of regulation that enjoy preferential treatment. Accordingly, the task is to distinguish compensable from non-compensable regulation. This task is carried out on the basis of a case-study of expropriation claims.

The research question addressed is whether regulatory measures constitute an exception from the normal operation of an expropriation doctrine in the sense that states should not pay compensation for regulatory measures. If regulatory measures do not constitute such general exception, the task is to determine if, nevertheless, there are certain circumstances – or types of regulation – that are granted preferential treatment, i.e. are presumed to be non-compensable. The analysis of how to distinguish compensable from non-compensable regulation may provide input to the solution of the more overall stability–flexibility dilemma of international investment law. In other words, this part seeks to come up with suggestions for a more unified approach to the law in the form of a balanced interpretation of the expropriation standard.

This part initially explains the concept of indirect expropriations. Subsequently, the distinction between compensable and non-compensable regulation is addressed on the basis of an analysis of BITs and arbitral practice. A general, clear-cut distinction between compensable and non-compensable regulation is not viable. Nevertheless, determinative factors can be deduced from BITs and arbitral practice. The expectations of the investor are of vital importance in arbitral practice. Hence, the concept of legitimate expectations is dealt with, focusing on the determination of the implications for the right to regulate.

Chapter 5 also explores how policy issues have paved their way into arbitral practice. By applying the theoretical approach of the gravitational pull explained in Chapter 2, it will become more clear what factors should be taken into account as contextual elements for interpreting the substantive provisions. This includes human rights obligations addressed in Chapter 4 and international policy trends addressed in Chapter 3. Accordingly, this chapter contains considerations *de lege lata* as well as suggestions *de lege ferenda*.

2. Forum for arbitration – ICSID as a preferred venue

The number of investment disputes has been increasing.[1] Most commonly, cases are brought against developing or transition economies,[2] and initiated by investors from developed countries.[3]

BITs typically contain various venues for solving investment disputes. Most BITs contain an access to settlement of investment disputes at the International Centre for Settlement of Investment Disputes (ICSID), the autonomous institution of the World Bank Group established in 1966 under the Convention on the Settlement of Investment Disputes between States and Nationals of Other States (the ICSID Convention). The case is initiated by the private investor requesting arbitration.[4] When investment arbitration is commenced the home state is left behind.[5] ICSID awards are binding and final and not subject to review, except under the narrow conditions provided by the ICSID Convention itself in articles 49–52.

Investment arbitration may also take place in other fora, and a variety of rules and institutions exist, such as the International Court of Arbitration under the International Chamber of Commerce (ICC), the Permanent Court of Arbitration, the London Court of International Arbitration, or the Stockholm Chamber of Commerce, which increasingly serves as an institutional venue for arbitration in investment disputes.[6] The focus of the expropriation case-study is limited to ICSID cases, since it appears as the most transparent system. Though with some limitations arbitration under the ICSID allows for third party interventions and many awards are publicly available.[7]

3. Conceptual challenges to 'expropriation'

For clarifying purposes some of the main terms should be explained. It is not only helpful but also necessary to make theoretical distinctions. In arbitral practice, however, the legal terms do not always strictly follow these categorizations. The

---

1 At least 46 new cases were initiated in 2011, constituting the highest number of known treaty-based disputes ever filed in one year, cf. "Latest Developments in Investor–State Dispute Settlement," UNCTAD, no. 1, April 2012.

2 38 out of 46 new cases according to UNCTAD; cf. "Latest Developments in Investor–State dispute settlement," UNCTAD, no. 1, April 2012, p. 2.

3 35 of the 46 new cases were filed by investors from developed countries according to UNCTAD, cf. "Latest Developments in Investor–State Dispute Settlement," UNCTAD, no. 1, April 2012, p. 2.

4 ICSID Convention article 36.

5 The right of the home state to exercise diplomatic protection is suspended but can be regained for instance if the investor decides to withdraw the claim or a later stage with regards to the enforcement of the right; cf. ICSID Convention article 27(1) *in fine*. See also Dolzer and Schreuer, *Principles of International Investment Law*, 238–9.

6 Dolzer and Schreuer, *Principles of International Investment Law*, 242–4.

7 Awards are not published automatically. ICSID publishes awards only if both parties agree. However, the parties are free to release awards and other decisions, e.g. at a company's webpage, unless it is otherwise agreed.

term *'expropriation'* refers to a state's taking of property – something of value – away from its owner.[8] The terms *'direct expropriation'* and *'indirect expropriation'* have been referred to above, the latter being the most relevant in practice today. Where the expression 'expropriation' is used in the following (without referring to whether it is a direct or indirect expropriation), it refers to both of these concepts taken together as an overarching expression. Both direct and indirect expropriations require compensation. The difference between direct and indirect expropriation consists in whether the legal title of the owner is affected or not, i.e. whether there has been a cease or transfer of ownership. In terms of indirect expropriation the investor is deprived *utility* or the *value* of the investment is undermined to such an extent by the governmental action as to deprive the investor of the reasonably expected benefits of the investment. The definition of indirect expropriation is controversial, but is further explained below. In terms of interferences these are often described as *'takings'*. So, 'measures', 'interferences' and 'takings' are all referring to actions by the host state that somehow affect the investor or the investment, however, with no legal qualification of whether the action is an expropriation or not. For the purpose of this research, a taking does not in itself contain any assessment as to whether the interference qualifies as an expropriation. Indirect expropriations cover various forms of expropriations such as *'regulatory expropriations'* and *'creeping expropriations'*. Regulatory expropriations are regulatory measures, interferences or takings typically based on new onerous legislation that reaches the threshold of the requirement to compensate. Regulation is considered 'onerous' when it contains an economic burden to the investor or a burden that has economic consequences to the value of the investment. Conversely, *'regulatory takings'* do not contain any qualification as to whether the taking amounts to expropriation but is merely referring to a taking that has its basis in regulation. Another term used below is the term *'police powers'*, which refers to the fact that states as sovereigns under international law can use their police powers to regulate.

Since the requirement to compensate is considered a prerequisite for the legality of expropriations, all expropriations – independently of how they are referred to – will be considered compensable. The distinction between *'compensable'* and *'non-compensable'* regulation thus refers to regulatory takings, which may or may not amount to expropriation. In this context, *'measuring the scope of the right to regulate'* thus refers to the question of whether imposed regulation triggers compensation or not. It is this distinction that is critical to the case-study of expropriation claims below.

4. Protected investment

Before examining the scope for intervening in protected investments it is a prerequisite to explain what is the subject protected against expropriations.

---

8 Krista Nadakavukaren Schefer, *International Investment Law: Text, Cases and Materials*, 1st ed. (Cheltenham: Edward Elgar Publishing, 2013), 168.

This question relates to the definition of an 'investment', the *ratione materiae* of an investment dispute. Whereas general international law has typically referred to the protection of 'property, rights and interests'[9] and human rights treaties to 'property', the term 'investment' in BITs often covers a broad range of interests, including intangible assets of economic value. Accordingly, investments that may be expropriated by states also comprise immaterial rights and interest, such as contractual rights. Generally, two approaches can be identified in BITs, the 'illustrative approach' with an open-ended list containing examples of investment or the 'closed list approach' with an exhaustive list of investments. The closed list approach has been adopted in only few BITs. The illustrative list typically includes five categories of assets that fall within the definition of investment.[10] A sixth category appears in some BITs.

First category typically includes:	Moveable and immovable property.[11] (For example land, facilities, equipment) Interests in property. (For example mortgages, liens, pledges and leases) Some BITs refers to tangible and intangible property, which is equally meant to include all forms of property.
Second category typically includes:	Companies and interests in companies, both debt and equity interests.[12] BITs rarely require the interest may be a controlling one. The language nearly

9 Dolzer and Schreuer, *Principles of International Investment Law*, 60.
10 The list is often redundant in places, with some assets belonging to more than one category. For instance, intellectual property rights in the third category are typically embraced within the first category as well. However, this technique is useful because it ensures particular attention to protection accorded to this form of property. The five categories are further explained in Vandevelde, *Bilateral Investment Treaties*, 122–57. For the definition of investment see also Engela C. Schlemmer, "Investment, Investor, Nationality, and Shareholders," in *The Oxford Handbook of International Investment Law*, ed. Peter Muchlinski, Federico Ortino, and Christoph Schreuer (Oxford: Oxford University Press, 2008), 51–69; Dolzer and Schreuer, *Principles of International Investment Law*, 60–8, 248; Mclachlan et al., *International Investment Arbitration*, 163–96.
11 E.g. Burkina Faso–Chad BIT, article 1(a); Belgium and Luxembourg–Algeria BIT, article 2(a), United States of America–Ecuador BIT, article 1(a)(i); Finland–Armenia BIT, article 1(1)(a).
12 E.g. Germany–Botswana BIT, article 1(b); Sweden–Pakistan BIT, article 1(b); Denmark–Egypt BIT, article 1(ii); El Salvador–Nicaragua BIT, article 1(a); United States of America–Ecuador BIT, article 1(a)(ii); Netherlands–Ethiopia BIT, article 1(a)(iv); Switzerland–Algeria BIT, article 1(2)(d); United Kingdom–Sierra Leone BIT, article 1(iii).

	always is broad enough to include direct and portfolio investment.
Third category typically includes:	Intellectual property rights.[13] (For example patents, copyrights, trademarks and trade secrets) Some BITs explicitly include goodwill and many include know-how.
Fourth category typically includes:	Claims to money as well as claims to performance having an economic value.[14] This category demonstrates that the definition includes not only property rights but also contractual rights.
Fifth category typically includes:	Concessions, a particular form of contracts rights.[15]
Sixth category typically includes:	Licences and permits.[16] This category appears only in a smaller number of BITs.

The typical BIT imposes actually only one condition for an asset to gain treaty protection, namely the asset must be foreign-owned or controlled.[17] Many definitions entail the assumption of risk.[18] By definition then, an investment may fail, but the fact that it failed does not make it less of an investment. Above all, BITs promote the movement of control over capital rather than the movement of the capital itself. Change in the form of an investment, e.g. change in organizational form or corporate structure of an investment, does not affect its character as an investment. In addition, if ICSID is chosen as the venue of arbitration, there has to be an 'investment', as defined by article 25 of the ICSID Convention. However, article 25 of the ICSID Convention refers to *"any legal dispute arising directly out of an investment"*, without clarifying the concept of an investment.[19] The most common perception of the definition of a direct investment involves 1) substantial commitment; 2) a certain duration; 3) assumption of business risk; 4) significance

---

13 E.g. El Salvador–Nicaragua BIT, article 1(d); Denmark–Egypt BIT, article 1(iv); United Kingdom–Sierra Leone BIT, article 1(iv); Italy–Nicaragua BIT, article 1(1)(d); Thailand–Indonesia BIT, article 1(d).

14 E.g. Sweden–Pakistan BIT, article i(c), Denmark–Egypt BIT, article 1(iii); Russia–Greece BIT, article 2(c); Austria–Armenia BIT, article 1(2)(e); Belgium and Luxembourg–Algeria BIT, article 2(c).

15 E.g. Germany–Botswana BIT, article 1(e); Denmark–Egypt BIT, article 1(v); Hungary–India BIT, article 1(e); Thailand–Indonesia BIT, article 1(e).

16 E.g. Egypt–Zambia BIT, article 1(1)(e).

17 Vandevelde, *Bilateral Investment Treaties*, 129.

18 *Ibid.*

19 Further on the definition of an investment pursuant to article 25 of the ICSID Convention see Dolzer and Schreuer, *Principles of International Investment Law*, 65–78.

for the host state's development.[20] Defined negatively, an investment does not cover sale of goods or services, portfolio investment (no management) or short-term financial transactions. Controversy has particularly centred on development as a criterion[21] and the fundamental contention that investment may sometimes not deserve protection due to the case of fraud or corruption. For the purpose of this expropriation case-study, protected investment should be understood as covering a broad range of economic activities, including protected rights pursuant to contractual undertakings, concessions and licences with a contractual or quasi-contractual nature. In terms of contractual undertakings, it will be demonstrated that the standard of expropriation becomes rather a protection of the investor's legitimate expectations.

5. Expropriation in international investment law

In general international law expropriation is not unlawful per se but subject to certain conditions.[22] Likewise, the paradigm of international investment law allows for states to expropriate foreign investments, provided that certain conditions are fulfilled. Most BITs do not explicitly articulate a rule allowing states to expropriate foreign investments but lay down the conditions hereof, thereby implicitly recognizing the rule under customary international law that states as sovereigns may interfere with foreign property rights.

5.1. *The legality of the expropriation*

The four requirements generally recognized in BITs as conditions for the legality of an expropriation are:

- that an expropriation must be for a *"public benefit"*, *"public purpose"* or *"social interest"*;[23]
- *"non-discriminatory"*;[24]

---

20 *Salini v Morocco*, Decision on Jurisdiction, 23 July 2001, para. 52.
21 See e.g. *LESI & ASTALDI v Algeria*, Decision on Jurisdiction, 12 July 2006, para. 72, where the tribunal finds that the promotion of the host state's economy is not a requirement.
22 See Chapter 2, section 6.4 and Chapter 3, section 4.2.
23 E.g. US Model BIT (2012), article 6(1)(a); German Model BIT (2008), article 4(2); Columbian Model BIT (2007), article VI(1); Indian Model BIT (2003), article 5(1); Italy–Morocco BIT, article 5(2); Australia–Lithuania BIT, article 7(1)(a); Finland–Algeria BIT, article 4(1); Switzerland–Benin BIT, article 8; Canada–Russia BIT, article VI.
24 E.g. US Model BIT (2012), article 6(1)(b); Columbian Model BIT (2007), article VI(1); Indian Model BIT (2003), article 5(1); Italy–Morocco BIT, article 5 (2); Australia–Lithuania BIT, article 7(1)(b); Finland–Algeria BIT, article 4(1); Switzerland–Benin BIT, article 8; Canada–Russia BIT, article VI.

- *"in accordance with due process of law"*[25]
- and followed by *"prompt, adequate and effective"* compensation.[26]

This is the most common approach to expropriation found in BITs, although these four conditions do not appear in all BITs.[27] Furthermore, some BITs may include additional requirements.[28]

The requirement of public interest prevents, for example, a taking of property for the private use of a dictator. However, this requirement is rarely raised in investment disputes when alleging expropriation. In the case of *Siemens v Argentina*,[29] the tribunal did touch upon the lack of public purpose (e.g. the permanent suspension of printing identity cards, and the forced contract changes by the government of Argentina), but in any case, due to the failure to grant compensation, the investor had a viable claim.

The requirement of non-discrimination prevents states from treating foreign nationals in a less preferential manner than nationals in cases of expropriation. This requirement reflects the general principle not to discriminate as found throughout the BIT, namely in the requirement of national treatment and MFN treatment.

The requirement of due process of law adds additional protection compared to due process in national law and is thus an international law standard of due process. This includes notice, a fair hearing and non-arbitrariness.

The requirement of compensation to be 'prompt' is usually described in BITs as a requirement to pay 'without delay' or 'without undue delay' or with references to payment to be made at or prior to the time of which the expropriation occurs. 'Adequate' compensation generally means that the compensation must be the full value of the investment, i.e. the fair market value of the investment. Whereas some BITs use the term 'adequate', others use the terms 'just' or 'full' compensation but these words seem to be synonyms. In terms of assessing the fair market value a number of methods exist.[30] The requirement that compensation must be 'effective' is aimed at ensuring that the investor is able to make use of the benefit of the compensation by requiring compensation to be paid in freely convertible currency, i.e. a currency that is exchanged on the principal

---

25 E.g. US Model BIT (2012), article 6(1)(d); Columbian Model BIT (2007), article VI(1); Australia–Lithuania BIT, article 7(1)(a); Finland–Algeria BIT, article 4(1); Canada–Russia BIT, article VI.

26 E.g. US Model BIT (2012), article 6(1)(c); German Model BIT (2008), article 4(2); Indian Model BIT (2003), article 5(1); Italy–Morocco BIT, article 5(2); Australia–Lithuania BIT, article 7(1)(c); Finland–Algeria BIT, article 4(1); Switzerland–Benin BIT, article 8; Canada–Russia BIT, article VI.

27 The due process requirement is not always explicitly mentioned.

28 For instance, the Columbian Model BIT adds 'good faith'; see the Columbian Model BIT (2007), article VI(1).

29 *Siemens v Argentina*, Award, 17 January 2007.

30 Vandevelde, *Bilateral Investment Treaties*, 274.

foreign exchange markets of the world.[31] Accordingly, the *Hull Formula* has been considered the applicable standard, even without a clear stipulation in the treaty. For instance, in *CME v Czech Republic*[32] article 5(c) of the BIT between the Netherlands and the Czech Republic merely provided for payment of *"just compensation"*, equivalent to the *"genuine value"* of the investment taken:[33]

> *"[T]he measures are accompanied by provision for the payment of just compensation.*
> *Such compensation shall represent the genuine value of the investments affected and shall, in order to be effective for the claimants, be paid and made transferable, without undue delay, to the country designated by the claimants concerned and in any freely convertible currency accepted by the claimants."*

However, the majority of the tribunal emphasized that this had to be interpreted as a strict requirement of fair market value in accordance with the Hull Formula.

5.2. The concept of indirect expropriation

Though the wording may vary, most IIAs recognize both a concept of 'direct' and 'indirect' expropriation. For example, article 1110 of the NAFTA refers to *"directly or indirectly"* nationalizations or expropriations as well as *"measures tantamount to nationalization or expropriation"*. Equivalent formulations are found in the Energy Charter Treaty, which in article 13 refers to *"nationalization or expropriation"* as well as *"measures having effect equivalent to nationalization or expropriation"*.

Likewise, most BITs recognize the concepts of direct as well as indirect expropriation. For example, India's Model BIT from 2003 states in article 5 that investment of investors of either contracting party *"shall not be nationalised, expropriated or subjected to measures having effect equivalent to nationalisation or expropriation"*. Article 4(2) of the German Model BIT from 2008 states that investments *"may not directly or indirectly be expropriated, nationalized or subjected to any other measure the effects of which would be tantamount to expropriation or nationalization"* unless the conditions referred to above are fulfilled. The 2012 US Model BIT prohibits the contracting parties to *"expropriate or nationalize a covered investment either directly or indirectly through measures equivalent to expropriation or nationalization"*, except when the conditions are complied with.

Other concrete examples are e.g. the BIT between Denmark and Algeria that states in article 5(1) that investments *"shall not be nationalized, expropriated or subject to measures having effect equivalent to nationalisation or expropriation"*. An equivalent formulation is found for instance in article 5(1) in the BIT between

---

31 *Ibid.*, p. 276; Schefer, *International Investment Law*, 189.
32 *CME Czech Republic BV v Czech Republic*, Final Award, 2003.
33 *Ibid.*, para 496–7.

United Kingdom and Bangladesh. The BIT between Switzerland and Ecuador refers in article 3 to *"des mesures d'expropriation, de nationalisation ou de dépossession, directes ou indirectes"*. A slightly different wording can be found in the BIT between Switzerland and Lebanon referring in article 4 to *"directly or indirectly, measures of expropriation, nationalization or any other measures having the same nature or the same effect against investments of investors"*. The BIT between Germany and Bosnia–Herzegovina refers in article 4 to *"directly or indirectly expropriated, nationalized or subject to any other measure the effects of which would be tantamount to expropriation or nationalization"*.

Direct expropriations or nationalizations have become relatively rare owing to the fact that direct expropriation appears to be a drastic step and a severe measure, which gives rise to negative publicity with possibly adverse impact on the investment climate.[34] An example of a direct expropriation is the 1979 Iranian nationalization of banks and insurance companies that gave rise to a number of cases brought before the Iran–US Claims Tribunal. Developments in Bolivia and Venezuela concerning governmental plans to expropriate foreign investors in the energy sector constitute examples of direct expropriations as the exceptions confirming the rule of rarity.

The concept of indirect expropriation is referred to in most BITs with references to measures 'tantamount to', 'equivalent to' or having 'the same effect' as expropriation thereby pointing to an assessment of the actual effects, typically without mentioning the intentions of the state. In general, BITs provide little guidance to arbitral tribunals as to the definition of indirect expropriation. A genuine attempt to clarify the scope was made in *Tecmed v Mexico*,[35] where the investor, Tecmed, claimed that the denial of renewal of a licence to operate a landfill amounted to expropriation. Relying on a general understanding of the terms *"equivalent to expropriation"* or *"tantamount to expropriation"* the tribunal found it to refer to *"indirect expropriation"* or *"creeping expropriation"*, as well as to *de facto* expropriation.[36] According to the tribunal, the general understanding of these forms of expropriation was that *"they materialize through actions or conduct, which do not explicitly express the purpose of depriving one of rights or assets, but actually have that effect"*. In addition, the tribunal explained the concept of creeping expropriation as a special type of indirect expropriation. Indirect expropriation *"may be carried out through a single action, through a series of actions in a short period of time or through simultaneous actions"*.

To determine whether an indirect expropriation has occurred, the measures imposed have to be examined on a case-by-case basis. In *Parkerings-Compagniet AS v Lithuania*[37] indirect expropriation was explained as the negative effect of governmental measures on the investor's property rights, which does not

---

34 Dolzer and Schreuer, *Principles of International Investment Law*, 101; Salacuse, *The Law of Investment Treaties*, 297f.
35 *Técnicas Medioambientales (TECMED) v Mexico*, ICSID Award, 29 May 2003.
36 *Ibid.*, para 114.
37 *Parkerings-Compagniet AS v Lithuania*, Award, 12 October 2005.

involve a transfer of property but a deprivation of the enjoyment of the proper-ty.[38] Salacuse mentions interferences with contractual rights, disproportionate tax increases, and unjustified interference with the management of the investment and the revocation or denial of government permits or licences as typical types of governmental measures, which may constitute indirect expropriation.[39] Regula-tion, onerous to the investor, may fall within the ambit of indirect expropriations if the effects are 'equivalent to' a direct expropriation.

Since the most common factual situation of taking of property today has switched from physical direct deprivations to indirect or creeping measures hav-ing equivalent effects, it could be expected that BITs would increasingly address the question of indirect expropriation. However, this has yet not been the case.

6. The challenge of today: Regulatory measures and indirect expropriation

Claims of indirect expropriation initiated within the last years display an increasing desire among investors to test regulatory measures. As earlier explained, the trend towards testing regulatory measures transpired in the context of the NAFTA. The investment claims initiated against Uruguay and Australia's tobacco-control legislation[40] as well as against Germany's nuclear phase-out[41] are notable exam-ples. Indeed, investments may be impaired for many reasons.

This is confirmed in arbitral practice where regulatory interferences cover a variety of measures, such as environmental policy,[42] urban policy,[43] monetary policy[44] and taxation.[45]

As a main rule, states do not incur responsibility for legitimate and *bona fide* exercise of certain types of basic regulation, such as general tax measures and security regulation. In *Feldman v Mexico*[46] a NAFTA tribunal recognized that governments must be free to act in the broader public interest through new or modified tax regimes.[47]

---

38 *Ibid.*, para. 437.
39 Salacuse, *The Law of Investment Treaties*, 300–7.
40 *Philip Morris v Uruguay*, initiated in March 2010 on the basis of the Switzerland–Uruguay BIT; *Philip Morris v Australia* (UNCITRAL), initiated in June 2011 at the Permanent Court of Arbitration under the UNCITRAL rules on the basis of the Australia–Hong Kong BIT.
41 *Vattenfall v Germany*. The case was brought under the ECT.
42 *Metalclad Corporation v Mexico*, Award, 30 August 2000; *Methanex Corporation v United States of America*, Final Award, 3 August 2005.
43 *MTD v Chile*, Award, 25 May 2004.
44 *CMS v Argentina*, Award, 12 May 2005.
45 *Occidental Exploration and Production Company v Ecuador*, Final Award, 1 July 2004.
46 *Feldman v Mexico*, Award, 16 December 2002.
47 *Ibid*, para. 103. See also Andrew Newcombe, "The Boundaries of Regulatory Expropriation in International Law," *ICSID Review* 20, no. 1 (2005): 1–57.

The existence of a legitimate public purpose is essential for the assessment of whether regulation can be viewed as non-compensable or amounts to an indirect expropriation. However, and most importantly, as the case-study reveals, the existence of a legitimate public purpose is not the only condition for regulation to be non-compensable. It still has to be measured against the severity of the interference vis-à-vis a concrete investor. As held by the tribunal in *ADC v Hungary* *"a sovereign state possesses the inherent right to regulate its domestic affairs".*[48] However, as the tribunal stated, *"the exercise of such right is not unlimited and must have its boundaries".*[49]

From the perspective of the foreign investor, regulatory measures can be designed in ways that have as severe an effect on the investment as a direct expropriation. From the perspective of the host state, regulatory measures could arguably be perceived either as exemptions to expropriation and thus not compensable, or as a mitigating factor to lower the amount of compensation.

7. Distinguishing compensable from non-compensable regulation

The following aims at determining the scope of the right to regulate. As a legal question, the determination of the scope of the right to regulate is concerned with establishing the distinction between compensable and non-compensable regulation. However, this distinction cannot be made on a general basis. What can be done on a general basis is to establish indicative factors for this distinction. The following therefore seeks to establish the indicative factors that elucidate when regulatory takings amount to an indirect expropriation. Initially, the question is analysed through an examination of a regional representative extract of model BITs and BITs. Hereafter, the question is addressed through the examination of expropriation claims in investment disputes. Accordingly, the more general question of establishing the scope of the right to regulate is answered on the basis of the more limited and concrete legal question. While acknowledging that there may be other ways to answer the more general question, the answer provided here in the form of indicative factors serves as a useful component to this question.

7.1. The distinction addressed in BITs

The examination of BITs shows that the vast majority of BITs and model BITs do not contain any references to a lower limit of regulatory measures that are non-compensable. Thus, there is no explicit recognition that states may adopt regulatory measures that do not call for compensation. Less do BITs provide any guidance on how to distinguish compensable from non-compensable regulation.

---

48 *ADC v Hungary*, Award, 2 October 2006, para. 423.
49 *Ibid.*

Yet, a notable trend in some BITs that entered into force within the new millennium is traceable. The reference to the notion that states may adopt *bona fide* regulation 'within their police power' has appeared in more recent investment protection treaties.[50] Though many of the more recently negotiated investment protection treaties follow the traditional approach and remain silent on this issue, the findings of BITs that actually address this question is noteworthy. The reason for this is that it exemplifies how major issues in policy discussions may evolve as legal rules in BITs. In other words, some states have chosen to address the policy issues dealt with above in Chapter 3 by articulating new legal rules in BITs. As will be demonstrated below, BITs that actually address non-compensable regulation have typically done this through the adoption of a *rule of presumption*, a *rule of interpretation* or a *rule of applicability*.

The BIT examination also reveals how policy considerations in some BITs articulated in the preamble, have evolved into substantive legal norms. For instance, in the BIT between the United States of America and Rwanda the preamble of the BIT refers to the *"protection of health, safety, the environment and promotion of labour rights"* as central policy concerns. In terms of indirect expropriations, three of these four concerns are articulated as substantive legal rules providing that non-discriminatory regulatory actions that are designed and applied to protect legitimate public welfare objectives, such as public 'health, safety, and the environment', only exceptionally constitute indirect expropriations.[51] Conversely, labour regulation is not considered an exceptional measure for cases of indirect expropriation. Another observation is that some BITs contain these policy concerns in the preamble without addressing the issue any further in the substantive parts of the treaty.[52]

Yet, the fact that BITs do not explicitly allow host states to adopt regulation does not mean that they cannot regulate. This is established in general international law as an inherent part of states' right to act in their sovereign capacities whereby not all interferences per se trigger the duty to compensate.[53] The fact

---

50 See for instance the Canadian Model BIT from 2004 and the US Model BIT from 2012. The police power doctrine is further explained below.

51 United States–Rwanda BIT, Annex B(4)(b).

52 E.g. the BIT between Finland and Kyrgyzstan from 2004, where the parties in the preamble agrees that *"a stable framework for investment will contribute to improving the effective utilisation of economic resources and increase living standards"* and *"promote respect for internationally recognised labour rights"*, while the parties agree *"that these objectives can be achieved without relaxing health, safety and environmental measures of general application. . . "*. Another example is the BIT between Sweden and Armenia from 2006, which in the preamble recognizes that *"the development of economic and business ties can promote respect for internationally recognized labour rights"* and *"that these objectives can be achieved without relaxing health, safety and environmental measures of general application"*. See also the BIT between Sweden and Georgia from 2009.

53 See above in Chapter 2.

that only few BITs and model BITs address this question calls for an examination of how this legal problem is resolved in practice.

7.1.1. As a rule of presumption

The BITs and model BITs that contain more detailed language addressing the delimitation between regulatory measures and indirect expropriation are adopted more recently, i.e. since the beginning of the new millennium.

For instance, the 2004 Canadian model provides in Annex B.13(1) as follows:

"The Parties confirm their shared understanding that:

a)   *Indirect expropriation results from a measure or series of measures of a Party that have an effect equivalent to direct expropriation without formal transfer of title or outright seizure;*

b)   *The determination of whether a measure or series of measures of a Party constitute an indirect expropriation requires a case-by case, fact-based inquiry that considers, among other factors:*

   i)   *the economic impact of the measure or series of measures, although the sole fact that a measure or series of measures of a Party has an adverse effect on the economic value of an investment does not establish that an indirect expropriation has occurred;*

   ii)   *the extent to which the measure or series of measures interfere with distinct, reasonable investment-backed expectations; and*

   iii)   *the character of the measure or series of measures;*

c)   *Except in rare circumstances, such as when a measure or series of measures are so severe in the light of their purpose that they cannot be reasonably viewed as having been adopted and applied in good faith, non-discriminatory measures of a Party that are designed and applied to protect legitimate public welfare objectives, such as health, safety and the environment, do not constitute indirect expropriation."*

Pursuant to this model BIT, the evaluation of whether states are duty-bound to pay compensation calls for an assessment of the concrete facts. At the same time, the BIT lists the factors that should be taken into account in the delimitation of compensable vs. non-compensable regulation. The first factor is the *effect* of the measure focusing on the economic impact, while at the same time recognizing that mere economic interferences that adversely affect the value of the investment do not call for compensation. The second factor is the extent to which the measures interfere with the *investment-backed expectations* of the investor. These expectations will indeed depend on the specific circumstances, taking into account the general legal and political framework of the country. For instance, it may be relevant whether the investor made its investment in a state with democratic institutions and judicial mechanisms to enforce legal claims. In addition, the expectations of the investor will depend on whether it is a country of high political instability, where an investor should expect a considerable risk of a strong sovereign-oriented ruling or frequent changes in the ruling of the state and the attitude towards foreign investors. In addition to the general legal and political framework at the time of the investment, the expectations of the investor may be safeguarded through individual guarantees (e.g. stabilization clauses in investment contracts, addressed below) granted to the foreign investor. Since the concept of investment-backed expectations, constitute an imperative in investment disputes this is further dealt with below under the concept of legitimate expectations.[54] The third factor concerns the *character* of the measure. One may question what is meant by character of the measure, but at least it could cover elements such as the intentions of the host state, the public purpose invoked and the type of regulation (fiscal or non-fiscal).

Besides articulating these three factors, the Canadian Model BIT creates a rule of presumption against compensation for non-discriminatory regulation such as – but not exclusively – regulation to protect health, safety and the environment. These concerns are also referred to in the model BIT as general concerns outside the context of expropriations, which the parties should mutually recognize as inappropriate to relax in order to encourage investment. Article 11 of the model BIT thus allows either state party to request consultations in terms of (offer to) waiver of or derogation from these considerations. These policy concerns (health, safety and the environment) are, however, not explicitly referred to in the preamble of the model BIT, which emphasizes the aim of promoting *"sustainable development"*. While recognizing that the definition of sustainable development is surrounded by controversy, these three policy considerations (health, safety and the environment) seem to be embodied in the concept of sustainable development. Accordingly, the rule of presumption against compensation for regulation to protect health, safety and the environment thus seem to follow the policy considerations in the preamble. The Canadian model exemplifies how policy considerations expressed in the preamble (promoting sustainable development) is expressed as legal rules of presumptions against payment of compensation for regulation to safeguard these social welfare objectives. The Canadian Model BIT also exemplifies how these policy considerations contained in the preamble might be of a more general character or broader scope than what is articulated in the substantive rules of the BIT. The approach laid down by Canada in its model BIT is also largely followed in more recent Canadian BITs, e.g. the 2012 Canada–China BIT.[55]

Likewise, the more recent 2012 US Model BIT contains further elaboration on the concept of expropriation in Annex B, with language similar to the 2004 Canadian Model BIT. This is, however, not something new, since the 2004 version of the US Model BIT equally contains this Annex B. Just as in the preamble of the

---

54 See section 8.
55 See Annex B.10.

2004 version, the 2012 US Model BIT enunciates specific policy concerns by referring to health, safety, and the environment, and the promotion of internationally recognized labour rights. The rule of presumption against compensation for non-discriminatory regulatory takings for the purpose of safeguarding health, safety and environment corresponds to the rule of presumption laid down in the 2004 Canada Model BIT. However, it does not create a rule of presumption in terms of regulation adopted to promote labour rights. Consequently, the US 2012 Model BIT seem to indicate that regulation to safeguard health, safety and the environment enjoys preferential treatment over regulation to promote labour rights or other types of regulation. By preferential treatment here is meant that there is an underlying assumption that regulation to safeguard health, safety and the environment is non-compensable. No such assumption can be employed for labour regulation.

This approach of having a rule of presumption against compensation for general regulatory measures to protect public health, safety and the environment is also followed in recent concrete BITs by the United States,[56] however not persistently.[57]

7.1.2. *As a rule of interpretation*

The 2007 Norwegian Draft Model BIT encompasses a provision with the heading 'Right to Regulate' in article 12, which states the following:[58]

> *"Nothing in this Agreement shall be construed to prevent a Party from adopting, maintaining or enforcing any measure otherwise consistent with this Agreement that it considers appropriate to ensure that investment activity is undertaken in a manner sensitive to health, safety or environmental concerns."*

This clause thereby explicitly articulates the right to regulate and is generally applicable. It applies to all substantial rules, including – but not limited to – the expropriation clause. Accordingly, this clause has a wider scope than the above-mentioned exceptional clause in e.g. the Canadian Model BIT, which is applicable only in the context of expropriation. The approach chosen in the Norwegian Draft Model BIT is thus an approach even more favourable to regulatory measures by host states. It applies to all types of regulatory interferences in the substantive rules of investment protection covered by the model BIT, including the FET standard.

This approach, embracing a general rule of interpretation, can also be found in concrete BITs. The BIT between Finland and Zambia from 2005 is one example

---

56 BIT between United States and Uruguay from 2006, Annex B(4)(b).
57 The BIT between the United States and Czech Republic contains no such rule of presumption even though social welfare policy concerns are enunciated in the preamble of the treaty. See also the BIT between United States and Honduras 2000, the BIT between United States and Lithuania 2001, the BIT between the United States and Croatia 2001, the BIT between the United States and Jordan 2003 and the BIT between the United States and Mozambique 2005.
58 Norwegian Draft Model BIT from 19 December 2007.

in this regard. This BIT contains a general derogation provision, which emphasizes that measures not constituting a disguised restriction on investment that are
neither discriminatory nor arbitrary should not *"be construed to prevent"* a state
party from adopting measures to maintain *"public order, or to protect public health
and safety, including environmental measures necessary to protect human, animal
or plant life"*.[59]

The mentioned provisions in the Norwegian Draft Model BIT as well as in the
Finland–Zambia BIT are technically rules of interpretation, not rules of presumption. Consequently, the question arises what the difference is between a rule of
interpretation and a rule of presumption. If we compare the provisions in the
Norwegian Model BIT with the mentioned provision in the Canadian Model
BIT a key difference in these types of rules is that whereby the provision in the
Norwegian Draft Model BIT is generally directed toward the substantive provisions of the treaty, the Canadian provision is concerned with a particular factual
subsumption of a case of expropriation. For the arbitrators, a rule of interpretation drags the interpretation of a legal norm in a specific direction. A rule of presumption, on the contrary, is more linked with a determination of the evidence
of a case. Employing a presumption, arbitrators are tasked with *not* to interpret,
unless there are circumstances that questions the presumption employed. In practice, this is a vicious circle because in order to determine *if* there are circumstances
that rule out the general presumption, arbitrators necessarily have to interpret the
normative rule. Hence, the approach of incorporating a regulatory norm either as
a rule of presumption or as a rule of interpretation will in practice lead to the same
result. The rule will serve as raising the bar for regulation relating to the policy
concerns enunciated (health, safety and environment in the examples found). To
conclude, one may infer that both approaches imply that arbitrators must interpret the legal norm with an underlying presumption that regulation relating to
the policy concerns articulated does not constitute indirect expropriation. Hence,
these types of regulations are presumed not to be compensable.

7.1.3. As an applicability rule

Apart from the two types of approaches expressing either a rule of presumption
or a rule of interpretation, a third approach can be observed. This approach
focuses on declaring that regulation applies and that the substantive standard of
treatment should not preclude or restrict this. For example, article 12 of the BIT
between Swaziland and Mauritius contains a formulation that basically expresses
the applicability of security, health and environmental regulation by declaring
that:

> *"The provisions of this Agreement shall not in any way limit the right of either
> Contracting Party to apply prohibitions or restrictions of any kind or take any*

---

59 BIT between Finland and Zambia, 2005, article 14(2).

other action which is directed to the protection of its essential security interests, or to the protection of public health or the prevention of diseases and pests in animals or plants in conformity with the laws of each Contracting Party."

This rule might indicate a higher threshold for non-compensation since the term used is *"essential security interests"* in contrast to the previously mentioned *"safety"* considerations. In terms of environmental regulation this might have a broader and more general scope than the considerations *"to prevention of diseases and pests in animals or plants"*.

The fundamental nature of this applicability rule is that it refers to applicability of two sets of policy concerns: economic and non-economic. Consequently, this rule states that investment protection standards should not be applied so as to bar explicitly mentioned types of regulation. The question of applicability of a rule naturally comes before the question of interpretation. In terms of regulatory expropriations, this type of rule thus states that arbitrators cannot ignore the existence of other non-economic concerns and international obligations relating the promotion of social development within these policy areas. Consequently, this rule requires the arbitrators to employ a balanced approach to interpretation.

7.1.4. Preliminary conclusions

Current BIT practice does not generally support the idea that certain regulatory measures should be granted preferential treatment and thus be considered non-compensable. Most states do not address the question at all. The states that have chosen to address the question have done this 1) by using the balanced approach to preambles expressing economic as well as non-economic concerns 2) by employing a rule of interpretation in the substantive parts of the treaty or 3) a rule of presumption or 4) a rule of applicability. These approaches are sometimes combined. Through these approaches, or a combination hereof, some BITs have established legal rules that appear to favour certain types of regulation, especially regulatory measures linked with policy concerns such as health, safety, environment and labour rights. So, even though BITs rarely address the delimitation of compensable regulation from non-compensable regulation, the BIT examination demonstrates some support of the view of preferential treatment for regulation of general applicability employed to enhance social welfare objectives such as security, health and the environment.

As recalled, Chapter 3 explained that there were two approaches to BIT preambles – the traditional approach and the balanced approach. Whereas the traditional approach focuses on investment promotion and protection, the balanced approach refers to preambles, which add further non-economic policy concerns to that of investment promotion and protection. The BIT analysis confirms that most BITs follow the traditional approach with no explicit consideration to policy concerns. BITs belonging to the category of treaties with traditional preambles are also silent in terms of acknowledging that some instances of regulation may be non-compensable. These BITs do not address the distinction between compensable and non-compensable regulation. Contrariwise, BITs that actually address this distinction are typically the BITs belonging to the category of BITs that deviate from the original approach to BIT preambles. Accordingly, BITs containing references to both economic and non-economic policy concerns in the preambles seem to link this with provisions addressing regulation and the delimitation of compensable vs. non-compensable regulation. This is oftentimes done by declaring that non-discriminatory measures to protect policy concerns enunciated in the preamble do not constitute regulatory expropriation (or indirect expropriation).[60] This shows how policy concerns in the preamble, constituting contextual elements for the interpretation of treaties, can develop into substantive legal rules.

7.2. *Indicative elements in practice*

The distinction between compensable and non-compensable regulation has been explained above on the basis of the BIT examination. The distinction is now addressed in the following on the basis of an examination of arbitral practice of expropriation claims in investment disputes. Though the distinction is largely decided on a case-by case basis, some indicative factors can be deduced from practice.

The review of arbitral case practice shows that the following principles can be identified in terms of establishing an obligation to pay compensation for regulatory expropriation:

- the form of the measure is not determinative;
- the measure must amount to substantial deprivation;
- the measure is not covered by the police powers exception;
- the expectations of the investor to be compensated for regulation support a claim for compensation if legitimate.

Below, the lower threshold for which regulation does not trigger compensation (referred to as the police power doctrine) is explained. This is followed by an analysis of the indicative elements deduced from practice.

7.2.1. *The police power doctrine in international investment law*

Not every measure imposed on the investor by the host state having adverse effect on foreign investors' business operation can be compensated. Such a requirement would severely impair the state in its sovereign functions. As explained in Chapter 1, the concept of risk is an inherent element in international investment law.

---

60 E.g. this is the approach laid down in the recently adopted US Model BIT from 2012, Annex B, article 4(b).

Foreign investors must thus accept to engage in activities that involve an element of business risk and political risk. By investing in a host state, the investor thus assumes an element of risk associated with the state's regulatory regime. The contentious issue is, however, this 'element of' risk, which certainly does not entail that investors must accept whatever the host state decides to do.

Alleged expropriations oftentimes involve regulation and could in principle fall into the category of a so-called 'regulatory taking'. The most practical situation is that the investment is affected by new or changed regulation onerous to the investor. Arbitral practice shows the advancement of basic principles that states are entitled to regulate foreign investment within their jurisdiction, even if it may be burdensome or even have injurious consequences for an investor. This is in practice an acknowledgement of 'the right to regulate', an inherent power of the state, conceptualized as the *police power doctrine*.[61]

According to the police power doctrine a measure adopted by the host state in the exercise of that state's police power will not make the state liable for a claim for expropriation as a result of that measure. It remains controversial whether this is because the exercise of police powers precludes the measure being regarded as an expropriatory act,[62] or whether it merely provides an exception to the rule that compensation must be paid for expropriation.[63] Relying on the view that the obligation to pay compensation is one of the conditions (and thus not consequences) of an expropriation to be lawful, it seems more convincing to perceive the police power doctrine as a concept that precludes measures being regarded as expropriatory acts. Accordingly, the police power doctrine should thus be seen as referring to minor interferences not reaching the threshold of indirect expropriations. Nevertheless, for the investor, the end result is the same and this question is thus more theoretical.

As demonstrated in Chapter 4, the right to regulate under the human right paradigm reveals the existence of a *duty* for states to regulate. This duty to regulate could also be understood under the concept of the police power doctrine. This is because it has become common to presume the police power doctrine as indicating a justification of specific regulatory measures that injures private rights and assets without being accompanied by compensation. For instance, this was expressed by the tribunal in the *Tecmed* case:[64]

> *"The principle that the State's exercise of its sovereign powers within the framework of its police power may cause economic damage to those subject to its powers as administrator without entitling them to any compensation whatsoever is undisputable."*

61 Dolzer and Schreuer, *Principles of International Investment Law*, 120–3.
62 *Saluka v Czech Republic*, Partial Award, 17 March 2006, para. 262.
63 Ian Brownlie, *Principles of Public International Law*, 5th ed. (Oxford: Clarendon Press, 1998), 624.
64 *Tecmed v Mexico*, Award, 29 May 2003, para. 119.

The contentious issue relating to the police power doctrine is not so much the existence hereof but rather the scope of the doctrine. One extreme view is that all types of *bona fide*, non-discriminatory regulation in the public interest fall within the scope of the doctrine.[65] Some authorities have set forth a general rule of presumption disfavouring compensation for regulation in general. For instance, in the *S.D. Myers* case, the two arbitrators expressing the majority decision observed that *"[t]he general body of precedent usually does not treat regulatory action as amounting to expropriation"*.[66] Regulatory conduct by public authorities was therefore perceived as unlikely to be the subject of a legitimate complaint under article 1110 of the NAFTA, although the tribunal did not rule out that possibility. This view needs to be taken with a pinch of salt. It might be, that the arbitrators here implicitly refers to a specific type of regulation but to say that regulation in general is supported by precedent of presumption against compensation is not convincing. Even non-discriminatory tax regulation may for example impose such a heavy burden upon the investor that it may contravene the legitimate expectations of an investor, in particular if the investor received additional guarantees. Various types of measures may, according to the host state, be considered as social welfare regulation within the police power exception. Nevertheless, such regulation may in fact constitute a discriminatory measure against foreign companies. The views expressed by the majority in the *S.D. Myers* case thus seem of too high level of generalization. If all regulatory takings were to be exempted from compensation, the number of viable claims would be close to zero. Clearly, a blanket exception for regulatory measures would create a gaping loophole in the international protection against expropriation.[67]

It is not plausible, however, to infer a general principle of non-compensation for general regulatory measures. Such inference would undermine the actual commitment, which is laid down by a state in a BIT. Conversely, a rule of presumption against compensation for certain types of regulation is a more persuasive argument. The police power doctrine is concerned with the lower threshold of which regulation does not trigger the duty to compensate the investor. The following explains the identified indicative elements to be used for establishing the threshold for whether a measure should be compensated.

7.2.2. The requirement of 'permanence'

Arbitral practice shows that for the assessment of whether a measure should be followed by compensation or not the duration of the measure is an essential factor, i.e. whether the measure is permanent or of a temporary character. This is because the duration is indicative of the 'seriousness' of the

---

65 *Methanex v USA,* Final Award, 3 August 2005, Part IV, Chapter D, p. 4, para. 7.
66 *S.D. Myers v Canada,* NAFTA, Partial Award, 13 November 2000, para. 281.
67 *Pope & Talbot Inc v Canada,* Interim Award, 26 June 2000, para. 99.

measure. In order to express the requirement that measures should have this permanent character to constitute an indirect expropriation, tribunals have referred to the requirement of 'permanence'[68] or used the terms 'irreversible' or 'non-ephemeral'.[69]

The requirement of a permanent character of the measure was addressed in the case of *Santa Elena v Costa Rica*.[70] A central issue was the amount of compensation to be paid by Costa Rica to the investor for expropriation.

The property (Santa Elena) was located in Costa Rica. The property was home to a variety of flora and fauna, many of which were indigenous to the region. The investor was formed in 1970 with the primary purpose of purchasing Santa Elena and with the intention of developing a tourist resort and residential community. After acquiring the property the investor undertook various financial and technical analyses of the property with a view to its development. Costa Rica, however, decided to preserve the area against tourism and issued an expropriation decree for Santa Elena offering to pay an amount in compensation that the investor later challenged in ICSID arbitrations.

In this case the tribunal emphasized the permanent character of the measure by declaring that *"the practical and economic use of the Property by the Claimant was irretrievably lost, notwithstanding that* [the investor] *remained in possession of the Property"*.[71] Moreover, the tribunal stated that the property could not be used for development purposes for which it was originally acquired, nor did it possess any significant resale value.

In *Feldman v Mexico*,[72] a case concerning a dispute regarding the application of tax laws by Mexico to the export of tobacco products by a Mexican company owned and controlled by Mr Marvin Feldman, an American citizen, the tribunal equally stressed the requirement of permanence. The tribunal stated that the investor, Feldman, was no longer able to engage in his business of purchasing Mexican cigarettes and exporting them. Hence, Feldman had thus been deprived *"completely and permanently"* of any potential economic benefits from that particular activity.[73]

---

68 See arbitral practice below.
69 The Iran–US Claims Tribunal have ruled that the appointment of a temporary manager by the host state against the will of the foreign investor will constitute a taking if the consequential deprivation is not "merely ephemeral"; see *Tippetts, Abbett, McCarthy, Stratton v TAMS-AFFA Consulting Eng'rs of Iran*, 6 Iran–US Claims Tribunal Reports, 1984, p. 219ff; *Wena Hotels v Egypt*, Award, 8 December 2000, para. 99 and *Azurix v Argentina*, Award, 16 July 2006, para 313. See also Dolzer and Schreuer, *Principles of International Investment Law*, 124f; Salacuse, *The Law of Investment Treaties*, 310f; Katia Yannaca-Small, "Indirect Expropriation and the Right to Regulate: How to Draw the Line?," in *Arbitration Under International Investment Agreements: A Guide to the Key Issues*, ed. Katia Yannaca-Small (Oxford: Oxford University Press, 2010), 467f.
70 *Santa Elena v Costa Rica*, Award, 17 February 2000.
71 *Ibid.*, para. 81.
72 *Feldman v Mexico*, Award, 16 December 2002.
73 *Ibid.*, para. 109.

The case of *Siemens v Argentina*[74] from 2007 was one of more than 40 arbitrations against Argentina related to measures taken during its financial crisis in 2001–2002, although the financial crisis was more peripheral to the facts of this case than it was to most of the others.

In 1996 Argentina called for bids to provide an immigration control system. In accordance with the bidding terms, Siemens A.G. incorporated an Argentine company (SITS) for the purposes of the bid. Argentina selected the bid, but SITS was faced with several challenges. The immigration control system started to operate in February 2000 but was stopped shortly thereafter by the government. In May 2001 Argentina terminated the contract by a decree under the terms of the *2000 Emergency Law*. SITS filed an administrative appeal, which was rejected by another decree, so in May 2002 Siemens initiated ICSID arbitration.

In this case the tribunal held that Argentina had used its superior power to interfere with the investment contract in a number of ways, e.g. by permanently suspending the printing of national identity cards, forcing changes in the contract, and lastly by terminating the contract by decree.[75] The tribunal thus here stressed that it was a *"permanent measure"* with the effect to terminate the contract.[76]

Cases might occur where the measures imposed are intended to have a temporary character. The freezing of assets due to economic sanctions to counter terrorism is one example of such measures. Assets freeze is in principle a temporary measure but at some point the sanction may turn into a *de facto* permanent deprivation.[77] Where bank accounts are frozen on the ground that it is necessary to do so for investigating a crime, the interference would be justified. Where it is done, however, in the process of an expropriation of the property of the foreign investor, the investor may have a strong case for the view that the freezing of assets amounts to a taking of property.[78] The question here again is whether the measures *de facto* can be perceived as permanent.

The duration of the governmental measure is indeed relevant and arbitral practice shows that as a main rule 'the taking' must have a permanent character. Nevertheless, there are also arbitral precedents supporting that partly or temporary measures may constitute expropriation. The case of *S.D. Myers v Canada*[79] is an important precedent in this regard.

The case of *S.D. Myers* concerned the closing of the borders between the United States and Canada with regards to import and export of PCBs (a synthetic chemical compound know as polychlorinated biphenyl) and PCB waste for disposal. The border was closed temporarily and, as a consequence, the

---

74 *Siemens v Argentina*, Award, 17 January 2007.

75 *Ibid.*, paras 245–60.

76 *Ibid.*, para. 271.

77 As a response to the Al Qaeda attack on the World Trade Center in 2011, the UN Security Council imposed a binding obligation on states to freeze financial assets of individuals and entities suspected for having committed, for planning or otherwise supporting terrorism.

78 Sornarajah, *The International Law on Foreign Investment*, 406.

79 *S.D. Myers v Canada*, First Partial Award, 13 November 2000.

American investor's venture into the Canadian market was postponed for around 18 months.

In this case the tribunal held that expropriation usually amounts to a lasting removal of the ability of the investor to make use of its economic rights, although it may be that, in some contexts, it would be appropriate to view a deprivation as amounting to an expropriation, even if it were partial or temporary.[80] The temporary character of the import/export ban was considered to be a decisive element, meaning that the measure was not characterized as an expropriation within the terms of article 1110 of the NAFTA.[81]

In *Middle East Cement v Egypt*,[82] a Greek corporate investor, which had established a branch in Egypt to carry out the business of importing, storing and selling cement, was deprived by a legislative decree of rights it had been granted under a licence agreement, at least for a period of four months. The measure was considered tantamount to expropriation by the tribunal.[83]

In *LG&E v Argentina*[84] the tribunal equally stressed duration of the measure as an important criterion for assessing the degree of interference:[85]

> *"Similarly, one must consider the duration of the measure as it relates to the degree of interference with the investor's ownership rights. Generally, the expropriation must be permanent, that is to say, it cannot have a temporary nature, unless the investment's successful development depends on the realization of certain activities at specific moments that may not endure variations."*

Accordingly, the tribunal was open to some measures being expropriatory even though they were not completely permanent.

In *Alpha v Ukraine*[86] from 2010 the events that gave rise to the arbitration were a series of commercial arrangements involving the Austrian investor Alpha and the state-owned Hotel Dnipro in Ukraine and other parties. The dispute concerned the renovation of the hotel. Two key issues of the case were 1) the temporary suspension of payments under the agreements regarding the reconstruction and renovation of some of the floors at the hotel, and 2) the transfer of management of the hotel to the 'State Administration' and cessation of payments of the contracts with the investor. On the basis of several incidents occurring subsequently, the measures were considered a creeping expropriation with the tribunal declaring that *"all evidence indicates that the cessation of payments is permanent".*[87] Hence, the various measures taken together, at least at the time of

---

80 *Ibid.*, para. 283.
81 *Ibid.*, para. 284.
82 *Middle East Cement Shipping and Handling Company v Egypt*, 12 April 2002.
83 *Ibid.*, para. 107.
84 *LG&E v Argentina*, Decision on Liability, 3 October 2006.
85 *Ibid.*, para. 193.
86 *Alpha v Ukraine*, Award, 8 November 2010.
87 *Ibid.*, paras 409–10.

the cessation of payments, had a permanent character, a determinative factor for finding an expropriation.

To conclude, the duration of the measure is an indicative element, though not the sole criterion. The determinative factor is rather on persistence of its negative effects. The failure to re-establish the situation and consequently terminate the temporary measure may thus constitute decisive elements for finding an expropriation. As the lower threshold, tribunals have held that a substantial deprivation should last *"for at least a meaningful period of time"*.[88] In practice, arbitral tribunals have considered that a measure is not ephemeral if the property was out of the control of the investor for a year[89] or an export licence was suspended for four months,[90] or that the measure was ephemeral if it lasted for three months.[91] These cases involved a single measure. When considering multiple measures, it will depend on the duration of their cumulative effect.[92] As expressed by the tribunal in *Azurix v Argentina*: *"Unfortunately, there is no mathematical formula to reach a mechanical result. How much time is needed must be judged by the specific circumstances of each case."*[93]

7.2.3. The requirement of 'substantiality'

Another key factor indicating that compensation should be paid concerns the substantiality of the measure imposed. In the assessment of an expropriation claim most tribunals would look at the substantiality as a measurement for severity of the economic impact caused by a governmental action.

In practice, tribunals have laid down a requirement that there must be a certain substance to the measure imposed for it to trigger the duty to compensate. Tribunals have used terms like 'radical', 'fundamental', 'in significant part', 'substantial' or 'serious'. The substantial interference typically concerns the investor's economic rights, i.e. ownership, use, enjoyment or management of the business, whereas restrictions on property rights do not constitute a taking.[94]

The requirement of substantiality was identified in the context of NAFTA, where the tribunal in *Pope & Talbot* stressed that mere interference is not expropriation. Rather, a significant degree of deprivation of fundamental rights of ownership is required. As expressed by the tribunal *"the test is whether that interference is sufficiently restrictive to support a conclusion that the property has been 'taken' from the owner"*.[95] The Canadian export restrictions on lumber were considered

---

88 *Deutsche Bank AG v Sri Lanka*, Award, 31 October 2012, para. 503.
89 *Wena Hotels v Egypt*, Award, 8 December 2000.
90 *Middle East Cement Shipping and Handling Company v Egypt*, 12 April 2002.
91 *S.D. Myers v Canada*, First Partial Award, 13 November 2000.
92 *Azurix v Argentina*, Award, 14 July 2006.
93 *Ibid.*, para 313.
94 *Pope and Talbot v Canada*, Award, 26 June 2000, para. 102; *Metalclad v Mexico*, Award, 30 August 2000, para. 103; *CMS v Argentina*, Award, 12 May 2005, para. 262.
95 *Pope and Talbot v Canada*, Award, 26 June 2000, para. 102.

to constitute an interference resulting in reduced profits. However, the tribunal noted that the investor continued to export substantial quantities of lumber and to earn substantial profit on the sales. On this basis the tribunal found that the degree of interference with the investment due to the export control did not reach the level of expropriation.[96] Even if the introduction of export quotas resulted in a reduction of profits for Pope & Talbot, sales abroad were thus not entirely prevented and the investor was still able to make profits. Accordingly, the measures affecting property interests' has to be of a certain "magnitude or severity".[97]

In *Feldman v Mexico* the tribunal attached determinative importance to the degree of interference and stressed that regulation in order to constitute expropriation *"may significantly interfere with an investor's property rights"*.[98] In *Occidental Exploration v Ecuador*[99] the investor claimed that the Ecuadorian authorities' refusal to refund the tax that it was entitled to under Ecuadorian law constituted an expropriation. The tribunal, however, found that Ecuador did not adopt measures that could be considered as amounting to direct or indirect expropriation since there was *"no deprivation of the use [. . .] of the investment, let alone measures affecting a significant part of the investment"*.[100] The requirement of 'substantial deprivation' was thus not fulfilled in this case.

In the same way, the substantiality of the measure imposed was crucial in the case of *Telenor v Ukraine*.[101] As a response to the alleged expropriations, the tribunal held that an interference *"must be such as substantially to deprive the investor of the economic value, use or enjoyment of its investment"*.[102]

In *Alpha v Ukraine*[103] the tribunal attached significant importance not only to the duration of the measure but also the fact that the investor had been deprived of *"substantially all remaining economic value in the agreements"*.[104]

In the case of *Railroad Development Corporation v Guatemala* from 2012 the tribunal cited a range of authorities in the support of the view that the effect of the measures must be that the investor is deprived substantially of the use and benefits of the investment.[105] The tribunal held that the effect on the investors' investment *"does not rise to the level of an indirect expropriation"*.[106] The wording of the tribunal thus again confirms that interferences can appear in various degrees or with different intensities.

---

96 *Ibid.*
97 *Ibid.*, para. 96.
98 *Feldman v Mexico*, Award, 16 December 2002, para. 100.
99 *Occidental Exploration and Production Company v Ecuador*, Award, 1 July 2004.
100 *Ibid.*, para. 89.
101 *Telenor v Hungary*, Award, 13 September 2006.
102 *Ibid.*, para. 65.
103 *Alpha v Ukraine,* Award, 8 November 2010.
104 *Ibid.*, paras 409–10.
105 *Railroad Development Corporation v Guatemala*, Award, 29 June 2012, para. 151.
106 *Ibid.*, para. 152.

Investment tribunals have also linked the substantial taking with the legitimate expectations of the investor, by emphasizing that the substantial effect of an intensity that reduces or removes the legitimate benefits of the investor amount to indirect expropriation.[107] To conclude, an insignificant, minor restriction or interference with the investment does not constitute indirect expropriation, but there is no clear-cut distinction between the extremes of total deprivation of ownership rights and the mere interference. Obviously, not every burden imposed on the foreign investor requires compensation. Nor does the duty to compensate depend on a total loss of property, but practice in investment arbitrations shows that the interference must be substantial.[108]

7.2.4. *The issue of control*

Another indicative factor relevant for determining whether a measure constitutes indirect expropriation and thus obliges the host state to compensate the investor is the element of control. In situations involving allegation of indirect expropriation it is not uncommon that the investor retains control over its investment, e.g. a company, but the company loses its economic viability. In fact, a significant form of indirect appropriation is state's acquisition of an investor's basic rights to manage and control its investment. Where a state exerts managerial control over an investment, for example through the appointment of managers, supervisors or administrators, and the appointment is not temporary, the state in actual fact acquires the investor's fundamental management rights.[109]

In several cases, tribunals have found that continued control of an enterprise by the investor strongly militates against a finding of indirect expropriation.[110] For instance, in *Azurix v Argentina* the tribunal found that breaches of a water concession did not constitute indirect expropriation due to the investor's continued control over the enterprise. Despite the fact that the management of the water concession was affected, it was *"not sufficiently for the Tribunal to find that Azurix's investment was expropriated"*.[111] Likewise, in *LG&E v Argentina* the host state had violated the terms of concessions for the distribution of gas but the investor continued the control. The tribunal stressed that an *"interference with*

---

107 *RFCC v Morocco,* Award, 22 December 2003, para. 69.
108 See also August Reinisch, "Expropriation," in *The Oxford Handbook of International Investment Law*, ed. Peter Muchlinski, Federico Ortino, and Christoph Schreuer (Oxford: Oxford University Press, 2008), 438; Salacuse, *The Law of Investment Treaties*, 311–13; Yannaca-Small, "Indirect Expropriation and the Right to Regulate," 460–7.
109 Dolzer and Schreuer, *Principles of International Investment Law*, 117–18; Salacuse, *The Law of Investment Treaties*, 308–10.
110 *Feldman v Mexico*, Award, 16 December 2002, paras 142, 152; *Occidential Exploration and Production co. v Ecador*, Award, 1 July 2004, para. 89; *CMS Gas Transmission Company v Argentina*, Award, 12 May 2005, paras 263–4; *LG&E v Argentina*, Decision on Liability, 3 October 2006, paras 188, 199.
111 *Azurix v Argentina*, Award, 14 July 2006, para. 322.

the investment's ability to carry on its business is not satisfied where the investment continues to operate, even if profits are diminished".[112]

In *Middle East Cement v Egypt* the claim by Egypt that the investor remained in control and could have continued the supply of cement was not perceived by the tribunal as an economically feasible alternative.[113] Accordingly, this award demonstrates that though the element of control might be indicative of whether measures should be considered a taking or not, this element cannot be the sole criterion.

In *Feldman v Mexico* the registered foreign trading company and exporter of cigarettes from Mexico was allegedly denied the benefits of the law that allowed certain tax refunds to exporters. The tribunal found that there was no expropriation but attached vital importance to the fact that the investor was not deprived the control of the company.[114]

In the case of *CMS v Argentina*, the element of control was also a decisive factor for not finding an expropriation. In this case the tribunal found that the Argentine government did not manage the day-to-day operation of the company but the investor had full ownership and control over the investment. Hence, there was no substantial deprivation.[115]

Oftentimes, the issue of control is an indicative factor to be assessed together with the other indicative factors. If the host state for example substantially deprives the investor of the value of the investment but the investor maintains full control, the deprivation may, nevertheless, be substantial and of a permanent character. Under such circumstances where the investment in reality constitutes no more than a shell of the former investment, the interference may amount to expropriation. Practice thus shows that continued control is in principle detrimental to the finding of an expropriation.[116] At the same time, arbitral practice proves that control is an indicative element, though not necessarily the decisive criterion.[117]

7.2.5. The requirement of a fair process

Another significant element is the requirement of regulatory acts to be consistent with due process. The requirement of a fair process appears to cover fundamental

---

112 *LG&E v Argentina*, Decision on Liability, 3 October 2006, paras 188, 191.
113 *Middle East Cement Shipping and Handling Company v Egypt*, Award, 12 April 2002, para. 168.
114 *Feldman v Mexico*, Award, 16 December 2002, para. 142.
115 *CMS v Argentina*, Award, 12 May 2005, paras 262–3.
116 *Feldman v Mexico*, Award, 16 December 2002, paras 142, 152; *CMS Gas Transmission Company v Argentina*, Award, 12 May 2005, paras 263–4.
117 Some tribunals have interpreted expropriation narrowly and preferred to find a violation of the FET standard. For example in *Azurix v Argentina* the tribunal rejected that breaches of a water concession agreement amounted to an indirect expropriation. The tribunal based its argument on the fact that the investor had retained control over the enterprise, but the tribunal found, however, other breaches of the United States of America–Argentina BIT, including a breach of the FET standard. See *Azurix v Argentina*, Award, 14 July 2006.

legal principles such as legality, transparency and consistency. Fair procedure is usually an elementary requirement of the rule of law and an element of the FET standard embracing the customary international law concept of denial of justice.[118] Yet, it may also acquire some importance with regards to expropriations claims. For example, in *Metalclad v Mexico* the tribunal found that the measures by Mexico[119] reached the threshold of regulatory expropriation because the acts were carried out in a non-transparent manner:[120]

> *"The measures, taken together with the representation of the Mexican federal government, on which Metalclad relied, and the absence of a timely, orderly or substantive basis for the denial by the Municipality of the local construction permit, amount to an indirect expropriation."*

In terms of cancellation of licences or permits, the lack of due process (combined with discrimination and violation of specific commitments made to the investor) could also amount to a compensable taking.[121] Accordingly, it cannot be ruled out that the lack of a fair process, such as lack of transparency, in itself may cause regulatory measures to be perceived an indirect expropriation. This issue came also up in the *Feldman v Mexico* case.[122] Though it is questionable whether mere transparency concerns may trigger compensation for indirect expropriations, transparency considerations may constitute an additional element as an indicative factor that, taken together with other elements, can support the finding of a regulatory expropriation.[123]

7.2.6. Preliminary conclusions on the indicative elements

Investment arbitration tribunals seem to suggest reaching a threshold as an imperative to find that an indirect expropriation has occurred. Reaching this threshold is dependent on elements such as the significance of interference with economic use or benefit and duration of the measure as well as control. On the basis of a review of arbitral practice, it appears that the mentioned elements constitute indicative factors in the determination of the scope of the police power doctrine, the distinction between compensable and non-compensable regulation. However, this distinction cannot be made on the basis of the above-mentioned criteria alone. Regulation is e.g. through the adoption of new laws by nature of a permanent character, and regulation rarely affects the control of the investment. Interferences might actually be significant, but nevertheless fall into the police

118 Dolzer and Schreuer, *Principles of International Investment Law*, 154.
119 1) a set of events that cumulatively denied the company a permit to operate and 2) a state-level act that essentially converted the property of Metalclad into an ecological reserve.
120 *Metalclad v Mexico*, Award, 30 August 2000, para. 107.
121 Sornarajah, *The International Law on Foreign Investment*, 402.
122 *Feldman v Mexico*, Award, 16 December 2000.
123 Salacuse, *The Law of Investment Treaties*, 315f.

power exception. At all times, the analysis is a function of comparing the investment prior to and after the imposed measure, an *ex post* evaluation weight against an *ex ante* evaluation.

As will be shown below, the question of whether regulatory measures require the state to compensate the investor greatly depends on the expectations of the investor concerned. These expectations can be enhanced through particular legal mechanisms, such as the insertion of an umbrella clause in a BIT or on the basis of contractual commitments.

In addition to these indicative factors, there are two essential approaches in practice that have been adopted to establish whether the imposed measure constitutes an indirect expropriation or not – 'the sole effect doctrine' and 'the balanced approach'. These two approaches require further attention.

7.3. The sole effect doctrine and implications for the regulatory space of manoeuvre

The difficulties in distinguishing compensable from non-compensable regulation is recognized in practice but the approaches to solving the problem diverge, especially in terms of the relevance of the state's purpose or rationale behind the measure adopted.

In addition to the above-mentioned indicative criteria, two main approaches can be found for distinguishing regulatory expropriation from non-compensable regulation. One approach focuses solely on the effects of regulation, whereas the other adopts a more contextual approach by including a test of proportionality between purpose of the measure and the effects. These two approaches are explained below. These approaches have diverging consequences for the regulatory space of manoeuvre, the scope of the right to regulate, i.e. the extent to which states can act as sovereigns without being liable to compensate the investor.[124]

The one approach, deduced from arbitral practice, is referred to as *the sole effect doctrine*.[125] According to the sole effect doctrine only the effects on the investor's control over or profits from its investments should be taken into account. This approach explicitly excludes any assessment of the host state's purpose, the public interest or necessity of the regulation. According to the sole effect doctrine, whenever the effect upon the economic value of the investment or upon the control over the investment is substantial and lasts for a significant period of time, it will be assumed *prima facie* that a taking of property has occurred.

Tribunals have in several instances pointed out what mattered for an indirect expropriation was only the effect of the measure and that any intention to expropriate was not decisive. For instance, the tribunal stressed in *Siemens v Argentina*

---

124 See also Salacuse, *The Law of Investment Treaties*, 316–18; Dolzer and Schreuer, *Principles of International Investment Law*, 112–15.
125 Schefer, *International Investment Law*, 208ff; Reinisch, "Expropriation," 444–7.

that the treaty (the German–Argentina BIT) referred to indirect expropriation, *"measures that have the effect of an expropriation"*, but had no reference to the intent of the state to expropriate.[126] Similarly the *Pope & Talbot* case supports the proposition that the threshold of interference required to show an indirect expropriation is that the effect of the measure must be the same as if the property had been taken.[127]

The sole effect doctrine is not new under the BIT regime but can be traced back to the cases by the Iran–US Claims Tribunal.[128] A key argument in favour of the sole effect doctrine has been that since the purpose of the measure is one of the factors of the legality of an expropriation, it cannot at the same time be a justification for non-compensation. Pursuant to this approach, regulatory expropriation is thus an expropriation notwithstanding how praiseworthy the purpose of the measure is. An important precedent for this school of thought is the *Metalclad* case,[129] where the tribunal applied a test that focuses on the effect in terms of the economic impact of the measures together with the protection of the investor's expectations:[130]

> *". . . interference with the use of property which has the effect of depriving the owner, in whole or in significant part, of the use or reasonably-to-be-expected economic benefit of property. . . ."*

In continuation hereof, the tribunal explicitly found, it was not needed to decide or consider the motivation or intent of the measure imposed (the adoption of the Ecological Decree).[131] Contrariwise, the tribunal attached crucial importance to the economic impact.

Other decisions support this strong emphasis on the economic effects of the measure as a decisive criterion. In *Telenor v Hungary*,[132] the tribunal noted that the conduct complained of *"must be such as to have a major adverse impact on the economic value of the investment"*.[133]

The case arose from various regulatory initiatives taken by Hungary between 2001 and 2003 to bring its telecommunications regime into line with European Union's norms, as part of the EU accession process. Among other things, Hungary introduced a programme where telecommunications providers should

---

126 *Siemens v Argentina*, Award, 6 February 2007, para. 270.
127 *Pope and Talbot Inc. v Canada*, Interim Award, 26 June 2000, para. 102.
128 Dolzer and Schreuer, *Principles of International Investment Law*, 103; Reinisch, "Expropriation," 445.
129 *Metalclad v Mexico*, Award, 30 August 2000.
130 *Ibid.*, para 103. In this regard, the *Metalclad* case is in direct conflict with later cases, most notably the *Methanex* case, which will be explained below.
131 *Ibid.*, para. 111.
132 *Telenor v Hungary*, Award, 13 September 2006.
133 *Ibid.*, para. 64.

pay a minor portion of their revenue into a central fund, which would be used to compensate fixed-line service providers for providing below-cost telephone access to individuals in poor areas.

In the assessment of whether the measures amounted to expropriatory acts the tribunal emphasized the duration and intensity of the measure.[134] Not much consideration was given to the purpose the measure. This case thus exemplifies how some tribunals have chosen to look only at a very narrow definition of the effect of the measure, i.e. the economic impact. Likewise, in *Spyridon Roussalis v Romania*[135] the tribunal focused on the economic effect of the measure as the decisive factor.[136]

While practice shows that (mere) economic impact generates a *prima facie* 'taking', it does not create a *prima facie* expropriation claim. This principle was established in the case of *Feldman v Mexico*.[137] In this case, the tribunal emphasized that *"many business problems are not expropriations"*,[138] and that investors may be disappointed in their dealings with public authorities. These difficulties might even amount to great difficulties without violating international law. Consequently, the tribunal held that regulatory measures, including changes in the law or changes in the application of existing laws that makes it uneconomical to continue a particular business, is not a *prima facie* expropriation claim.[139] Subsequent practice supports this view. For example, in *Telenor v Hungary* the tribunal found that it was *"well established that the mere exercise by government of regulatory powers that create impediments to business or entail the payment of taxes or other levies does not of itself constitute expropriation"*.[140]

All in all, the concept of the sole effect doctrine allows for a broad definition of expropriation, which may significantly limit legitimate non-compensable regulation. Since the focus of the sole effect doctrine is the economic impact of the measure, the sole effect doctrine does not allow a differentiation between various types of regulation. Consequently, according to this approach the scope of the right to regulate is not dependent on the type of regulation imposed. This approach thus does not allow for a wider regulatory space of the state in terms of regulation to promote human rights. The obligation to compensate the investor for regulation to promote human rights or development concerns is thus decided according to the same criteria as for regulation to promote economic development, such as tax regulation.

---

134 *Ibid.*, para. 70.
135 *Spyridon Roussalis v Romania*, Award, 7 December 2011.
136 *Ibid.*, para. 328.
137 *Feldman v Mexico*, Award, 2000.
138 *Ibid.*, paras 112–14.
139 *Ibid.*
140 *Telenor v Hungary*, Award, 13 September 2006, para. 64.

7.4. *A balanced approach and the implications for the regulatory space of manoeuvre*

The purpose for interfering with an investment is oftentimes invoked by host states in investment disputes as a main argument against an indirect expropriation. A central question is therefore how much weight should be given to the rationale behind the (claimed) noble intentions of the host state. Though tribunals have strongly emphasized the effect of the measure, other decisions display a more differentiated approach. Where the debate originated in the discussion of whether the effect or intentions should be the decisive criterion, an alternative and more nuanced approach has developed, i.e. the balanced approach. This approach takes into account the broader context of the measure. Whereas intentionally discriminatory regulation against a foreign investor fulfils a key requirement for establishing expropriation, the balanced approach thus requires an assessment of several factors taken together. So, this approach does not aim to throw overboard the sole effect doctrine. On the contrary, it does include the (economic) effect of the measure imposed, however not as a sole criterion, and not necessarily the decisive criterion either, but as one element among others.

In the *Methanex* case the arbitral tribunal explicitly spelled out – in what appears as an *obiter dictum* – the conditions for regulation to be non-compensable according to this approach.[141] Relying on general international law, the tribunal noted that regulation is not compensable provided that:

1) it is non-discriminatory;
2) it is for a public purpose;
3) it is enacted in accordance with due process; and
4) there are no specific commitments given by the regulating government to the foreign investor that the government would refrain from such regulation.[142]

The tribunal thus stressed that regulatory measures as a main rule do not constitute indirect expropriations provided that the regulation is non-discriminatory. Accordingly, the tribunal rejected the sole effect doctrine as earlier imposed by the tribunal in the *Metalclad* case. On the contrary, the tribunal highlighted the motives and intentions of the host state and concluded that the policy decision to ban the MTBE *"was motivated by the honest belief, held in good faith and on reasonable scientific grounds that MTBE contaminated groundwater and was difficult and expensive to clean up".*[143] In continuation hereof, the tribunal found that the investor, Methanex, enjoyed no protected legitimate expectation to continue the production and sale of the chemical substance prohibited by the Californian authorities. The tribunal in the *Methanex case* thus seems to create a presumption that non-discriminatory regulation is not expropriation, even if it

---

141 *Methanex v USA*, Final Award, 2005, Part IV, Chapter D, p. 4, para. 7.
142 *Ibid.*
143 *Ibid.*, para. 102.

has an economic impact on the investor, provided that the measure is taken in a *bona fide* manner, i.e. that the host state acts in good faith. The tribunal does not, however, elaborate further on what is decisive for regulatory measures to be deemed non-discriminatory. Does it suffice that the government did not intend to discriminate? Or is the key element that the regulation is not *de facto* discriminatory? In order not to support a stringent, formalistic notion, the better view seems to be to focus on actual discrimination, i.e. whether measures *de facto* are discriminating or not.

These contextual aspects articulated in the *Methanex* case have been supplemented by other tribunals taking into account the proportionality of the measure. In this regard, tribunals have examined whether the challenged measure is reasonably proportional to the purpose the government seeks to achieve. In other words, tribunals have assessed the excessiveness of the individual loss or burden placed on specific investors taking into consideration the purpose of the measure. As explained above in Chapter 4, the proportionality test is found in the jurisprudence of the ECtHR.[144]

In the *S.D. Myers* case, the tribunal implied a proportionality test taking the various concerns into account by stressing that it was required to look at *"the real interests"* involved and the purpose and effect of the government measure.[145]

The proportionality test was later spelled out in *Tecmed v Mexico*.[146] In this case the tribunal held that the government's intention was relevant though 'less important'.[147] The intention was thereby given some priority, though just a lower priority than the effect of the measures. Like the *Metalclad* case, the *Tecmed* case, stressed the actual effects of the measure. The cases concerned comparable issues.[148] However, in *Tecmed* the tribunal held that the effect did not by itself sufficiently establish that the decision to revoke a permit could be deemed expropriatory. In this regards, the *Tecmed* tribunal drew on the jurisprudence by the ECtHR and held that the decisive factor was whether the measures were proportionate in view of their purpose and effect:[149]

> *"There must be a reasonable relationship of proportionality between the charge or weight imposed to the foreign investor and the aim sought to be realized by any expropriatory measure."*

In line with the jurisprudence of the ECtHR in the *James and Others* case,[150] the tribunal emphasized that foreigners are more vulnerable to domestic legislation

---

144 See also Alvik, *Contracting With Sovereignty*, 268; Salacuse, *The Law of Investment Treaties*, 313–15; Yannaca-Small, "Indirect Expropriation and the Right to Regulate," 472–4.
145 *S.D. Myers v Canada*, NAFTA, Partial Award, 2000, para. 285.
146 *Tecmed v Mexico*, Award, 29 May 2003.
147 See also Schefer, *International Investment Law*, 210–18.
148 In *Tecmed*: Denial of an extension of an existing licence. In *Metalclad*: Revocation of a permit to operate a landfill.
149 *Tecmed v Mexico*, Award, 29 May 2003, para. 122.
150 *James and Others v United Kingdom*, ECtHR, 21 February 1986, para. 63.

than nationals since foreign investors are not entitled to exercise political rights, such as voting for decision-making authorities. According to the tribunal, this factor is part and parcel of the proportionality test. This perception supports the early view by Foighel.[151] The balanced approach laid down in the *Tecmed* case has subsequently been endorsed by other arbitral tribunals.

For example, the need for balancing the effect with the causes of the measure was explicitly emphasized by the tribunal in *LG&E v Argentina*:[152]

> *"The question remains as to whether one should only take into account the effects produced by the measure or if one should consider also the context within which a measure was adopted and the host State's purpose. It is this Tribunal's opinion that there must be a balance in the analysis both of the causes and the effects of a measure in order that one may qualify a measure as being of an expropriatory nature."*

In *Azurix v Argentina*,[153] the tribunal also adopted the proportionality test as enunciated in the *Tecmed* case. The tribunal emphasized that the public purpose criterion together with the effect of the measure had to be accompanied by something more. The tribunal criticized the tribunal in the *S.D. Meyers* case for its emphasis on *bona fide* regulation within the accepted police powers of the state as a criterion for distinguishing between compensable and non-compensable regulation. As stressed by the tribunal in *Azurix v Argentina* this criterion was *"insufficient"*. The tribunal then held that a test of proportionality would *"provide useful guidance for purposes of determining whether regulatory actions would be expropriatory and give rise to compensation"*.[154]

In terms of distinguishing compensable regulation from non-compensable regulation the balanced approach allows for several factors to be taken into account. However, this approach does not solve the question of how much weight should be granted to the various criteria and which criteria should be decisive. Some tribunals seem to have adopted a general perception that regulation for social or welfare purposes allows for a wider regulatory space. In *LG&E v Argentina*, for example, the tribunal seemed to support the view that states have the right to adopt social welfare regulation with the implications that measure must be accepted without any imposition of liability, except in cases where the state's action *"is obviously disproportionate"* to the need being addressed.[155] The relevant proportionality test for questions regarding the right to regulate is thus whether the measures are proportional to the public interest protected vs. the legal protection accorded to investments.

---

151 See above section 8.4 See also Foighel, *Nationalization: A Study in the Protection of Alien Property in International Law.*
152 *LG&E v Argentina*, Decision on Liability, 3 October 2006, para. 194.
153 *Azurix v Argentina*, Award, 16 July 2006.
154 *Ibid.*, para. 310–12.
155 *LG&E v Argentina*, Decision on Liability, 3 October 2006, para. 195.

In general, it can be inferred from arbitral practice that the intentions of the host state do play a significant role. Allowing more weight to the intentions of the host state can also be an argument in favour of certain types of regulation. This can be explained through the example of tax regulation vs. environmental regulation. For instance, while acknowledging that both types of regulation aim at preserving public interest, one might say that the intentions of a state adopting environmental regulation due to an imminent risk or scientific proof of certain chemicals being dangerous to the life of citizens or the environments, carry more weight than the motive to finance the state, the latter imposing a less imminent risk for the state. At the same time, however, the purpose of the measure is not primarily what conditions its legitimacy, but whether it is a result of legitimate authority.[156] Upon review of arbitral practice, it is found that an approach of balancing various factors seems to be predominant.[157] All in all, a balanced approach is also favourable to a more unified approach to the law since it takes into account a broader range of concerns.

8. The concept of legitimate expectations and the implications for the right to regulate

Whereas the balanced approach to the law emphasizes the need for taking into account the various contextual factors, it does not articulate what weight should be granted to the various elements. What determine the weight is case-specific where the expectations of the investor play a pivotal role.

As explained earlier, the concept of expropriation covers not only open and deliberate takings of property but also indirect measures in the form of *"covert or incidental interference with the use of property which has the effect of depriving the owner, in whole or in significant part, of the use or reasonably-to-be-expected economic benefit of property even if not necessarily to the obvious benefit of the host State".*[158] The concept of *'reasonably to be expected economic benefit'* has increasingly received attention in practice and has been referred to as the more broadly *'concept of legitimate expectations'.*[159] The way in which the legitimate expectations have been dealt with in arbitral practice is as an element included in the proportionality test. The concept of legitimate expectations play a key role in interpreting the fair and equitable treatment standard, but to some point also as a part of the law governing indirect expropriation.[160] Moreover, it has sometimes been considered as a part of the general principles of international law.[161]

---

156 See also Alvik, *Contracting With Sovereignty*, 268.
157 Dolzer and Schreuer, *Principles of International Investment Law*, 114.
158 *Metalclad v Mexico*, Award, 30 August 2000, para. 103.
159 Schefer, *International Investment Law*, 218ff; Dolzer and Schreuer, *Principles of International Investment Law*, 145–60; Reinisch, "Expropriation," 448f; Salacuse, *The Law of Investment Treaties*, 311–13.
160 Salacuse, *The Law of Investment Treaties*, 311.
161 Dolzer and Schreuer, *Principles of International Investment Law*, 115.

The following deals with the concept of legitimate expectations and the implications for the regulatory scope of the host state.

8.1. Public–private perspective: From vitiating circumstance to legitimate expectations

Host states make various commitments to investors. Some of these are embodied in formal bilateral agreements with an investor, such as investment accords, development contracts, public service concessions or tax stabilization agreements. Other commitments may be found in unilateral acts, like foreign investment legislation, licences and regulatory permissions or more indirectly through the behaviour of the government or principal state organs. Not surprisingly, foreign investors rely on such undertakings in their decision-making, and the willingness of host states to respect these commitments may often be vital to the profitability of an investment. These various commitments are typically governed by the national law of the host state. It may therefore be questionable whether the law of the host state provides sufficient protection for the investor. The continued viability is premised on the assumption that the host state will refrain from unilaterally altering or terminating the agreements, but the investor is likely to be uncertain about this. Rights to operate granted for one year may be cancelled the year after. This uncertainty may be further substantiated with regards to the likelihood that an agreement made with one government may be cancelled by a subsequent government.[162]

There are various reasons why governments should decide unilaterally to modify or terminate agreements. One reason might be that revenues do not meet governmental expectations after a few years of operation. Another reason might be that public opposition towards the project become strong and persistent. The host state may then choose to terminate or alter the conditions. Yet, such conduct is not without risks, since it may negatively impede on the investment climate.[163]

Oftentimes an investment project is established on a contractual basis. For various reasons, the contracting party of the host state may fail to perform the contract causing a breach of contract. From a private law perspective, an issue of contractual expectations is a question about the governing law on implied conditions in contract law, the *concept of vitiating circumstances*. From an international law perspective, these considerations become relevant under the *concept of legitimate expectations*. It may thus be said that the concept of vitiating circumstances transforms into the concept of legitimate expectations. This transformation entails consequences as to the rules that govern the problem. The following deals with two essential mechanisms: umbrella clauses in BITs and stabilization clauses in investment contracts. These legal mechanisms have consequences for the right to regulate.

---

162 Salacuse, *The Law of Investment Treaties*, 271–3.
163 *Ibid.*

8.2. General expectations of investors in a long-term investment project

Investors' expectations may vary largely depending on the project. Yet, as an implied condition, investors can at least expect to be treated in accordance with the minimum standard of treatment under customary international law.[164] In general, investors will always have some minimum expectations of economic benefits and legal stability. Otherwise, the investor would not have made the decision to invest; but, as held by Dolzer and Schreuer, to the extent that this state of law was transparent and did not violate minimum standards of treatment at the time of making the investment, an investor will hardly convince a tribunal that the proper application of that law has led to an expropriation.[165] It is thus the *changes* in the regulatory environment, either through changes in practice or through the adoption of new laws and regulations, which is at stake.

As mentioned, there are various elements that may be added to the basic expectations. Obviously, in an investment dispute one cannot attach importance to every expectation the investor may have. This is specifically found in the requirement that the expectations have to be 'legitimate'. For example, in the *Revere Copper v OPIC*,[166] the host state had given explicit contractual assurances not to increase taxes and royalties to the investor. The tribunal relied on these contractual assurances as a basis for the legitimate expectations of the investor. In the *Tecmed* case the tribunal emphasized that the investor *"had legitimate reasons to believe"* that the operation of the landfill would extend over the long term.[167] For expectations to be legitimate it requires the presence of 'something more' than the mere general legal framework, e.g. that the investor received an explicit promise or guarantee from the host state or, if implicitly, that the host state made assurances or representations that the investor took into account in making the investment.[168] Thus, assurances need to be a determinative factor at the time of making the decision to invest. When referring to "the concept of legitimate expectations" of the investor it thus entails a legal assessment of the expectations that the investor had.

A pertinent question then is whether the investor can expect that the state will *not* regulate? As a general rule, there is no legitimacy in an expectation that laws will not change. In a long-term project there is even more need for adapting terms and conditions to maintain the economic viability of the project as well as sustainability. Hence, it cannot be a general expectation that the state will not regulate, and regulation may even be economically burdensome. Phrased positively: as a fundamental basis, the investor should expect regulation having an

---

164 See above Chapter 2, section 6.
165 Dolzer and Schreuer, *Principles of International Investment Law*, 115.
166 *Revere Copper v OPIC*, Award, 24 August 1978.
167 *Tecmed v Mexico*, Award, 29 May 2003, para. 149. See also *Metalclad v Mexico*, Award, 30 August 2000; *Azurix v Argentina*, Award, 16 July 2006.
168 *Parkerings-Compagniet AS v Lithuania*, Award, 7 September 2007, para. 331.

economic impact on the investment. Yet, the extent of the economic burden has a limit, a threshold above which the duty to compensate will be triggered.

The following will show that this limit is not fixed but flexible. This means that a general threshold cannot be found. Rather, the threshold is case-specific. The parameters, which have an impact on this limit, are either general mechanisms applicable to all investors or specific mechanisms applicable *inter partes* between the host state and a concrete investor. The following will display such parameters, which can adjust the threshold, i.e. increasing or decreasing the legitimacy of the expectations that the investor may have.

8.3. *The expectations of the investor as a legal factor embraced in BIT practice*

Though born out of judicial practice, the concept of legitimate expectations has been incorporated into BIT practice by some countries. For example, references to the concept can be found in the model BITs of the United States, Canada and Colombia:

2012 American Model BIT Annex B, 4(a)(ii) *"reasonable investment-backed expectations"*.

2004 Canadian Model BIT, Annex B 13(1)(b)(ii) *"reasonable investment-backed expectations"*.

2009 Colombia Model BIT, Article VI, (2)(b)(ii) *"reasonable and distinguishable expectations concerning the investment"*.

Contrariwise, the model BITs by Italy (2003), Germany (2009), India (2003), Denmark (2005) or Sweden (2008) contain no such reference to the concept.

The concept of legitimate expectations has also found its way into concretely negotiated BITs. One example is the BIT between Columbia and Belgium, which mirrors the approach of the Columbian Model BIT in article IX(3)(b) of the BIT.[169] The BIT between Columbia and China refers in the same manner to the concept in article 4(2)(b)(ii).[170]

The concept of legitimate expectations is also covered by a provision in Annex B, 4(a)(ii) to the 2008 BIT between the United States and Rwanda. Pursuant to this provision, the extent to which the government action interferes with *"distinct, reasonable investment-backed expectations"* should be a factor in the determination of an indirect expropriation. A similar provision is found in Annex B, 4(a)(ii) to the 2006 BIT between the United States and Uruguay.

Pursuant to Annex A, (b)(ii) to the 2012 BIT between Canada and the Slovak Republic, the determination of whether a measure or series of measures constitute an indirect expropriation requires a case-by-case, fact-based inquiry that

---

169 The BIT was signed in 2009. Data is not available as to whether it is (yet) in force.
170 The BIT entered into force in 2012.

considers, inter alia, *"the extent to which the measure or series of measures interfere with distinct, reasonable, investment-backed expectations"*.

8.4. BIT mechanisms affecting the assessment of investors' expectations

The general legal mechanisms that may add to the minimum expectations of the investor are referred to as general because they are not directed towards a specific investor, a specific project or a specific investment. These mechanisms are found in the legal framework as such. Not surprisingly, the legal framework provided by the host state will be an important source of expectations on the part of the investor. Apart from national legislation adopted by the host state, an *international* general legal mechanism is the mere adoption of IIAs, such as BITs, in which the host state on a bilateral level agrees to the mutual protection of foreign investors and their investment. The adoption of the traditional liberal BIT approach generates expectations of protection of the investment. The long-term nature of BITs also supports the expectations of the investor.[171]

General legal mechanisms in BITs, which can have an impact on investors' expectations, are:

- a reference to the right to regulate;
- provisions articulating a presumption of non-compensations for specific types of regulation;
- the enunciation of specific public policy goals in the preamble;[172]
- the insertion of an umbrella clause.

An explicit right to regulate is an expression of the inherent right for states to regulate as sovereigns. The inclusion of such reference thereby generates a general expectation that the substantive provisions in a BIT are not intended to deviate from that right. Notwithstanding whether the right to regulate is referred to or not, states may exercise their right to regulate, but *if* the BIT contains an explicit reference to this right, it has an impact on what could be considered the legitimate expectations of the investor. The Norwegian Draft Model BIT is one example in this regard.[173]

As explained above, BITs containing a rule of interpretation or a rule of presumption against compensation for social welfare regulation (safety, health and the environment) provide a general expectation that the investor should not be compensated for these types of regulation.

In terms of explicitly referring to specific non-economic policy goals, this would create an expectation that the investor should anticipate regulation within these areas. For instance, the preamble of the 2012 American Model BIT stresses

---

171 See also Dolzer and Schreuer, *Principles of International Investment Law*, 115–17.
172 The aforementioned balanced approach, see Chapter 3, section 7.
173 See article 12 of the Draft.

the desire to achieve investment promotion and protection *"in a manner consistent with the protection of health, safety, and the environment, and the promotion of internationally recognized labour rights"*. Another example is the 2003 Swedish Model BIT, which in the preamble underlines that investment promotion and protection *"can be achieved without relaxing health, safety and environmental measures of general application"*. Consequently, preambles embracing a balanced approach can arguably affect the 'legitimacy' of the investor's expectations. This is because the investor's expectations, in terms of not being confronted with regulation within the stated non-economic policy areas, no longer are legitimate.

An example hereof is Rwanda and its BITs with the United States and Germany, respectively. Rwanda is an African state, which has been referred to as a 'lion-economy',[174] which implies an economy rapidly on the rise and thus appealing for future foreign investments. The USA–Rwanda BIT from 2008 explicitly outlines in the preamble that protection of foreign investment must be achieved consistent with other key policy objectives:

> *"Desiring to achieve these objectives in a manner consistent with the protection of health, safety, and the environment, and the promotion of internationally recognized labor rights."*

Accordingly, this BIT relies on the balanced approach to preambles.[175] This balancing of interests is thus explicitly referred to and must be taken into account in the interpretation of the substantive rights of the treaty.

The earlier Germany–Rwanda BIT from 1967 on the contrary relies on the traditional approach to preambles:

> *"IN DEM WUNSCH, die wirtschaftliche Zusammenarbeit zwischen ihren beiden Staaten zu vertiefen,*
>
> *IN DEM BESTREBEN, günstige Bedingungen für Kapitalanlangen von Staatsangehörigen und Gesellschaften des einen Staates im Hoheitsgebiet des anderen Staates zu schaffen, und*
>
> *IN DER ERKENNTNIS, daß die Förderung dieser Kapitalanlagen geeignet ist, die privatwirtschaftliche Initiative zu beleben und den Wohlstand beider Völker zu mehren –"*

In contrast to the USA–Rwanda BIT, the Germany–Rwanda BIT thus does not declare that investment protection must be consistent with other key policy objectives. On the basis of these differences, one could argue that a German investor may have a more solid basis for legitimate expectations, i.e. that social

---

174 *The Economist*, "The Sun Shines Bright; Africa's Hopeful Economies," 3 December 2011, pp. 82–4. See also the report by McKinsey Global Institute, "Lions on the Move: The Progress and Potential of African Economies," June 2010.
175 Chapter 3, section 7.

regulation will not inhibit the investment compared to an American investor, who as a main rule must accept that investment protection cannot compromise raising social standards such as health, safety and promotion of environmental standards and labour rights enunciated in the preamble of the USA–Rwanda BIT. However, this is not to say that the German investor should not accept new and economically burdensome requirements imposed by the host state (Rwanda) to promote social standards, namely with regards to realizing human rights under the ICESCR. No such guarantee is given. The host state can still exert its right to regulate as a sovereign right under general international law, but in terms of an investment dispute one could argue that it makes a difference for the assessment of the legitimacy of the investor's expectations and accordingly the distinction between compensable and non-compensable regulation.

Besides the preamble, substantive clauses may have implications for the expectations of the investor and thereby for the assessment of whether investors' should be compensated for regulation or not. Umbrella clauses are essential in this regard. The umbrella clause is therefore dealt with in this respect below.

8.4.1. Umbrella clauses and the impact on investors' legitimate expectations

It is a well-established principle of international law that a breach of a state contract is not per se considered a breach of international law.[176] Many BITs include a provision requiring each party to the treaty 'to observe any obligation' into which it has entered with respect to an investment.[177] This kind of provision is known as an 'umbrella clause', since it may bring contractual commitments within the coverage, or umbrella, of the BIT.[178] The umbrella clause is thus an exception to the well-established principle of international law. These clauses pave the way for contractual undertakings having an impact upon the regulatory scope of host states.

Historically, the purpose of the umbrella clause was to ensure that disputes under investment contracts would be resolved in a neutral forum and enforced as a matter of international law. The idea of using investment treaties to give effect to the protection of contractual rights in international law can be traced back to negotiations concerning the Iranian oil nationalization disputes and to the Abs–Shawcross draft from 1959.[179]

---

176 See above Chapter 2, section 6.4.
177 Salacuse, *The Law of Investment Treaties*, 277; Katia Yannaca-Small, "What About This 'Umbrella Clause'?," in *Arbitration under International Investment Agreements: A Guide to the Key Issues*, ed. Katia Yannaca-Small (Oxford: Oxford University Press, 2010), 483. With regards to BITs by member states of the EU, see Angelos Dimopoulos, *EU Foreign Investment Law*, 2nd ed. (Oxford: Oxford University Press, 2011), 57.
178 Dolzer and Schreuer, *Principles of International Investment Law*, 166.
179 See e.g. Mclachlan et al., *International Investment Arbitration*, 93; Salacuse, *The Law of Investment Treaties*, 276f; Yannaca-Small, "What About This 'Umbrella Clause'?," 481–3.

The umbrella clause was included in the first BITs in the 1960s and is now found in a vast number of BITs, in particular in Western model BITs. Notably, the provision is absent in many non-Western BITs.[180] It appears in the Energy Charter Treaty[181] but not in the NAFTA. A typical formulation of an umbrella clause is found in the Denmark–Egypt BIT, stating in article 2(3): *"Each contracting party shall observe any obligation it may have entered into with regard to investments of investors of the other contracting party."* Though other formulations of the umbrella clause can be found, the language of the observance of obligations provision is virtually identical in most BITs. There are two common factors in the wording of the umbrella clause: 1) the use of mandatory language (e.g. *"shall observe"*) and 2) the fact that the clause relates to obligations undertaken by the state, and therefore do not refer to obligations between private individuals.

A pertinent question in this respect is how an umbrella clause in a BIT may materially affect the regulatory space of the host state. To assess this, it is necessary to have a closer look at the interpretation of the clause in practice. The most contentious issues with regards to the umbrella clause concern whether and to what extent the provision itself make the breach of an obligation in an investment contract between the host state and the investor a breach of international law.[182] If so, the umbrella clause can turn a claim based on the contract to a claim under the BIT. One may question the need for an enforcement of the obligations to preserve contractual obligations since these are already binding pursuant to the international law norm of *pacta sunt servanda*.[183] In recognition of this international law principle, the observance of obligations provision, the umbrella clause, arguably goes further and provides for additional protection. For example, it is possible that the umbrella clause imposes further obligations upon the state to the extent that it is violated by mere breaches of contract not constituting an expropriation.[184]

The case of *SGS v Pakistan*[185] (2003) was one of the first cases to discuss the meaning of an umbrella clause in the BIT between Switzerland and Pakistan.

---

180 For instance it does not appear in the Sri Lanka Model BIT, Chinas Model BIT or the Model BIT of Chile. In contrast, it is found in the UK Model BIT, the French Model BIT and the US Model BIT. See also Mclachlan et al., *International Investment Arbitration*, 94; Alvik, *Contracting With Sovereignty*, 177.

181 Article 10(1).

182 Dolzer and Schreuer, *Principles of International Investment Law*, 166.

183 See above Chapter 2, section 4.2.

184 Vandevelde, *Bilateral Investment Treaties*, 259. For the interpretation of umbrella clauses by investment tribunals see also Maria Cristina Griton Salias, "Do Umbrella Clauses Apply to Unilateral Undertakings?," in *International Investment Law for the 21st Century: Essays in Honour of Christoph Schreuer*, ed. Christina Binder, Ursula Kriebaum, August Reinisch, and Stephan Wittich (Oxford: Oxford University Press, 2009), 490–6; Dolzer and Schreuer, *Principles of International Investment Law*, 166–78; Salacuse, *The Law of Investment Treaties*, 279–83.

185 *SGS v Pakistan*, Decision of the Tribunal on Objections to Jurisdiction, 6 August 2003, para. 11.

In 1994 Pakistan entered into a contract with Société Générale de Surveillance S.A. (SGS) whereby SGS agreed to provide 'pre-shipment inspection' services with respect to goods to be exported from certain countries to Pakistan. SGS undertook to inspect such goods i) abroad through its offices and affiliates; and ii) at Pakistani ports of entry jointly with Pakistani Customs. When Pakistan unilaterally terminated the contract, SGS initiated ICSID arbitration under the BIT between Pakistan and Switzerland.

In this case the tribunal made a quite restrictive interpretation of the given umbrella clause, which stated: *"Either Contracting Party shall constantly guarantee the observance of the commitments it has entered into with respect to the investments of the investors of the other Contracting Party."*[186] Strikingly, the tribunal declined to interpret the clause in accordance with its ordinary meaning. The tribunal thus rejected SGS's contention that the referred clause elevated breaches of a contract to breaches of the treaty.[187] If it were to be read literally, the tribunal noted, the text of the umbrella clause would be applicable to any commitment by the state or any conduct attributable to the state.[188] Allowing contract claims to turn into treaty claims would lead to a flood of lawsuits before international tribunals and obviate the meaning of other guarantees contained in investment treaties.[189] In addition to this, the tribunal attached significant importance to the location of the umbrella clause towards the end of the treaty, which, according to the tribunal, was an argument against a far-reaching obligation.[190] This argument, however, does not seem convincing. On the contrary, placing the umbrella clause towards the end of the treaty emphasizes the very rationale behind the clause, i.e. to be considered more like a 'catch-all' clause. At least, placing the umbrella clause towards the end of the treaty demonstrate that it captures further infringements and provides further treaty protection than measures not covered by other substantive parts of the treaty.

In continuation hereof, the tribunal found that contract claims were not to be accepted as treaty claims in the absence of clear and convincing evidence that this was actually the intention of the drafting parties. Drawing on WTO jurisprudence, the tribunal found that the proper mode of interpretation of a BIT was "in the case of doubt for the restrictive view".[191] Accordingly, the tribunal reversed the usual presumption in favour of interpreting treaty language in accordance with its meaning.

The tribunal in *SGS v Pakistan* did not preclude the possibility that under exceptional circumstances, a violation of certain provisions of a state contract with

---

186 Article 11 in the BIT. See also Dolzer and Schreuer, *Principles of International Investment Law*, 157f.
187 *SGS v Pakistan*, Decision of the Tribunal on Objections to Jurisdiction, 6 August 2003, para. 166.
188 *Ibid.*, para 168.
189 *Ibid.*
190 *Ibid.*, para. 169.
191 *Ibid.*, para. 171, note 178.

an investor of another state might constitute a violation of a treaty provision.[192] However, the tribunal refrained from making it clear when such 'exceptional measures' would occur. In reaction to the award, the Swiss Government (home state of the investor) sent a letter to ICSID stating that it was *"alarmed about the very narrow interpretation"* given to the provision by the tribunal, which was contrary to Switzerland's intention in concluding the BIT.[193]

There are two major reasons why the view of the tribunal in *SGS v Pakistan* does not seem convincing. *Firstly*, the VCLT is – as explained in Chapter 2[194] – the primary tool for interpreting treaties. The VCLT does not support a restrictive view in case of doubt. *Secondly*, the fact that the tribunal finds some support for this approach in the jurisprudence by the WTO[195] is not completely convincing, since it is a different system with a different procedure by the appellate body.

Shortly after the award in *SGS v Pakistan* another tribunal took quite a different approach in *SGS v Philippines* (2004).[196] This umbrella clause was a bit different: *"Each Contracting Party shall observe any obligation it has assumed with regard to specific investments in its territory by investors of the other Contracting Party."*[197] Even though the tribunal recognized the differences in the wording, it criticized the *SGS v Pakistan* award as being *"unconvincing"*, *"highly restrictive"* and *"failing to give any clear meaning to the umbrella clause"*.[198] In contrast to *SGS v Pakistan*, the tribunal in its decision on jurisdiction ruled that, in the presence of an umbrella clause, a violation of an investment contractual agreement would lead to a violation of the treaty.[199] In *SGS v Philippines* the tribunal thus took a wider reading of the scope of the umbrella clause.

While the *SGS v Philippines* did adopt a wider interpretation of the scope of the umbrella clause, the *SGS v Pakistan* case should not be considered an isolated decision, and it has subsequently been supported in other awards.[200] For instance, the tribunals in *El Paso v Argentina*[201] and *Pan American v Argentina*[202] indicated that only certain types of public contracts are covered by umbrella clauses. In *El Paso v Argentina* the tribunal did not permit contractual breaches as a breach of the umbrella clause in the BIT. The award of *Pan American v Argentina* followed the same approach. Here the tribunal introduced a

---

192 *Ibid.*, para. 172.
193 The letter is quoted in the *Eureko v Poland*, Partial Award, 19 August 2005, para. 254.
194 Chapter 2, section 9.3.
195 *SGS v Pakistan*, Decision of the Tribunal on Objections to Jurisdiction, 6 August 2003, para. 171, note 178.
196 *SGS v Philippines*, Decision of the Tribunal on Objections to Jurisdiction, 29 January 2004.
197 BIT between Philippines and Switzerland, Article X(2).
198 *SGS v Philippines*, Decision of the Tribunal on Objections to Jurisdiction, 29 January 2004, paras 119 and 125.
199 *Ibid.*, para. 128.
200 *El Paso Energy v Argentina*, Decision on Jurisdiction, 27 April 2006; *Pan American v Argentina*, Decision on Preliminary Objections, 27 July 2006.
201 *El Paso Energy v Argentina*, Decision on Jurisdiction, 27 April 2006.
202 *Pan American v Argentina*, Decision on Preliminary Objections, 27 July 2006.

distinction between the *state as a merchant* and the *state as a sovereign*, where investment arbitration should only cover disputes where the state acts as a sovereign.[203] In that way the tribunals accepted that obligations in investor–state contracts are covered by the clause to the extent that they bind the state in its sovereign capacity. This, however, raises the question of how to distinguish measures that are merchant acts vs. measures falling into the category of sovereign acts. Since investment agreements by nature are for commercial purposes it is difficult to make that distinction in investment law. In terms of regulatory measures, the adoption of laws and regulations seems to fall into the category of sovereign acts.

In *Noble Ventures v Romania*[204] the tribunal adopted a broad interpretation of an umbrella clause in a BIT between Romania and the United States and stressed that there was no doubt that the umbrella clause was intended to create obligations beyond those specified in other provisions of the BIT itself.[205] With reference to the principle of effectiveness, the tribunal emphasized that any other interpretation of the umbrella clause would deprive it of practical content.[206]

In a more recent case from 2012 of *SGS v Paraguay*,[207] the tribunal had to determine whether there was a breach of contract due to 1) the failure by Paraguay to meet its payment obligations,[208] and 2) additional promises by the host state to pay SGS's invoices through various oral and written representations during and after the termination of the contract.[209] The tribunal adopted a wide recognition of the applicability of an umbrella clause to contractual commitments, since the intentions of the umbrella clause was to provide an additional substantive protection to foreign investments *"in addition to whatever rights the investor could negotiate for itself in a contract or could find under domestic law"*.[210]

8.4.2. Umbrella clauses may enhance imbalance

As shown, umbrella clauses may allow investors to bring a claim and to obtain compensation for the non-performance of state obligations. In general, the umbrella clause can be perceived as the link between international law and contractual undertakings or as a clause in BITs that may draw contracts out of the confines of national law by transforming them into an obligation under international law.[211] Accordingly, umbrella clauses should be given the effect that originally was the intention to cover contractual obligations. It is up to the states when

---

203 *Ibid.*, para. 108.
204 *Noble Ventures, Inc. v Romania*, Award, 12 October 2005.
205 *Ibid.*, para. 51.
206 *Ibid.*, para. 52.
207 *SGS v Paraguay*, Award, 10 February 2012.
208 According to the claimant, SGS, such breach in itself amounted to a breach of the umbrella clause.
209 According to the claimant, SGS, these additional representations were enforceable commitments under the umbrella clause.
210 *SGS v Paraguay*, Award, 10 February 2012, para. 76.
211 Alvik, *Contracting With Sovereignty*, 177–92.

they negotiate BITs to decide whether an umbrella clause should be included and, in the affirmative, how broad any given umbrella clause should be. Yet, if the clause is there, the investor may potentially use the clause to elevate a breach of contract to the level of international arbitration. However, as demonstrated above, recent awards[212] and discussions[213] show that the interpretation of umbrella clauses is a matter that has not been entirely resolved. Therefore, the insertion of clear language in new BITs would be a much-needed development.

What can be found in practice is a considerable support for the view that umbrella clauses potentially may broaden the substantive investment protection to cover contractual agreements. Umbrella clauses in BITs may thus indirectly impede on the regulatory space of manoeuvre by strengthening investment protection. It can also be said that umbrella clauses may substantiate expectations by the investor that even contractual breaches might be covered.

In the view of the investor, the insertion of an umbrella clause in a BIT changes the general risk perception for investors planning and assessing the opportunities to enter the market of the host state. States may thus choose to provide the additional guarantees to observe contractual commitments through the inclusion of an umbrella clause in a BIT. One may therefore conclude that the umbrella clause is an element objectively strengthening the legitimate expectations of the investor. In that way, umbrella clauses enhance the stability aspect in BITs, which is already the stronger aspect of the treaty. Yet, formulations may be undesirably broad and intrude on what states consider their right to regulate. As mentioned, many BITs include a provision formulated as an umbrella clause. In terms of future EU investment agreements, umbrella clauses will in all likelihood be included.[214] From the perspective of the unification of the international investment law regime, it is, however, doubtful whether the inclusion of umbrella clauses in BITs is desirable.

8.5. Specific commitments affecting the assessment of investors' expectations

Whereas umbrella clauses generally apply to all foreign investors, there may also be specific agreements with concrete investors that have an impact on the

---

212 In *SGS v Pakistan* ICSID, (2003) the tribunal made a quite restrictive interpretation of the umbrella clause found in the BIT between Switzerland and Pakistan. Soon after this award another tribunal took a different approach in *SGS v Philippines* (2004) adopting a wide interpretation of the umbrella clause in the BIT between Switzerland and Philippines allowing the ICSID tribunal jurisdiction for contractual claims.

213 See, inter alia, Crawford, "Treaty and Contract in Investment Arbitration," 351–74; Jarrod Wong, "Umbrella Clauses in Bilateral Investment Treaties: Of Breaches of Contract, Treaty Violations, and the Divide Between Developing and Developed Countries in Foreign Investment Disputes," *George Mason Law Review* 14, no. 1 (2006): 135–77; OECD Working Paper, *"Interpretation of the Umbrella Clause in Investment Agreements,"* October 2006.

214 According to Dimopoulos; see Dimopoulos, *EU Foreign Investment Law*, 57.

legitimate expectations of an investor. These legal mechanisms are referred to as specific since they only affect the relation between the host state and a specific investor.

The specific legal mechanisms that can be identified as having an impact on the investor's legitimate expectations are for example specific guarantees and contractual undertakings. Practice supports that specific commitments given by the host state can switch the balance by enhancing investor's legitimate expectations. For example, in the *Methanex* case the tribunal stressed that *"as a matter of general international law, a non-discriminatory regulation for a public purpose, which is enacted in accordance with due process and, which affects . . . a foreign investor or investment is not deemed expropriatory and compensable unless specific commitments had been given by the regulating government to the then putative foreign investor contemplating investment that the government would refrain from such regulation".*[215] Besides concrete legal mechanisms, specific measures of a non-legal character, such as the conduct towards an investor, specific behaviour or statements by public authorities may have an influence on the investor's expectations.

Again, conduct and behaviour will typically belong to the facts of a specific case. Where such commitments take the form of conduct or behaviour by the state, it may be less clear whether such conduct even expresses a commitment by the host state. If commitments are laid down in an investment contract, investors are likely to have a more solid basis for proving the existence of a commitment and that they relied on such commitment. Another contentious aspect of host state commitments concerns how to identify 'the state'. It may, for instance, be less clear where commitments include undertakings by other governmental bodies, which may or may not be separate legal entities, as well as state-owned enterprises.

Specific legal mechanisms generating expectations towards an investor are oftentimes contained in contractual devices in contracts between the state and the investor.[216] Sometimes, however, such concrete guarantees are not explicitly declared. For example, in a recent case, *Railroad Development Corporation (RDC) v Guatemala*[217] from 2012 the tribunal stated that in a situation where three contracts relate to the same operation, an investor (RDC, a privately owned railway investment and management company) who had won all three through international public bidding, two of which had been approved by the respondent or its agencies, could reasonably expect that the third contract would also be ratified.[218] It thus follows that legitimate expectations may be created not only by explicit undertakings on the part of the host state in contracts but also implicitly by specific commitments to an investor.[219]

---

215 *Methanex Corporation v United States of America*, Final Award, 3 August 2005, Part IV, Chapter D, para. 7.
216 See below with regards to stabilization clauses, section 8.5.1.
217 *Railroad Development Corporation (RDC) v Guatemala*, Award, 2012.
218 *Ibid.*, para. 120.
219 See also *Azurix v Argentina*, Award, 14 July 2006, para. 318.

Determining the weight that should be given to investors' legitimate expectations is commonly an issue in indirect expropriation claims. The question is whether the foreign investor could reasonably have expected that the economic value of its property would have been lost either in whole or in significant part by the regulatory measures taken by the state. In this assessment, specific guarantees may be crucial.

In the *Metalclad* case, the tribunal addressed the concept of legitimate expectations in the context of an indirect expropriation. The case concerned two sets of separate governmental measures imposed on the investor operating a landfill; one being addressed at the specific investor (a set of events that cumulatively denied the company a permit to operate), and another being of general character (a state-level act that essentially converted the property into an ecological reserve, taking all private rights away from Metalclad). In this case, the tribunal stressed the importance of the expectations created by the government's assurances to Metalclad:[220]

> *"These measures, taken together with the representations of the Mexican federal government, on which Metalclad relied, and the absence of a timely, orderly or substantive basis for the denial by the Municipality of the local construction permit, amount to an indirect expropriation."*

Likewise, in the *Tecmed* case, the tribunal attached significant importance to the expectations of the investor in the determination of whether an investment had been expropriated:[221]

> *"... upon making its investment, the Claimant had legitimate reasons to believe that the operation of the Landfill would extend over the long term. The political and social circumstances [. . .] could not have reasonably been foreseen by the Claimant with the scope, effects and consequences that those circumstances had. There is no doubt that [. . .] the Claimant's expectation was that of a long-term investment relying on the recovery of its investment and the estimated return through the operation of the Landfill during its entire useful life."*

States may thus through various acts provide investors with guarantees or specific commitments that the investor will rely on when making the investment.

8.5.1. Stabilization clauses and the regulatory space of manoeuvre

The following addresses the right to regulate from a private law perspective showing how contractual devices in the form of stabilization clauses can generate specific commitments that limit the scope of states' right to regulate. As it appears, this may be an unintended outcome for states using stabilization clauses.

---

220 *Metalclad v Mexico*, Award, 30 August 2000, para. 107.
221 *Tecmed v Mexico*, Award, 29 May 2003, para. 149.

The concept of protection of 'acquired rights' is a concept that is closely linked with the concept of legitimate expectations. On a closer scrutiny by Alvik, the concept of acquired rights applied to contractual undertakings in respect of investments *"is not so much reminiscent of a strict sanctity of contracts approach as a notion of legitimate expectations based on reliance..."*.[222] Protection of contractual undertakings is thus part of the equation when it come to the assessment of the investor's legitimate expectations. According to *Waste Management v Mexico*,[223] the non-performance by a state party to a contract does not per se constitute an expropriation but 'something more' is required.[224] A stabilization clause could in principle constitute this 'something more'.

As laid down in Chapter 1, under the stability–flexibility dilemma it is a central concern for investors to safeguard the stability of the investment project. Changes in the legal framework may therefore constitute a critical legal risk, and investors may employ several methods to mitigate that risk. Whereas the opportunity for investors to influence the drafting of a BIT may – at least in principle – be uncertain, investors may be in a better position to control the terms and conditions of the contractual layer. One option relates to the choice of law applicable to the contract. Another contractual mechanism is the dispute resolution clause determining where contractual disputes should be settled. A third option is the insertion of a 'stabilization clause' in an investment contract.[225]

Stabilization clauses are contractual devices that could be described as a special variant of a choice-of-law clause in an investment contract and thereby basically a matter of private law. These clauses are relevant since they may oblige host states to compensate foreign investors for regulation, which may not otherwise be considered a taking in the form of indirect expropriation. In combination with an umbrella clause that is designed to protect the investor against violations of a contractual arrangement, a violation of a stabilization clause may trigger an international claim for compensation in investor–state arbitration.[226] Contractual clauses that potentially restrict states' right to regulate thereby become an international law issue.

Since there is no stabilization clause as such and formulation of the clause may vary,[227] stabilization clauses are considered from a more general perspective. The focus of the analysis here is to determine the potential legal effects of the clause on the right to regulate. Stabilization clauses may read: *"The laws of the state of Utopia are applicable as in force of 1 January 2013."* Stabilization clauses thus 'stabilize' or 'freeze' the applicable law, typically from the time of making an investment. Stabilization clauses thus enhance the stability aspect. The pertinent

---

222 Alvik, *Contracting With Sovereignty*, 219.
223 *Waste Management v Mexico*, Award, 30 April 2004.
224 *Ibid.*, paras 159–60.
225 See further in Dolzer and Schreuer, *Principles of International Investment Law*, 82–5; Sornarajah, *The International Law on Foreign Investment*, 281–4.
226 Mclachlan et al., *International Investment Arbitration*, 116.
227 Dolzer and Schreuer, *Principles of International Investment Law*, 82.

question, however, is whether investors in fact achieve the certainty and stability that is expected from such a clause.

Though stabilization clauses can be drafted in various ways, two more common categories of stabilization clauses can be identified:[228]

Freezing clauses

Freezing clauses fix or freeze for the term of the project the applicable domestic legislation or regulations affecting the project to those in effect as of the date of the investment contract. Under these clauses, legislation adopted after the date of the investment contract is not applicable to the foreign investors or the project unless the investor agrees.

Economic equilibrium clauses

Economic equilibrium clauses come in two versions. Under a rigid economic equilibrium clause, changes in law occurring after the execution of the investment contract apply to the project and its foreign investors, except that the host state must compensate the investor for the cost of complying with them. For instance, the host state may impose new emissions standards concerning a power plant, but the costs of modifying the plant's design or customizing the plant will be borne by the host state. Under a more flexible equilibrium clause, the host state and the investor would commit to conducting future negotiations with the goal of recalibrating the original allocation of risks or losses/gains, based on the reality of the new legislation. This type of stabilization clause has emerged in more modern agreements.

In essence, it is not crucial to determine which category the clause belongs to. Rather, this is to show that there are diverging formulations of stability clauses, and accordingly the degree to which the clause actually freezes the applicable law varies. Therefore, the actual legal effect of the clause depends on the wording of the clause.

8.5.2. Stabilization clauses enhance legitimate expectations of the investor

The extent to which a stabilization clause may affect the expectations of the investor is controversial. As stated by the tribunal in *Paushok v Mongolia*[229] concerning tax regulation *"investors cannot legitimately expect that the taxation environment*

---

228 Andrea Shemberg, "Stabilization Clauses and Human Rights" (International Finance Corporation, report by the World Bank Group, 27 May 2009): 5.
229 *Paushok v Mongolia*, Award, 28 April 2011.

which they face at the time of their first investment will not be substantially altered with the passage of time and the evolution of events".[230] Likewise, investors cannot expect that changes will not occur in the non-fiscal environment. On the contrary, the tribunal concluded in *Impregilo v Argentina*[231] that *"the legitimate expectations of foreign investors cannot be that the State will never modify the legal framework".*[232] In addition, the tribunal seemed to imply that in situations of severe economic crisis in the host country, investors should even expect increased regulation.[233]

In *Parkerings-Compagniet v Lithuania,*[234] the arbitrators recognized the right for states to modify their laws but implicitly acknowledged that a stabilization clause might bar regulation:[235]

> *"It is each State's undeniable right and privilege to exercise its sovereign legislative power. A state has the right to enact, modify or cancel a law at its own discretion. Save for the existence of an agreement, in the form of a stabilisation clause or otherwise, there is nothing objectionable about the amendment brought to the regulatory framework existing at the time an investor made its investment. As a matter of fact, any businessman or investor knows that laws will evolve over time. What is prohibited however is for a State to act unfairly, unreasonably or inequitably in the exercise of its legislative power."*

According to the tribunal, states are free to exercise their right to regulate. When they have not made explicit commitments toward an investor, investors should even expect to be met by regulatory changes. Investors must accept such changes, as long as they are fair, reasonable and equitable. Contrariwise, when specific commitments not to regulate in the form of stabilization clauses exist, investors should not accept such regulatory changes. In these instances investors can expect to be compensated, even if regulatory changes are fair, reasonable and equitable. In addition hereto, the tribunal particularly highlighted that in circumstances with a country in transition, no expectation that the laws would remain unchanged could be perceived legitimate.[236] The investor had the opportunity to protect its legitimate expectations, for instance through a stabilization clause into

---

230 *Ibid.*, para. 370.
231 *Impregilo v Argentina*, Award, 21 June 2011.
232 *Ibid.*, para. 291.
233 *Ibid.*
234 *Parkerings-Compagniet v Lithuania*, Award, 7 September 2007.
235 *Ibid.*, paras 331–3. Instead of referring to the protection of foreign investments against unlawful expropriations, the tribunal seems to categorize a potential breach of stabilization clause in contract as a breach of *"the duty to grant full protection and fair and equitable treatment"*; see para. 244.
236 The political environment in Lithuania was characteristic of a country in transition from its past being part of the Soviet Union to candidate for the European Union membership. Under these circumstances, legislative changes were far from being unpredictable, but on the contrary regarded as likely; *Parkerings-Compagniet v Lithuania*, Award, 7 September 2007, para. 335.

the investment agreement, but with no such guarantee, the investor was considered to have taken the business risk to invest, notwithstanding the possible legal and political instability.[237]

In a case from 2012, *Toto v Lebanon*,[238] the tribunal indirectly touched upon stabilization clauses as a factor, which would increase the expectations of the investor. Here the tribunal stressed specifically that the investment contract did not contain a stabilization clause, nor provided that custom duties and taxes would not be changed. The investor could therefore not legitimately expect to be compensated for price increases beyond what the contract provided for.[239]

8.5.3. The legal effect of stabilization clauses

The legal implications of stabilization clauses are controversial. This is because it remains unclear to what extent stabilization clauses may freeze the applicable law. Interpreted literally, freezing clauses do not allow attention to the purpose of the regulation. So, freezing clauses do thus not distinguish between various types of regulation.

In principle, the legal effect of an economic equilibrium stabilization clause is that it adjusts the threshold as to when the state is duty-bound to compensate the investor. This means that an economic equilibrium clause lowers the threshold for when states should compensate investors.[240]

Depending on the specific formulation of a stabilization clause, clauses obliging states to compensate investors for changes in the laws, such as economic equilibrium clauses, may affect the following factors:

- The *character* of governmental interference, which would then entail a duty to compensate the investor even in the case of non-discriminatory regulation in the public interest that do not usually require payment of compensation.
- As for requirements concerning the *impact* of the governmental interference, stabilization clauses result in a shift from usually requiring substantial deprivation of rights before triggering the duty to compensate, to covering less intrusive forms of governmental action affecting the economic equilibrium of the investment project.
- With regards to the considerations of the *expectations* of the investor, the presence of a stabilization clause creates legitimate expectations that the investor will not be burdened with costs based upon regulation.

---

237 *Parkerings-Compagniet v Lithuania*, Award, 7 September 2007, paras 335–6.
238 *Toto v Lebanon* Award, 7 June 2012.
239 *Ibid.*, para. 241.
240 See also Lorenzo Cotula, "Stabilization Clauses and the Evolution of Environmental Standards in Foreign Investment Contracts," *Yearbook of International Environmental Law* 17, no. 1 (2006): 127.

In conclusion, stabilization clauses should be considered legal risk allocation tools, designed to increase the predictability of the regulatory environment in which the investor will be operating. From the perspective of the investor, stabilization is thus a way to mitigate political risk. Consequently, the existence of a stabilization clause enhances the legitimate expectations of the investor of a stable and predictable legal environment.[241]

8.5.4. Stabilization clauses and implications for human rights or social welfare regulation

In principle, the state is free to adopt and change its policies provided that investors are compensated for losses. It may be, though, that the state has restricted its capacity to regulate. This has led to the question of whether a state may actually bind its sovereign powers in this manner, especially when states seek to enhance general social welfare or promote human rights.[242]

Practice does not support a general contention that stabilization clauses are invalid in international law, but some conditions have been spelled out, namely that stabilization clauses should be limited in time and material scope.[243] Still, it does not seem clear whether such conditions should generate a rule of validity[244] or a rule of interpretation.[245] In practice, the issue of stabilization clauses has come up in international arbitration concerning nationalizations of concession contracts, which are already granted for a limited period of time.[246]

The use of stabilization clauses as a tool to assist investors in managing risks associated with future changes in law appears frequently.[247] Research supports that stabilization clauses are drafted in a way that either allows investors to avoid compliance with, or seek compensation for compliance with, laws designed to

---

241 See also Taillant and Bonnitcha, "International Investment Law and Human Rights," 63.
242 Sornarajah, *The International Law on Foreign Investment*, 298; Alvik, *Contracting With Sovereignty*, 252.
243 *Kuwait v American Independent Oil Company (Aminoil)*, 66 ILR 1982, *The Validity of Decree Law No. 124*, p. 525 and para. 95, p. 589.
244 Meaning that only stabilization clauses that are limited in time and scope are valid in international law.
245 Meaning that stabilization clauses should always be narrowly interpreted and thereby being limited in time and material scope.
246 *Libyan American Oil Company (LIAMCO) v Libya*, 62 ILR 1977; *Texaco Overseas Petroleum Company and California Asiatic Oil Company v Libya*, 53 ILR 1979; *Kuwait v American Independent Oil Company (Aminoil)*, 66 ILR 1982.
247 In a joint study by the UN Special Representative on Business and Human Rights, John Ruggie, and the International Finance Corporation (IFC) led by Andrea Shemberg, this was further investigated through the examination of stabilization clauses in investment contracts and the effect they have on a state's action to implement its international human rights obligations. The findings of the study were published first in a consultation draft in March 2008, and then in a final report in May 2009. See Shemberg, "Stabilization Clauses and Human Rights," 39.

promote environmental, social, or human rights goals.[248] Stabilization clauses are largely found in agreements with developing and transition states.[249] Two main reasons can be identified to explain this fact. Firstly, the more foreign investors perceive a government as unstable and unreliable, the more the use of stabilization methods will be desired. Secondly, in the competition to attract foreign investors developing countries may be relatively more weak in terms of bargaining power thereby accepting conditions that developing states would not consider.[250]

Stabilization clauses may bar applicability of human rights or social welfare regulation or require the state to compensate investors for this type of regulation. Hence, stabilization clauses may enhance the risk of a regulatory chill.[251] This is particularly problematic for developing countries since the consequences of non-regulation are more severe to a country in a developing stage. Another problematic aspect of these clauses is that the stabilization commitments often are unknown to the general public due to lack of transparency in the negotiation of state contracts. Hence, this can reduce democratic accountability in policy-making processes.

It thus appears that stabilization clauses may have far-reaching consequences for implementing human rights and for promoting social welfare. Though these clauses do not *generally* limit the state's right to regulate, they may potentially constitute an obstacle for states, since these clauses may oblige the state to compensate the investor for regulation that seeks to enhance these objectives.

A possible way to challenge the validity of stabilization clauses under international law concerns the clauses that are indefinite in terms of time and material scope.[252] Another option for challenging stabilization clauses is to apply the concept of sovereignty as modified by human rights treaties, previously referred to as the concept of *internal absolute alienability*. As mentioned, this concept focuses on the will of the population. If we apply the concept of *internal absolute alienability*, two types of stabilization clauses are barred: 1) clauses that exempt the investor from non-discriminatory *bona fide* regulation such as human rights regulation and 2) the variant of the economic equilibrium clause that requires the state to pay compensation at a level that would cause catastrophic economic consequences for the host state and its population.[253] However, in practice it may be difficult to determine 1) what *in concreto* is considered *bona fide* human rights regulation and 2) the level of compensation in terms of assessing what is 'reasonable' to avoid crossing a limit, which would have catastrophic economic consequences for the host state and its population.

---

248 *Ibid.*, para. 146, p. 39.
249 Kyla Susanne Tienhaara, "Unilateral Commitments to Investment Protection: Does the Promise of Stability Restrict Environmental Policy Development?," *Yearbook of International Environmental Law* 17, no. 1 (2006): 146.
250 *Ibid.*, p. 147.
251 See Chapter 3, section 2.
252 Apart from challenging stabilization clauses contractually, the clauses may also be challenged from a private law perspective according to the applicable rules of contract law.
253 See above Chapter 2, section 7.6.

8.6. *Expectations of the host state*

While addressing the concept of legitimate expectations, it is also necessary to pay attention to the other side of the coin, i.e. the expectations of the host state. From the unification approach to international investment law this element is inevitable.

It may be that the host state expects to have a wide discretion for regulatory measures to enhance general social welfare and regulation to promote human rights. It may also be that the host state did not foresee that commitments to investors laid down in a BIT could entail a duty to compensate for regulatory measures. Hence, a pertinent question is whether host states may be lifted from BIT obligations, for example under the concept of fundamental change of circumstances, *rebus sic stantibus*.[254] It is likely that the host state did not consider that it could be required to compensate investors even for social welfare regulation. Pursuant to the VCLT article 62(2)(b) a fundamental change of circumstances cannot be invoked if the change is the result of a breach by the party invoking it of another international obligation. So, even when states seek to regulate to live up to their commitments under the duty to regulate within the human rights regime, it does not lift the state from its obligation under a BIT on the basis of the principle of *rebus sic stantibus*. With regards to general regulation to promote social welfare, this type of regulation can hardly be characterized as an unforeseen event either. This is because it is up to the state itself to decide whether it wants to promote social welfare or not. It is not an event of an unforeseen character. Hence, it is likely that the host state anticipated to be able to impose human rights regulation or social welfare regulation. Nevertheless, the principle of *rebus sic stantibus* does not lift the host state as such from obligations under a BIT.

Expectations of the host state may also find their way into claims of *ordre public*, such as when invoking the defence of necessity. Moreover, in terms of future developments of the international investment law regime, expectations of the host state could be an aspect of counterclaims in investment arbitration.

Besides that, expectations of the host state are also relevant under the current international investment law regime. The argument in this regard is that where host states have explicitly committed to international human rights obligations, the investor should generally expect that the state will live up to those commitments. In this way, it may be held that investors should be expected to consider the human rights framework at the time of making the decision whether to investor or not. This is part of the political risk that investors must accept.

Some support for this argument might be found in the *Methanex* case concerning environmental regulation. In this case, California was renowned for being active on environmental matters. Hence, the tribunal stressed that the investor knew or should have known that California attached high political importance to this specific policy area. The tribunal thus explicitly emphasized the predictability

---

254 See above Chapter 2, section 4.3.

of the regulatory change. All investors in the area should thus anticipate that its activities, if found to be detrimental to the environment, would become the subject of public debate and regulation. The tribunal concluded that the environmental regulation in California was foreseeable for the Canadian investor, which entered *"a political economy"* where environmental regulation was *"widely known, if not notorious"*.[255] In terms of human rights regulation or general social welfare regulation, arbitrators should thereby take into account whether the regulatory change was foreseeable, whether the investor should anticipate regulatory change within a specific policy area (e.g. on the basis of a BIT referring to this particularly non-economic policy goal) and whether the investor was assured against such regulatory change (e.g. in the form of a stabilization clause).

In addition to assessing the legal framework, other factors may be relevant. Elements that may generate expectations that the state will regulate within a specific area may for instance become visible through the general policy of the host state, the yearlong tradition for specific political priorities or values or proclaimed new goals by a new government. Such factors are also elements that potentially can affect the expectations of the investor. However, in terms of an examination of the regulatory space of the host state in an investment dispute, all these non-legal factors technically belongs to the facts of a case.

Under the current international investment law regime, expectations of the host state can be and are given some weight in investment arbitrations while taking into account the intentions of the host state, the rationale behind the imposed regulation. In terms of enhancing a more unified approach to the law under the current legal regime, an argument is thus to attach more weight to the expectations of the host state as part of the intentions of the state.

8.7. Preliminary conclusion

The concept of legitimate expectations is a *legal factor* with its roots in practice where it has been articulated by arbitral tribunals in investment disputes. In addition hereto, the concept of legitimate expectations is also a potential *regulatory barrier* since a host state may refrain from adopting new regulation based on the guarantees it may have given a foreign investor through specific contractual commitments.

The more substantive evidence that can be presented for the legitimate expectations of the investor, the higher the risk that the host state might be liable to compensate the investor for adopting new regulation. In other words, the higher the legitimate expectations of the investor, the lower the regulatory space of manoeuvre. In essence, the right to regulate vs. the concept of legitimate expectations is two sides of the same coin, which basically demonstrates the fundamental tension between *legal stability* and *flexibility*.

---

255 *Methanex v USA*, Final Award, 2005, Part IV, Chapter D, paras 9–10.

Various factors have now been identified as having an impact on the concept of legitimate expectations. General legal mechanisms can be identified that could either have a positive or negative impact on the legitimate expectations of the investor. In other words, there are provisions that could be inserted in BITs having the effect that the investor 'loses' its legitimacy in terms of the expectations not to be met with certain types of regulatory interferences. Besides general legal mechanisms, other specific commitments may impact on the legitimate expectations of the investor. The parameters, which affect the threshold of when states should compensate investors, may for example be altered as the consequence of umbrella clauses in BITs and contractual devices such as stabilization clauses. Moreover, non-transparent procedures or unreasonable application of laws might lead a tribunal to conclude that a specific measure amounts to expropriation. In general, investors cannot expect not to face regulatory changes, especially in long-term projects. All in all, the question is whether the changes were predictable for a prudent investor at the time of the investment. To establish a more balanced and unified approach to the law, arbitrators in investment disputes should attach weight to the expectations of the host states as well.

9. Applying a 'gravitational pull' theory for alleged expropriations of investments

The theory of gravitational pull was explained above in Chapter 2. According to this theory, BITs should be interpreted in a harmonizing manner with human rights obligations. The interpretation should be based on the positive presumption that general principles of law apply and the negative presumption against inconsistencies. The interpretation must take into account the particular context of the case as well as inherent limitations to treaty standards such as avoiding catastrophic economic consequences for the host state and its population.

This theory is applied below in order to solve the legal dilemma of distinguishing compensable from non-compensable regulation in investment claims for expropriation.

9.1. *The duty to compensate: The question of whether regulation amounts to regulatory expropriation*

The theory of gravitational pull may have something to offer as a response to the stability–flexibility dilemma of international investment law. Applying this theory, the starting point would be the presumption that BITs are intended to produce effects in accordance with existing rules of international law. The qualification of legal norms encompassed in a BIT, i.e. the provision containing protection against 'expropriations and measures tantamount to expropriations', is then guided by external factors thus having a steering effect on the interpretation of the substantive rule of protection. This requires BITs to be interpreted teleologically, taking into account all aspects such as the words, intentions, aims and the object and purpose of the treaty. A key objective of the interpretation of the expropriation standard is to produce effects that are most coherent with other international obligations, in particular binding obligations incumbent upon the host state. In addition thereto, policy concerns expressed in non-legally binding instruments may even have a steering effect on the interpretation of the BIT as contextual elements.

In expropriation claims the protective standards encompassed in the BIT should be interpreted to grant effective – though not unlimited – rights to investors. Policy concerns may direct the interpretation of a BIT.

The key policy concerns of contemporary international investment law have been displayed above in Chapter 3. One of the trends defined was the expectation that companies should perform their business in a socially responsible manner. For companies that have voluntarily adopted CSR policies, codes of conduct or committed to instruments such as the UN Global Compact, there may be even further support for treaty interpretation founded on a general presumption that the investor should not be compensated for legitimate public welfare regulation.

For BITs with a preamble encompassing the 'balanced approach', the arbitrator is obliged to adopt a balanced approach to the interpretation. For example, the arbitrators may be tasked with the interpretation of a BIT stating that *"investment promotion and protection should not be detrimental to the protection of health, safety and the environment"*. The inclusion of several purposes in the preamble generates the need to prioritize among divergent purposes. Again some support may be found in the contextual elements, i.e. for corporations that have chosen a specific CSR strategy expressed in a code of conduct for example with a focus to ensure that responsible business conduct should not be detrimental to the protection of the environment. In this case, the arbitrators could attach a higher priority to protection of the environment in the prioritization of policy concerns in a preamble.

However, if the preamble – as in most BITs – follows the traditional approach to preambles with no references to social welfare purposes the question is if the gravitational pull theory imposes any limits to the interpretation of substantive rights. This question should be answered in the affirmative. Even when BITs are silent on the question of the right to regulate, states enjoy their right to regulate under the general international law paradigm as a fundamental cornerstone of the concept of sovereignty. If the parties do not appear to have intended otherwise, the gravitational pull theory would require the arbitrator to adopt the interpretation that coheres with previously existing rules, including human rights obligations etc. The legitimate expectations of the investor constitute a part of the context and a key element in a balanced approach to interpreting the expropriation standard. So, the well-established practice of the ECtHR (external rules to the investment law regime) may exhort gravitational pull on the interpretation of a BIT and thereby advance the adoption of a balanced approach to interpretation, in particular for delimiting legitimate regulation from regulatory expropriation.

9.2. The standard of compensation: Determining the extent to which investors should be compensated

A question left unresolved in terms of indirect expropriation is the question of compensation. As explained above in Chapter 2 the standard of compensation for expropriation in the BIT regime has most commonly followed the Hull Formula requiring 'prompt, adequate and effective compensation'.[256]

However, the gravitational pull theory is more conducive for enhancing coherence. For determining the standard of compensation the balanced approach is therefore more useful to ensure the most coherent effect of the interpretation. Additional support for a balanced approach to assessing the amount of compensation is found in the Separate Opinion by Brownlie in the *CME* case on his views relating to avoiding 'catastrophic economic consequences'.[257]

If we apply this theory to the interpretation of stabilization clauses in investment contracts, the effect is that an implied limitation occurs. This limitation means that the scope of the stabilization clause for clauses that oblige the state to compensate the investor for regulatory changes ('economic equilibrium clauses') should always be interpreted as to avoid catastrophic economic consequences for the state. Applied to the standard of expropriation an implied limitation would equally occur. Compensations for indirect expropriations could thereby not go beyond a certain limit, above which they would have 'catastrophic economic consequences'.

So, even for BITs following a traditional approach with no reference to policy considerations, the gravitational pull theory may lay down an inherent limitation 1) for the qualification of the expropriation clause and 2) for the determination of compensation.

9.3. Illustrative case: Health regulation in PMI v Uruguay

Governments' attempt to improve public health is an issue that is increasingly being subject to regulation. For instance, governments may want to promote healthy eating to fight obesity by restricting corporate food advertising or ban trans-fat in response to expensive corporate marketing campaigns that promote the consumption of high calorie food. Another example is governments that may engage in social marketing or impose counter-advertising duties, where health warnings on cigarette packaging are widely known. As a result of increasing regulation, companies more and more seek to test health regulation. A current example is the disputes initiated by the tobacco company, Phillip Morris International, a company that has filed several claims against states. One of them is initiated as an ICSID investment claim against Uruguay.[258] Until now, safeguarding public health has primarily been

---

256 See above Chapter 2, section 6.4.1.
257 See above Chapter 2, section 7.6.
258 *Philip Morris v Uruguay*, initiated in March 2010 on the basis of the Switzerland–Uruguay BIT.

linked with environmental protection. The claims initiated by the tobacco company might provide further clarification as to what extent public health could be perceived a general legitimate public purpose in investment disputes.

The basic facts of the case are these.[259]

In March 2010 the tobacco company Philip Morris International (PMI) filed a claim against Uruguay at ICSID.

The three measures that form the basis of the PMI claim are the following:

Firstly,

The increase in the size of the health warnings on the cigarette packet from 50% to 80% of the surface of the front and back of the packages.

Secondly,

The obligation to display graphic images (pictograms) that are purported to illustrate the adverse health effects of smoking.

Thirdly,

The existing prohibition on the use of misleading product names (such as "light" or "mild") is extended so it includes colour codes. The use of brands is thus limited to a single line of products (plain packaging).

PMI's headquarters is based in Switzerland, which allows the company to rely on a BIT between Switzerland and Uruguay from 1991. According to the BIT each country guarantees certain minimum standards of treatment for the other country's investors, and agrees to resort to international arbitration to resolve disputes with individual investors over alleged failures to live up to those commitments. PMI contends that the use of their investments has been unreasonably impaired; the value of their investments has been expropriated without compensation; and they have been deprived of fair and equitable treatment.[260] From the view of Uruguay, anti-smoking campaigns and tobacco control has been a high level political priority for decades. The country considers itself as leading

---

259 The facts of the case are based upon the *"Request for Arbitration"* made by the Swiss law firm, Lalive representing the claimant, 19 February 2010 and T. Weiler, *"Expert Opinion: An Analysis of Tobacco Control Measures in the Context of International Investment Law"*, 28 July 2010. It is thus vital to take into account a critical view on these sources. Yet, deducing the fact on the basis of these two documents seems reasonable from a research perspective since the first source represents the view of the claimant and the second the view of an expert (likely paid) on behalf of an NGO, Physicians for a Smoke Free Canada. These documents are publicly available at: <http://www.italaw.com/cases/460>.

260 *PMI Public Statement and Background Information Regarding the Company's Bilateral Investment Treaty (BIT) Claim Against the Government of Uruguay*, 5 October 2010.

in this regard and as an inspiration for other states in the region. Uruguay, thus, contends that the regulation is within their policy space and follows from their ratification and obligation to implement the WHO Framework Convention on Tobacco Control (FCTC) as well as the International Covenant on Economic, Social and Cultural Rights (ICESCR).

The preamble of the Switzerland–Uruguay BIT (1991) reads:

> *"Le Conseil fédéral suisse et le Gouvernement de la République orientale de l'Uruguay,*
>
> *Désireux de renforcer, entre les deux Etats, la coopération économique fondée sur le droit international et la confiance mutuelle,*
>
> *Reconnaissant le rôle complémentaire important des investissements de capitaux privés étrangers dans le processus du développement économique et le droit de chaque Partie Contractante de déterminer ce rôle et de définir les conditions dans lesquelles les investissements étrangers pourraient participer à ce processus,*
>
> *Reconnaissant que la seule manière d'établir et de maintenir un flux international de capitaux adéquat est d'entretenir mutuellement un climat d'investissement satisfaisant, et, pour ce qui est des investisseurs étrangers, de respecter la souveraineté et les lois du pays hôte ayant juridiction sur eux et d'agir de manière compatible avec les politiques et les priorités adoptées par le pays hôte, et de s'efforcer de contribuer de façon importante à son développement,*
>
> *Dans l'intention de créer des conditions favorables à l'investissement de capitaux dans les deux Etats,*
>
> *Désireux d'intensifier la coopération entre ressortissants et sociétés, privées ou de droit publie, des deux Etats, notamment dans les domaines de la technologie et de l'industrialisation,*
>
> *Reconnaissant la nécessité de protéger les investissements des ressortissants et sociétés des deux Etats en vue de promouvoir la prospérité économique de ces derniers,*
>
> *Sont convenus de ce qui suit."*

This preamble is based on the traditional liberal approach to preambles since it does not contain explicit references to regulation, social welfare concerns in the form of human rights or references to sustainable development. Yet, this view could be slightly modified by the fact that the preamble mentions the need to respect the sovereignty of the host state[261] and for investors to strive for contribution to development[262] as the only way to establish and maintain a mutually beneficial investment climate. Accordingly, the reference to state sovereignty and development concerns may implicitly express the parties' acknowledgment of a

---

261 *"de respecter la souveraineté et les lois du pays hôte ayant juridiction sur eux et d'agir de manière compatible avec les politiques et les priorités adoptées par le pays hôte."*

262 *"et de s'efforcer de contribuer de façon importante à son développement."*

right to regulate, not only for promoting economic development but also social development.

The expropriation clause of the BIT reads:

> *"Art. 5 Dépossession, compensation*
>
> *(1) Aucune des Parties Contractantes ne prendra, directement ou indirectement, des mesures d'expropriation, de nationalisation ou toute autre mesure ayant le même caractère ou le même effet, à l'encontre d'investissements appartenant à des investisseurs de l'autre Partie Contractante, si ce n'est pour des raisons d'intérêt public tel que défini par la loi et à condition que ces mesures ne soient pas discriminatoires, qu'elles soient conformes aux prescriptions légales et qu'elles donnent lieu au paiement d'une indemnité effective et adéquate. Le montant de l'indemnité, intérêt compris, sera réglé dans la monnaie du pays d'origine de l'investissement et sera versé sans retard à l'ayant droit."*

The expropriation clause obliges the host state to compensate the investor for takings, including regulatory measures, which have the same character or effect as a direct expropriation.[263] The provision does not mention non-compensable regulation.

9.3.1. Identification of the relevant factors exhorting gravitational pull

For the purpose of delimiting compensable from non-compensable regulation the theory of gravitational pull may add some support. In applying the theory to the illustrative case, the first step of the process is to identify the factors that may exhort a gravitational pull on the investment protection. As explained above in Chapter 2, factors that may exhort a pull on the interpretation of the BIT standard concerning expropriation can generally be divided into two categories: 1) legally binding human rights norms; and 2) non-legally binding policy concerns.

Identifying key factors with steering effect on the interpretation of the expropriation standard:

Legal norms:

Both state parties are members of the ICESCR without reservations. Uruguay signed the ICESCR in 1967 and ratified the ICESCR in 1970. Switzerland acceded to the ICESCR in 1992.

Both parties have the duty to implement the ICESCR pursuant to the state obligations under ICESCR article 2. Likewise, both parties have committed themselves to realizing the right to the highest attainable health pursuant to article 12 of the ICESCR.

Both parties have committed themselves to the WHO Framework Convention on Tobacco Control (FCTC), though to varying degrees. Uruguay signed

---

263 *"ou toute autre mesure ayant le même caractère ou le même effet."*

the FCTC in 2003, ratified in 2004 and the FCTC entered into force in 2005. Switzerland signed the FCTC in 2004 but has not ratified the convention.

In sum:

- Uruguay and Switzerland are obliged to strive to the maximum of available resources to implement economic, social and cultural rights under the ICESCR;
- Uruguay and Switzerland are obliged to realize the right to health;
- Uruguay is obliged fully to implement the FCTC;
- Switzerland is obliged not to contravene the object and purpose of the FCTC.[264]

Policy concerns:

- CSR is a significant policy issue in this case – tobacco companies are explicitly discouraged from participation in the UN Global Compact initiative due to *"the serious health effects of tobacco use"*. Since tobacco is a legal product whose use UN member states have not yet outlawed, the Global Compact Office cannot exclude tobacco companies from the initiative if they wish to join. The Global Compact Office does not accept funding from tobacco companies or permits tobacco companies to make presentations at global events or to use the global brand in any other way to raise their profile.[265]
- Provided that proof thereof can be established other national policy issues may have an impact on the expectations of the investor. E.g. in this case, it would be relevant to determine to what extent health regulation has been a governmental priority by Uruguay.

The second step is to determine the way these various concerns interact in the specific case in the adoption of a balanced approach to interpretation.

264 This is the legal consequence of signing but not ratifying a treaty; see VCLT article 18(a).
265 <http://www.unglobalcompact.org/AboutTheGC/faq.html>.

6 Collecting the pieces

1. Introduction

This last chapter aims at drawing the larger picture on the basis of the findings and the preliminary conclusions of the earlier parts. Some remarks are provided as recommendations to BIT negotiators and adjudicators in investment disputes.

2. Sovereignty revised?

In general international law, the right to regulate is basically concerned with what states can do as sovereigns and the question of when exercising that right involves a duty for states to compensate foreign investors. As laid down in Chapter 2, the right to make a binding commitment is the foundation of state sovereignty. The conclusion of a BIT, by which a state undertakes to protect foreign investors and their investments, is not a renouncement of sovereignty but rather an attribute of state sovereignty. And clauses of investor–state dispute settlement that remove the dispute settlement from national jurisdictions to international arbitration constitute a confirmation of the authority of states. As laid down in Chapter 4, the evolution of the international human rights regime has placed community interests and the will of the people at the forefront and international adjudication has gradually become more open to human rights concerns. In particular, human rights have paved their way into the jurisprudence of the ICJ.

As shown, human rights can be said to have had an impact on the perception of sovereignty in general international law. The main focus on human rights has led scholars to argue a process of 'humanization' of international law.[1] In this way, the human rights regime has altered the concept of sovereignty by forming an underlying assumption that states can make binding commitments (e.g.

---

1 See in general, Theodor Meron, *The Humanization of International Law*, 1st ed., vol. 3, The Hague Academy of International Law Monographs (Nijhoff: Brill Nijhof, 2006). See also Cassese, *International Law*, 396; Menno T. Kamminga, "Final Report on the Impact of International Human Rights Law on General International Law," in *The Impact of Human Rights Law on General International Law*, ed. Menno T. Kamminga and Martin Scheinin (Oxford: Oxford University Press, 2009), 2f.

by concluding BITs), provided that they can still take measures to comply with international obligations to make certain minimum policy prioritizations (under the duty to regulate).

An essential point is not to consider the concept of sovereignty as an absolutism, i.e. that either the state may regulate or it may not. As a sovereign, a state may choose to impose regulation to enhance development and the general social welfare. As a sovereign, a state may also choose to negotiate binding BITs. In this connection, it cannot be generally assumed either that the will of the population, the public interest, takes precedence over commitments to foreign investors (e.g. on the basis of a contract) or to other states for the reciprocal promotion and protection of investments (e.g. in a BIT). Such assumption fails to take into consideration the public interest in attracting foreign investment through an attractive investment climate furnished by legal protection of foreign investments. In the great competition for foreign investments one cannot presume that states' establishment of a legal framework that actually makes it attractive to foreign investors is per se detrimental to the will of the population. There is oftentimes a substantial risk involved in foreign investments, which is largely confined to the investor, and the fact that investors are willing to incur such risk may be highly beneficial to the population.

To conclude, there is no need for a revised perception of the concept of sovereignty as such, but the humanization of international law affects the right to regulate in general international law by adding this element of the underlying human rights presumptions.

3. From 'contractual' thinking to 'public policy' thinking

In its origin, the BIT regime was developed on the basis of a *contractual way of thinking*, lifting contractual claims out of a domestic context and into an international law context. The BIT regime could thereby provide both strong international rules of protection and a strong mechanism to enforce the rules in investment arbitration, like a parallel to international commercial arbitration. In contrast thereto, multilateral treaties are negotiated on the basis of *political opinion* and governmental policies founded in consensus on broader goals and values as the basis for legally binding rights and obligations. Human rights treaties or international environmental agreements are examples in this regard.

Considering the international investment law regime from its original contractual perspective, regulatory measures imposed by the host state should be perceived as an implied condition. As part of the initial risk assessment the investor must thereby expect certain types of regulation. The regulation that the investor should expect is fundamental regulation to safeguard basic human rights concerns, i.e. the measures falling within the duty to regulate, referred to as the duty to make certain policy prioritizations. Hence, the investor must expect a minimum level of regulation imposed to ensure a minimum standard of living, such as a basic health regulation, environmental regulation and labour regulation, which should therefore not be compensated. Accordingly, even from a private law perspective, the investor cannot expect a completely frozen legal framework in long-term investment projects, especially when investing in projects relating to the management and performance of functions that are fundamental to the needs of society, such as for example providing public transportation,[2] technology and telecommunication,[3] water and sanitation,[4] or handling hazardous waste.[5] As demonstrated above in Chapter 4, states are obliged to pursue development concerns, and this obligation becomes even more apparent in long-term relations. In these situations, one could argue that the investor assumes an obligation to pursue these development concerns as a complementary duty bearer of human rights protection. In practice, this aspect could have an impact on the assessment of the expectations of the investor.

For human rights regulation, which goes beyond the minimum duty to regulate, it is less clear if a general presumption of non-compensation can be applied. The context is particularly relevant in this regard, including the text of a BIT and the extent to which the investor has been given specific guarantees that could alter such presumption. As explained, umbrella clauses in BITs and stabilization clauses in investment contracts may constitute such guarantees. In essence, a fundamental point is that the investor already at the initial stage of a long-term project should expect that the state is going to safeguard basic development concerns. As found in Chapter 5, it may be questionable whether stabilization clauses provide the stability that was intended. This is primarily due to the uncertainty about their interpretation and scope. A frozen legal framework does not provide stability in the sense of legal certainty. On the contrary, legal stability can be addressed in a better way through flexible legal devices. From the contractual perspective, one option to preserve the sanctity of contracts might be for the parties to agree on a renegotiation clause, and there seems to be an increasing tendency to include such clauses.[6] This would allow greater flexibility into the contractual relation so as to ensure realization of the contractual terms rather than performance of the contract. Yet, adjusting contracts are just one aspect to the stability–flexibility dilemma.

As this research has demonstrated, the traditional public–private dichotomy, found in general international law, is not suitable under the paradigm of international investment law. Investors are increasingly perceived as participants of international law. Investors assume the role as caretakers of basic public functions, become complementary duty bearers of human rights promotion and protection and have legal standing to sue states in investment arbitration for

---

2 E.g. *Railroad Development Corporation v Guatemala*, Award, 29 June 2012.

3 E.g. *Siemens v Argentina*, Award, 17 January 2007; immigration control, personal identification system, electoral information service.

4 E.g. *Aguas del Tunari v. Bolivia*, Award, Decision on Respondent's Objections to Jurisdiction, 21 October 2005.

5 *Tecmed v Mexico*, Award, 29 May 2003.

6 Dolzer and Schreuer, *Principles of International Investment Law*, 85f.

regulatory measures. This development is sometimes detrimental to the governmental sphere of influence. What seems apparent is the need for a legal regime that encapsulates both public and private law perspectives. The legal challenge is to strike an appropriate balance between the host states' regulatory space and investment protection.

On this basis, it appears that the international investment law regime, which has to accommodate diverging interests, cannot rely on a traditional public international law regime that merely safeguards the sovereign rights of states. This balancing of rights and obligations must be supported by the preservation of basic principles of private law. This could for example include fundamental principles of contract law,[7] such as rules relating to *pacta sunt servanda*,[8] foreseeability,[9] good faith and fair dealing[10] and the concept of change of circumstances or hardship.[11] From an international investment law perspective, such principles are basically covered by the concept of legitimate expectations of the investor.

To view international investment law through the lenses of public international law is thus inadequate. Yet, the international investment law regime cannot be regulated purely under private law either, since it lacks fundamental aspects of the public law regime. Choosing between contractual stability and a regulatory need is not a question that can be generally resolved. This question needs to be settled on a case-by-case basis allowing due consideration to the specific facts, the regulatory interest and the existing legal framework. What can be resolved on a more general and principled basis, however, is the balancing of rights and obligations through the formation of rules of presumption.

All things considered, it appears that the BIT regime has moved away from the traditional contractual way of thinking, which was the foundation for creating the system. Today, the BIT regime should be considered an expression of a state's policy with respect to foreign investment as an element of the state's economic policy. BITs may include references to policy issues, including non-economic policies. Even if they do not contain references to policy issues they still have to be interpreted in their particular policy context. As explained, non-economic policy issues were traditionally not included in BITs. Yet, it appears

---

7 Basic principles of private law pertaining to the fundamental rules of the law of obligations can be found in codifications, such as the UNIDROIT Principles by UNIDROIT, an intergovernmental organization on harmonization of private international law. Other legal instruments relevant in this regard is the American Uniform Commercial Code (AUCC), which was first published in 1952, and which was intended to harmonize the law of sales and other commercial transactions in the United States and the Principles of European Contract Law (PECL), which equally embraces basic rules of contract law and more generally the law of obligations, which most European legal systems hold in common.
8 UNDROIT Principles article 1.3.
9 See e.g. PECL article 9:503.
10 See e.g. PECL article 1:102, PECL article 1:106, PECL article 1:201; UNIDROIT Principles article 1.7; the AUCC § 1–201 (20) and § 1–304.
11 See e.g. PECL article 6.111; UNIDROIT Principles articles 6.2.1, 6.2.2 and 6.2.3.

that states have become aware of the long-term implications of signing BITs. Consequently, states seek to integrate other policy areas in order to address the nature of these long-term commitments. This means that BITs are gradually more and more concluded with a view to other policy issues than merely safe-guarding contractual rights at an international law level. Accordingly, BITs seem to have moved more in the direction of being legal instruments expressing a general state policy in line with multilateral treaties and in contrast to contracts imposing obligations on the parties. The fact that some states wish to make references to other policy concerns than investment promotion and protection constitutes an express choice to do so. BITs with a balanced policy approach demonstrate a shift in this regard, from a contractual way of thinking of BITs to a public policy way of thinking.

4. Reconciling the international investment law regime and the human rights regime

The two legal regimes – international investment law and the human rights regime – have progressed significantly over the last decades. There is no indica-tion that these legal regimes will not develop further in the future. The expansion of rules, institutions and enforcement mechanisms in both regimes has led to arguments that international law as an holistic system is in the process of frag-mentation and there is a high risk that international law might dissolve into *"a series of discrete localised or limited systems with little or no interrelationship"*.[12] Globalization is perceived as an essential causative factor in this regard. Yet, as identified in this research, other essential factors can be identified. On the policy level, various trends were identified in Chapter 3 with some issues contributing to policy coherence and others to further fragmentation or a high risk hereof. From a legal perspective, the rules laid down in the international investment law regime have long been fertilizing further fragmentation of international law. Though some states have responded to these concerns in the drafting of BITs and some arbitrators in their approach to treaty interpretation, this dysfunction of the sys-tem has not yet been settled. This is a fundamental problem for a society founded in the rule of law. Accordingly, there is a need to strive for greater coherence between international obligations under the international investment law regime vs. the human rights regime.

This research shows that the investment law regime is not a completely closed legal circuit. As a paradigm or a sub-system, the international investment law regime does, and must, interact with other areas of general international law, such as the human rights regime. As laid down in Chapter 4, human rights are in various ways intruding into the international investment law regime and this has become quite apparent in investment arbitration. The human rights regime has proved its impact on the international investment law. This humanization of international investment law could thus be considered a spillover effect of the human rights impact on general international law.

Striving towards unification of international law presupposes reconciliation of international investment law and human rights. For international law to enjoy widespread recognition and acquire legitimacy as the law of the international community, international law has to become more reflective of the interests and values of a wider range of actors than states only. The various intersections of human rights and international investment law that materialize in investment arbitrations prove the changing perceptions of international law from a state-centred system based on bilateral obligations towards a normative system reflecting the interests and values of a wider range of actors, including the national and international community. This 'community interest' perspective embraces an even broader aspect than the humanization of international law.[13] Additional to the human rights perspective, a 'community interest' perspective covers international peace and security and protection of the environment.[14]

In order to correspond to the developments in general international law, there is a need for international investment law to reflect these broader interests and values, i.e. the humanization and the 'community interest' perspective. Accordingly, a unified approach to the law is required. The human rights regime has something to offer by serving as a tool for enhanced legitimacy of international investment law.

From a theoretical perspective there seems to be two central unifying factors of international investment law, the VCLT and the human rights regime. Using the VCLT as a basis for unification is a credible solution due to its root in general international law, whereas some scepticism may be attached to allowing one specialized system (the human rights system) as a 'controlling' factor of another specialized system (international investment law). The VCLT is mainly expressing customary international law and thus enjoys widespread support. On the other hand, the VCLT is written as if only the interests of states matter, which as shown is hardly the case of international law today. Using the VCLT as the unifying factor is not very human rights oriented, and could be criticized for not reflecting the humanization of international law.[15] The impact of human rights

---

13 More generally on the 'community interest' perspective in international law, see Ulrich Fastenrath et al., *From Bilateralism to Community Interest: Essays in Honour of Bruno Simma*, 1st ed. (Oxford: Oxford University Press, 2011).

14 Simma defines community interest as *"a consensus according to which respect for certain fundamental values is not to be left to the free disposition of States individually but is recognized and sanctioned by international law as a matter of concern to all States."* Simma also lists 'solidarity between developed and developing countries' as a community interest. See further in Bruno Simma, *From Bilateralism to Community Interests in International Law*, 1st ed., vol. 250, Collected Courses of the Hague Academy of International Law (Leiden: Brill Nijhof, 1994), 217.

15 In a report by the Committee on International Human Rights Law and Practice, a body under the International Law Association, concerning the relationship between general international law and human rights, the Committee questions the VCLT as the unifying factor of the fragmentation of international law as perceived by the ILC, Kamminga, "Final Report

law on general international law appears on the contrary as a process, which is just in its initial phase.[16] The humanization of international law is likely to gain further importance and the human rights regime may therefore serve well as the unifying factor representing the interests and values of a broader range of international actors. Hence, the human rights regime, which allows for a balance of interests, may contribute to the coherence of international law.[17]

The argument here is that both approaches seem valid and one needs not to exclude the other. Whereas the VCLT only regulates how a state may react to the other state's performance under a treaty and is silent on the role of other actors, it may still function as the key tool for interpreting treaties. Moreover, it does allow human rights to have an impact on the interpretation of a treaty through article 31(3)(c).[18] Relying on the VCLT thus does not exclude taking human rights into account. So, whereas the VCLT may primarily serve as a unifying factor of international law regulating inter-state relations, the human rights regime is more constructive as the unifying factor of the relationship between states and other international actors.

5. Unification – human rights in arbitral practice

Until now, the lack of a general legal framework, which resolves the stability–flexibility dilemma, has led to a situation where the dilemma is dealt with on an ad hoc basis in arbitral practice. With no *stare decisis* doctrine this is not a solid approach to the law in cases involving general public policy matters. Though patterns of *jurisprudence constante* can be identified, there is a need for moving away from pragmatic solutions to the law towards a more principled approach to international investment law, which embraces the mentioned public–private dichotomy. International investment tribunals have not yet developed a coherent approach to the standard of review applicable to investment disputes. In terms of regulatory measures to fulfil national policies, it is particularly questionable if or to what degree the review of such measures really can be entrusted to three independent arbitrators mostly having commercial expertise and rarely an insight into human rights.

As demonstrated in Chapter 4, some investment tribunals have drawn on human rights jurisprudence and relied on the principle of proportionality, adopting 'the fair balance test' for the determination of a breach of a BIT standard.[19] This approach allows for taking broader societal considerations into account and is thereby conducive for a process of coherence. In cases where vital social

---

on the Impact of International Human Rights Law," 21f. For the work of the Committee on International Human Rights Law and Practice, see <http://www.ila-hq.org/en/commit tees/index.cfm/cid/20>.

16 *Ibid.*, p. 4.
17 *Ibid.*, p. 21f.
18 See above Chapter 2, section 7.5.
19 *Ibid.*

concerns are at stake, the fair balance test, which allows for a margin of appreciation for states to regulate, thus appears plausible.

From the perspective of the unification of international law, allowing for a margin of appreciation appears persuasive since states are better acquainted with the national circumstances, debates and sensitivities. Hence, states are in principle in a better position to decide the means to fulfil their goals. More generally, there appears to be a growing acceptance of international courts and tribunals of the fair balance test and the margin of appreciation doctrine.[20] However, the doctrine of the margin of appreciation seems suitable only for certain types of norms and e.g. obviously not for absolute norms with the status of *jus cogens*. With a view to state obligations under the two central covenants, the ICESCR and the ICCPR, arbitrators may adjust the scope of the margin of appreciation doctrine depending on whether states act to prevent (imminent) physical harm to citizens, or whether the state adopts social and economic policies to further general development. The covenants themselves suggest this prioritization in terms of obligations for states to implement the rights enshrined. In addition, the level of development of the host state may serve as an added argument for allowing a broader margin of appreciation, especially in situations of emergency. Finally, the scope of the margin of appreciation may potentially change over time, particularly in the light of emerging norms.

The case-study in Chapter 5 shows that not all government regulatory activity, which either complicates or makes it impossible for an investor to carry out a particular business, is an expropriation.[21] Even in situations where an investment has become of no value, it does not mean per se that it amounts to an act of expropriation because investment always entails an element of risk. The case-study highlighted key parameters that have been taken into account in arbitral practice for delimiting compensable from non-compensable regulation. What the case-study also showed was that the scope of the right to regulate – i.e. the question of when states should compensate investors for regulation – could be decided on the basis of a more unified approach to the law, i.e. through the balanced approach to interpretation.

In essence, BIT interpretation should be based on the theory of gravitational pull since this will enhance policy coherence as well as legal coherence. This entails first of all that BITs should be interpreted in a harmonizing manner with human rights obligations. This can only be done through a balanced approach to interpretation that allows taking into account a broader range of interests. The interpretation should be based on the positive presumption that general

20 E.g. by the European Court of Justice (ECJ) and within the WTO by Dispute Settlement Body (DSB) panels and the Appellate Body (AB), whereas the concept is more unclear in the context of the ICJ. See Yuval Shany, "Toward a General Margin of Appreciation Doctrine in International Law?," *European Journal of International Law* 16, no. 5 (2005): 907–40.
21 *Feldman v Mexico*, Award, 16 December 2002, para. 112. See also Todd Weiler, *International Investment Law and Arbitration: Leading Cases from the ICSID, NAFTA, Bilateral Treaties and Customary International Law*, 1st ed. (London: Cameron May, 2005), 632–4.

principles of law apply and the negative presumption against inconsistencies. The interpretation of the BIT must take into account the particular context of the case, namely whether the host state has provided the investor with specific guarantees. The interpretation should also include human rights commitments by the investor as contextual elements if such commitments are declared, for example in CSR policies of the company. The interpretation must take into account inherent human rights limitations. Accordingly, certain types of regulation that fall within the duty to regulate under the human rights regime, for example measures to ensure basic health care under the right to health, should be presumed non-compensable. Moreover, compensation should be balanced as well so as not to bring about catastrophic economic consequences for the host state and its population.

According to the theory of gravitational pull, it would be a mistake not to distinguish between the various types of regulation, i.e. the purpose of the measure, though this does not in itself release host states from their BIT obligations. Hence, there are certain types of regulation that should be presumed to be non-compensable. This includes regulation that fall under the duty to regulate in the human rights regime and regulation to further non-economic policy goals enunciated in the preamble of a BIT (e.g. as references to health, safety and the environment).

As shown, human rights have indeed paved their way into international investment arbitration. There are many ways to give importance to human rights concern in investment arbitrations, for example by allowing a margin of appreciation, applying the principle of proportionality, allowing states to raise counterclaims, enhancing third party interventions, modifying or drafting new BITs with explicit references to non-economic concerns and more elaborated investment protection rules. When BITs do not address the relationship between standards of protection, such as indirect expropriation, and the host state's right to regulate, the tribunals lack guidance upon the applicable standard of review. Hence, the theoretical framework concerning the unification of international law and the exhortation of gravitational pull can serve as a way to balance rights and interests. In this way, arbitrators may consider the human rights regime that calls for investment protection based on inherent limitations to investment protection.

So, one of the major conclusions by the ILC in the report relating to Fragmentation of International Law was that increasing attention would have to be given to the collision of norms and regimes and the rules, methods and techniques for dealing with such collisions.[22] This research serves this purpose. The suggestion of a theoretical background explained as the theory of gravitational pull does not resolve all dysfunctions of the legal regime of international investment law. Yet, it does serve well as a basis for a more unified approach to the law and as a way

---

22 The International law Commission, "Fragmentation of International Law: Difficulties Arising from the Diversification and Expansion of International Law," *op. cit.*, 248–56.

to identify the factors that should be taken into account when interpreting the investment protection standards in a BIT.

6. International investment law and the right to regulate – quintessence of fragmentation

This research has provided light and shade to the intersections of the two international law regimes, international investment law and human rights. It has been clarified how states are obliged to protect foreign investments as a minimum, how states may provide protection to investors through IIAs such as BITs and how this protection may sometimes be an obstacle to the state that also wishes to make other prioritizations. Most states have committed to fundamental human rights instruments, such as the two covenants, the ICCPR and the ICESCR, requiring states to adopt regulation to promote human rights and, as shown, human rights have gradually paved their way into international law and investment arbitrations evidencing the humanization of international law.

This research shows that it is detrimental to fundamental values and the ethos of international law, when states seek to promote human rights through regulatory measures that either do not apply to investors or require states to compensate investors pursuing such goals. The problem is aggravated if the regulating party is a developing state. This problem becomes a legal problem to the extent that states are duty-bound to make certain policy prioritizations to safeguard core human rights while being duty-bound to protect foreign investments. In international investment law this problem is currently left with the arbitrators, who do not necessarily appear to acknowledge the problem at all. Yet, if the international investment law regime does not respond to present day conditions, further fragmentation is a great risk, but as this research has shown there is ample opportunity for remedying the problem. The theory of gravitational pull is a legal response hereto.

7. Recommendations to BIT negotiators

There are a number ways to improve the BIT regime to accommodate the right to regulate in international investment law. Three essential options should be highlighted in terms of incorporating the right to regulate in the BIT regime.

First and foremost, the right to regulate should be reflected in the preamble of BITs. Indeed, it is desirable to adjust the BIT regime so it reflects the interests of all stakeholders incorporating an appropriate balance between investment protection and the right of governments to pursue legitimate public policy objectives. Preambles should therefore include non-economic policies of major importance to the state. Accordingly, BITs should identify the overall purpose of the BIT regime in a more elaborate way.

References to key economic as well as non-economic concerns in the preamble of the BIT oblige treaty interpreters, i.e. the arbitrators, to take non-economic policy objectives into account while interpreting the substantive provisions. Like-wise, human rights could be integrated in the preamble with explicit references to soft law instruments that highlight aspects of corporate social responsibility. Yet, there are drawbacks in referring to specific soft law instruments, like e.g. the OECD Guidelines for Multinational Enterprises, since it may lead to the conclusion that it suffices for corporations to commit to the Guidelines. This might be an unintended outcome. Nevertheless, by referring to non-economic policy objectives and human rights, the preamble could set a benchmark for striking the balance between investment protection and a sufficient degree of flexibility to the host state.

Besides including non-economic policy goals in the preamble, the right to regulate in international investment law could be included in the operative part of the agreement explicitly stating 'the right to regulate'. The advantage of includ-ing such a provision is that it constitutes a general recognition of the right to regulate as an inherent right underlying the substantive investment protection standards. However, it is questionable what such provision actually adds. As shown, states' right to regulate is part of general international law and adding such reference may exacerbate uncertainty, unless it is supported by further clari-fication as to what it entails.

Another option is to include the right to regulate in the operational parts of the treaty as an integrated part in the respective standards of protection. This approach is already followed by some states in more recent BIT negotiations. Indeed, it is advisable to develop clearer rules that address legitimate regulatory purposes, which should be presumed non-compensable. It is, however, not only relevant to incorporate the right to regulate in the expropriation standard, since it is likely to be relevant to other standards of treatment as well.

8. Recommendations to adjudicators

This research shows that there is an inherent problem in entrusting the balance of rights and obligations to arbitrators without further guidance. Though gen-eral international law recognizes the right for states to regulate, it is surrounded by much controversy when it comes to interpretation of the vaguely formulated standards of protection. Arbitrators may therefore draw on the considerations concerning the theory of gravitational pull.

The gravitational pull theory is plausible due to three main considerations: The first aspect of the theory ensures a general principle-based approach to interna-tional investment law embracing its public international law nature. The second aspect of the theory allows for taking into account the business context, including specific guarantees provided to the investor. The third aspect of the gravitational pull theory makes allowance for broader societal considerations in terms of policy coherence and a consequential aspect.

In terms of the first aspect, the gravitational pull theory requires that BITs should be interpreted in a harmonizing manner with human rights obligations. The VCLT article 31(3)(c) constitutes the legal basis for such interpretation. In addition hereto, the interpretation of the standards of protection contained in BITs should be based on the positive presumption that general principles of law apply and the negative presumption against inconsistencies. Hence, this aspect adds the general presumption that certain types of regulation are non-compensable.

In relation to the second aspect, the interpretation must take into account the particular context of the case. This aspect allows for attention to the business context in the form of the expectations of the investor. The legitimate expectations of the investor are a flexible device, which can be adjusted by legal mechanisms, such as for example the inclusion of stabilization clauses in investment contracts or umbrella clauses in BITs.

The third aspect concerns the policy context. The interpretation must take into account inherent limitations to treaty standards, so as to avoid catastrophic economic consequences for the host state and its population. On this basis, the investor must accept regulatory measures under the duty to make certain policy prioritizations. The policy considerations expressed in the preamble of the BIT should be given special attention. In addition, the host state's level of development may be a relevant factor.

All in all, a balanced approach to interpretation would require that arbitrators allow these aspects to be taken into account. These aspects are relevant for the assessment of whether a regulatory interference gives rise to compensation as well as the determination of the amount of compensation.

Bibliography

Abi-Saab, Georges. "Permanent Sovereignty Over Natural Resources and Economic Activities." Chap. 27 In *International Law: Achievements and Prospects*, edited by Mohammed Bedjaoui, 597–618. Dordrecht: Martinus Nijhoff Publishers, 1991.

Akande, Dapo. "International Organizations." Chap. 9 In *International Law*, edited by Malcolm D. Evans, 269–97. Oxford: Oxford University Press, 2003.

Alexandrov, Stanimir. "Breach of Treaty Claims and Breach of Contract Claims: Is It Still Unknown Territory?" Chap. 14 In *Arbitration Under International Investment Agreements: A Guide to the Key Issues*, edited by Katia Yannaca-Small, 323–50. Oxford: Oxford University Press, 2010.

Alston, Phillip. "Downsizing the State in Human Rights Discourse." In *Democracy and the Rule of Law*, edited by Norman Dorsen and Prosser Gifford, 357–68. Washington, DC: Congressional Quarterly Press, 2001.

Alvarez, Jose E., and Karl P. Sauvant. *The Evolving International Investment Regime: Expectations, Realities, Options*. 1st ed. Oxford: Oxford University Press, 2011.

Alvik, Ivar. *Contracting With Sovereignty: State Contracts and International Arbitration*. Studies in International Law. 1st ed. Vol. 31. Oxford: Hart Publishing, 2011.

Arai-Takahashi, Yutaka. *The Margin of Appreciation Doctrine and the Principle of Proportionality in the Jurisprudence of the ECHR*. 1st ed. Antwerpen: Intersentia, 2002.

Augenstein, Daniel, and David Kinley. "When Human Rights 'Responsibilities' Become 'Duties': The Extra-Territorial Obligations of States That Bind Corporations." Chap. 11 In *Human Rights Obligations of Business: Beyond the Corporate Responsibility to Respect?*, edited by Surya Deva and David Bilchitz, 271–94. Cambridge: Cambridge University Press, 2013.

Barbary, Victoria, and Bernardo Bortolotti. "Sovereign Wealth Funds and Political Risk: New Challenges in the Regulation of Foreign Investment." Chap. 8 In *Regulation of Foreign Investment: Challenges to International Harmonization*, edited by Zdenek Drabek and Petros Mavroidis. World Scientific Studies in International Economics, 307–39. Singapore: World Scientific Publishing, 2013.

Barbour, Paul Antony, Persephone Economou, Nathan M. Jensen, and Daniel Villar. "The Arab Spring: How Soon Will Foreign Investors Return?" *Columbia FDI Perspectives*, no. 67 (2012), available at <http://ccsi.columbia.edu/files/2014/01/FDI_67.pdf>.

Bedi, Shiv. *The Development of Human Rights Law by the Judges of the International Court of Justice*. Studies in International Law. 1st ed. Oxford: Hart Publishing, 2007.

Bernasconi-Osterwalder, Nathalie. "Transparency and Amicus Curiae in ICSID Arbitrations." Chap. 9 In *Sustainable Development in World Investment Law*, edited by Marie-Claire Cordonier Segger, Markus W. Gehring, and Andrew Paul Newcombe. Global Trade Law Series, 189–210. Alphen aan den Rijn: Kluwer Law International, 2011.

Bertea, Stefano. "The Arguments from Coherence: Analysis and Evaluation." *Oxford Journal of Legal Studies* 25, no. 3 (2005): 369–91.

Bhuta, Nehal. "The Role International Actors Other Than States Can Play in the New World Order." Chap. 6 In *Realizing Utopia: The Future of International Law*, edited by Antonio Cassese, 61–75. Oxford: Oxford University Press, 2012.

Bjorklund, Andrea K. "Emergency Exceptions: State of Necessity and Force Majeure." Chap. 12 In *The Oxford Handbook of International Investment Law*, edited by Peter Muchlinski, Federico Ortino, and Christoph Schreuer, 459–523. Oxford: Oxford University Press, 2008.

———. "Assessing the Effectiveness of Soft Law Instruments in International Investment Law." Chap. 4 In *International Investment Law and Soft Law*, edited by Andrea K. Bjorklund and August Reinisch, 51–81. Cheltenham: Edward Elgar Publishing, 2012.

Boven, Theo van. "Categories of Rights." Chap. 7 In *International Human Rights Law*, edited by Sangeeta Shah, Sandesh Sivakumaran, and Daniel Moeckli, 143–56. Oxford: Oxford University Press, 2010.

Brejning, Jeanette. *Corporate Social Responsibility and the Welfare State: The Historical and Contemporary Role of CSR in the Mixed Economy of Welfare*. 1st ed. Burlington: Ashgate Publishing, 2012.

Brems, Eva. *Human Rights: Universality and Diversity*. International Studies in Human Rights. 1st ed. Vol. 66. Nijhoff: Brill Nijhof, 2001.

Brown, Chester. *Commentaries on Selected Model Investment Treaties*. Oxford Commentaries on International Law, edited by Philip Alston and Vaughan Lowe. 1st ed. Oxford: Oxford University Press, 2013.

Brownlie, Ian. *Principles of Public International Law*. 5th ed. Oxford: Clarendon Press, 1998.

Cameron, Iain. *An Introduction to the European Convention on Human Rights*. 5th ed. Uppsala: Iustus Forlag, 2006.

Cassese, Antonio. *International Law*. 2nd ed. Oxford: Oxford University Press, 2004.

———. *International Criminal Law*. 2nd ed. Oxford: Oxford University Press, 2008.

———. "A Plea for a Global Community Grounded in a Core of Human Rights." Chap. 11 In *Realizing Utopia: The Future of International Law*, edited by Antonio Cassese, 136–43. Oxford: Oxford University Press, 2012a.

———. *Realizing Utopia: The Future of International Law*. 1st ed. Oxford: Oxford University Press, 2012.

Chen, Tai-Heng. "Precedent and Control in Investment Treaty Arbitration." *Fordham International Law Journal* 30, no. 4 (2007): 1014–49.

Christoffersen, Jonas. *Fair Balance, Proportionality, Subsidiarity and Primarity in the European Convention on Human Rights*. 1st ed. Leiden: Martinus Nijhoff Publishers, 2009.

Clapham, Andrew. *Human Rights Obligations of Non-State Actors*. Collected Courses of the Academy of European Law. 1st ed. Oxford: Oxford University Press, 2006.

————. "Non-State Actors." Chap. 26 In *International Human Rights Law*, edited by Sangeeta Shah, Sandesh Sivakumaran, and Daniel Moeckli, 531–49. Oxford: Oxford University Press, 2010.

Clark, Dana L. "The World Bank and Human Rights: The Need for Greater Accountability." *Harvard Human Rights Journal* 15, no. 1, Spring (2002): 205–26.

Cordonier, Marie-Claire, Markus W. Gehring, and Andrew Newcombe. *Sustainable Development in World Investment Law*. Global Trade Law Series. 1st ed. Alphen aan den Rijn: Kluwer Law International, 2011.

Cotula, Lorenzo. "Stabilization Clauses and the Evolution of Environmental Standards in Foreign Investment Contracts." *Yearbook of International Environmental Law* 17, no. 1 (2006): 111–38.

Crane, Andrew, Abagail McWilliams, Dirk Matten, Jeremy Moon, and Donald S. Siegel. *The Oxford Handbook of Corporate Social Responsibility*. Oxford Handbooks in Business and Management. 1st ed. Oxford: Oxford University Press, 2008.

Crawford, James. "Treaty and Contract in Investment Arbitration." *Arbitration International* 24, no. 3 (2008): 351–74.

————. "Continuity and Discontinuity in International Dispute Settlement." Chap. 40 In *International Investment Law for the 21st Century: Essays in Honour of Christoph Schreue*, edited by Christina Binder, Ursula Kriebaum, August Reinisch, and Stephan Wittich, 801–17. Oxford: Oxford University Press, 2009.

————. *Brownlie's Principles of Public International Law*. 8th ed. Oxford: Oxford University Press, 2012.

Crawford, James, and Simon Olleson. "The Nature and Forms of International Responsibility." Chap. 15 In *International Law*, edited by Malcolm D. Evans, 441–71. Oxford: Oxford University Press, 2003.

Darrow, Mac. *Between Light and Shadow: The World Bank, the International Monetary Fund and International Human Rights Law*. Studies in International Law. 1st ed. 8 vols. Vol. 1. Oxford: Hart Publishing, 2006.

Dennis, Michael J., and David P. Stewart. "Justiciability of Economic, Social, and Cultural Rights: Should There Be an International Complaints Mechanism to Adjudicate the Rights to Food, Water, Housing, and Health?" *American Journal of International Law* 98, no. 3 (2004): 462–515.

Dennys, Nicholas, Mark Raeside, and Robert Clay. *Hudson's Building and Engineering Contracts*. 12th ed. London: Sweet & Maxwell, 2010.

Dijk, Pieter Van, Fried van Hoof, Arjen van Rijn, and Leo Zwaak. *Theory and Practice of the European Convention on Human Rights*. 4th ed. Antwerpen: Intersentia, 2006.

Dimopoulos, Angelos. *EU Foreign Investment Law*. 2nd ed. Oxford: Oxford University Press, 2011.

Dixon, Martin, and Robert McCorquodale. *Cases and Materials on International Law*. 4th ed. Oxford: Oxford University Press, 2003.

Dolzer, Rudolf, and Yun-I Kim. "Germany." Chap. 7 In *Commentaries on Selected Model Investment Treaties*, edited by Chester Brown. Oxford Commentaries on International Law, 289–319. Oxford: Oxford University Press, 2013.

Dolzer, Rudolf, and Christoph Schreuer. *Principles of International Investment Law*. 2nd ed. Oxford: Oxford University Press, 2012.

Drabek, Zdenek, and Petros Mavroidis. *Regulation of Foreign Investment: Challenges to International Harmonization*. 1st ed. Singapore: World Scientific Publishing, 2013.

Dumberry, Patrick, and Gabrielle Dumas-Aubin. "How to Impose Human Rights Obligations on Corporations Under Investment Treaties? Pragmatic Guidelines for the Amendment of BITs." Chap. 14 In *Yearbook on International Investment Law & Policy 2011–2012*, edited by Karl P. Sauvant, 569–600. Oxford: Oxford University Press, 2010.

———. "When and How Allegations of Human Rights Violations Can Be Raised in Investor–state Arbitration." *The Journal of World Investment & Trade* 13, no. 3 (2012): 349–72.

Dupuy, Pierre-Marie. "Unification Rather Than Fragmentation of International Law? The Case of International Investment Law and Human Rights Law." Chap. 2 In *Human Rights in International Investment Law and Arbitration*, edited by Pierre-Marie Dupuy, Ernst-Ulrich Petersmann, and Francesco Francioni. International Economic Law Series, 45–62. Oxford: Oxford University Press, 2009.

Dworkin, Ronald. *Taking Rights Seriously*. 1st ed. Cambridge, Massachusetts: Harvard University Press, 1978.

———. *Law's Empire*. 1st ed. Cambridge, Massachusetts: Harvard University Press, 1986.

Echandi, Roberto. "What Do Developing Countries Expect from the International Investment Regime?" Chap. 1.1. In *The Evolving International Investment Regime: Expectations, Realities, Options*, edited by Jose E. Alvarez and Karl P. Sauvant, 3–21. Oxford: Oxford University Press, 2011.

Færdig, Ikke. "Jurisdiction." Chap. 7 In *International Law*, edited by Malcolm D. Evans, 173–201. Oxford: Oxford University Press, 2003.

Fastenrath, Ulrich, Rudolf Geiger, Daniel-Erasmus Khan, Andreas Paulus, Sabine von Schorlemer, and Christoph Vedder. *From Bilateralism to Community Interest: Essays in Honour of Bruno Simma*. 1st ed. Oxford: Oxford University Press, 2011.

Fitzmaurice, Malgosia. "The Practical Working of the Law of Treaties." Chap. 7 In *International Law*, edited by Malcolm D. Evans, 173–201. Oxford: Oxford University Press, 2003.

Foighel, Isi. *Nationalization: A Study in the Protection of Alien Property in International Law*. 1st ed. Copenhagen: Nyt Nordisk Forlag, 1957.

Franck, Susan D. "The Legitimacy Crisis in Investment Treaty Arbitration: Privatizing Public International Law Through Inconsistent Decisions." *Fordham Law Review* 73, no. 4 (2005): 1521–625.

Freeman, Michael. *Lloyd's Introduction to Jurisprudence*. 8th ed. London: Sweet & Maxwell, 2008.

Friedman, Milton. *Capitalism and Freedom: Fortieth Anniversary Edition*. 1st ed. Chicago: University of Chicago Press, 2002.

Fujita, Sanae. "The Challenges of Mainstreaming Human Rights in the World Bank." *International Journal of Human Rights* 15, no. 3 (2011): 374–96.

Garner, Bryan A. *Black's Law Dictionary*. 7th ed. Minnesota: West Group, 1999.

Gaukrodger, David. "Foreign State Immunity and Foreign Government Controlled Investors." In *OECD Working Papers on International Investment 2010/2*. Paris: OECD, 2010, available at <http://papers.ssrn.com/sol3/papers.cfm?abstract_id=1629251>.

Geiger, Rainer. "Multilateral Approaches to Investment: The Way Forward." Chap. 2.6. In *The Evolving International Investment Regime: Expectations, Realities, Options*, edited by Jose E. Alvarez and Karl P. Sauvant, 147–92. Oxford: Oxford University Press, 2011.

Ghandhi, Sandy. "Human Rights and the International Court of Justice the Ahmadou Sadio Diallo Case." *Human Rights Law Review* 11, no. 3 (2011): 527–55.

Gianviti, François. "Economic, Social, and Cultural Human Rights and the International Monetary Fund." Chap. 4 In *Non-State Actors and Human Rights*, edited by Philip Alston. Collected Courses of the Academy of European Law, 113–38. Oxford: Oxford University Press, 2005.

Haider, Ziad. "Corporate Liability for Human Rights Abuses: Analyzing Kiobel & Alternatives to the Alien Tort Statute." *Georgetown Journal of International Law* 43, no. 4 (2012): 1361–90.

Harris, David J., Michael O'Boyle, and Colin Warbrick. *Law of the European Convention on Human Rights*. 2nd ed. Oxford: Oxford University Press, 2009.

Harrison, James. "Human Rights Arguments in 'Amicus Curiae' Submissions: Promoting Social Justice?" Chap. 17 In *Human Rights in International Investment Law and Arbitration*, edited by Pierre-Marie Dupuy, Ernst-Ulrich Petersmann, and Francesco Francioni. International Economic Law Series, 396–421. Oxford: Oxford University Press, 2009.

Harten, Gus Van. *Investment Treaty Arbitration and Public Law*. Oxford Monographs in International Law, edited by Catherine Redgewell, Dan Sarooshi, and Stefan Talmon. 1st ed. Oxford: Oxford University Press, 2007.

———. "Five Justifications for Investment Treaties: A Critical Discussion." *Trade, Law and Development* 2, no. 1 (2010): 19–58.

Heindl, Jennifer A. "Toward a History of NAFTA's Chapter Eleven." *Berkeley Journal of International Law* 24, no. 2 (2006): 672–86.

Henckaerts, Jean-Marie, and Louise Doswald-Beck. *Customary International Humanitarian Law*. Customary International Humanitarian Law, edited by International Committee of the Red Cross. 1st ed. 2 vols. Vol. 1. Cambridge: Cambridge University Press, 2005.

Hepburn, Jarrod, and Vuyelwa Kuuya. "Corporate Social Responsibility and Investment Treaties." Chap. 24 In *Sustainable Development in World Investment Law*, edited by Marie-Claire Cordonier, Markus W. Gehring, and Andrew Newcombe. Global Trade Law Series, 585–610. Alphen aan den Rijn: Kluwer Law International, 2011.

Hermans, Leon M., and Scott W. Cunningham. "Actor Models for Policy Analysis." Chap. 8 In *Public Policy Analysis: New Developments*, edited by Wil A. H. Thissen and Warren E. Walker. International Series in Operations Research & Management Science, 185–213. New York: Springer, 2013.

Jack Coe, Jr., and Noah Rubins. "Regulatory Expropriation and the Tecmed Case: Context and Contributions." Chap. 17 In *International Investment Law and Arbitration: Leading Cases from the ICSID, NAFTA, Bilateral Treaties and Customary International Law*, edited by Tod Weiler, 597–667. London: Cameron May, 2005.

Jacobs, Francis G., and Robin C.A. White. *The European Convention on Human Rights*. 2nd ed. London: Clarendon Press, 1996.

James, Stephen Andrew. *Universal Human Rights: Origins and Development*. 1st ed. New York: LFB Scholarly Publishing, 2007.

Jandhyala, Srividya, Witold J. Henisz, and Edward D. Mansfield. "Three Waves of BITs: The Global Diffusion of Foreign Investment Policy." *Journal of Conflict Resolution* 55, no. 6 (2011): 1047–73.

Jenks, Clarence Wilfred. "The Conflict of Law-Making Treaties." *British Yearbook of International Law* 30 (1953): 401–53.

Jolowicz, John Anthony. *On Civil Procedure*. Cambridge Studies in International and Comparative Law, edited by James Crawford and John S. Bell. 1st ed. Vol. 13. Cambridge: Cambridge University Press, 2000.

Joubin-Bret, Anna, Marie-Estelle Rey, and Jörg Weber. "International Investment Law and Development." Chap. 2 In *Sustainable Development in World Investment Law*, edited by Marie-Claire Cordonier Segger, Markus W. Gehring, and Andrew Paul Newcombe. Global Trade Law Series, 13–32. Alphen aan den Rijn: Kluwer Law International, 2011.

Kammerhofer, Jörg. "The Theory of Norm Conflict Solutions in International Investment Law." Chap. 5 In *Sustainable Development in World Investment Law*, edited by Marie-Claire Cordonier, Markus W. Gehring, and Andrew Newcombe. Global Trade Law Series, 81–98. Alphen aan den Rijn: Kluwer Law International, 2011.

Kamminga, Menno T. "The Evolving Status of NGOs under International Law: A Threat to the Inter-State System?" in Non-State Actors and Human Rights, edited by Philip Alston, Collected Courses of the Academy of European Law, 93–111. Oxford: Oxford University Press, 2005.

———. "Final Report on the Impact of International Human Rights Law on General International Law." Chap. 1 In *The Impact of Human Rights Law on General International Law*, edited by Menno T. Kamminga and Martin Scheinin, 1–22. Oxford: Oxford University Press, 2009.

Khalfan, Ashfaq. "International Investment Law and Human Rights." Chap. 4 In *Sustainable Development in World Investment Law*, edited by Marie-Claire Cordonier Segger, Markus W. Gehring, and Andrew Paul Newcombe. Global Trade Law Series, 53–6. Alphen aan den Rijn: Kluwer Law International, 2011.

Khaliq, Urfan, and Robin Churchill. "The Protection of Economic and Social Rights: A Particular Challenge?" Chap. 5 In *Un Human Rights Treaty Bodies: Law and Legitimacy*, edited by Helen Keller and Geir Ulfstein. Studies on Human Rights Conventions. Cambridge: Cambridge University Press, 2012.

Kinley, David. *Civilising Globalisation: Human Rights and the Global Economy*. 1st ed. Cambridge: Cambridge University Press, 2009.

Kokko, Ari. "Globalization and FDI Policies." In *The Development Dimension of FDI: Policy and Rule-Making Perspectives*, edited by Americo Beviglia Zampetti and Torbjörn Fredriksson, 29–40. New York: UNCTAD, 2003.

Krajewski, Markus. *Wirtschaftsvölkerrech [International Economic Law]*. 3rd ed. Heidelberg: C.F. Müller, 2012.

Kriebaum, Ursula. "Privatizing Human Rights, the Interface Between International Investment Protection and Human Rights." In *The Law of International Relations – Liber Amicorum Hanspeter Neuhold*, edited by August Reinisch and Ursula Kriebaum, 165–89. Utrecht: Eleven International Publishing, 2007.

———. "Human Rights of the Population of the Host State in International Investment Arbitration." *The Journal of World Investment & Trade* 10, no. 5 (2009): 653–77.

———. "Foreign Investments & Human Rights – The Actors and Their Different Roles." *Transnational Dispute Management (TDM)* 10, no. 1 (2013), available at <http://www.transnational-dispute-management.com/article.asp?key=1925>.

Langa, Pius. "Taking Dignity Seriously: Judicial Reflections on the Optional Protocol to the ICESCR." *Nordic Journal of Human Rights* 27, no. 1 (2009): 29–38.

Lauterpacht, Hersch. *The Development of International Law by the International Court*. 1st. ed. Cambridge: Cambridige University Press, 1996.

———. *The Development of International Law by the International Court.* Grotius Classic Reprint Series. Reis. ed. Cambridge: Cambridge University Press, 2011.

Leinhardt, Stephanie. "Some Thoughts on Foreign Investors' Responsibilities to Respect Human Rights." *Transnational Dispute Management (TDM)* 10, no. 1 (2013), available at <http://www.transnational-dispute-management.com/article.asp?key=1927>.

Lowe, Vaughan. "Jurisdiction." Chap. 11 In *International Law*, edited by Malcolm D. Evans, 329–55. Oxford: Oxford University Press, 2003.

Lowenfeld, Andreas F. *International Economic Law.* International Economic Law Series, edited by John Jackson. 2nd ed. Oxford: Oxford University Press, 2008.

Malanczuk, Peter. *Akehurst's Modern Introduction to International Law.* 7th rev. ed. London: Routledge, 1997.

Mann, Howard. "Civil Society Perspectives: What Do Key Stakeholders Expect from the International Investment Regime?" Chap. 1.2 In *The Evolving International Investment Regime: Expectations, Realities, Options*, edited by Jose E. Alvarez and Karl P. Sauvant, 22–9. Oxford: Oxford University Press, 2011.

Markert, Lars. "The Crucial Question of Future Investment Treaties: Balancing Investors' Rights and Regulatory Interests of Host States." Chap. 10 In *International Investment Law and EU Law*, edited by Marc Bungenberg, Joern Griebel, and Steffen Hindelang. European Yearbook of International Economic Law 2011, 145–71. Berlin: Springer, 2011.

Mavroidis, Petros C. "All Clear on the Investment Front: A Plea for a Restatement?" Chap. 2.2. In *The Evolving International Investment Regime: Expectations, Realities, Options*, edited by Jose E. Alvarez and Karl P. Sauvant, 95–103. Oxford: Oxford University Press, 2011.

———. "Regulation of Investment in the Trade Régime: From ITO to WTO." Chap. 1 In *Regulation of Foreign Investment: Challenges to International Harmonization*, edited by Zdenek Drabek and Petros Mavroidis. World Scientific Studies in International Economics, 13–55. Singapore: World Scientific Publishing, 2013.

McLachlan, Campbell, Laurence Shore, and Matthew Weiniger. *International Investment Arbitration: Substantive Principles.* Oxford International Arbitration Series, edited by Loukas A. Mistelis and Clive M. Schmitthoff. 1st ed. Oxford: Oxford University Press, 2007.

Meron, Theodor. "On a Hierarchy in International Human Rights." *American Journal of International Law* 80, no. 1 (1986): 1–23.

———. *The Humanization of International Law.* The Hague Academy of International Law Monographs. 1st ed. Vol. 3. Nijhoff: Brill Nijhof, 2006.

Michaels, Ralf, and Joost H.B. Pauwelyn. "Conflict of Norms or Conflict of Laws? Different Techniques in the Fragmentation of International Law." Chap. 2 In *Multi-Sourced Equivalent Norms in International Law*, edited by Tomer Broude and Yuval Shany. Studies in International Law, 19–44. Oxford: Hart Publishing, 2011.

Miles, Kate. "Soft Law Instruments in Environmental Law: Models for International Investment Law?" Chap. 5 In *International Investment Law and Soft Law*, edited by Andrea K. Bjorklund and August Reinisch, 82–108. Cheltenham: Edward Elgar Publishing, 2012.

Mitra, Rahul. "Framing the Corporate Responsibility-Reputation Linkage: The Case of Tata Motors in India." *Public Relations Review* 37, no. 4 (2011): 392–8.

Moss, Giuditta Cordero. "Soft Law Codifications in the Area of Commercial Law." Chap. 6 In *International Investment Law and Soft Law*, edited by Andrea K. Bjorklund and August Reinisch, 109–47. Cheltenham: Edward Elgar Publishing, 2012.

Muchlinski, Peter. "Policy Issues." Chap. 1 In *The Oxford Handbook of International Investment Law*, edited by Peter Muchlinski, Federico Ortino, and Christoph Schreuer, 3–48. Oxford: Oxford University Press, 2008.

———. "Regulating Multinationals: Foreign Investment, Development and the Balance of Corporate and Home Country Rights and Responsibilities in a Globalizing World." Chap. 1.3. In *The Evolving International Investment Regime: Expectations, Realities, Options*, edited by Jose E. Alvarez and Karl P. Sauvant, 30–59. Oxford: Oxford University Press, 2011.

Nelson, Timothy G. "Human Rights Law and BIT Protection: Areas of Convergence." *Transnational Dispute Management (TDM)* 10, no. 1 (2011), available at <http://www.transnational-dispute-management.com/article.asp?key=1936>.

Newcombe, Andrew. "The Boundaries of Regulatory Expropriation in International Law." *ICSID Review* 20, no. 1 (2005): 1–57.

Newcombe, Andrew, and Lluís Paradell. *Law and Practice of Investment Treaties: Standards of Treatment*. 1st ed. Austin: Kluwer Law International, 2009.

Nowrot, Karsten. "Transnational Corporations as Steering Subjects in International Economic Law: Two Competing Visions of the Future." *Indiana Journal of Global Legal Studies* 18, no. 2 (2011): 803–42.

O'Neill, Onora. "Agents of Justice." *Metaphilosophy* 32, no. 1–2 (2001): 180–95.

Ortino, Federico. "The Social Dimension of International Investment Agreements: Drafting a New BIT/MIT Model?" *International Law FORUM du droit international* 7, no. 4 (2005): 243–50.

———. "Non-Discriminatory Treatment in Investment Disputes." Chap. 15 In *Human Rights in International Investment Law and Arbitration*, edited by Pierre-Marie Dupuy, Ernst-Ulrich Petersmann, and Francesco Francioni. International Economic Law Series, 344–66. Oxford: Oxford University Press, 2009.

———. "Italy." Chap. 8 In *Commentaries on Selected Model Investment Treaties*, edited by Chester Brown. Oxford Commentaries on International Law, 321–46. Oxford: Oxford University Press, 2013.

———. "Public Services, Investment Liberalization and Protection." Chap. 11 In *Regulation of Foreign Investment: Challenges to International Harmonization*, edited by Zdenek Drabek and Petros Mavroidis. World Scientific Studies in International Economics, 395–416. Singapore: World Scientific Publishing, 2013.

———. "Refining the Content and Role of Investment 'Rules' and 'Standards': A New Approach to International Investment Treaty Making." *ICSID Review* 28, no. 1 (2013): 152–68.

Paparinskis, Martins. "Regulatory Expropriation and Sustainable Development." Chap. 13 In *Sustainable Development in World Investment Law*, edited by Marie-Claire Cordonier, Markus W. Gehring, and Andrew Newcombe. Global Trade Law Series, 295–328. Alphen aan den Rijn: Kluwer Law International, 2011.

Paulsson, Jan. "The Role of Precedent in Investment Arbitration." Chap. 26 In *Arbitration Under International Investment Agreements: A Guide to the Key Issues*, edited by Katia Yannaca-Small, 699–718. Oxford: Oxford University Press, 2010.

Peterson, Luke Eric. "Human Rights and Bilateral Investment Treaties: Mapping the Role of Human Rights Law Within Investor–state Arbitration." *Montreal:*

Rights & Democracy (2009), available at <http://publications.gc.ca/collections/collection_2012/dd-rd/E84-36-2009-eng.pdf>.

Poulsen, Lauge Skovgaard. "The Importance of Bits for Foreign Direct Investment and Political Risk Insurance: Revisiting the Evidence." Chap. 14 In *Yearbook on International Investment Law & Policy 2009–2010*, edited by Karl P. Sauvant, 539–74. Oxford: Oxford University Press, 2010.

Ranjan, Prabhash, and Deepak Raju. "The Enigma of Enforceability of Investment Treaty Arbitration Awards in India." *Asian Journal of Comparative Law* 6, no. 1 (2011): 1–33.

Reiner, Clara, and Christoph Schreuer. "Human Rights and International Investment Arbitration." Chap. 4 In *Human Rights in International Investment Law and Arbitration*, edited by Pierre-Marie Dupuy, Ernst-Ulrich Petersmann, and Francesco Francioni. International Economic Law Series, 82–96. Oxford: Oxford University Press, 2009.

Reinisch, August. "The Changing International Legal Framework for Dealing with Non-State Actors." Chap. 2 In *Non-State Actors and Human Rights*, edited by Philip Alston. Collected Courses of the Academy of European Law, 37–89. Oxford: Oxford University Press, 2005.

———. "Expropriation." Chap. 11 In *The Oxford Handbook of International Investment Law*, edited by Peter Muchlinski, Federico Ortino, and Christoph Schreuer, 407–58. Oxford: Oxford University Press, 2008.

———. "The Proliferation of International Dispute Settlement Mechanisms: The Threat of Fragmentation Vs. The Promise of a More Effective System? Some Reflections from the Perspective of Investment Arbitration." Chap. 7 In *International Law Between Universalism and Fragmentation: Festschrift in Honour of Gerhard Hafner*, edited by Isabelle Buffard, James Crawford, Alain Pellet, and Stephan Wittich, 107–26. Leiden: Martinus Nijhoff Publishers, 2008.

Reisman, Michael W. "Sovereignty and Human Rights in Contemporary International Law." *American Journal of International Law* 84, no. 4 (1990): 866–76.

Riley, Stephen. *Legal Philosophy*. 1st ed. Harlow: Pearson, 2012.

Rubagotti, Gianluca. "Non-Governmental Organisations and the Reporting Obligation under the International Covenant on Civil and Political Rights." *Non-State Actors and International Law* 5, no. 1 (2005): 59–76.

Salacuse, Jeswald W. *The Law of Investment Treaties*. Oxford International Law Library. 1st ed. Oxford: Oxford University Press, 2010.

Salias, Maria Cristina Griton. "Do Umbrella Clauses Apply to Unilateral Undertakings?" Chap. 25 In *International Investment Law for the 21st Century: Essays in Honour of Christoph Schreuer*, edited by Christina Binder, Ursula Kriebaum, August Reinisch, and Stephan Wittich, 490–6. Oxford: Oxford University Press, 2009.

Schadendorf, Sarah. "Human Rights Arguments in Amicus Curiae Submissions: Analysis of ICSID and NAFTA Investor–state Arbitrations." *Transnational Dispute Management (TDM)* 10, no. 1 (2013), available at <http://www.transnational-dispute-management.com/article.asp?key=1935>.

Schefer, Krista Nadakavukaren. *International Investment Law: Text, Cases and Materials*. 1st ed. Cheltenham: Edward Elgar Publishing, 2013.

Schill, Stephan W. *The Multilateralization of International Investment Law*. Cambridge International Trade and Economic Law., edited by Lorand Bartels, Thomas Cottier and William Davey. 1st ed. Cambridge: Cambridge University Press, 2009.

————. *International Investment Law and Comparative Public Law.* 1st ed. Oxford: Oxford University Press, 2010.

————. "W(h)ither Fragmentation? On the Literature and Sociology of International Investment Law." *European Journal of International Law* 22, no. 3 (2011): 875–908.

————. "Enhancing International Investment Law's Legitimacy: Conceptual and Methodological Foundations of a New Public Law Approach." *Virginia Journal of International Law* 52, no. 1 (2011): 57–102.

————. "The Public Law Challenge: Killing or Rethinking International Investment Law?". *Columbia FDI Perspectives*, no. 58 (2012), available at <http://www.ohchr.org/EN/Issues/Pages/ListOfIssues.aspx>.

Schlemmer, Engela C. "Investment, Investor, Nationality, and Shareholders." Chap. 2 In *The Oxford Handbook of International Investment Law*, edited by Peter Muchlinski, Federico Ortino, and Christoph Schreuer, 49–88. Oxford: Oxford University Press, 2008.

Schneiderman, David. *Constitutionalizing Economic Globalization: Investment Rules and Democracy's Promise.* Cambridge Studies in Law and Society, edited by Sally Engle Merry, Chris Arup, and Susan S. Silbey. 1st ed. Cambridge: Cambridge University Press, 2008.

Schreuer, Christoph H., and Ursula Kriebaum. "From Individual to Community Interest in International Investment Law." Chap. 66 In *From Bilateralism to Community Interest: Essays in Honour of Bruno Simma*, edited by Ulrich Fastenrath, Rudolf Geiger, Daniel-Erasmus Khan, Andreas Paulus, Sabine von Schorlemer, and Christoph Vedder, 1079–96. Oxford: Oxford University Press, 2011.

Schreuer, Christoph H., and Matthew M. Weiniger. "A Doctrine of Precedent?" Chap. 30 In *The Oxford Handbook of International Investment Law*, edited by Peter Muchlinski, Federico Ortino, and Christoph Schreuer, 1188–206. Oxford: Oxford University Press, 2008.

Schutter, Olivier De. *International Human Rights Law: Cases, Materials, Commentary.* 1st ed. Cambridge: Cambridge University Press, 2010.

Segger, Marie-Claire Cordonier, and Avidan Kent. "Promoting Sustainable Investment Through International Law." Chap. 30 In *Sustainable Development in World Investment Law*, edited by Marie-Claire Cordonier Segger, Markus W. Gehring, and Andrew Paul Newcombe. Global Trade Law Series, 771–92. Alphen aan den Rijn: Kluwer Law International, 2011.

Shan, Wenhua, and Norah Gallagher. "China." Chap. 4 In *Commentaries on Selected Model Investment Treaties*, edited by Chester Brown. Oxford Commentaries on International Law, 131–81. Oxford: Oxford University Press, 2013.

Shany, Yuval. "Toward a General Margin of Appreciation Doctrine in International Law?" *European Journal of International Law* 16, no. 5 (2005): 907–40.

Shaw, Malcolm N. *International Law.* 6th ed. Cambridge: Cambridge University Press, 2008.

Shemberg, Andrea. "Stabilization Clauses and Human Rights." International Finance Corporation, World Bank Group, 2009.

Simma, Bruno. *From Bilateralism to Community Interests in International Law.* Collected Courses of the Hague Academy of International Law. 1st ed. Vol. 250. Leiden: Brill Nijhof, 1994.

————. "Mainstreaming Human Rights: The Contribution of the International Court of Justice." *Journal of International Dispute Settlement* 3, no. 1 (2012): 7–29.

Simma, Bruno, and Theodore Kill. "Harmonizing Investment Protection and International Human Rights: First Steps Towards a Methodology?" Chap. 36 In *International Investment Law for the 21st Century: Essays in Honour of Christoph Schreuer*, edited by Christina Binder, Ursula Kriebaum, August Reinisch, and Stephan Wittich, 678–707. Oxford: Oxford University Press, 2009.

Sinclair, Ian McTaggart. *The Vienna Convention on the Law of Treaties*. Melland Schill Monographs in International Law. 2nd ed. Manchester: Manchester University Press, 1973.

Sohn, Louis B., and Richard Baxter. *Convention on the International Responsibility of States for Injuries to Aliens (Preliminary Draft With Explanatory Notes)*. 1st ed. Cambridge: Harvard Law School, 1959.

Sornarajah, Muthucumaraswamy. *The Settlement of Foreign Investment Disputes*. 1st ed. The Hague: Kluwer Law International, 2000.

———. *The International Law on Foreign Investment*. 3rd ed. Cambridge: Cambridge University Press, 2010.

———. "Starting Anew in International Investment Law." *Columbia FDI Perspectives*, no. 74 (2012), available at <http://ccsi.columbia.edu/files/2014/01/FDI_74.pdf>.

Spiermann, Ole. "International voldgift under Danmarks bilaterale investeringsoverenskomster." *Juristen* 9 (2003): 325–40.

———. "Individual Rights, State Interests, and the Power to Waive ICSID Jurisdiction under Bilateral Investment Treaties." *Arbitration International* 20, no. 2 (2004): 179–211.

———. "Applicable Law." Chap. 3 In *The Oxford Handbook of International Investment Law*, edited by Peter Muchlinski, Federico Ortino, and Christoph Schreuer, 89–118. Oxford: Oxford University Press, 2008.

———. *International Legal Argument in the Permanent Court of International Justice: The Rise of the International Judiciary*. Cambridge Studies in International and Comparative Law, edited by James Crawford and John S. Bell. 1st ed. Cambridge: Cambridge University Press, 2010.

Suda, Ryan. "The Effect of Bilateral Investment Treaties on Human Rights Enforcement and Realization." Chap. 3 In *Transnational Corporations and Human Rights*, edited by Olivier De Schutter. Studies in International Law, 73–160. Oxford: Hart Publishing, 2006.

Sureda, Andrés Rigo. "Precedent in Investment Treaty Arbitration." Chap. 42 In *International Investment Law for the 21st Century: Essays in Honour of Christoph Schreuer*, edited by Christina Binder, Ursula Kriebaum, August Reinisch, and Stephan Wittich, 830–42. Oxford: Oxford University Press, 2009.

Taillant, Jorge Daniel, and Jonathan Bonnitcha. "International Investment Law and Human Rights." Chap. 4 In *Sustainable Development in World Investment Law*, edited by Marie-Claire Cordonier Segger, Markus W. Gehring and Andrew Paul Newcombe. Global Trade Law Series, 53–80. Alphen aan den Rijn: Kluwer Law International, 2011.

Thirlway, Hugh. "The Sources of International Law." Chap. 4 In *International Law*, edited by Malcolm D. Evans. Oxford: Oxford University Press, 2003: 99–122.

Tienhaara, Kyla. "What You Don't Know Can Hurt You: Investor–state Disputes and the Protection of the Environment in Developing Countries." *Global Environmental Politics* 6, no. 4 (2006): 73–100.

———. "Unilateral Commitments to Investment Protection: Does the Promise of Stability Restrict Environmental Policy Development?" *Yearbook of International Environmental Law* 17, no. 1 (2006): 139–67.

———. *The Expropriation of Environmental Governance: Protecting Foreign Investors at the Expense of Public Policy.* 1st ed. Cambridge: Cambridge University Press, 2009.

Trebilcock, Michael J., and Robert Howse. *The Regulation of International Trade.* 3rd ed. London: Routledge, 2005.

Vandevelde, Kenneth J. "Investment Liberalization and Economic Development: The Role of Bilateral Investment Treaties." *Columbia Journal of Transnational Law* 36, no. 3 (1998): 501–27.

———. *U.S. International Investment Agreements.* 1st ed. Oxford: Oxford University Press, 2009.

———. *Bilateral Investment Treaties: History, Policy, and Interpretation.* 1st ed. Oxford: Oxford University Press, 2010.

Vermeer-Künzli, Annemarieke. "As If: The Legal Fiction in Diplomatic Protection." *European Journal of International Law* 18, no. 1 (2007): 37–68.

Viotti, Paul R., and Mark V. Kauppi. *International Relations Theory.* 5th ed. Harlow: Pearson, 2011.

Waincymer, Jeff. "Balancing Property Rights and Human Rights in Expropriation." Chap. 13 In *Human Rights in International Investment Law and Arbitration,* edited by Pierre-Marie Dupuy, Ernst-Ulrich Petersmann, and Francesco Francioni. International Economic Law Series, 275–309. Oxford: Oxford University Press, 2009.

Wälde, Thomas W. "Interpreting Investment Treaties." Chap. 38 In *International Investment Law for the 21st Century: Essays in Honour of Christoph Schreuer,* edited by Christina Binder, Ursula Kriebaum, August Reinisch, and Stephan Wittich, 724–81. Oxford: Oxford University Press, 2009.

Wälde, Thomas W., and Borzu Sabahi. "Compensation, Damages, and Valuation." Chap. 26 In *The Oxford Handbook of International Investment Law,* edited by Peter Muchlinski, Federico Ortino, and Christoph Schreuer, 1049–124. Oxford: Oxford University Press, 2008.

Weeramantry, J. Romesh. *Treaty Interpretation in Investment Arbitration.* Oxford International Arbitration Series, edited by Loukas A. Mistelis. 1st ed. Oxford: Oxford University Press, 2012.

Weidemaier, Mark C. "Toward a Theory of Precedent in Arbitration". *William and Mary Law Review* 51, no. 5 (2010): 1895–958.

Weiler, Todd. *International Investment Law and Arbitration: Leading Cases from the ICSID, NAFTA, Bilateral Treaties and Customary International Law.* 1st ed. London: Cameron May, 2005.

Weiss, Friedl. "Trade and Investment." Chap. 6 In *The Oxford Handbook of International Investment Law,* edited by Peter Muchlinski, Federico Ortino, and Christoph Schreuer, 182–223. Oxford: Oxford University Press, 2008.

White, Robin C.A., and Clare Ovey. *The European Convention on Human Rights.* 5th ed. Oxford: Oxford University Press, 2010.

Wilson, Timothy Ross. "Trade Rules: Ethyl Corporation V. Canada (NAFTA Chapter 11) Part 1: Claim and Award on Jurisdiction?" *Law and Business Review of the Americas* 6, no. 1 (2000): 52–71.

———. "Trade Rules: Ethyl Corporation V. Canada (NAFTA Chapter 11) Part 2: Are Fears Founded?" *Law and Business Review of the Americas* 6, no. 2 (2000): 205–41.

Wong, Jarrod. "Umbrella Clauses in Bilateral Investment Treaties: Of Breaches of Contract, Treaty Violations, and the Divide Between Developing and Developed Countries in Foreign Investment Disputes". *George Mason Law Review* 14, no. 1 (2006): 135–77.

Yannaca-Small, Katia. "Annulment of ICSID Awards: Limited Scope But is There Potential?" Chap. 23 In *Arbitration Under International Investment Agreements: A Guide to the Key Issues*, edited by Katia Yannaca-Small, 603–34. Oxford: Oxford University Press, 2010.

———. "Indirect Expropriation and the Right to Regulate: How to Draw the Line?" Chap. 18 In *Arbitration under International Investment Agreements: A Guide to the Key Issues*, edited by Katia Yannaca-Small, 445–78. Oxford: Oxford University Press, 2010.

———. "What About This 'Umbrella Clause'?" Chap. 19 In *Arbitration Under International Investment Agreements: A Guide to the Key Issues*, edited by Katia Yannaca-Small, 479–503. Oxford: Oxford University Press, 2010.

Zampetti, Americo Beviglia, and Colin Brown. "The EU Approach to Investment." Chap. 12 In *Regulation of Foreign Investment: Challenges to International Harmonization*, edited by Zdenek Drabek and Petros Mavroidis. World Scientific Studies in International Economics, 417–51. Singapore: World Scientific Publishing, 2013.

Zhan, James, Jorg Weber, and Joachim Karl. "International Investment Rulemaking at the Beginning of the Twenty-First Century: Stocktaking and Options for the Way Forward." Chap. 2.8 In *The Evolving International Investment Regime: Expectations, Realities, Options*, edited by Jose E. Alvarez and Karl P. Sauvant, 193–212. Oxford: Oxford University Press, 2011.

Zhan, James Xiaoning. "The Spread of BITs and Their Changing Face." *ICSID Review* 24, no. 2 (2009): 339–46.

Appendix 1
Decisions and awards

Aguas del Tunari v. Bolivia, Award, Decision on Respondent's Objections to Jurisdiction, 21 October 2005

Alpha v Ukraine, Award, 8 November 2010

Azurix v Argentina, Award, 16 July 2006

Bernhard von Pezold v Zimbabwe, Procedural Order No. 2, 26 June 2012

Biloune v Ghana, Award, 27 October 1989

Biwater Gauff (Tanzania) Ltd. v Tanzania, Procedural Order No. 5, 2007

Biwater Gauff (Tanzania) Ltd. v Tanzania, Award, 24 July 2008

Border Timbers Limited v Zimbabwe, Procedural Order No. 2, 26 June 2012

CMS v Argentina, Award, 12 May 2005

Deutsche Bank AG v Sri Lanka, Award, 31 October 2012

El Paso Energy v Argentina, Decision on Jurisdiction, 27 April 2006

Eureko v Poland, Partial Award, 19 August 2005

Feldman v Mexico, Award, 16 December 2002

Impregilo v Argentina, Award, 21 June 2011

LG&E v Argentina, Decision on Liability, 3 October 2006

Metalcald v Mexico, Award, 30 August 2000

Methanex v USA, Final Award, 3 August 2005

Mondev v United States of America, Award, 11 October 2002

Noble Ventures, Inc. v Romania, Award, 12 October 2005

Pan American v Argentina, Decision on Preliminary Objections, 27 July 2006

Parkerings-Compagniet v Lithuania, Award, 7 September 2007

Paushok et al v Mongolia, Award, 28 April 2011

Piero Foresti, Laura de Carli and Others v South Africa, Letter Regarding Non-Disputing Parties, 5 October 2009

Pope & Talbot Inc v Canada, Interim Award, 26 June 2000

Railroad Development Corporation v Guatemala, 29 June 2012

Revere Copper v OPIC, Award, 24 August 1978

RFCC v Morocco, Award, 22 December 2003

Ronald Lauder v Czech Republic, Award, 3 September 2001

Santa Elena v Costa Rica, Award, 17 February 2000

S.D. Myers v Canada, NAFTA, Partial Award, 13 November 2000

SGS Société Générale de Surveillance S.A. v Pakistan, Decision of the Tribunal on Objections to Jurisdiction, 6 August 2003

SGS Société Générale de Surveillance S.A. v Paraguay, Award, 10 February 2012

SGS Société Générale de Surveillance S.A. v Philippines, Decision of the Tribunal on Objections to Jurisdiction, 29 January 2004

Siemens v Argentina, Award, 6 February 2007
Spyridon Roussalis v Romania, Award, 7 December 2011
Tecmed v Mexico, Award, 29 May 2003
Toto Costruzioni Generali v Lebanon Award, 7 June 2012
Trinh Vinh Binh v Vietnam, Award, 1 March 2007, UNCITRAL
Wena Hotels v Egypt, Award, 8 December 2000
White Industries Australia Limited v India, Award, UNCITRAL, 30 November 2011

ECtHR

Agrotexim Hellas S.A. and others v Greece, no. 14807/80, 12 February 1992
Al-Adsani v United Kingdom, no. 35763/97, 21 November 2001
Beyeler v Italy, no. 33202/96, 5 January 2000
Bramelid and Malmström v Sweden, no. 8588/79 and 8589/79, 12 October 1982
Carbonara and Ventura v Italy, no. 24638/94, 30 May 2000
Chassagnou v France, no. 25088/94 28331/95 28443/95, 29 April 1999
Fredin v Sweden, 12033/86, 18 February 1991
Hentrich v France, no. 13616/88, 22 September 1994
Holy Monasteries v Greece, no. 13092/87; 13984/88, 9 December 1994
James and Others v United Kingdom, no. 8793/79, 21 February 1986
Kaplan v United Kingdom, Commission's Report, 17 July 1980
Lithgow and Others v United Kingdom, no. 9006/80 9262/81 9263/81 9265/81 9266/81 9313/81 9405/81, 8 July 1986
Loizidou v Turkey, Preliminary Objections, no. 15318/89, 23 March 1995
Marckx v Belgium, no. 6833/74, 13 June 1979
Mellacher and Others v Austria, no. 10522/83 11011/84 11070/84, 19 December 1989
Melnychuk v Ukraine, no. 28743/03, 5 July 2005
Norris v Ireland, no. 10581/83, 26 October 1988,
Pudas v Sweden, no. 10426/83, 27 October 1987
Selmouni v France, no 25803/94, 28 July 1999
Smith Kline and French Laboratoires v Netherlands, no. 12633/87, 4 October 1990
Soering v United Kingdom, no. 14038/88, 7 July 1989
Sporrong and Lönnroth v Sweden, Commission's Report, 8 October 1980, para 105
Sporrong and Lönnroth v Sweden, no. 7151/75; 7152/75, 23 September 1982
Tre Taktörer Aktiebolag v Sweden, no. 10873/84, 7 July 1989
Tyrer v United Kingdom, no. 5856/72, 25 April 1978
Van Marle and Others v Netherlands, no. 8543/79 8674/79 8675/79 8685/79, 26 June 1986
Wiggins v United Kingdom, no. 7456/76, 8 February 1978
Yukos v Russia, no. 14902/04, 29 January 2009 and Final Judgment, no. 14902/04, 8 March 2012

Permanent Court of International Justice

S.S. Wimbledon, (United Kingdom, France, Italy, Japan v. Germany), Permanent Court of International Justice, 28 June 1923

S.S. Lotus (France v. Turkey), Judgment, Permanent Courts of International Justice, 7 September 1927

ICJ

Coard et al. v United States, Inter-American Commission of Human Rights, 29 September 1999

Corfu Channel (*United Kingdom of Great Britain and Northern Ireland v Albania*), ICJ, Judgment, 4 April 1949

Elettronica Sicula S.p.A. (ELSI) (United States of America v. Italy*)*, ICJ, Judgment 20 July 1989, ICJ Reports, 1989.

Factory of Chorzòw, ICJ, Judgment, 13 September 1928

Fisheries Jurisdiction (*United Kingdom and Northern Ireland v Iceland*), ICJ, Judgment of 2 February 1973

Gab íkovo-Nagymaros Project (*Hungary v Slovakia*), ICJ, Judgment of 25 September 1997

Harry Roberts (USA) v Mexico, 2 November 1926

Jalapa Railroad and Power Co. (*US v Mexico*), US–Mexican Claims Commission

Kiobel v Royal Dutch Petroleum, proceedings and orders can be found at <http://www.scotusblog.com/case-files/cases/kiobel-v-royal-dutch-petroleum/>

Kuwait v American Independent Oil Company (Aminoil), 66 ILR 1982

Legal Consequences of the Construction of a Wall, Advisory Opinion, 9 July 2004

LFH Neer and Pauline Neer (*US v Mexico*), US–Mexican Claims Commission, 15 October 1926,

Libyan American Oil Company (LIAMCO) v Libya, 62 ILR 1977

Norway v United States of America, PCA, Award, 13 October 1922

Paramilitary Activities in and Against Nicaragua, Judgment, 27 June 1986, ICJ Reports

Spanish Zone of Morocco Claims, General Decisions (Principles of State Responsibility), RIAA, 1925

Texaco Overseas Petroleum Company and California Asiatic Oil Company v Libya, 53 ILR 1979

Tippetts, Abbett, McCarthy, Stratton v TAMS-AFFA Consulting Eng'rs of Iran, 6 Iran–US Claims Tribunal Reports, 1984

United States of America vs. Carl Krauch et al. (I.G. Farben), 30 July 1948, see <http://werle.rewi.hu-berlin.de/IGFarbenCase.pdf>

United States–Venezuela Mixed-Claims Commission, 1903, <http://legal.un.org/riaa/cases/vol_IX/113-318.pdf>

United States v Krupp, 31 July 1948, see <http://werle.rewi.hu-berlin.de/KRUPP-Case%20Judgment.pdf>

US Military Tribunal Nuremberg, Judgment, 19 February 1948, Trials of War Criminals before the Nuremberg Military Tribunals under Control Council Law No. 10, Volume XI/2, p. 1241, see <https://www.loc.gov/rr/frd/Military_Law/pdf/NT_war-criminals_Vol-IV.pdf>

Appendix 2
List of bilateral investment treaties (BITs)

A geographical representative extract of BITs entered into force post year 2000. The BITs were the subject to an examination of the right to regulate focusing on policy concerns enunciated in the preamble and the expropriation clause.

BITs and Model BITs can be found in the UNCTAD database: <http://invest mentpolicyhub.unctad.org/IIA>

at Investment Treaty Arbitration: <http://www.italaw.com/investment-treaties>

or in Chester Brown ed. *Commentaries on Selected Model Investment Treaties.* Oxford Commentaries on International Law, edited by Philip Alston and Vaughan Lowe. 1st ed. Oxford: Oxford University Press, 2013.

1.	Algeria	Argentina
2.	Algeria	Denmark
3.	Algeria	Finland
4.	Angola	Italy
5.	Argentina	Guatemala
6.	Argentina	Nicaragua
7.	Argentina	South Africa
8.	Argentina	Costa Rica
9.	Argentina	Guatemala
10.	Argentina	India
11.	Argentina	Indonesia
12.	Argentina	Morocco
13.	Argentina	Nicaragua
14.	Argentina	Panama
15.	Argentina	Philippines

16.	Argentina	Russian Federation
17.	Argentina	Senegal
18.	Argentina	South Africa
19.	Argentina	Thailand
20.	Argentina	Morocco
21.	Armenia	Finland
22.	Armenia	Egypt
23.	Australia	Mexico
24.	Australia	Egypt
25.	Australia	India
26.	Australia	Lithuania
27.	Australia	Uruguay
28.	Australia	Egypt
29.	Austria	Mexico
30.	Austria	Ethiopia
31.	Austria	Uzbekistan
32.	Austria	Libya
33.	Azerbaijan	Finland
34.	Azerbaijan	Italy
35.	Azerbaijan	United States
36.	Bahrain	China
37.	Bahrain	Italy
38.	Bahrain	Czech Republic
39.	Bahrain	United States
40.	Bangladesh	Uzbekistan
41.	Belarus	Finland
42.	Belarus	Mexico
43.	Belarus	Venezuela
44.	Belgium–Luxembourg	Mexico
45.	Belgium–Luxembourg	Uzbekistan
46.	Belgium–Luxembourg	South Africa
47.	Belgium–Luxembourg	China
48.	Belgium–Luxembourg	Venezuela
49.	Belgium–Luxembourg	Egypt
50.	Belgium–Luxembourg	Kuwait

(continued)

51.	Belgium–Luxembourg	Libya
52.	Belgium–Luxembourg	Morocco
53.	Bolivia	United States
54.	Bosnia and Herzegovina	Finland
55.	Bosnia and Herzegovina	Italy
56.	Bosnia and Herzegovina	Czech Republic
57.	Bosnia and Herzegovina	Denmark
58.	Bosnia and Herzegovina	Sweden
59.	Bosnia and Herzegovina	Egypt
60.	Bosnia and Herzegovina	Kuwait
61.	Bosnia and Herzegovina	China
62.	Bulgaria	China
63.	Bulgaria	Czech Republic
64.	Bulgaria	Egypt
65.	Bulgaria	Kuwait
66.	Burundi	Mauritius
67.	Cambodia	China
68.	Cambodia	Czech Republic
69.	Canada	Czech Republic
70.	Canada	Croatia
71.	Canada	Czech Republic
72.	Canada	Jordan
73.	Canada	Latvia
74.	Canada	Peru
75.	Canada	Romania
76.	Canada	Slovakia
77.	Chile	Guatemala
78.	Chile	Nicaragua
79.	China	Guatemala
80.	China	Mexico
81.	China	Ethiopia
82.	China	Cuba
83.	China	Czech Republic
84.	China	Finland
85.	China	France

86.	China	Germany
87.	China	Guyana
88.	China	Iran
89.	China	Democratic People's Republic of Korea
90.	China	Korea
91.	China	Latvia
92.	China	Madagascar
93.	China	Myanmar
94.	China	Netherlands
95.	China	Qatar
96.	China	Romania
97.	China	Russian Federation
98.	China	Slovakia
99.	China	Spain
100.	China	Switzerland
101.	China	Syrian Arab Republic
102.	China	Trinidad and Tobago
103.	Congo	Italy
104.	Costa Rica	Venezuela
105.	Costa Rica	Czech Republic
106.	Croatia	Finland
107.	Croatia	Czech Republic
108.	Croatia	Denmark
109.	Croatia	Sweden
110.	Croatia	United States
111.	Cuba	Guatemala
112.	Cuba	Mexico
113.	Cuba	Venezuela
114.	Cyprus	Czech Republic
115.	Czech Republic	Guatemala
116.	Czech Republic	Mexico
117.	Czech Republic	Nicaragua
118.	Czech Republic	El Salvador
119.	Czech Republic	Georgia
120.	Czech Republic	Democratic People's Republic of Korea

(continued)

121.	Czech Republic	India
122.	Czech Republic	Jordan
123.	Czech Republic	Macedonia
124.	Czech Republic	Mauritius
125.	Czech Republic	Moldova
126.	Czech Republic	Nicaragua
127.	Czech Republic	Panama
128.	Czech Republic	Paraguay
129.	Czech Republic	Romania
130.	Czech Republic	Saudi Arabia
131.	Czech Republic	Serbia
132.	Czech Republic	Syria
133.	Czech Republic	Turkey
134.	Czech Republic	Ukraine
135.	Czech Republic	United States
136.	Czech Republic	Uruguay
137.	Czech Republic	Vietnam
138.	Czech Republic	Yemen
139.	Denmark	Mexico
140.	Denmark	Nicaragua
141.	Denmark	Egypt
142.	Denmark	Ethiopia
143.	Denmark	Kuwait
144.	Denmark	Mexico
145.	Denmark	Nicaragua
146.	Denmark	Slovenia
147.	Denmark	Uganda
148.	Djibouti	Italy
149.	Dominican Republic	Morocco
150.	Ecuador	Italy
151.	Ecuador	Sweden
152.	Egypt	Italy
153.	Egypt	Finland
154.	Egypt	Germany
155.	Egypt	India

156.	Egypt	Malaysia
157.	Egypt	Mali
158.	Egypt	Malta
159.	Egypt	Mongolia
160.	Egypt	Portugal
161.	Egypt	Russian Federation
162.	Egypt	Singapore
163.	Egypt	Slovakia
164.	Egypt	Sudan
165.	Egypt	Thailand
166.	Egypt	Turkey
167.	Egypt	Vietnam
168.	El Salvador	Morocco
169.	Eritrea	Italy
170.	Estonia	Italy
171.	Ethiopia	Finland
172.	Ethiopia	Yemen
173.	Ethiopia	Sweden
174.	Finland	Guatemala
175.	Finland	Indonesia
176.	Finland	Kyrgyzstan
177.	Finland	Lebanon
178.	Finland	Nigeria
179.	Finland	Serbia
180.	Finland	Mexico
181.	Finland	Morocco
182.	Finland	Slovenia
183.	Finland	Tanzania
184.	Finland	Tunisia
185.	Finland	Ukraine
186.	Finland	Uruguay
187.	Finland	Vietnam
188.	France	Guatemala
189.	France	Mexico
190.	France	Nicaragua

(continued)

191.	France	Venezuela
192.	Gabon	Italy
193.	Gabon	Morocco
194.	Germany	Mexico
195.	Germany	Nicaragua
196.	Germany	Kenya
197.	Germany	Morocco
198.	Greece	Mexico
199.	Greece	South Africa
200.	Greece	Morocco
201.	Guatemala	Korea
202.	Guatemala	Netherlands
203.	Guatemala	Spain
204.	Guatemala	Switzerland
205.	Guatemala	Italy
206.	Honduras	United States
207.	Hungary	Uzbekistan
208.	Hungary	Morocco
209.	Iceland	Mexico
210.	India	Mexico
211.	India	Sweden
212.	India	Kuwait
213.	India	Morocco
214.	Indonesia	Morocco
215.	Iran	South Africa
216.	Iran	Italy
217.	Iran	Venezuela
218.	Italy	Mexico
219.	Italy	Jordan
220.	Italy	Lebanon
221.	Italy	Libya
222.	Italy	Malta
223.	Italy	Moldova
224.	Italy	Morocco
225.	Italy	Mozambique

226.	Italy	Nigeria
227.	Italy	Pakistan
228.	Italy	Panama
229.	Italy	Qatar
230.	Italy	Russian Federation
231.	Italy	Serbia
232.	Italy	Syria
233.	Italy	Tanzania
234.	Italy	Turkey
235.	Italy	Yemen
236.	Italy	Morocco
237.	Japan	Uzbekistan
238.	Japan	Korea
239.	Japan	Lao
240.	Japan	Mongolia
241.	Japan	Pakistan
242.	Japan	Peru
243.	Japan	Russian Federation
244.	Japan	Vietnam
245.	Jordan	Morocco
246.	Jordan	United States
247.	Kazakhstan	Sweden
248.	Korea	Mexico
249.	Korea	Nicaragua
250.	Kuwait	Lebanon
251.	Kuwait	Lithuania
252.	Kuwait	Netherlands
253.	Kyrgyzstan	Sweden
254.	Lebanon	Sweden
255.	Libya	Portugal
256.	Libya	Switzerland
257.	Lithuania	United States
258.	Malaysia	Uzbekistan
259.	Mexico	Panama
260.	Mexico	Portugal

(continued)

261.	Mexico	Slovakia
262.	Mexico	Spain
263.	Mexico	Trinidad and Tobago
264.	Mexico	United Kingdom
265.	Mexico	Uruguay
266.	Mexico	Sweden
267.	Morocco	Sweden
268.	Morocco	Romania
269.	Morocco	Spain
270.	Morocco	Turkey
271.	Morocco	Ukraine
272.	Morocco	United Kingdom
273.	Mozambique	United States
274.	Netherlands	Suriname
275.	Netherlands	Nicaragua
276.	Nicaragua	Switzerland
277.	Nicaragua	United Kingdom
278.	Oman	Uzbekistan
279.	Pakistan	Uzbekistan
280.	Panama	Sweden
281.	Portugal	Uzbekistan
282.	Romania	Sweden
283.	Rwanda	United States
284.	Slovenia	Uzbekistan
285.	Slovenia	Sweden
286.	Spain	Uzbekistan
287.	Sweden	Uzbekistan
288.	Sweden	Thailand
289.	Sweden	United Arab Emirates
290.	Sweden	Uzbekistan
291.	United Arab Emirates	Uzbekistan
292.	United States	Uruguay
293.	Uruguay	Venezuela

Appendix 3
List of Model BITs

Austria Model BIT 2008
Canada Model BIT 2004
China Model BIT 2003
Colombia Model BIT 2007
Denmark Model BIT 2005
France Model BIT 2006
Germany Model BIT 2008
India Model BIT 2003
Italy Model BIT 2003
Norway Draft Model BIT 2007
Sweden Model BIT 2003
United Kingdom Model BIT 2005
United States Model BIT 2012

Index

For Product Safety Concerns and Information please contact our EU
representative GPSR@taylorandfrancis.com Taylor & Francis Verlag GmbH,
Kaufingerstraße 24, 80331 München, Germany

Printed and bound by CPI Group (UK) Ltd, Croydon, CR0 4YY
08/05/2025
01864347-0002